A GUILTE

A GUILTED AGE

APOLOGIES FOR THE PAST

Ashraf H. A. Rushdy

TEMPLE UNIVERSITY PRESS
Philadelphia • Rome • Tokyo

TEMPLE UNIVERSITY PRESS
Philadelphia, Pennsylvania 19122
www.temple.edu/tempress

Published 2015

Library of Congress Cataloging-in-Publication Data

Rushdy, Ashraf H. A., 1961–
A guilted age : apologies for the past / Ashraf Rushdy.
pages cm
Includes bibliographical references and index.
ISBN 978-1-4399-1321-5 (hardback : alk. paper) — ISBN 978-1-4399-1322-2 (paper : alk. paper) — ISBN 978-1-4399-1323-9 (e-book) 1. Apology—Political aspects. 2. Restorative justice. 3. Reparations for historical injustices. I. Title.
BF575.A75R87 2015
302'.17—dc23

2015007949

♾ The paper used in this publication meets the requirements of the American National Standard for Information Sciences—Permanence of Paper for Printed Library Materials, ANSI Z39.48-1992

Printed in the United States of America

9 8 7 6 5 4 3 2 1

For Amgad

CONTENTS

PREFACE

Consider these four scenes from four continents.

We begin with Africa. The Acholi people in Northern Uganda have a ritual called *nyono tong gweno*. Literally translated as "stepping on the egg," the rite was originally understood as a purification ritual for travelers returning home, as a way of cleansing the impurities from beyond, that was essential for the health of the individual and the community. The Acholi have other rituals for purification that are also meant to provide various forms of reconciliation, including *moyo kum* (cleansing the body), *moyo piny* (cleansing an area), and *gomo tong* (bending the spear). The core belief about these rites of conflict resolution, writes James Latigo, is that they provide a forum for the wrongdoer to acknowledge and accept responsibility for the harm and then remake "relations of trust and the restoration of social cohesion" through "the act and process of forgiveness." Recently, the Acholi have implemented the full range of these rites in a more concerted and widespread way to welcome back to the community those child soldiers who were abducted to serve in Joseph Kony's Lord's Resistance Army. After brushing against the branch of a pobo tree and then stepping over a pole, Charles Otim, for instance, who had been abducted eighteen years earlier when he was sixteen, addressed the village chiefs: "I ask for your forgiveness. We have wronged you." In other cases, those seeking forgiveness and permission to return to the community step on an egg as a symbol of cleansing. What used to be a rite for creating reconciliation between individuals and within families has now become a ritual for the thousands of former members of Kony's

Army who have accepted the government's offer of amnesty and must be forgiven to return to their communities and their lives.[1]

Let us now turn to Europe. In an address in 2001, Pope John Paul II made a statement to the bishops of the Greek Orthodox Church in which he begged God to forgive the sins that the Catholic Church had committed against the Greek Orthodox Church. These events, he noted, "have left deep wounds in the minds and hearts of people to this day." He then specified one event in particular—"the disastrous sack of the imperial city of Constantinople" by the Catholic warriors who were seeking a secure path to Jerusalem for the Fourth Crusade. This event of 1204, the pope believed, still resonated in a powerfully destructive way: "To God alone belongs judgment, and therefore we entrust the heavy burden of the past to his endless mercy, imploring him to heal the wounds which still cause suffering to the spirit of the Greek people." This "healing" is necessary, the pope perorated, "if the Europe now emerging is to be true to its identity, which is inseparable from the Christian humanism shared by East and West." Two years before the pope's address, an informal group of four hundred Christians completed what they called the Reconciliation Walk, in which, from 1996 to 1999, they traced the exact path and chronology of those who had set off nine hundred years earlier on the First Crusade (1096–1099). Arriving in Jerusalem on the nine hundredth anniversary of the arrival of the Crusaders, they offered religious leaders in the Old City framed statements of their apology for the Crusaders' slaughter of Jewish and Muslim inhabitants of the Holy Land.[2]

Let us next consider America. On January 14, 1993, at Sand Creek, Colorado, a group of congregants gathered to commemorate the slaughter of the Native Americans that occurred on that site in 1864, when a large regiment of the Colorado Territory militia killed a peaceful village of Cheyenne and Arapaho people. The leader of the congregation led the group in confession and prayer and then directed them as they sought "forgiveness in the presence of the Lord" and from the Native Americans gathered for the occasion. He described how "one woman stretched herself out in the sand, touching the feet of an Indian pastor; deeply ashamed she wept for the lost generation that was cut off in this place." At the end of the day, the congregation took communion together and then walked in pairs to where the dead had been placed by the creek. The leader poured out the remainder of the communion wine to commemorate the spot where blood had been shed.[3]

Finally, let us go down under to Australia. In memory of the white settler nation's history of oppression of the Aboriginal peoples, and especially in the wake of the government-sponsored removal of Aboriginal children from their birth families (the so-called "stolen generations"), Australian citizens formed civil society groups to urge the government to apologize for these acts. The Conservative Party leader refused. After the Labor Party finally won the election in 2007, the prime minister offered an official apology. Meanwhile, in the absence of official atonement, the citizens undertook their own acts of penance. Hundreds of thousands of people each sponsored a plastic "hand" in the multicolored "Sea of Hands" placed on the lawn of the Parliament House to symbolize an act of "collective apology" for the theft of the land. Some of the hands were inscribed with people's names, others with political programs, such as "Hands Up for Indigenous Rights." Thousands signed their names in "Sorry Books," where they recorded their own contrition. Each May 26 since 1998, Australia has celebrated "National Sorry Day."[4]

These four scenes differ in significant ways. The first is about preparing to welcome an individual back into the community through a process of purification, while the second is about retracing unholy historical pathways in a journey of reconciliation. One uses purification to permit return, while the other uses return to produce purification (the modern Crusaders' "return" to Jerusalem through the same path followed by the original Crusaders to alter the meaning of the first event). Most of them are religious rituals, but there are also political ceremonies. In the Colorado case, the religious group seeks to exorcise the ghosts of a historical event and sanctify the haunted site where it occurred, while in Australia a set of quasi-constitutional acts enables people to affirm their sense of what citizenship means by inscribing their names into a text as part of a new civic holiday.

Yet despite the apparent differences, these scenes all also exhibit a shared commitment to the ideals and practices of contrition and redemption or, in the less religiously inflected language commonly used to describe them, to the practices of public apology and forgiveness. Each of these acts was an apology or a request for forgiveness witnessed by a community, by a group other than the offender and the victim. This is what makes them "public."

For anyone who has followed the news in any media for the past quarter century, such scenes have become increasingly common representative moments in what appears to be a global process of apology and forgiveness. Acts such as these inspired me to undertake my research for *The Guilted Age*. What, I sought to understand, did such rituals of atonement mean, and to what extent might they constitute a coherent practice? Beyond acts of atonement, however, I was interested in the specific forms of interaction people used to apologize and to beg for someone's forgiveness. What I inelegantly call the apology-forgiveness dynamic is familiar to all of us, since we apologize daily—some of us, because of our nationality, more than others. Canadians are reputed to be particularly prone to apologizing (full disclosure: Canadian is one of my identities). The recent film *Anchorman 2* (2013) parodies this widespread belief with Canadian news anchors who apologize each time they shoot a hockey puck at the people they are targeting. What I wanted to understand is how this regular practice in personal life came to be applied to political and historical events and what that meant. It was easy enough to parody these public apologies; after all, they were using the same discursive form ("I am sorry") to express contrition for the Crusades, the Holocaust, and slavery that we use when we accidentally step on someone's shoe. How could this expression possibly be meaningful in this new context? And parodied these events certainly were, as pundits made them a regular feature of their columns.[5]

Some editorials proclaimed 1995 as "the year of the apology." Then they dubbed 1997 the same. Then 2000 got the label. And then their writers stopped, realizing, it seems, that this was not an annual fad, but something larger and more comprehensive. These public apologies became a common enough feature of contemporary life that they warranted even larger parodies than short editorials could provide. Two novels undertook the task: Jay Rayner's *Eating Crow* (2004) and Jonathan Dee's *A Thousand Pardons* (2013).[6] Punditry and parody did some important work, but more was needed to understand precisely what was being mocked. I set out to investigate what this new development in our modern world was, why it was happening, and what it meant.

In *The Guilted Age*, I make five major arguments. First, I argue that the "guilted age" exists. In other words, we can understand the proliferation of nations' and churches' apologies for past events as a historical phenomenon. These apologies for the past are not, as pundits frequently claim, aberrations or delusions, nor are they a passing and perverse fad with no rational explanation for why they began to appear when they did. These public apologies are a practice that emerged at a specific moment, out of particular social and intellectual conditions that we can identify, and they express what I argue is a widespread sensibility that is a product of and response to that historical moment. We apologize, in other words, because we live in a "guilted age." And that guilted age is largely a postwar phenomenon, beginning, as Jacques Derrida and Pascal Bruckner note, shortly after 1945.[7]

Second, I argue that two types of apologies have emerged in the guilted age and that one has evolved from the other. The first type consists of apologies offered by groups for crimes committed *just before* the guilted age, and the second consists of apologies for crimes committed *well before* the guilted age. In the first category, for example, fall apologies by Germany for the actions of the Third Reich and apologies by Austria and France for complicity with the Third Reich. In the second category, for example, fall apologies by Australia for the separation of Aborigines from their families, by the United States for its overthrow of the Hawaiian monarchy in 1893, by England for its indifference during the Irish potato famine, and by the Vatican for the Counter-Reformation. One category, which I call *political apologies*, is for crimes of the recent past; the other category, which I call *historical apologies*, is for crimes of the distant past. A caveat is in order here: I do not mean to say or imply that apologies for events in the distant past (historical apologies) are not also political. They most certainly are; leaders who hold political office make these apologies, and they are themselves expressions of an interpretation of the past that is meant to imply some policy or resolution toward the effects of that past.

Time, of course, is relative, and the distinction between what is recent and what is distant is somewhat arbitrary. A slightly less arbitrary way to make the distinction is to note whether anyone at the time of the apology was living at the time of the event that is the reason for the apology—if yes, then it is a political apology; if no, it is a historical one.[8] The distinction is worth making to show how nations and churches that began by apologizing for political crimes in which their leaders and constituents could be implicated eventually turned to apologizing for historical crimes in which they could not. That shift—from political to historical apologies, from recognizing responsibility for the immediate past to accepting it for the distant past—demonstrates the quality of guilt in the guilted age, how it expands its reach and broadens and deepens a particular kind of historical sensibility.

Third, I argue that each type of apology—political and historical—has a particular dynamic and strategy. They differ not only in the chronological proximity of the events for which they are offered—events that occurred during the two world wars or events that occurred during the previous millennium—but also in the discursive properties and meanings that each kind of apology expresses. Clearly, they share a great deal, since they represent the same kind of moral act for which the agent is contrite, but they differ substantially in how their agents frame the events, how these agents claim responsibility for the acts, and how the agents see the apology doing a specific kind of ethical and political work. The political apology that I use as my case study—Japan's apologies to the nations it colonized prior to and during World War II—shows how these apologies figure in a long and tortured debate about the nature of responsibility in a polity based on empire. When Japanese prime ministers apologize on the anniversary of the end of World War II in the Asian theater each August 15, they implicitly address issues that are both contemporary (how the apology will affect current relations with

South Korea or China) and profoundly enduring (what the apology says or does not say about Japan's Shōwa-era politics). The historical apology that is the center of this book's focus—the apologies offered by churches, Congress, presidents, and families for American chattel slavery—reveals a sensibility different from that of the political apology, as it addresses key questions about inheritance and the meaning of bearing citizenship or clinging to a sense of belonging within a nation founded on the institution of enslavement. The passage of time seems to change questions that are explicitly political in one case into questions that are ethical as well as political in the other.

Fourth, I argue that these apologies address a particular metaphysical question: the question of what apology and forgiveness *do* to the past events they respectively apologize for and forgive. In personal acts, when someone apologizes for and someone forgives a particular act, that act seems to undergo some transformation. Indeed, the apology-forgiveness dynamic is premised on the idea of transformation. The person apologizing is changed from perpetrator to penitent, and the person forgiving is changed from resentful to merciful. Many philosophers argue that in the midst of all this transformation, the event is somehow *undone*. In some cases, this means that the *effects* of it are undone (the folk wisdom of "forgive and forget" articulates this idea), but in other cases, philosophers argue, the undoing is more mystical and the event itself—the thing that happened—is undone. I set out to understand the theoretical meaning of this argument and its implications when we look at a particular case that demonstrates the dangerous dynamics involved in thinking of forgiveness as undoing.

Finally, I argue that there might be a telling categorical error that explains what these apologies are attempting and frequently fail to do. Sorrow is how we express both guilt and grief ("I am sorry for having done that" and "I am sorry for your loss"). English is not the only language in which the two terms for expressing guilt and mourning are etymologically connected. By returning to the key, formative scenes of political apologies in contemporary Europe—what I think can be aptly described as the inaugurating events of the guilted age—we can see how these particular moments manifest something ambiguous between guilt and grief. By examining the contexts in which they occur, we are better able to see what this conflation and confusion can tell us about the deeper dynamics and desires that mark the guilted age.

ACKNOWLEDGMENTS

I thank everyone at Temple University Press for making the process of completing and publishing this book such a great pleasure. From the very beginning, the acquisitions editor Micah Kleit was enthusiastic and supportive, and his interest in this book made it possible. I also thank Sara Jo Cohen for her help through the process, Kate Nichols for creatively managing the cover design, and Gary Kramer for his helpful advice in managing the publicity for the book. Joan Vidal and Heather Wilcox edited the manuscript with elegance, attention, and generosity. I am truly grateful for all of these thoughtful people who exhibited such caring professionalism on behalf of this book.

I was fortunate in having two wonderfully gifted readers for this book. Christina Sharpe and Brian Weiner have written books that have moved me, and moved me to think, about the nature of our engagements with politics, representations, and representations of politics. I thank them for their extremely helpful suggestions for how to improve this book and for the quality and clarity of their own thinking on related topics.

I have read parts of this book at conferences and invited lectures, and I thank all those who were kind enough to listen and help me in thinking through the problems of the topic of apologies for the past. In particular, I thank Judith Misrahi-Barak and Claudine Raynaud, who convened wonderful conferences that allowed me to test some of these ideas on engaged and attentive audiences.

I thank Bob Levine, who invited me to deliver a lecture in the New Americanists Series at the University of Maryland–College Park. He was a gracious and thoughtful host during the whole of my stay. Finally, I was privileged to have an opportunity to share some of this work with colleagues at my home institution. I thank President Michael Roth for inviting me to address my friends at the President's Lunch Talks Series at Wesleyan University, and I thank my friends for being such a congenial and receptive audience. I deeply appreciate all of the people who listened to the talks, asked probing questions, and made me rethink some positions I experimentally presented in these lectures. Their intellectual engagement was heartening and necessary.

What also made this book possible was the more material assistance of two provosts who have been extremely generous with the university's resources. I am grateful to Rob Rosenthal and Ruth Weissman for their generosity with research funding that made this work possible and, equally, for their unstinting intellectual support of my work. I also thank the numerous librarians at Wesleyan University's Olin Library, particularly the officers at the Interlibrary Loan Office, as well as the librarians at Yale's Sterling Library. As many of us who spend a lifetime reading do, I have a special place in my heart for librarians, and I am fortunate in having had the assistance of such wonderful ones.

As usual, my colleagues at Wesleyan have been remarkable. Unfortunately, I cannot name all the people whose conversation and writing have inspired and informed my work, but I do appreciate them, deeply. I thank, especially, Khachig Tölölyan, Nat and Erness Brody, Sean McCann, Joel Pfister, Lois Brown, Andy Curran, Joyce Jacobsen, and Peter Gottschalk. I also thank Joan Chiari, Elizabeth Tinker, Maureen Zimmer, Eloise Glick, and Joy Vodak for providing warm and terrifically expert help in more ways than I can name.

I am grateful for the close and meaningful friendships that I have with those who have talked with me about this book, and with those who have never talked with me about it. I especially thank Ted Abel, Jeff Kerr-Ritchie, Shani Mott, Nathan Connolly, Rochelle Gurstein, and Robert Greenhill for always being there and always being who they are.

My family, as always, has been wonderful and supportive and loving. My mother and father, Amal and Hassan, have been role models in every way, from intellectual to ethical engagements. My aunts and uncles—Khalo Mohsen, Tante Felicity, Amo Enayat, Tante Ensuf, Uncle Booker, Aunt Gail, Aunt Augustine, Uncle Roy, Aunt Gwen—have been safe havens throughout the world, which their presence makes better. My nieces and nephews consistently uplift my heart and life, as do my sisters, Janice and Senait. Nevolia Ogletree and Kassahun Checole have been terrific, as they always are, providing me with exemplary support, help, and models to imitate.

This book was written on a computer that was constantly surrounded by reminders of what is most important in life. I look up from the screen and see photographs of my beloved sons, Zidane and Aziz, on my desk; I look around and see glorious works of art they have produced taped to my walls; and almost every day I start the process of writing by examining the most recent of an endless series of remarkable, magnificent LEGO creations that they have deposited right next to my computer mouse. I marvel at the creativity and ingenuity of their minds, find constant solace and hope in their voices and laughter, and am ever renewed and humbled by their unquestioning love. They are a shining, precious presence for which I am deeply, wholly thankful.

My wife, Kidan, makes many more things—many more *important* things —possible than this book. But what she has done for this book is inestimable. She has helped me in every possible way—from ensuring that I had the time and quiet to write it to stimulating me with her always profound insights into all sorts of matters integral and related to the subject of my study. I am thankful for her intelligence, her conversation, her thoughts, and the lessons she has taught me that have made this book better than it would have been otherwise. Even more, much more, I am thankful for having her soulful presence in all the things wholly unrelated to this book. I am deeply, hopelessly, and eternally in love with her and grateful for everything she has done for me in our life together. Every day, I marvel that she has given me everything—our sons, my happiness—and every day I am joyful that I wake to her presence and love. A character in Toni Morrison's *Beloved* says of his own beloved: "She is a friend of my mind. She gather me, man. The pieces of me I am, she gather them and give them back to me in all the right order." Kidan, you are the friend of my mind and the love of my life. Thank you.

Finally, I dedicate this book to my brother, Amgad. Everything in my life—from my childhood and adolescence to my adulthood—has been made richer and better because of his kindness, his thoughtfulness, and his consistent and unwavering love. My brother is one of the most caring and concerned people I know, one of the most truly generous in the world. He has set examples for me time after time and exemplified what it means to be a perfect older brother. Having him in my life from its beginning has made me who I am. Everyone who knows my brother loves him; I was lucky enough to know him from the moment I was born.

A GUILTED AGE

INTRODUCTION

The first year of the new millennium unfolded in the following way: In May 2001, the French parliament passed a law calling slavery and the slave trade "crimes against humanity." It was widely perceived to be that nation's apology for slavery. That same month, the Vatican explicitly apologized for its complicity in the murder of Jews in Poland during World War II. Later that year, the director of the Max Planck Institute apologized for that organization's involvement in medical experiments in the concentration camps (June); the Russian parliament voted to apologize to the ethnic Germans who were forcibly resettled (July); former Khmer Rouge leader Khieu Samphan apologized for his role in the regime's atrocities at the same time that the United Nations World Conference against Racism, Racial Discrimination, Xenophobia, and Related Intolerance, held in Durban, South Africa, also called slavery and the slave trade "crimes against humanity" (August); the leaders of the Myōshin-ji sect of Zen Buddhism apologized for their ties to Japan's militarist past (September); the Japanese prime minister apologized to China for acts committed during World War II (October); and the Canadian House of Commons apologized for the execution of Canadian soldiers charged with cowardice during World War I (December).[1]

Other apologies were issued during this year, but I have listed only the political and historical apologies from World War II and earlier, not politicians' apologies for contemporary events, such as the American apology to China for the U.S spy plane that collided with a Chinese fighter jet in April, or the American apology to Japan for an American submarine's collision with a Japanese fishing boat in February. Even where apologies were not offered, they were contemplated. Eleven nations of the European Union had prepared what was described as "a straightforward apology for the transatlantic trade in slavery" in September, but four of the member states demurred, wishing the statement to be more temperate in its contrition—that is, to express "regret" without "responsibility." It is perhaps not surprising that the four demurring nations—Britain, Spain, the Netherlands, and Portugal—also happen to be the nations that profited most from the slave trade.[2] The point, however, is that apology had become a routine, expected form. That development is a novel thing, and one, I argue, that defines the guilted age.

What might such a furious attempt to come to terms with the past in this mode of apologizing for it mean? First, I would draw attention to the two most evident kinds of apologies—the political ones for events connected to World War II and the historical apologies for events in the distant past. As I argue in this book, the historical apologies evolved from the political apologies sometime in the 1980s. Thereafter, numerous nations apologized for what they now defined as the crimes of their past. These included institutions (slavery, most notably) as well as political strategies to decimate aboriginal cultures within their borders. Church leaders also apologized for the sins of their past. Some were political apologies, as in the Vatican's apology noted above for inaction during the Holocaust, and some were historical apologies, as Pope John Paul II apologized for specific events (the Counter-Reformation, the Crusades, the slave trade) as well as long-standing trends (the oppression of women). That distinction between political and historical apologies is admittedly an arbitrary one; events that are of the recent past now will eventually recede into the distant past. But the distinction is not without significance for the guilted age, since it alerts us to the fact that these nations and churches feel the pressures of two distinct pasts—one clearly connected to the present, events around World War II that largely defined our world (prewar, postwar), and the other less clearly connected. As I say above, I believe that the historical apology emerged from the political and that the second sense of connection to the distant past evolved from the first. Institutions and nations that felt guilty for the roles they played or failed to play around 1945 learned to accept a wider sense of guilt for the roles they played a century or five centuries prior.

Second, I would draw attention to the fact that these are *apologies*. By the end of the millennium, they had become routine, and, as I show in the Preface, routinely mocked, but we must not fail to recognize that these public apologies are a recent phenomenon, and the fact that they are so pervasive must tell us something about the epoch in which they first and most fully appeared in these forms. These public apologies for events of the recent and distant past, I argue, are the transcendent practice that has emerged as a defining feature of our *guilted* age. The guilted age that began around 1945 is to some extent defined by precisely that—a widespread global feeling of guilt, not an existential guilt unmoored to anything, but a moral guilt that emerges from particular political conditions. The practice that the guilted age has developed to assuage that feeling of guilt is a particular kind of contrition that first takes the form of the political apology and then later the historical apology. *The Guilted Age*, then, is a study of what Martha Nussbaum calls a "political emotion." The emotion with which she is concerned is love, and the practice through which she believes love is politically expressed in a meaningful way is justice.[3] The emotion with which I am concerned here is guilt, and the practice through which that guilt is manifest and expressed is the public apology.

In the next chapter, I show which forces led to the emergence of guilt as that distinctive quality by looking more intently at the development of particular judicial institutions that defined key terms for that age and the expression of a specific kind of philosophy that argued for an ethics of guilt on the basis of those terms. This chapter first asks, however, in what sense we can speak of an era as being marked by a peculiar attitude and tries to shed light on how this age may be said to be defined by guilt.

In suggesting a name for an epoch as I do here, I gratefully acknowledge that I am humbly and tepidly following the masterly example of Eric Hobsbawm, who has virtually made a career of naming each of the eras of the long nineteenth century (1789–1914): the age of revolution, the age of capital, and the age of empire. At the end of a long and magnificent career, he turned to the short twentieth century (1914–1991), and divided what he called the "age of extremes" into two epochs: the age of catastrophe (1914–1945), and the golden age (1945–1990). Timidly, I disagree. What he is calling "golden," I am calling "guilted." I am certainly not denying that it was also golden in its technical achievements, and in describing the material and technological and economic accomplishments of the second half of the century, Hobsbawm more than hints that all that glitters is not gold. (Someone more inclined to punning would have said that Hobsbawm implies that the golden was also a gilted age.) Pierre Nora describes that same era in a different way, calling it the "era of commemoration," which is marked, he writes, in the "passage from the historical to the remembered and the remembered to the commemorative." In other words, what happened is transformed from an existential thing (it happened) to a cognitive thing (it is remembered) to a symbolic thing (it is commemorated). We see that this dynamic aptly describes the processes of the guilted age, where what happened is remembered frequently in the form of the public apology. Commemoration becomes an expression of guilt.[4]

Writing shortly after the end of World War II, Albert Camus sees the emergence of the primary themes of the twentieth century in terms similar to the ones I am employing here. While the nineteenth was "the century of rebellion," he writes, the twentieth has become "the century of justice and ethics"—in which, he adds ominously, "everyone indulges in self-recrimination." The "question of the twentieth century," he concludes at mid-century, is "how to live without grace and without justice." A world racked by war and devastated by genocide must feel guilt—indeed, what Camus calls "universal guilt"—both because it was a witness to those atrocities, and, he argues more specifically, because that is what the Third Reich ultimately produced. As he looks around him at the close of the war, he sees the inevitable response to universal guilt—that is, universal contrition. When perpetrators are guilty because of what they have done, and victims are made to feel guilty by what the perpetrators have done, the "concept of innocence disappears from the world," replaced by guilt and despair. "That is why an unworthy and cruel penitence reigns over this world where only the stones are innocent," Camus perorates. The rest of the twentieth century, and the beginning of the twenty-first, saw that penitence develop a formal and discursive means by which it would attempt to expiate its "universal guilt."[5] Camus is prescient here, as in so much else, about a world where heroic rebellion has been superseded, a century that has lost its innocence in what Camus entitles *The Fall*, is ill with what he calls *The Plague*, and generally is marked by exile, anomie, and despair. Other observers of the unfolding of the postwar world found the same manifestations of guilt.

In a 1967 article entitled "Generation without a Past," Gitta Sereny, an Austrian-born Hungarian journalist who lived through parts of the Third Reich and then worked in postwar Germany, describes just what a profound sense of malaise there was in a country tense with faithlessness. She interviews several students born in the years after the war who are afraid to ask their parents just what happened, lest they find out things they would rather not know. As one of her interviewees puts it, "It would mean saying to those we love: 'We accuse you.'" At the same time, many trials of former Nazis were underway in several cities in West Germany, all struggling to complete their adjudication and sentencing before the impending statute of limitations was reached in 1970 (the statute of limitations was extended in Germany and then later abolished for crimes against humanity, but these were trials usually of lesser charges of simple murder). At the same time, these courts recognized the futility of what they were doing. They could not charge the two groups of people everyone knew to be guilty—that is, the *Schreibtischtäter* (the desk murderers) who issued and signed the orders that led to the murder of millions and the major Nazi criminals who had already been found guilty in the military tribunal courts of the Allies in the 1940s and then amnestied in the early 1950s. Those who signed the death orders could not be tried because of technicalities, while those who killed could not be retried because of the Allied treaty forbidding Germans from repealing any Allied legal decision. And, in any case, as the prosecuting attorneys Sereny interviews notes, what difference does it make? What sentence could mean anything in the face of the crimes? In the "final analysis," they conclude, "any punishment handed out belittles the crime."[6]

Sereny is an acute observer who spent her adolescence witnessing the spectacle of National Socialism. As a preteen, she accidently wandered into a rally in Nuremberg when the train taking her to London had mechanical difficulties. She was in Vienna when the Nazis took over the city, and she volunteered as an Allied nurse during the war. After the war, she worked with the agencies trying to identify and return the children who were stolen from Polish families and given to German families as adoptees. Heinrich Himmler had established the policy of identifying which children had what he called "racial potential" and then giving them to families for what was called "Germanization." Sereny, then, witnessed Germany at the beginning and at the end of the Nazi era and helped redress some of what Nazi policies had done. As an outsider, and someone with a keen ear and shrewd intelligence, she is able to see what lies underneath what her interviewees are telling her. She senses a country that in many ways is immature, precisely because the generation that should be arising to activity and endeavor is mired in a relationship with its parents that has never been resolved. "In other countries," she writes, "a man of twenty-seven or thirty is an adult—in Germany the term 'youth' must apply even to those of thirty-five and over" because the "only valid point of division is who was part—and who was not part—of the Hitler era."[7] Sereny, in 1967, describes a country that is profoundly stalled.

It was also a country that was suffering a particular and dynamic kind of travail. "Contrary to popular belief abroad," she asserts, "the Germans are consumed by impotent guilt." She finds that guilt etched into the very geography and chronology of the nation: "They are a country not only geographically divided, but divided from their own history and divided, what is more, into sharply defined age groups, each with an entirely separate and yet primarily evasive perspective of their past and present." Although Sereny is not particularly given to drawing on the language of psychoanalysis, she sees this situation in precisely those terms: All German generations are in separate states of denial (each one evading what it fears to confront, its own responsibility, its parents' complicity), and that denial only augments and deepens that primal guilt: "The nation's guilt—entirely unresolved—has become the nation's trauma."[8]

Sereny describes a number of different kinds and qualities of guilt in this society. There are those who are criminally guilty—found so and then freed and amnestied, or on trial and likely to meet punishments that will mock rather than fit the crime. There are those who are morally guilty—who cannot confront their children because they know that they have led a life of ethical corruption, of accepting the unacceptable. And there are those who are politically guilty—those who supported the regime or failed to resist its most obvious and obnoxious actions. These, as it happens, are three of the four categories of guilt that the philosopher Karl Jaspers identifies in his 1948 book *The Question of German Guilt.* (I discuss this book in greater detail in the next chapter; the fourth category is metaphysical guilt.) It was, in other words, a society that was guilty in no simple sense, not merely guilty of having pursued a particular course of action, but one guilty in a fundamental and complex way and with a guilt that festered and was turning pathological. When Primo Levi's *Survival in Auschwitz* was published in a German edition in 1961, he received about a letter a month from German readers in the first three years his book was in print. Many of these letters state directly, as one representative example does, "We are guilty," or accepts, in the words of another, "what we recognize to be our guilt before God and mankind."[9] It is telling that so many sought to confess their moral guilt to someone they could clearly identify as a victim of their nation's political guilt.[10]

Part of the reason is that this guilt had not been addressed in the institutions where it most reasonably might have been—namely, the courts. Consider two of the most reflective and thoughtful defendants in the first Nuremberg trial. At the end of his testimony, Hans Frank, the minister of justice for the Third Reich, famously prophesied that a "thousand years will pass and still this guilt of Germany will not have been erased." It is a striking statement, a moment of seemingly resolute recognition and penitence. Some of his fellow defendants were skeptical and wondered why Frank resorted to a grand claim of national guilt instead of acknowledging a more personal one. In any case, by the end of the trial, in his closing statement before sentencing, Frank returned to this question and gave a rather different assessment. He reminded his listeners of his earlier claim and then suggested that he would like to modify it: "Every possible guilt incurred by our nation has already been completely wiped out today," he now claimed, by virtue of the ongoing "mass crimes" against the German people in the aftermath of the war. In a matter of weeks, Frank went from penitence to resentment, from a millennial guilt to an indignant absolution.

The other defendant, Albert Speer, is often cast as the one Nazi who accepted responsibility at Nuremberg and lived his life thereafter in consistent atonement. And yet in his testimony at Nuremberg, he was remarkably unclear and, as shown later, dishonest about what he knew. In a redirect after the cross-examination, Speer's lawyer Hans Flächsner sought clarity about a statement Speer made during the cross-examination about "common responsibility." Did Speer want to say that he was claiming a "measurable guilt or coresponsibility under the penal law" or rather that he was noting Germany's "historical responsibility"? Speer acknowledged that the "question is a very difficult one to answer"—and then didn't answer it. Here, then, were the two most confident acknowledgments of responsibility at Nuremberg, and both came to nothing. Neither Frank nor Speer revoked their "not guilty" pleas when they accepted responsibility and guilt, and neither, in the end, maintained that responsibility for long, or honestly. The next generation would pay for that. One of the people Sereny interviews for a later article, Dirk, is the son of the head of the Gestapo in Braunschweig. His father had been found guilty and hanged in 1948. More than forty years later, his son is still haunted. Nazis like his father, he claims, "were incapable of shame or repentance and therefore left us alone with nothing but the heritage of their awful guilt." He had joined a group counseling session led by an Israeli psychologist, Dan Bar-On, to find some resolution to that guilt. The guilt that was found or not found, claimed or unclaimed, in the courtroom was now appearing on the therapist's couch.[11]

Three years before Sereny published her 1967 essay on Germany's postwar malaise, Japan had undergone a similar moment of reflection around an enigmatic moment in its postwar history. In 1964, Japan awarded American Air Force General Curtis LeMay the highest honor a non-Japanese citizen could receive, the First Class Order of the Rising Sun. Both Emperor Hirohito and Prime Minister Satō Eisaku and his cabinet approved the award. The Japanese Diet was aghast. LeMay, after all, had planned and executed the bombing campaign against Japanese cities, including the firebombing of Tokyo, which he had masterminded without consulting Washington. That campaign, conducted on the night of March 9–10, 1945, involved flying 334 aircraft at low altitudes with incendiary bombs that created fires so intense that, as one historian of the war puts it, "canals boiled, metal melted, and buildings and human beings burst spontaneously into flames." It was the most devastating bombing raid during World War II, and the second-largest "urban conflagration in recorded history." LeMay had also planned Operation Starvation, in which American planes dropped mines in the waterways that transported Japanese food distribution. Finally, he was also the one who relayed the presidential order to drop the atomic bombs on Hiroshima and Nagasaki. How could Japan honor this person, whose missions under his command had killed somewhere around half a million Japanese civilians? Members of the Diet demanded that the honor be retracted. The Foreign Ministry and the Self-Defense Agency responded to their request in an odd way, reportedly replying, "There is no limit to talking about what occurred during the war."[12] If this is their true reply, it is a profound statement, and, if apocryphal, just as profound.

In Japan, this anecdote reveals, there were at least two ways of talking and thinking about the war. One involved something like forgiveness, and the other something like resentment. Honoring someone who had done so much damage to the country and its citizens could mean only an exorbitant act of acceptance, a willingness to forego indignation that amounted to an act of forgiveness at the very highest levels of the polity. The emperor approved. Those who saw this act of honoring the enemy as a violation, an affront to their history and the meaning of the lives of their fellow citizens, felt a righteous resentment. The Diet seethed.

In the background of these events in 1964 were two different kinds of politics. One was immediate: Tokyo was hosting the 1964 Olympics, and some believed that this act was a way of establishing a tenor for the type of gracious host Japan would prove to be as the world arrived. The other was less recent and directly connected to the events of 1945: Like Germany, Japan too had developed a guilt complex. The filmmaker Itami Mansaku published an article in 1946 in which he contests the prevailing idea that Japanese people had been deceived by their war leaders and were therefore not responsible in any way for the crimes their country had committed in the war. Itami argues for a more robust and stringent sense of responsibility, more akin to the one that Jaspers would produce for German guilt.[13] A people are held responsible for what their leaders do, and the leaders are also responsible for what they do. This, in Japan, was a toxic issue, since the leader whose responsibility was primarily the topic of debate was Emperor Hirohito. As I discuss later, the question of Hirohito's "responsibility" would haunt Japan for decades—indeed, for the rest of the Shōwa era, and beyond. So, the odd politics of 1964, where the Japanese emperor who refused to apologize for what he did to begin the war seemed to be forgiving the American general who had devastated his country at the end of that war, echoed back to debates that had begun in 1945 and would continue well into the new millennium.

Jaspers and Itami are early theorists of national responsibility, at the dawn of the era I am calling the guilted age. And yet Germany and Japan both came to their guilt late. Devastated beyond belief at the end of the war, neither nation had the physical, mental, and spiritual resources to respond quickly to the historical events many elsewhere in the world believed that they had to acknowledge. That guilt would be expressed, in conscious and unconscious ways, over the next several decades. (The LeMay incident might well be an unconscious expression of it.) And the strategies that both nations employed to express that guilt and in some ways address it would also develop over the course of those decades. At the heart of those strategies was the hallmark of the guilted age: Acts of atonement and redress manifest most often in the political apology. Both nations believed that the way out of guilt was repentance. And that repentance, like the feeling of guilt it was meant to assuage, was long in coming, and its unfolding is the unfolding of the guilted age. As Sereny views the sort of industriousness with which Germany had achieved its remarkable economic success by the mid-1960s, she notes that it appears to her that this work ethic, this drive to produce and succeed, was, as she puts it, "not because of, but instead of repentance." Likewise, in 1946, the Japanese scholar of French literature Watanabe Kazuo published an essay in which he ponders whether Japan and Germany would be returned to the international community if they did not express "repentance," which he believes that the Japanese at least did not sufficiently comprehend.[14] Japan's similar "economic miracle" might well have caused some to reflect, as Sereny does of Germany, whether this was another case of industriousness in lieu of penance.

Despite, or maybe because of, the fact that there had been no "war responsibility" clause in the aftermath of World War II, as there had disastrously been in the Treaty of Versailles, the issue of responsibility and guilt became more amorphous and free-floating. Because it was not encased in a formal document, the sense of responsibility appears to have been more diffuse and, in some ways, more potent for that very reason. Germany and Japan are extreme cases, not paradigmatic ones. And yet their experiences, the evolution of their strategies for returning to the global order, I think define what would happen to a lesser degree in other nations over the seven decades following the end of the war. The sense of guilt that Germans and Japanese exhibited, and also bitterly disputed and contested, formed a discourse that spread to other nations and defined the new sensibility of the guilted age. The way out of that guilt, as I show, was through symbolic acts of atonement, particularly the political apology that both Japanese and German leaders would offer and offer again to the nations they injured, and to the world in general.

It would be that kind of atonement that many nations would express in the decades following 1945. The political apology was obviously not the only practice that developed for healing the wounds of the past or assuaging the guilt for it. Many other forms were available and developed, especially when a collective body, usually a nation, had to confront the major divisions and widespread complicities in its past. This has been most clearly the case in those nations in which notorious regimes of all sorts—military juntas, police states, totalitarian societies—have undergone a transition to a new regime. These polities have had to confront the fact that many of their citizens were active agents in the previous regime—sometimes as police agents, sometimes as spies, and sometimes as what in East Germany were called *Inoffizielle Mitarbeiter* ("unofficial collaborator"). The processes for dealing with those agents have ranged from "de-Nazification" in Germany in the late 1940s, to contested amnesties in many Latin American nations in the 1980s, to lustration and what was called "de-communization" in the European countries emerging from communist rule in the early 1990s, to truth and reconciliation commissions in both South America and South Africa at the fin de siècle.[15] In some cases, these processes were made forms of entertainment. In 1992, French television aired an episode of the television program *Marche de Siècle* on which appeared two Poles on polar sides of politics in Poland, General Wojciech Witold Jaruzelski and Adam Michnik, to discuss whether forgiveness was an apt response to the political transition. The German station Sudwestfunk broadcast another interview between two people, one a spy and the other his victim, that it titled "My Friend the Stasi Informer."[16]

The scholarship assessing what constitutes justice when the creators of law are turned out and their rule of law shown to be wholly coercive has come to be called "transitional justice."[17] The point of studies conducted in that field is to demonstrate the range of options such societies have when they undergo these transitions and to gauge to what extent such societies are torn between making a choice to pursue retributive justice or a choice to nurture a fragile democracy, between rigorously punishing those who operated the previous regime's often terrorist machinery or tepidly attempting to establish the grounds for a new social order. That choice, sometimes cast between amnesty and justice, and, more recently, between truth (for amnesty) and justice, has struck some as based on a logical flaw.[18] That debate is not my concern, though.

My concern is that these transitional societies undergo particular kinds of travails precisely because the citizens in them feel guilty, and that guilt manifests itself in specific ways and inspires particular courses of action. These cases, like those of Japan and Germany, show us the dynamic that formed and extended the guilted age. No period of recorded history has witnessed more such transitions than the period following the end of what Hobsbawm insightfully calls "the thirty-one years' world war," that period of history between Austria's declaration of war on Serbia in July 1914 and Japan's surrender in August 1945.[19] First, and most crucially, Germany and Japan were both occupied, both put on trial (the Nuremberg and Tokyo trials), and both subjected to a forced transition from one regime to the next (de-Nazification in Germany, demilitarization in Japan). Neighboring countries like Austria and France likewise underwent transitions, from the First to the Second Republic in the former, from Vichy to the Fourth Republic in the latter. Thereafter, in a series of waves, we saw global transitions.

The first wave that followed 1945 spelled the end of colonization. England lost Jordan in 1946; the crown jewel of its empire, India, in 1947; its other Asian holdings in Burma, Ceylon (now Sri Lanka), and Indonesia in 1948; and then shortly thereafter the rest of its empire in Africa. France lost Syria and Lebanon in 1945, the states of Indochina in 1946 (although the wars over it would continue to the 1970s), and then its North African holdings in Morocco, Tunisia, and Algeria from 1956 to 1962. The Netherlands lost its East Indies colonies in 1950, while the United States lost the Philippines in 1946. Political decolonization was followed by intellectual—that is, how to decolonize the mind—and then by pointed questions about what to do with that past, how a nation cobbled together by the colonizer could establish a unity of that diversity, and how to address just what colonization meant for the lack of development in that nation. In other words, here were nations that demanded at the very least an acknowledgment that their histories had been compromised.

The next wave came in the fall of totalitarian regimes in the 1980s and 1990s, including the fall of the communist bloc, the fall of military juntas in South America, and the fall of apartheid. These events inspired the formation of the concept of "transitional justice" and posed the questions about how to address widespread cases of complicity with the mechanisms of a judicial system that were simply inadequate to define and process those kinds of allegations.

The final wave, at the time of this writing, is what is being called the "Arab Spring," which led to the fall of several long-standing tyrannies in Libya, Tunisia, Algeria, Egypt, and Yemen. As the citizens of other nations in the region, notably Syria, continue to attempt the overthrow of their corrupt governments, we will likely witness another set of tribunals, commissions, and debates about how each of these countries can emerge from the destructive rule of its previous regime.

In the midst of the decolonization of the 1960s and 1970s also emerged an important social movement in which we saw the rise of consciousness of oppressed peoples worldwide (women, the working class, ethnic and racial minorities). In the United States, out of the civil rights, Black Power, feminist, antiwar, and indigenous peoples' movements came a new sense that there was a long history of oppression that required more than legal redress. The 1960s also marked a changing of the guard in the historical profession and the emergence of a new social history that took seriously the idea of examining the past "from the bottom up"—that is, using the testimony of the oppressed, and not the victors only, to tell the nation's story. These would be histories of accusations and not celebrations, of crimes and not destiny, of guilt and not innocence. The French student uprising, like the American one, addressed the Vietnam War, but it also wanted to dismantle the myth of France's wartime experience, the "resistance" account that bracketed Vichy as an anomaly that could be denied. Likewise, the German student movement was antiwar, and it also seemed to be about more than only the Vietnam War; the students in Germany simultaneously raised difficult questions about their parents' wartime conduct under National Socialism. The "youth revolt of 1968," as the future president of West Germany writes, "brought about a new, more honest response to the Nazi past."[20] The social movements of the 1960s, then, constituted another moment when members of a generation came to question their nations' past and to demand answers to what to do with that past—whether it was the Nazi past, the Vichy past, or the slave past.

All these transitions raised precisely the kinds of questions that were raised in 1945. What does one do with the guilty, and what does one do with the guilt? That sense of guilt is sometimes criminal, and sometimes moral, to employ the categories Jaspers suggests in the wake of World War II. It some cases, the guilt is felt by individuals who were agents of the state, who did the nasty work of policing, surveilling, disappearing, and exterminating particular populations. Theirs is the guilt of the betrayed warrior, whose cause has been definitively shown to be corrupt and riddled with lies that now appear transparent. People like Franz Stangl, the commandant of the Treblinka extermination camp, or Eugene de Kock, a colonel in the South African Police, specializing in murdering perceived insurgents against apartheid, express that kind of guilt. They recognize that what they did was wrong and that the social order they were trying to uphold was wrong, but they also feel singled out as sacrifices to a new morality. These are cases of criminal guilt. The more widespread sentiment, though, is one of moral guilt, of those who believe that they lived compromised lives under those regimes, within those social orders. They feel an uneasiness that they were somehow complicit in what they knew to be wrong. Some were more active than others; some, for instance, were recruited to operate in the spying networks of their societies, while others were simply willing to look the other way. In either case—as informal agents of the state or unquestioning citizens of it—they believe that they have not done the better part, and therefore feel a gnawing moral guilt. The question is what to do with it.

In the face of unprecedented inhumanity, what possibilities could there be for the institutions and practices that humans had previously used to define, punish, and show mercy? Trials? If almost an entire society can be seen as complicit in what happened, it would be unfair to single some out as more culpable than others—the quislings, the collaborators, the insufficiently resistant. To put only some on trial when almost all were guilty to varying extents would be manifestly unjust, but to put none on trial would also be manifestly unjust. What other practice besides justice might serve in these critical situations? One answer, a tragic one that was not theoretical but practiced widely, was summary justice. Throughout Europe, people pursued a policy of vengeance against their fellow citizens. People perceived to have collaborated or slept with the enemy were killed by mobs; subjected to ritual humiliations, their hair shorn, stripped, tarred and feathered; and made to suffer other indignities. This aggressive vindictiveness was massively widespread, as recent works on the postwar period demonstrate. It was in light of those debates—and in the midst of those acts of summary justice—that some thinkers proposed the possibility of forgiveness. The French philosopher Vladimir Jankélévitch, who published his book on forgiveness, *Le Pardon*, in 1967, first turned to the subject around 1945. His translator notes that the "subject of forgiveness begins to appear in Jankélévitch's works after World War II," starting with his book *Le Mal* in 1947.[21]

In one notable instance in 1944–1945, in post-Vichy France, two former members of the French Resistance, François Mauriac and Albert Camus, debated whether it was better for France to pursue strict justice and punish those who committed crimes against the nation or to be more forbearing, accept the human condition of sinfulness, and forgive their enemies. In the editorials he wrote for *Combat*, Camus maintains that charity at this moment would destroy the nation. To extend forgiveness or mercy—*une charité divine*—would be to deny the French people of the justice they deserve and to frustrate the creation of a new society. In his columns in the pages of *Le Figaro,* Mauriac holds the opposite but fears that such forgiveness is simply impossible at this moment: *"La charité se retire tous les camps à la fois."*[22] It is significant that both thinkers, writing at the end of one regime, Vichy, and at the dawn of the one that would replace it, the Fourth Republic, are irresistibly drawn to the eighteenth century of the First Republic to ground their arguments.

Mauriac immediately draws on the example of the Terror of 1793–1794 to compare the desire for retribution with another moment of France's desire to purify itself through violence. Camus returns to this point a few years later in *The Rebel.* Citing Louis Antoine de Saint-Just, one of the leaders of the Terror before he became its victim, Camus notes that Saint-Just's dream for "a republic of forgiveness" in revolutionary times—like 1945, one is meant to infer—leads "with implacable logic, to the republic of the guillotine." Camus recognizes that "there is a certain ambiguity in the case of Saint-Just," as there is in Camus's own argument. A few years later, Camus would write passionately against the death penalty in his "Reflections on the Guillotine," and so it is not entirely clear what he means by citing Saint-Just's opposition to it, if his point is simply to show that such opposition in times that call for strict justice can consume all those who wish to temper it.[23] It could be that Camus holds more tenuously in 1951, when he wrote *The Rebel,* the position he holds more firmly in 1957, when he wrote his anti–death penalty manifesto. Or it could be that he is working out in 1951 the issues he had raised in 1944, about the place of forgiveness in cases of transitional justice. Could forgiveness appear in a world that required but could not find justice? Or, in the terms Camus himself uses, could forgiveness have a place in a world racked with "universal guilt" and exhibiting only "cruel penitence"?

We can see, then, that the postwar world was consistently defined by a series of political transitions that inspired key questions about the place of mercy and amnesty and forgiveness in societies where it was hard to identify the appropriate measures of justice for crimes that beggared the imagination as much as they mocked the insufficiency of any punishment that could be imposed on those who performed them. That postwar world, which I am calling the guilted age, did not answer those questions in a uniform way, nor did it develop the primary practice that would mark that age—the political and historical apology—in the immediate aftermath of the war. It took the unfolding of the decades, and the deepening of the political guilt, and then the expansion of the historical guilt, for those strategies to emerge in the fullness witnessed in the scenes described at the beginning of this chapter. Political events at the beginning of the 1970s, and then further developments in the mid-1980s, began to reveal the potential for the public apology as a practice.

Moreover, when that sense of guilt began to manifest itself in the form of political and historical apologies, as I show later, it was deeply contested—the apologies were rebutted by some who saw them as unnecessary because the guilt was wrongly ascribed, and they were condemned by others who saw them as inadequate because the guilt was too deep and the apologies insufficient. Those who see them as inadequate often make the argument for the propriety of more concrete forms of reparation, which is a topic unto itself. What is important for this study is to recognize that the advocates for reparations accept the terms of the debate about guilt and responsibility and challenge instead the forms of the resolution that the debate takes. Those who see the apologies as unnecessary, on the other hand, contest the terms of the debate itself, claiming that the key ideas of guilt and responsibility for the past are the wrong terms for us to use when assessing our sense of historical placement. We need, then, to have a better sense of how those terms—the crucial ideas and language that defined how to think about the particular dynamics of the guilted age—evolved in the postwar world. It is to those terms and the institutional and intellectual traditions from which they emerged that I now turn.

1

THE GUILTED AGE

I should acknowledge at the outset that the task of arguing for the existence, and the reasons for the existence, of a diffuse sensibility—that is, the guilt in the guilted age—is complicated because I am trying to demonstrate how a relatively diffuse emotion seems to have crept or seeped into political and popular discourses. Had it been a tangible political structure whose inauguration or changes I was trying to identify, or an intellectual trend, the task would have been easier. If, say, I was studying a political structure, I could trace its origins or its declines with a pretty high degree of certainty. If I wanted to know why the Soviet Union collapsed in the early 1990s, I would trace back from definable events that mark the moment of the collapse itself—the states actually seceding from it—to the political events that preceded those events. I would examine how Mikhail Gorbachev's reformist policy of *glasnost* and *perestroika*, as it entered our political lexicon, struck at precisely the points at which the Soviet Union was most fragile. And I would see how, as so often happens in the course of history, the final result was considerably greater than the hopes of those who set out to alter it in some way. What Gorbachev hoped only to reform underwent a dramatic revolutionary change.

Likewise, those who gathered in Tahrir Square in Cairo in 2011 did not imagine that their actions would bring down an autocratic presidency of thirty years' duration; they wanted to reform the system so that it would be less oppressive and give them greater voice. Those who set out to boycott segregated buses in Montgomery, Alabama, in 1955 might have *dreamed* of bringing down the entire edifice of American legal racism, but their stated plan was limited to changing the terms of the existing segregation on public transportation—that is, how the seating was arranged, not the very injustice of defining seating by race. In general, these lessons are encouraging because they show that the planners cannot anticipate the needs and demands of the people for whom they plan. But the specific point I am making is that these are all events that culminate in something, and therefore their origins can be traced.

The case is the same with an intellectual movement. If I wanted to know how Romantic poetry or Dadaism emerged, I would go back to the thinkers and artists associated with the movement and see in what ways they developed a theory in response to some felt need, how they identified the specific social constraint against which they rebelled, and how they theorized a particular kind of practice that would respond to that need and alter those constraints.

The guilted age, as I have been writing about it here, is neither a political structure nor an intellectual movement. It is primarily a widespread sensibility, which is considerably harder to trace to some origin. I necessarily have to be speculative in suggesting such an origin, and here, having offered the reader the requisite *caveat emptor*, is just where I can begin my speculating. My major questions are threefold: First, when did it begin, and why did it emerge then? Second, since the major tenet of guilted age discourse is the question of responsibility, how did the sentiment that there was such a thing as collective, communal responsibility emerge? Finally, how did the guilted age arrive at the belief that the form of redress most appropriate as a response to the felt need of the era was the apology (political and historical)? These questions, then, are about chronology and origins (when did it emerge), agency (who can be held responsible and why), and discourse (why apology).

I have suggested that the guilted age is a postwar phenomenon—that its origins, so to speak, can be traced back to 1945. Of course, what constitutes the "guilt" in the guilted age has to be traced back earlier to events that occurred from 1914 to 1945, what Eric Hobsbawm has helpfully called the "Thirty-One Years' War" that roiled one world and created another.[1] The question is: why then? Why in 1945 does something happen that led to the emergence of a new sensibility about guilt and the development of particular strategies for encompassing and redressing it? Germany did not apologize after World War I, and indeed it felt a particularly acute form of *ressentiment* precisely at what was called the "War Guilt Clause" of the Treaty of Versailles, which placed "responsibility" solely on Germany. Here were all the terms that later emerged in the discourse of the guilted age (guilt, responsibility, redress), and yet they did not coalesce into anything more than *ressentiment*, a sentiment that is precisely opposed to forgiveness. In the wake of World War II, German politicians assumed a very different attitude and employed a novel discursive strategy. They apologized, and kept apologizing from Chancellor Konrad Adenauer in 1949 to Chancellor Willy Brandt in 1970 to Chancellor Helmut Kohl in 1985. The obvious difference was the nature of the war and the event for which they apologized, the Holocaust. What they apologized for was not simply a war crime, and what they acknowledged was not simply "war guilt," but rather a different kind of national guilt for a different kind of crime—namely, a crime against humanity. And it is here, I think, that I can find some more firm ground for my speculations.

The specific legal category of "crimes against humanity" did not exist prior to 1945, and it was produced in 1945. The Allies proposed the idea that there was such a thing as "crimes against humanity" so that they could pursue a particular legal prosecution of Axis war leaders. Of course, the idea of crimes against humanity—that is, crimes that are not directed at individuals, not acts committed during war, and not covered by other legal statutes—is not a product of 1945. At the end of World War I, the British Prime Minister Lloyd George and the Australian Prime Minister W. M. Hughes both referred to the crimes committed by Kaiser Wilhelm II in starting the war as "high treason against humanity." Indeed, the term "crimes against humanity" was coined in the midst of World War I. When the Russian minister for foreign affairs, Sergei Sazonov, proposed the term crimes "against Christianity and civilisation" to describe the Turkish genocide against the Armenians, the British ambassador in Paris was concerned at the anti-Islamic sound of the phrase and suggested the alternative "crimes against civilization." To appease the British, Sazonov proposed the final wording of crimes "against humanity and civilisation." As early as 1915, then, that language was in use, and it became quite useful to a range of actors. The new Turkish grand vizier referred to the acts of the Ittihadist leaders he had arrested as "crimes against humanity and against liberty." Between 1915 and 1919, then, as Gary Jonathan Bass has admirably demonstrated, that newly minted term took hold in a range of different nations.[2]

It did not take hold as a legal category with force behind it, however, until 1945. In the Charter of the International Military Tribunal (popularly known as the Nuremberg Tribunal), signed into power on August 8, 1945, in London, "crimes against humanity" constitute the third and final category of crimes (following "crimes against peace" and "war crimes"). This category of crimes was indeed groundbreaking in three specific ways. First, it defined a new victim of crimes (humanity). The Tribunal defines "crimes against humanity" as including "murder, extermination, enslavement, deportation, and other inhumane acts committed against any civilian population, before or during the war, or persecutions on political, racial, or religious grounds." Second, it broke the grounds of national sovereignty; these acts would be considered crimes no matter what laws are in place in the nation or nations where they occurred ("whether or not in violation of the domestic law of the country where perpetrated").[3] In other words, it made domestic law subject to a new international set of laws that the Tribunal was in the process of establishing. Finally, it broke the grounds of chronology. The standard belief of all legal thinking is that for something to be a crime, a preexisting law has to define it as such. In the Latin phrase defining that principle, *nullum crimen, nulla poena sine praevia lege poenali* (no crime, no punishment without a preexisting penal law). But the Tribunal was establishing a new law that it would use to punish those who had committed a breach of it *before* it had been formulated. These, then, were the principles that we can associate with "Nuremberg," the city where the trials that gave force of law to these principles took place.

"Nuremberg," the shorthand for the war trials conducted there in the wake of World War II, occupies a special place in the guilted age. ("Tokyo," the place where the trials of Japan's Class A war criminals were conducted, never assumed the same status.) And "Nuremberg" as a term and an idea in the guilted age has largely been identified as a *negative* example. Nuremberg became shorthand for an unrelieved and unpromising sense of pyrrhic justice. In cases of what came to be called "transitional justice," and in institutions that put "reconciliation" in their titles, like the South African Truth and Reconciliation Commission, apology and forgiveness—the hallmarks of the guilted age sensibility—were proposed as an alternative to the prosecution that took place in Nuremberg. For the advocates of restorative justice, transitional justice, and emergent democracies, the options facing the world were either Nuremberg or forgiveness, either prosecution or mercy. And so Nuremberg came to define a sort of retributive justice that most advocates hinted would merely lead to the cycle of other kinds of retribution. What Desmond Tutu calls "the Nuremberg trial paradigm" came to signify precisely the polar opposite of reconciliation. In the kinds of political circumstances and transitions that marked the postwar era, what was needed was not strict, retributive justice but something else. In a debate over the viability of an international tribunal to try those guilty of the crimes committed during the atrocities in Bosnia, American National Security Advisor Anthony Lake cautioned against a legal strategy that would sacrifice "future lives on the altar of justice for the past."[4] The international tribunal that was contemplated when he uttered these words would have been, and eventually became, the first one since Nuremberg.

While these claims of the value of mercy might be appealing—and should be—they are often based on a misreading of the history in which Nuremberg took place. We should recall that the alternative to justice then was not mercy but sheer revenge. In his opening statement in the Nuremberg trials, Justice Robert Jackson saw the tribunal as necessary to "stay the hand of vengeance," as he eloquently put it. Nor was this mere rhetoric. The Allied leaders who finally decided on the International Military Tribunal had considered precisely that vengeance as a plausible alternative. Joseph Stalin in a speech at the meeting of the Allied leaders in Tehran had semiseriously declared that it would be necessary to liquidate fifty thousand German General Staff officers. The American diplomat Charles Bohlen, who spoke Russian, saw it as a joke, but Winston Churchill, who spoke *realpolitik*, took it as a serious proposal. That was in November 1943. When Franklin Roosevelt, Churchill, and Stalin met again in Québec in September 1944, they approved a memorandum in which those war criminals on an authorized list drawn up by the Allies would be summarily executed on proof of their identity. A little more than a month later, and largely because of Stalin's reconsideration of the plan, the memorandum was withdrawn. When those three met again, for the last time, at Yalta in February 1945, Churchill returned to the issue and argued that the leading Nazis ought to be shot without benefit of trial. It was only when Roosevelt died and Harry Truman assumed the presidency that the question of summary execution was removed from consideration and the Tribunal plan became focal. Meanwhile, of course, Europe in the wake of the war was awash with citizens of several nations killing thousands in lynchings, summary executions, and ritual acts of revenge against Germans and their collaborators.[5] One suspects that the advocates of forms of nonretributive justice would be more persuasive citing the Treaty of Versailles, since that document led precisely to the cycles of violence that the Nuremberg Tribunal ended.

What I am suggesting here, though, is that the Tribunal was also a *positive* example—or, if not an example, at least an expression of important elements of the sensibility of the guilted age. Here, encased in law, was a statement about *duration*. There were crimes where what was most important was that they *happened*—not the technicalities of where and when they happened. The Tribunal implied that these were crimes even though there were no laws to define them as such *before* they occurred. Nations would later pass laws that gave this category of crimes no statute of limitations (the Bundestag extended the statute of limitations in 1964 and 1969 and then abolished it in 1979; France defined such crimes as imprescriptible in 1964). There was simply no before and after in this category of laws—no *before* these acts were illegal, and no *after* during which they were not subject to prosecution. It was this latitude, this breadth of coverage that aligned the Tribunal laws with the sensibility of the guilted age. Although few would actually refer to them specifically, although many did use the term "crimes against humanity," the people who made historical apologies were implicitly abiding by the terms set by the Tribunal. It is no surprise, then, that many of the historical apologies were for precisely the crimes named in the Tribunal: enslavement, extermination, and racial and religious persecution. The Tribunal meant to identify those acts committed by the Nazi regime, which enslaved, exterminated, and founded a polity based on religious and racial persecution. But because of the openness of the language ("before or during the war"), and because of the implication that this category of crime simply existed in a timeless present, it was easily assumed that earlier atrocities and crimes of the past also fell within the inviting language of "crimes against humanity." If enslavement under the Nazis, why not enslavement of Africans? If extermination under National Socialism, why not earlier acts of extermination, like that of Armenians or Aborigines? If a crime was a crime, despite laws, borders, and time, then clearly the world's past needed to be reassessed. That became the imperative of the guilted age.

And so 1945 stands as a good year at which to date the dawn of the guilted age, because it represents the end of one set of atrocities for which certain nations would assume responsibility and guilt, and because it openly defined a new category of inhumanity that would provide language and inspiration for those who wished to identify a longer course of atrocities in world history for which nations, churches, and populations could be held accountable. It was obviously not the desire or aim of the minds behind the Tribunal to do any of these things. They wanted to create a legal category that would permit them to prosecute Nazis, but the idea they proposed greatly exceeded that original aim—like the bus boycott in Montgomery, and the occupation of Tahrir Square in Cairo, one is tempted to say. What this Tribunal established, I believe, is the *glasnost* and *perestroika* of the guilted age. By identifying a new victim (humanity), a new legal territory (the world), and a new statute of limitations (timeless), they created precisely the discourse that would come to define the guilted age. Let me be clear that I am not arguing a causal relationship here. The Tribunal did not create the guilted age, or its sensibility. Rather, it expressed, at the highest possible levels of authority and power, that sensibility and, in some cases, inspired it.

The Tribunal also defined a larger sense of responsibility and agency—the second of my concerns here. At the end of Article 6, which defines the three crimes (against peace, of war, and against humanity), the Tribunal states that "[l]eaders, organizers, instigators and accomplices participating in the formulation or execution of a common plan or conspiracy to commit any of the foregoing crimes are responsible for all acts performed by any persons in execution of such plans." In other words, there were two kinds of responsibility for those who devised such crimes: the responsibility for the creation of the plans, and the responsibility for the acts of those who executed these plans. Himmler was dually responsible, then, for what he created and for what those he ordered did. That principle, the Tribunal wished to make absolutely clear, did not absolve anyone who simply followed orders. The next two Articles continue to define what responsibility obtained for those who occupied particular offices and held specific authorities. Those who had some authority "as Heads of State or responsible officials in Government Departments" could not claim their offices as sanctuaries "freeing them from responsibility." They were responsible for what they did in those offices. Likewise, those who were led by those in authority—that is, those who simply followed orders given by their superiors—could not claim their status in extenuation of their guilt. Whoever "acted pursuant to order of his Government or of a superior" should not be considered freed "from responsibility," although that fact may mitigate the punishment.[6]

Shortly after the Tribunal defined what constituted responsibility and guilt for those who planned and executed the crimes of National Socialism, the German philosopher Karl Jaspers wrote a profoundly important book entitled *The Question of German Guilt*. In this book, Jaspers is meditating on the nature of responsibility as well as guilt—that is, both the moral conception of being accountable and the legal one of being liable to punishment. He identifies four kinds of guilt—criminal, political, moral, and metaphysical—and then determines which could be ascribed to any collective. Criminal guilt is the only one that is wholly individual. He declares it "nonsensical . . . to charge a whole people with a crime," since the "criminal is always only an individual." Moral guilt is a little more complex—Jaspers discusses whether "communities of language, customs, habits and descent" might be collectively considered as being morally responsible for some set of beliefs or actions. He concludes that that they cannot, and that moral guilt, like criminal guilt, cannot be ascribed to a whole people: "There is no such thing as a national character extending to every single member of a nation."[7] So, individuals can be criminally guilty and morally guilty, but not groups of people.

The focal point for Jaspers is political guilt. Groups of people, he argues, can be held politically guilty. "Everybody," he writes, "is co-responsible for the way he is governed." Even those who think of themselves as apolitical—who "live aloof from all politics, like monks, hermits, scholars, artists"—remain "politically liable, because they, too, live by the order of the state." There "is no such aloofness in modern states." Since "a people answers for its polity," he writes, the key question is to determine in what sense one can speak of being "collectively liable." His conclusion is not comforting, as he turns to the question in his title—that is, the question of "German guilt": "All Germans without exception share in the political liability," he concludes. (He also suggests that "probably every German" has some degree of moral and metaphysical guilt, too.) Indeed, part of the problem Jaspers has with the Nuremberg trials, of which he is mostly complimentary, is that they worked to "exonerate the German people" by focusing exclusively on the leaders and planners. "We were German nationals at the time when the crimes were committed by the régime which called itself German, which claimed to be Germany," he notes, and that makes each German, political or apolitical, knowledgeable or ignorant of what was done, liable for the polity that committed those atrocities. To be "German"—that is, all the "we" who share a "language, descent, situation, fate" and sense of "immediate solidarity"—is to be responsible and liable for what was done by Germany. Jaspers is unsparing in identifying the criteria of responsibility. It does not require positive affirmation, or active participation; it is merely being German in a nation that did those things. In the end, Jaspers mercilessly concludes, "we are responsible for our delusions."[8]

What Jaspers calls "metaphysical guilt" is in some ways the most intriguing and profound commentary he makes on the nature of human responsibility. Metaphysical guilt takes seriously the idea behind the term "humanity" that the Tribunal was proposing as the basis of the crimes Germany had committed—that is, "crimes against humanity." What could "humanity" mean except the "solidarity among men [and women] as human beings"? This feeling of solidarity with all other humans carries not only the comforting sense of being in a world in which we belong but also, more importantly, a sense that we are all responsible for each other. And that makes us, as he puts it, "co-responsible for every wrong and every injustice in the world." It is precisely around this sense of metaphysical guilt that Hannah Arendt later builds her case in *The Human Condition* regarding what constitutes human responsibility. Nor is Jaspers vague or utopic about this responsibility. He identifies a range of positions from which one can be found guilty. If an injustice happens and I "fail to do whatever I can to prevent" it, "I too am guilty." If an injustice has already taken place before I can prevent or end it, the fact that "I live after such a thing has happened weighs upon me as indelible guilt." Metaphysical guilt, he concludes, "is the lack of absolute solidarity with the human being as such—an indelible claim beyond morally meaningful duty." In some ways, and perhaps with desolate propriety in postwar Germany, Jaspers is describing something like survivors' guilt: "I am guilty of being still alive." He quotes a speech he gave in August 1945, immediately after the end of Third Reich, in which he reflects on what it means for him, and for other Germans, to be alive in 1945. Why did they not die "in 1933 when the Constitution was torn up, the dictatorship established"? Why did they survive June 30, 1934, "when the crimes of the régime became publicly apparent"? What did they do as they witnessed the "lootings, deportations and murders of our Jewish friends and fellow-citizens in 1938"? And how do they explain that they still draw breath in November 1938, when the "synagogues burned and Jews were deported for the first time"?[9] The unspoken answer is the one to *The Question of German Guilt.*

What is important to note right away is that Jaspers does *not* propose that metaphysical guilt in any way allays or reduces the political and moral guilt that each and every German should feel. In other words, he is not creating a hierarchy in which one kind of guilt (political and moral) is trumped by a considerably more encompassing one (metaphysical). He is not suggesting that citizens of the Allied countries should share in the guilt that Germans do or should feel, or, at least, not with the hope of spreading that guilt to such an extent that it lessens the importance of the political and moral guilt that he feels and believes that other Germans ought to feel. Rather, he is expressing what I think is the cardinal feature of the guilted age—that is, the belief that as human beings who belong in time, we are responsible, in some indefinable way, for what has occurred in the places we occupy, and the place we all occupy is the world. In developing an expansive sense of responsibility for other people, for their survival and well-being, Jaspers is giving impetus to the broad category of "humanity." And that category, he believes, cannot be empty of significance, simply a grandiloquent way of describing relationships that no one takes seriously because they transcend the biological ties, communal boundaries, and national borders that define the relationships we think matter more. That category of "humanity" matters, and it defines our place in the world. After all, it is that concept alone that gives any meaning at all to the legal category that the Tribunal established of "crimes against humanity."

Like the Tribunal, then, and the Nuremberg trials that he sees as a "feeble, ambiguous harbinger of a world order, the need of which mankind is beginning to feel," Jaspers offers a grander vision of what constitutes responsibility.[10] And by doing so, as the Tribunal also did, in terms of an open, temporal framework that challenges the simple legalistic order—for Jaspers, we can feel responsible for what happened before we arrived; for the Tribunal, crimes are crimes before they are defined so by laws—he also provides a formulation that would serve the guilted age. Two things were in place, then, at the dawn of the guilted age: a comprehensive belief in an encompassing and broadly defined responsibility that was formulated and empowered by a legal body in 1945 and was articulated as a philosophical principle in 1948.

The final question is why the *apology* was cast as the best way of expressing that responsibility and subjectivity. Reader, be forewarned: Here is where I am at my most speculative, since I am now trying to discern the evolution of a practice that seems to have been transformed from one sphere of activity to another.

The Tribunal, obviously, does not help here, since it expressed a set of principles that clearly argued against any *symbolic* forms of retribution or restitution, and the apology is unrelentingly symbolic. Nuremberg was about trials that were to determine the actual punishment that would be meted out. They represented pure justice—victors' justice, according to their critics, but justice in any case. It is precisely for that reason that later advocates of forgiveness would posit Nuremberg as their polar opposite, the faint justice to their robust mercy. As we leave the Tribunal, and with it the dawn of the guilted age, to make our way later in the postwar period, it is important to appreciate what the Tribunal did do: It created a new temporal framework and identified a new category of legal defendant. When later apologists used the term "crimes against humanity" to describe the atrocities of the distant past, they might or might not have had the Nuremberg principles in mind, but whether they did or did not is immaterial, since they were living, thinking, and acting in an era that had been defined by the intellectual principles embodied in that Tribunal.

So, how then can we explain the emergence of the political apology as *the* practice for responding to political atrocities and, later, historical atrocities? Let me suggest three ways: one that looks at institutions, one that looks at philosophies, and one that looks at practices.

The first way is the most obvious, and that is to trace the shift from what was routine in one sphere (the religious sphere) to what became a discursive possibility in another (the political sphere). We can understand the emergence of the political apology in the guilted age, then, by examining the sphere within which it had hitherto been most fully anchored, in religious institutions. Shortly after the revelations of the Holocaust became widely known, a wide range of Christian churches undertook a deep examination of what they had done or not done, what they had believed or not believed, that made the Holocaust possible. Both the Vatican and Protestant churches clearly perceived that they were responsible for a profound failure. As they explored the ways in which they had failed to provide material succor and sanctuary to those who needed them most critically, as they probed the ways in which their very liturgical practices and thinking about Judaism had in fact provided spiritual sustenance for those who wanted to act on their anti-Semitic hatred, these churches turned to the practices they identified as most fundamental to their mission—the practices of contrition, atonement, confession, apology, and forgiveness. It was, after all, necessary for the churches to distance themselves from those who committed this atrocity.

In September 2000, an interdenominational group of Jewish scholars issued a statement entitled *Dabru Emet* ("Speak the truth," Zechariah 8:16), with 170 signers, that answered that anxious hope of the churches: "Nazism was not a Christian phenomenon," *Dabru Emet* states. Although Nazism was certainly fed by the strains of "Christian anti-Judaism," and many Christians participated in or insufficiently protested the Holocaust, "Nazism itself was not an inevitable outcome of Christianity." Part of what inspired this statement was the sense that Christian churches had expressed atonement in terms recognizable to the Jewish scholars who signed the document—that is, they had been contrite and acted in ways that demonstrated that contrition. "In the decades since the Holocaust," *Dabru Emet* notes, "Christianity has changed dramatically." The scholars note with approval the "public statements of remorse" and the concerted effort to reform Church doctrine and practices so that they are purged of anti-Judaism and have greater appreciation of the meaning of Judaism on its own terms. What some saw, mistakenly, I think, as an act of Jewish forgiveness in response to the churches' concerted acts of apology for the Holocaust is not that; rather, it is an acknowledgment of what the churches had done and an offer of what future interfaith coordination was possible. One scholar who signed the statement, Michael Signer, said that *Dabru Emet* is more about reconciliation than forgiveness.[11] The main point, though, is that the statement provides acknowledgment of the numerous apologies that Christian churches had offered for the Holocaust and, tacitly, recognizes that it is precisely on this somewhat shared ground, between two faiths with traditions of contrition and forgiveness, that the future can be established.

This account of how the contrition that was native to the religious sphere migrated to the political sphere after an event that roiled the religious world in fundamental ways intuitively makes sense. But it also has some problems. For one thing, many of the *public* church apologies for the Holocaust have come in the 1990s, well into the guilted age. The information regarding whatever acts of contrition and penance might have been occurring in individual churches is not yet readily available to us, other than a few examples. So, for instance, in a different moment, Herbert Anderson and Edward Foley offer an account of a Milwaukee church that conducted a remarkable service in 1972, at the moment when the United States had renewed its massive bombing of Hanoi and Haiphong. As the congregation prays for forgiveness "for our sins against humanity, and for the violence our country perpetrates in our name," the minister responds that the "words are empty," and the actions continue. In a repeated ritual in which the congregation then states its repentance and requests absolution, the minister concludes: "I deny you absolution; I withhold the consolation of the church from you; I refuse to collaborate in your search for spiritual comfort, for though you may be repentant, you have not been reconciled with your enemies." We can notice the borrowing of the language that inaugurated the guilted age—"sins against humanity" and even "collaborate"—but, more importantly, we can see how the practice involves applying religious rituals to political conditions. In what many Protestant churches took to calling "identificational repentance," congregations began to undertake acts of atonement for the political crimes of their governments and the historical atrocities of their nations.[12] Future research might turn up such anecdotal evidence earlier in the guilted age and therefore permit us to see that migration of the practice more clearly. Until then, though, we can probably find some value in the second way of explaining the emergence of the political apology in the guilted age, which is not about particular institutions (churches and governments) but rather about a diffuse but clearly felt philosophical sensibility.

When we do turn to the philosophers, we discover a widespread, popular recognition that all the conventional strategies for responding to lesser atrocities have been exhausted and are clearly inappropriate, inadequate, and in some ways an affront to the reality they attempt to encompass. In the face of these events, this degree of damage and suffering, this kind of historical breach, what possible legal mechanism can work? What punishment can be meted out that is adequate? What account can account for what happened? These events were, in the language that is repeatedly used, "unspeakable." In a 1965 book appropriately titled *Language and Silence*, George Steiner argues that we could approach the concentration camp experience with only the latter. "The best *now*," he writes, "after so much has been set forth, is, perhaps, to be silent; not to add the trivia of literary, sociological debate, to the unspeakable." It is perhaps something like this sentiment that Theodor Adorno wants to capture when he offers his dictum that "to write poetry after Auschwitz is barbaric." To utter something, particularly something aspiring to comprehension and beauty, seems equally a betrayal of what it is to be human. To remain human after the inhumane has happened seems wrong. One collection of Adorno's writings is titled *Can One Live after Auschwitz?* Steiner indicates a similar shift when he notes that we "are post-Auschwitz *homo sapiens*."[13] The life of humanity has ineradicably changed—ended . . . devolved . . . something.

When Brandt fell to his knees in front of the Warsaw memorial in 1970, he described his motivation in similar terms: "I did what human beings do when speech fails them." What is "unspeakable" is also, inherently, "unforgivable." Steiner again states the case most concisely: "What the Nazis did in the camps and torture chambers is wholly unforgivable[;] it is a brand on the image of man and will last; each of us ha[s] been diminished by the enactment of a potential sub-humanity latent in all of us." It is worth noting the ways in which Steiner is echoing Jaspers's description of metaphysical guilt: All "humanity" is diminished; all were capable; all are beyond forgiveness. Even more explicitly drawing on Jaspers, Arendt likewise holds that when confronted with what Immanuel Kant calls "radical evil," we are at a loss. In the one skeptical moment in what is otherwise an optimistic account of the ways that forgiveness can liberate us existentially from being drowned in the past, Arendt notes that "men are unable to forgive what they cannot punish and that they are unable to punish what has turned out to be unforgivable."[14] She does not name the Holocaust, although it is arguably what she has in mind, and she does not resolve this dilemma in any way nor make an attempt to do so. It is a curious and faltering moment in Arendt's otherwise brisk, confident, and assured book. Steiner wrote on the twentieth anniversary of the end of World War II, Arendt shortly after the tenth. When we return even closer to the event and to the thinker Steiner echoes and on whom Arendt consistently draws, we can get an even more poignant sense of the despair with which Jaspers articulates the hope that contrition and apology *might* work, that redemption and forgiveness *might* be possible.

Writing three years after the end of the war, Jaspers first wants to ensure that his readers do not think that metaphysical guilt (which all humanity feels) somehow exonerates Germans from the political guilt they should feel. "It would, indeed, be an evasion and a false excuse," he writes, "if we Germans tried to exculpate ourselves by pointing to the guilt of being human." But what the guilt associated with "original sin" does provide, Jaspers implies, is a way of understanding what can possibly expiate and cleanse a people who feel it, who are aware of having faced and acted on the failure of will that Kant terms "radical evil." What is required in postwar Germany, Jaspers concludes, is an act of "purification." Again, like his former student Arendt, Jaspers is most hesitant here, at the crucial point where his argument can be resolved or dissolved. The answer, he argues, is truth; Germans must accept it. And, yet, the way to accept it, to prepare themselves psychologically to be capable of accepting it, is to renounce the medium in which truth is cast. In the face of the "unspeakable," one must not speak but, instead, pursue what Jaspers calls "unaggressive silence," since it is from "the simplicity of silence that the clarity of the communicable will emerge." The "communicable," it turns out, is incommunicable.

The truth that will be produced through this process will indeed accomplish purification. But, here again, Jaspers wavers. "If at this close of our discussions of guilt we ask what purification consists in," he writes, "no concrete reply is possible beyond what has been said." What "has been said" so far, as he recognizes, has been vague and elusive, and that, he concludes, is how it must be. The process is not rational, but something else. Purification "cannot be realized as an end of rational will but occurs as a metamorphosis by inner action." To describe that kind of transformation is impossible; "one can only repeat the indefinite, comprehensive figures of speech: uplift by illumination and growing transparency—love of man."[15] Jaspers recognizes that he has descended to the banal, and he accepts it as the only mode available to him. What Jaspers means when he says that he cannot say what purification means except by resorting to what he describes as inadequate and trite generalizations is that, faced with what he feels, he has no resources. The unspeakable cannot be spoken; the unimaginable cannot be imagined.

It is only when we fully accept that sense of acknowledged failure that we can appreciate just what is involved when Jaspers proposes the moral resolutions he does for "purification." Here, then, is the logical sequence that Jasper outlines: The silent acceptance of truth can lead to purification, which in turn leads to "political liberty," which in turn is based on "people feeling jointly liable for the politics of their community." It is, clearly, less a sequence than a circle. A sense of responsibility (the truth) leads eventually to a sense of responsibility. And at the beginning of that circle (and, because it is a circle, at the end of that circle too) is atonement: "Purification in action means, first of all, making amends." He talks about material reparations as part of what it means to "make amends," but he also talks about the intangible ways that contrition redefines life. "Essentially," he writes, "our life remains permitted only to be consumed by a task." Marked by humility, modesty, silence, and the abiding "consciousness of guilt," the person who makes amends, offers reparations, begs forgiveness—in a word, apologizes—is ready to face a desolate world that now offers no guarantees. Not freed of political, moral, or metaphysical guilt but continually making amends for the political, moral, and metaphysical sins that wrought it, the soul goes to live "in this tension: to know about the possible ruin and still remain tirelessly active for all that is possible in the world."[16] It is, at best, an irresolute resolution. These are terms and practices that used to have more force; they were not always "indefinite." But the world has changed, and humanity devolved. What Steiner calls "post-Auschwitz *homo sapiens*" do not have the same resources, capacities, or practices as "pre-Auschwitz *homo sapiens.*" That homo, less sapiens because of it, has now seen what humanity is capable of, what crimes against humanity it can commit, and that the spiritual, moral practices available to it are meager, but also all it has. Apology, in this sense, is the product not of making a conscientious effort to give moral restitution where it is deserved but of having no other options yet retaining a sense of needing some means to be delivered from the guilt of the guilted age.

Here, then, are the earliest theorists of the guilted age: Jaspers suggesting in 1948 that "making amends" is an "indefinite" way of addressing an otherwise unspeakable past, and Arendt claiming in 1957 that forgiveness is the only way to extricate ourselves from a past that is otherwise irreversible, even as she recognizes that the forgiveness she is espousing confronts the wholly "unforgivable" past from which *The Human Condition* is emerging. And both writers self-consciously stumble as they make their tepid proposals. Jaspers apologetically claims that he has to resort to the trite; Arendt leaves the concept of the "unforgivable" undigested and unassimilated in an argument that it clearly threatens to undermine. If the churches have provided limited data on the processes by which they arrived at apology as an answer, the philosophers have shown us how they have had to sacrifice clarity and logic. We should think of that answer—apology—in the same terms in which it was proposed: It is a product of despair.

The third and final way to understand the emergence of the political apology is by seeing the earliest examples of it, which seems counterintuitive since it is their emergence I am trying to explain. What the earliest attempts show, I think, is that they were not clearly understood by those who offered and those who witnessed them. What exploring these inchoate efforts reveals, in other words, is the formation of a practice that was in the earliest moments of its evolution, which can certainly help us understand what drove some to believe that this strategy in which philosophers place some futile hope might hold more than that.

As I suggest in the Preface and argue more fully in Chapter 7, the emergence of that practice might well be based on a categorical error, a mistaking and mislabeling of one especially poignant and meaningful act. If Brandt's *kniefall* is, as so many later commentators attest, the original act of political apology, and if, as I later suggest, it is primarily an act of mourning that has come to be understood as an apology, then we could say that the political apology is based on a mistake. There is some question of whether Brandt's act can be described as the first gesture by a politician to address the horrific past of World War II; there are those who think of Chancellor Adenauer's speech to the Bundestag on September 27, 1951, as an official apology. It was a speech specifically intended as a formal acceptance of the reparations treaty that West Germany had made with Israel, but it addressed the historical conditions that made the reparations necessary:

> The government of the Federal Republic of Germany and with it the great majority of the German people are aware of the immeasurable suffering inflicted upon the Jews in Germany and the occupied territories in the era of National Socialism. The large majority of the German people abhorred the crimes and did not participate in them. . . . [T]here were many Germans, despite endangering themselves out of religious reasons, the call of conscience, and shame at the dishonor of Germany's name, who showed a willingness to help their fellow Jewish citizens. In the name of the German people, unspeakable crimes were committed which create a duty of moral and material restitution.

At the end of the speech, almost all members of the Bundestag rose in silence. For some, the speech and silence could be understood as an apology and an act of repentance. For others, the speech attempted too much to exculpate the majority of Germans and offered a vague sense of agency in the passive voice ("unspeakable crimes were committed"), and the silence did not necessarily register as anything specifically connected to contrition.[17] (Although, I do note, a minute of silence in an assembly usually does denote an act of commemorative mourning.)

Moreover, whatever we can call Adenauer's speech, it also came from someone who was seeking consensus more than expressing contrition. This had been the tenor of his leadership from the very beginning. Adenauer had hinted at the need for Germany to move on from its recent history in his very first address as chancellor in 1949, a mere four years after the end of the war. While giving tacit acknowledgment that Germany still had to "draw out of the past all the necessary lessons" that it could provide, Adenauer seemed more comfortable in his affirmative statement that the "federal government is determined to let the past be past when it is defensible." And since the speech also stated that "de-Nazification" had done much harm and that the Bundestag was going to address the question of a "general amnesty," it was pretty clear that he thought it "defensible" now.[18] In any case, then, regardless of whether Brandt's 1970 *kniefall* was an apology and whether it was the first, it did mark a clear break with earlier German politicians' attempts to address the past in a tenor other than excusing or forgetting it. And if, as I later suggest, it was an act that was something other than an apology but has come to be subsumed into that category, perhaps we can learn something from that error of categorization.

Misconstruing the meaning of a historic act is one way of falling into the error of miscategorization. Misconstruing history itself is another. Consider these two apocryphal stories about Emperor Hirohito, one set in 1945 and the other some years later. In an August 1993 editorial on the week that Prime Minister Morihiro Hosokawa offered his political apology, *The Economist* claims that Emperor Hirohito had said the following at the first meeting with General Douglas MacArthur: "I come before you to offer myself to the judgment of the powers you represent, as one to bear sole responsibility for every political and military decision made and action taken by my people in the conduct of the war." *The Economist* gives no citation for the quotation. In 2006, a reporter for the *Salt Lake Tribune* interviewed ninety-three-year-old Lennox Tierney, who had been a cultural specialist in the U.S. Navy during the Occupation and had an office on the fifth floor of the Dai-Ichi Insurance Building in Tokyo where MacArthur also had his office. Tierney claims that near the end of the Occupation, Hirohito had come to the office to offer a formal apology for Japan's war conduct and for the bombing of Pearl Harbor, but that MacArthur had refused to admit or acknowledge him.[19]

These two stories—one about a rejected apology at the beginning of the Occupation and one about a denied apology at the end of it—do not ring true and certainly seem strikingly at odds with everything we know about Hirohito's behavior and sense of responsibility in the weeks and months after the surrender. No biography of Hirohito contains either anecdote. These are stories about cultural misunderstanding—about the tense encounter between a "shame" and a "guilt" culture—and intend to show, in the case of the Tierney interview, how America continues to exhibit unacceptable cultural arrogance as it pursues war after war in the new century. What these apocryphal stories most clearly reveal, however, are the ways in which particular crucial scenes in the past can be revised in light of guilted-age beliefs about the power of the political apology. Historically, we know that Hirohito came humbly to MacArthur's offices, as was suitable for the political situation, but that humility did not express an apology (and Hirohito consistently rejected any opportunity or invitation to apologize). Yet those visits, by some, can be read as an apology. Brandt, too, clearly exhibited another posture, one of grief and mourning, but his act also has been read as an apology. What we can see in these cases, I suggest, is the same thing we can see in the philosophers discussed above: The philosophers arrive at apology with the recognition that they have nothing else; these misinterpretations arrive at apology because they believe that other postures and attitudes can mean nothing else.

If these three attempts at explaining the origins of the turn to the political apology have any merit, what might they tell us about the inauguration of the guilted age? I would emphasize that one is about the insufficiency of the institutions within which contrition and redemption had been hitherto practiced; the second frankly admits that the practice it is espousing is exhausted, outmoded, and inadequate for the past it is trying to encompass and reconcile; and the third mistakes the meaning of a gesture of grief for penance. We must see these for what they are: a failure, a hope that knows itself to be futile, and a mistake. The guilted age began, then, in desperation because it was unmoored from the institutions, practices, and philosophies that had animated the world before the thirty-one years of world war produced an irreparable breach between that world, the "world we have lost," and this one, "the world we wish we had never found."

My answer, then, to the question of why the guilted age emerged and developed in the way it did, perhaps appropriately, is likely as weak as the resolutions I have teased out of the institutions, philosophies, and practices that confronted the problem of guilt at its dawning. What I can say with some confidence, though, is that it is clearly a staggered phenomenon. No one single moment—not even Brandt's *kniefall*—inaugurated the practice of the political apology, nor did one defining act transform the political apology into the historical apology. This is a history of halting steps, failed experiments, and deep anxiety. The reasons are not hard to identify. The steps were halting because, as Jaspers and Steiner and Arendt demonstrate, the discursive choices were limited and not entirely robust. The traditions that had given force to these practices of atonement were exhausted, the institutions that had housed them were bankrupt and complicit, and the rituals themselves seemed inadequate and sterile. It was a world looking for a new set of terms. The crimes had only recently found theirs. The term "racism" was coined in 1933, "genocide" in 1948. The means of answering those crimes was still unnamed, or at least undefined. "Atonement," "making amends," "contrition," and "apology" were all old terms, but they clearly were going to *mean* something new when applied as they were to political and historical events.

The source of anxiety was also not hard to discover. The alternative to the kind of acknowledgment on which apology is based is denial. Jaspers does not say it, or even suggest it, since he relies on the language of religion rather than therapy, but part of what contrition offers, I think, is a counter to denial. After all, one year after Jaspers published *The Question of German Guilt*, Chancellor Adenauer was already moving beyond that question and addressing the question of German amnesty. The question for the guilted age, then, was how to oppose denial, to encourage acceptance of the past, and to work forward from that. As I have shown, there was no easy answer, and it was clear that the process not only was staggered, as I suggest above, but also contained its own momentum. Let us conclude, then, by considering one nation to see that momentum from denial to apology at work.

At the dawn of the guilted age and well into the 1950s and 1960s, President Charles de Gaulle's France, like Adenauer's Germany, went through a similar strategy of denial about the meaning of Vichy, as he wished to focus on the present and created a patently false myth of a widespread French Resistance that permitted the nation to feel redeemed. At the same time that there was a denial, though, there was just as clearly a desire for an accounting. What Henry Rousso terms the "Vichy Syndrome" was an illness with manifestly conflicted symptoms—the desire simultaneously to escape and to embrace the object of its repulsion and attraction. When René Bousquet was murdered at his home before his trial for crimes as secretary general for police in the Vichy regime's Ministry of the Interior in June 1993, several French newspapers ran the headline, "The Trial of Vichy Will Not Take Place." I suspect that some headlines were celebratory, some dismayed. For Rousso, the courts are clearly the wrong place for French "history and memory" to be cross-examined; that is an interrogation that historians need to conduct. For others, it would have been symbolic, a first in the nation's confrontation with its past, a rejection of a particular mythology. When the *milicien* Paul Touvier was brought to trial in 1994 on charges of ordering the murder of seven Jews in reprisal for the Resistance's assassination of Vichy's propaganda minister, Phillippe Henriot, the newspapers described it as "The Last Trial of the Purge." The political work of 1944–1945 was being completed on its fiftieth anniversary. The French courts did not define the main term of the crime with which Touvier was charged, but instead drew on the United Nations' instrument that was itself a commentary on the Military Tribunal's original definition of the crime: "crimes against humanity." In 1994, fifty years after Vichy fell, Touvier became the first French citizen to be found guilty of that imprescriptible crime. In an interview, Touvier's lawyer shared a sentiment that is repeated throughout the period covered by this study: "Let forgiveness be more powerful than remembrance."[20] He lost, and the guilted age in France had its first guilty verdict.

There was no forgiveness for Touvier, just as there had been no trial for Bousquet. In lieu of a trial for the man responsible for the roundup of the Vel d'Hiv, France produced an apology, which is what President Jacques Chirac offered two years later in July 1995, at the fifty-third anniversary memorial of the place where thirteen thousand Jews had been rounded up and then transported in 1942. Chirac openly acknowledged what he called the French people's "collective error," affirming that Vichy was not coerced but had assisted (*secondeé*) in the Holocaust, and he lamented the fact that "France, the homeland of the Enlightenment and of the rights of man, a land of welcome and asylum, on that day committed the irreparable." That apology came about ten months after his predecessor, President François Mitterrand, had proclaimed, "I will not apologize in the name of France. The Republic had nothing to do with this. I do not believe France is responsible." These were two very differently situated politicians. Chirac had what Chancellor Kohl called the "blessing of a late birth" and had played no part in the war. Mitterrand had an ambiguous record in relationship to Vichy and had, in fact, had some kind of relationship with Bousquet during his first presidential campaign in 1965. Yet the point on which they differed was whether the transition from Vichy to the Fifth Republic altered the historical identity of the land they both led. For Chirac, but, sadly, not for the compromised Mitterrand, the France of the Enlightenment and the Fifth Republic was also the France of Vichy.

With this political apology on record, then, it was only a matter of time before the historical apology would come. And it came in 2001, when the French government passed a law condemning the slave trade and slavery. The first article of that law states: "The French Republic recognizes . . . that the transatlantic slave trade as well as the slave trade in the Indian Ocean; and . . . [the] slavery perpetuated against the populations of Africa, America, Madagascar and India . . . constitute a crime against humanity."[21] In a matter of seven years, after decades of denial in one case and centuries in the other,

France had acknowledged two "crimes against humanity"—one committed a half century earlier, just shortly before that term would assume the meaning it did, and one committed centuries ago, as a belated recognition of the humanity that had to be denied for slavery to exist. The law did not mention the Enlightenment, which coincided with the slave trade.

In one nation, then, and in a spurt of activity, we see the full dynamic of the guilted age. The crimes that inaugurated it—the crimes of World War II, or in the case of France, the crimes of Vichy—were tried and apologized for, which led, almost predictably, to the historical apology for the earlier crime against humanity, the slave trade. The discourse that mobilized a belated trial that would attempt to discover tangible and legal guilt of a Vichy official was the same discourse that moved politicians to address the intangible guilt of a nation's participation in the slave trade. France was a belated participant in the practices of the guilted age, largely because it had a robust tradition of mythical denial. As I show with examples of the political apology in Japan and the historical apology in the United States, those nations too had to struggle against equally robust traditions of denial. We turn now to those cases to see how they did so, how they differed, and what that difference tells us about the evolution of public apologies in the guilted age.

2

POLITICAL APOLOGIES I

Forgiveness and apology obviously occupy two poles of the same dynamic conceptual universe. Apology can be understood as asking for forgiveness, and forgiveness as accepting an apology. Both involve a splitting of the self—in the case of apology, the person who performed the harm becomes the person who recognizes the sinfulness of the harm; in the case of forgiveness, the person who was resentful becomes the person who forgoes resentment. And both are communicative acts: One apologizes to, and one forgives, someone. Apologies that are soliloquies, like forgiveness in the form of an unsent letter, may be particular kinds of acts, but for most of us they are not acts of apologizing or forgiving. They differ, obviously, in that one is an act involving penitence and the other an act involving grace, one an act of atonement and the other of redemption, one beseeching and the other giving, one changing the relation between the person and the act she or he committed and the other changing the relationship between two persons. I am concerned solely with political apology here, and not political forgiveness, because I believe that the political and historical *apology* has distinguished the guilted age. As we look back over the past seven decades, we find infinitely more cases of political apologies than political forgiveness. There are likely good reasons for that. Suffice it to say that this exponential ratio of apologies to forgiveness is part of what marks the era as a *guilted* age. An increase in forgiveness would distinguish it as a different kind of epoch.

What is common to political apologies and political forgiveness, though, is that both differ from interpersonal apologies and forgiveness in the same crucial way. To appreciate that difference, we can return to an important point Martha Nussbaum makes: that societies need, and need to manage, particular political emotions, both positive ones like love and negative ones like disgust and shame. Nussbaum urges us to consider the ways that societies can temper, augment, and control particular emotions through legislative and judicial acts as well as through more literally concrete means. She shows how societies temper fear and envy, for instance, through political rhetoric and urban architecture or how they create memorials to promote reconciliation and a space for sharing public grief. In any number of ways, then, societies at different times and through diverse strategies raise, divert, sometimes repress, and always manage the political emotions that all societies need to sustain themselves as living social bodies.[1] What I would like to emphasize about political emotions—at least the ones that are the subject of this study, the guilt that leads to apology—is that they undergo a dramatic transformation when they are raised from interpersonal acts to political ones.

First, I need to note how my concern here differs from Nussbaum's. Nussbaum is largely interested in seeing how citizens' emotions can be inspired, managed, controlled, and made productive. Either political rhetoric or the manipulation of the civic environment can do this work by altering the political or actual landscape of the polity. My concern here is with how politicians represent political emotions, not with the work these emotions do. And what politicians do as representatives is exactly what we might expect of them in that role—that is, they *represent* the emotions they express. And by "represent," I *do* mean to imply precisely that these are not "sincere" emotions. In an interpersonal apology, we expect sincere repentance since the person apologizing is doing so for a wrong he or she did. In a political apology, we get represented repentance since the person apologizing is acting as the representative of the corporation or polity on whose behalf he or she is apologizing. In other words, what distinguishes political emotions, in the way I am talking about here, is that they have no emotional content. They are performances, just as all acts by political representatives are.

When a politician apologizes, then, he or she does not express his or her own emotions but the emotions of the polity. More accurately, I suggest that he or she represents the emotions that the executive office has determined to be the ones that *should* represent the emotions of the polity. (I return to this problem of representing mixed emotions presently.) An effective political apology, of course, must resemble a sincere personal apology, since those are the terms by which the public judges it, but it is *not* a sincere personal apology. It is a political apology that has the patina of emotional expression, which, of course, can appear more or less successful depending on the abilities and sensibilities of the politician in question. President Bill Clinton was likely deeply grieved by what the nation had done to the victims of the Tuskegee experiment, but his grief was his own personal emotion. When he spoke on behalf of the nation, that grief came through, making the apology more resonant and effective. But we must distinguish between the person and the politician, between Clinton's own sincere grief and his represented penitence. This is a hard task, naturally, since we are talking about one voice and one body. In our current political climate, the most successful politicians are the ones who can most convince their constituency that there is no distance between themselves as persons and their role as political representatives (but that does not define the dynamic of political apology; it just says something unflattering about our age's political expectations). That difference exists, and it matters. They are, in the end, political actors, who don and shed the emotions they need for the occasions on which they need them. They are always representative, as are their emotions.

So, when we talk about political apology or forgiveness, we are talking about an event that does not rely on the same informal rules by which we assess personal apologies or forgiveness. This point is worth stressing because it is the source of much misunderstanding of exactly what is transpiring when a politician makes a political apology. Consider the critique Ernesto Verdeja offers, and his description of the problems that ensue when we make personal forgiveness an element of particular political discourses. When we "institutionalize forgiveness in public discourse or public policy," he writes, we do damage to its "transcendental and expiatory character." Because forgiveness "requires unpredictability"—that is, it is an act of free will and should not be expected—it cannot be comfortably made into political discourse, which requires standard procedures with expected outcomes. The "institutionalization and routinization" of forgiveness, he concludes, "will result in predictability" and consequently the "debasement" of forgiveness.[2] That is probably true, *if* we assume that the forgiveness in these institutional sites, in the mouths of representative politicians, is the same thing as the forgiveness that is offered by one person to another. My argument is that it is not. That is not to say that political forgiveness cannot be debased; it can and frequently is. But it is not debased because it does not conform to the dynamics of interpersonal forgiveness, such as unpredictability, but rather because corrupt use is made of what is a very different event—political forgiveness. Like other political acts and statements that become corrupt, political forgiveness becomes debased when it is put to improper use (but, again, this is improper use of *political* forgiveness, not the impropriety of personal forgiveness in political fora).

P. E. Diseger makes a compelling argument for precisely that sense of political forgiveness. Digeser argues for "forgiveness as a political concept" and for what he calls a "secular, performative notion of forgiveness" at the heart of it. Political forgiveness, he writes, requires "a relationship between at least two parties in which the appropriate party relieves a debt through appropriate signs or utterances." What makes it forgiveness rather than a payment of debt is that the "victim or creditor" does "not receive what is due." There is something forgiven. At the end of the process, past claims are settled, and there is a "restoration of a valued political relationship through the reinstatement of civic and moral equality or of the status quo ante." In this way, Digeser challenges what he calls the "commonsensical understanding of forgiveness," which he feels is overly "burdened with psychological and religious assumptions." One forgives when one has rid oneself of resentment, or, in some cases, in order to rid oneself of resentment, but, in either case, forgiveness is a relieving of an internal and felt state. For Digeser, though, "political forgiveness assumes that the success of this release [of debt] does not depend on the emotional or internal states of the forgiver."[3] Digeser recognizes that some people are going to have trouble with this definition, since he appears to be jettisoning the very heart of forgiveness. Can it make sense, they ask, to suggest that there is such a thing as a political forgiveness that does not redeem, and to affirm that there is such a thing as an impenitent political apology? No, it cannot. But that is neither what Digeser is suggesting about political forgiveness nor what I am arguing about political apologies. They both contain emotions, but they are not personal emotions; they are political and part of the performance of a political statement presented by a political actor whose most defining feature is that he or she is acting as a representative. In other words, the emotion is a representative emotion.

What political apologies can also reveal, though, are the kinds of tensions that continue to fester because the apology did not address—and, in many cases, could not address—the wrong for which it is tendered in a sufficiently meaningful way. Here, I am not interested in examining the performance and rhetoric of failed apologies—that is, those attempts at apology that do not succeed in their presentation for the same reasons interpersonal apologies fail; in other words, they do not evince genuine sincerity, they turn into excuses, they inadequately name and address the particular wrongs or misunderstand the harms those wrongs have done, or they are offered in a tone or manner that clearly demonstrates impenitence. There are many such failed political apologies, and they are well studied. Rather, what I want to focus on is a more general failure of political apologies, which is based on the distinctive features of *political* apologies—that is, those defining characteristics of acts that are avowedly political (that is, representative) by actors who are performing a political role (that is, bearing a certain kind of power).

The danger in making an unreflective shift from interpersonal to political apologies, as if the nation were a person enlarged, is that we employ the same terms and meanings for acts that are dramatically different. When a person apologizes, we have to assume that he or she is penitent and must demonstrate that penitence in the apology. We do not assume that only a percentage of that person is actually penitent; we would consider an apology that states that our wrongdoer is about 73 percent sorry to be unacceptable. The key distinction is that political apologies are representative acts by representative actors. When the president stands at a podium and offers an apology to the group whose forgiveness the nation seeks, he or she is, at that moment, the representative of the nation. Yet the nation's people are quite free to express their support or dissent in their own way. As I show later, there are cases where people do just that, performing acts that are intended to undermine the political apology at the very time it is being offered. These are circumstances that just do not occur in interpersonal apologies. It is hard for us to imagine someone standing in front of us, head bowed in an act of humble penitence, saying, "I am truly sorry," while her left leg is jitterbugging and her right hand is forming a fist and threatening us. We would assume that we are being confronted with either a person who is not truly penitent or someone with chorea. In political apologies, though, there is always a divided political body, sometimes in the form of public opinion polls that declare just what percentage of that body believes in the apology, or in other representative political actors' actions that demonstrate impenitence meant to undermine the executive's presentation of the apology. In other words, what is also distinctive about political apologies is that they are contestations of and struggles over power.

It should be clear, then, that political apologies differ from the practice that is often mistaken for them—namely, politicians' apologies. Not every apology made by a politician is a political apology, in the sense that I mean here. Consider two apologies that Richard Nixon made. The first, the famous "Checkers" speech that he made in a televised broadcast in 1952, although considered by some as the inaugurating event in politicians' apologies for their conduct, is not really an apology at all. It is a defense of his financial management and a political campaign speech urging his supporters to contact the Republication National Committee to keep him on the Eisenhower ticket. The only time he broaches the idea of apologizing is to say something about an entirely different matter, his role in prosecuting Alger Hiss, about which he says: "I have no apologies to the American people for my part in putting Alger Hiss where he is today." The second is the televised interview he gave in 1977 to David Frost during which he did apologize, albeit not for the criminal activities that he orchestrated but for putting the American people through the ordeal. Both of these cases are about political affairs, accusations of financial mismanagement in the first and proven criminal acts to disrupt the Democratic presidential campaign in the second. Yet, in neither case are these political apologies, in the sense in which I am using the term, but rather personal apologies made by a politician for political misconduct.

A later president can help us make that distinction even sharper. Consider two apologies Clinton made. The first apology was in the wake of the Monica Lewinsky affair, during which Clinton expressed tepid regret while defending himself as having misled but not lied to the Office of the Independent Counsel and the American people. (This apology produced a rousing and edifying public debate about what constituted truth, and what constituted sex.) Clinton's tepid regret and call for a *cordon sanitaire* around his private life was criticized, and eventually Clinton gave a more forthright, less defensive, less legalistic apology to the American people. This is a personal apology by a politician for a personal failing. It differs from Nixon's in that it is about private misconduct, not political. The second apology is the one Clinton delivered to the survivors of the Tuskegee experiment, in which African American men infected with syphilis were treated with a placebo to determine the life course of the virus. That apology, I argue, *is* a political apology. So, too, is Clinton's apology in his speech to the Rwandan survivors at the Kigali airport in March 1998. What, then, is the difference that makes one a politician's apology and the other a political apology?

What distinguishes the apologies is that in one case Clinton (like Nixon) is speaking as an individual, while in the other he is speaking as a representative of the nation of which he is the leader. When he says in the speech in Rwanda that America, like all the other nations in the international community, "must bear its responsibility for this tragedy," he is speaking as the executive of the nation and on its behalf. When he apologizes for misleading the American people about his dalliance with an intern, he is speaking in his nonrepresentative role. What makes an apology political, then, in the sense I am using it here, is that the apology is made by a representative for a crime for which he or she may have been responsible because of decisions he or she made or failed to make, but not always. Clinton is responsible for the decisions he made during the Rwandan genocide, but he is not responsible for the Tuskegee experiments. His apologies in both cases, though, are political apologies, precisely because he is speaking in his role as the representative of the apologizing entity.

By "role" here, I do not mean to imply that Clinton is not playing any other role in life or politics, nor that any of us is constricted to one role. Kenneth Burke has proposed a robust and compelling theory of dramatism to explain in what ways, and for what ends, we all assume representative roles (the "world's a stage"). This fact does not alter—and indeed reinforces—what I am arguing about the roles that an individual can assume in public. It is precisely because we can occupy a multitude of roles that we need to make a distinction about what each role expresses and bears. When Clinton apologizes for the Monica Lewinsky affair, for instance, he is occupying two roles: He is presenting himself as a contrite husband to his wife and as a penitent politician to his constituency. When he apologizes to the Tuskegee experiment or Rwandan genocide survivors, he is presenting himself as a symbolic penitent for the nation. It is only these examples, I argue, when he presents himself as representing the nation (or the corporate body that is offering the apology) that define a political apology.

This distinction is important to make to understand why one example that many writers argue constitutes a stellar case of political apologizing and forgiving—what some maintain might be the transcendent example of our era, in fact—is actually not, with one rare exception. That case is South Africa, which is often presented as being a haven of political reconciliation based on remorse, apology, and forgiveness. It is important for us to clarify just what happened in South Africa. South Africa did not offer either political apologies or forgiveness; what its government offered to its citizens was amnesty for political crimes if those state agents confessed to the crimes before the Truth and Reconciliation Commission (TRC), and if those crimes were in fact political and not personal crimes. That so much apologizing and forgiving took place had much to do with the religious principles brought to the TRC by its leaders. But the apologies that state agents made—while they were confessing to crimes of state—were offered by individuals, and were in fact personal apologies. Likewise, the forgiveness that was extended to those confessing—and sometimes to others—was likewise offered by individuals. In South Africa, then, what we saw were acts of interpersonal apology and forgiveness. What the TRC had as its mandate was reconciliation that might emerge from truth-telling; the apologizing and forgiving process was an effect of that imperative but not essential to it, and, most importantly, it was performed at the individual level of citizens, not at the state level. The one exception in South Africa is President F. W. de Klerk's apology for the crimes of apartheid, which he offered at a 1993 press conference while he was still president, and for the crimes of the nation.[4] The distinction, then, is that he was the representative and not only an agent of the state, as those who confessed before the TRC were. So, in the case of South Africa, I would call Eugene de Kock's apology to the widows whose husbands he killed a personal apology and de Klerk's apology for apartheid a political apology.[5]

I would also make two other distinctions before turning to an analysis of political apologies. The first concerns the identity and status of the person or institution apologizing: *Who* apologizes? Both executives (presidents or prime ministers in the case of nations, CEOs and generals in the case of corporations or armies, the pope or archbishops in the case of churches) and representative legislative bodies (Congress and the Senate in the United States, the Diet in Japan) have issued political apologies. (The field is more crowded in the case of historical apologies, which have been made by individuals and families as well as by executives and representative legislative bodies.) The second distinction concerns the identity and status of those who are receiving, accepting, or acknowledging the apologies: *To whom* are these apologies made? (I leave the vexing question of who receives historical apologies for Chapter 4.) Political apologies are often made to one of three groups: a small group of people who suffered a particular state-sanctioned crime, a subnational group that has suffered an enduring state-sanctioned oppression, or another nation. An example of the first is the apology President Clinton offered to the survivors of the Tuskegee syphilis experiment. Examples of the second include President George H. W. Bush's apology to the victims of the Japanese internment camps during World War II, the prime ministers of Canada's apology to its First Nations, and the prime ministers of Australia and New Zealand's apology to their respective Aboriginal peoples. An example of the third is Japan's apologies for the colonization of Korea, for the Rape of Nanking, and for crimes against the so-called comfort women.

With those distinctions in mind, then, I can turn now to the question of what purposes these political apologies serve.

Its advocates make several robust and compelling claims for the value of the political apology. I focus on two of these claims here. First, they argue that such apologies are transformative for the people affiliated with the apologizing nation, changing them and their relationship to the nation's past in much the same way that penitence can change each person who revisits, acknowledges, and atones for acts of harm she or he has committed. When a nation apologizes for its previous acts of aggression, oppression, and injustice, that act, according to Brian Weiner, "may transform us as a citizenry in our collective attempts to work through the ambiguous legacy left us by our political ancestors."[6] What is particularly admirable in this belief is that citizens are more able, and more forced, to understand their own roles as participants in an ongoing drama. Such a conception of citizenship responsible for the actions of its nation, a congregation for the sins of its church, or employees for the wrongs of their corporation gives substance and heft to the notion of *belonging*. Just as the executive must accept the kind of responsibility she or he does in the role of the representative, so does each of us accept a measure of responsibility in our role as the represented. So, the value of this idea is that political apologies give the weight of responsible citizenship to those on whose behalf they are made.

The second valuable work that such political apologies perform is that they can transform the relationships between corporate bodies, and thereby transform the possible futures of those bodies. This is certainly the motivation when a nation's leader apologizes to a subnational group within its borders. When America apologized to the Tuskegee experiment survivors, for instance, the apology was partly motivated by the hope that there will be a healthier relationship between the institutions of the state and the African American population that has so long been abused rather than served by those institutions. Clinton noted that crimes like the Tuskegee experiment have enduring legacies. In this case, that crime created distrust among African Americans of the state and of the medical institutions supported by the state. At the official ceremony at which the apology was offered, Clinton announced that the Department of Health and Human Services was going to create a center and give postgraduate grants for bioethics in research and healthcare as well as extend the charter of the National Bioethics Advisory Commission. What these reparative acts might do, he hoped, was "begin restoring lost trust." The most important legacy of the experiments is precisely that loss, and Clinton's intelligence was to see its deeper implications. "We cannot be one America," he said, echoing Abraham Lincoln, "when a whole segment of our nation has no trust in America." The apology was "the first step to rebuild that broken trust."[7] The American apology for the Japanese internment camps falls into the same category of a nation's apologizing to a subnational group for an egregious crime committed during the guilted age.

Political apologies from one nation to another nation are, likewise, strategies meant to produce reconciliation and amity. These are often diplomatic acts meant to address one particular event in the past relationship between two nations to promote a different future relationship. In the guilted age, these apologies have largely been offered by the Axis nations—particularly

Germany and Japan—and extended to those nations colonized and occupied by them. These have significantly been featured at treaty-signing ceremonies or as preludes to the creation of treaties. In other words, the political apology functions to repudiate the harmful criminal relations at the moment that the new treaty bespeaks a healthier future economic relation. The question is whether these political apologies are necessary for that kind of reconciliation. Most writers believe they are, but Jennifer Lind has challenged that belief by noting two things. First, such apologies can be counterproductive. In almost every case, the apology does not have the unanimous support of the constituency on whose behalf it is made, and in those cases there is frequently a domestic backlash that undermines the nation's apology. How, then, can the nation to which the apology is offered accept something that is tainted by the ambiguous context in which it is offered? Often, Lind argues, these compromised political apologies create a "spiral of acrimony that makes reconciliation even more elusive." Her second point is empirical. There is reconciliation between nations, and productive economic relationships, without any political apologies. She presents the example of West Germany and France, whose governments had developed "profound reconciliation" with "minimal contrition." In the era before Germany became the poster child of political apologizing, France had already forged a healthy relationship with its neighbor and former occupier. Likewise, nations that have not apologized to each other for the atrocities of World War II—Japan for bombing Pearl Harbor, or America for dropping the bombs on Nagasaki and Hiroshima, for instance—nonetheless have "extremely friendly relations and a solid military alliance."[8] In other words, political apologies can be costly and are sometimes unnecessary. That is unarguably true. But they also are sometimes necessary, even though they are always costly.

We have seen, then, that political apologies can be extended as acts of goodwill to mark an emergent reconciliation between former adversaries, and that these apologies serve to enhance, or at least are in play, in both the domestic and international contexts in which they take place. For some, political apologies enrich the sense of citizenship, while, for others, political apologies augment stronger international relations. Having seen what they are, what distinguishes these acts, and what they can do, let us turn now to the case study that exemplifies the possibilities and problems of political apology: the case of Japan's apologies to the victims of its aggressive colonization and prewar and wartime atrocities. What the case of Japan shows is not just that this was a nation's apology that failed for peculiar reasons—I list those reasons shortly—but that its failure indicates precisely how every political apology is in danger of failing, how every political apology is fraught with a peculiar burden and subject to peculiar pressures arising from both the current political climate and the enduring historical trajectory of the nation.

To appreciate and understand the dynamic of political apologies in this case study, I begin with the present and work backward. The prime minister of Japan at the time of this writing (2014), Shinzō Abe, is in his second term as premier. The first Japanese prime minister to be born after the war, he served as premier of Japan in 2005–2006 and then reassumed the office in 2012. Politically, he represents the more hawkish right-wing spectrum of his conservative nationalist party, the Liberal Democratic Party (LDP), and he does so with perhaps more vigor than his predecessors in the same party. What is important is to see specifically how he addresses the questions at the heart of Japan's tense relationship with its neighbors, in particular China and South Korea. The historical crimes at issue are Japan's colonization of Korea and Manchuria, the atrocities committed by the Imperial Army in Nanking and Manila, and the wartime Japanese government's coercing thousands of Korean women into prostitution for the army (the so-called comfort women).[9] In his short first tenure as prime minister, Abe aggressively challenged the mood of penitence that his predecessors had expressed, fearing that the historical record was emphasizing the wrong things and therefore promoting values that were damaging to the future of Japan. His two concerns were that Japan's educational curriculum should represent a celebratory historical record, and that its politicians should not feel bound to apologize for the crimes its soldiers and government committed during the war.

In public speeches in 2006, and in a book he published that year, entitled *Toward a Beautiful Nation*, he consistently questioned whether Japan was indeed the aggressor in World War II and whether the Class A war criminals found guilty in the Tokyo trials had actually committed any crimes under Japan's domestic laws. In his political campaign, Abe ran on a platform that emphasized the need to pass legislation on educational reform and develop curricula that would promote what in his book he ominously calls "national awareness." In that same year, as the leader of the Japanese Society for History Textbook Reform, Abe had first suggested that there might not have been that much coercion in recruiting the comfort women, a point that had been made repeatedly by nationalists and Korea-bashers in Japan. The Japanese novelist Kobayashi Yoshinoro, for instance, produced highly popular cartoon books (*manga* art) that represent Korean women as "smiling volunteers" who just wanted to help the brave Imperial soldiers relieve their sexual stress. In the face of public outrage, Abe grudgingly revised his statement and claimed that he accepted the official 1993 government report on the issue.[10]

These struggles over which version of history to teach Japanese students exemplify the kind of domestic politics we find everywhere that political apologies are tendered. The debate is frequently between conservatives and liberals who are both concerned about the effects textbooks will have on young minds and future citizens. At one meeting of the Society for History Textbook Reform in April 2004, for instance, one conservative plaintively asked: "Why are we teaching our children to hate Japan?" A common argument is that emphasizing the evils of a nation's past takes away the pride that the young should have in a nation, and its advocates often offer their conservative, celebratory counter-narrative. In the case of the colonization of Korea and China, for instance, such groups as the Society for History Textbook Reform and such war veteran associations as the Japan War-Bereaved Families Association have argued that "Japanese wartime occupation actually freed Asian countries from Western colonial oppression." And Abe, a leader in Society for History Textbook Reform before he became the leader of the nation, exemplified this same historical narrative when he maintained that Japan was not the aggressor in World War II and that those tried and executed at the Tokyo trials were found guilty only under "victors' justice," not valid law.[11]

When Abe became prime minister again in 2012, he resumed the use of his pulpit to address specific points about World War II to affirm the nationalist sentiments he endorsed. He created a new public holiday, Restoration of Sovereignty Day, on April 28, 2013, to celebrate the end of the American Occupation of Japan. He also began to hint that he would resume his visits to Yasukuni Shrine in an official capacity. Yasukuni Shrine, which honors the war dead of Japan, was inaugurated in 1869 by Meiji officials to honor those who died in the war to oust the shogunate in 1868. Its domestic critics, and China and South Korea, find the shrine notorious and proscribe official visits to it because it also honors the Class A war criminals executed in the wake of World War II. The shrine, then, serves as a symbol of a new militarism in Japan, an important icon for Japanese nationalists, and an important barometer for gauging the politics of Japanese politicians. Abe had refrained from visiting the shrine during his first premiership, although he had visited it frequently when he was not prime minister and, on one occasion, paid for a wreath that two of his cabinet ministers placed at the shrine. Early in his second term as premier, in August 2013, he had planned and then skipped a visit to Yasukuni Shrine on the anniversary of Japan's surrender on August

15, 1945, because it would have caused a disruption in Japan's relationship with China and South Korea. Emboldened six months later, he undertook an official visit to Yasukuni Shrine on December 26, 2013.[12]

Abe's visit was the first made by a sitting prime minister since 2006. Both the South Korean and Chinese governments immediately expressed dismay and concern. The South Korean Culture Minister Yoo Jin-ryong declared, "Our government cannot help but deplore and express anger over the fact that Prime Minister Abe ignored the concerns and warnings of the neighboring countries and the world community and paid respect at the Yasukuni Shrine, which glorifies Japan's colonial rule and war of aggression." The Chinese Foreign Ministry likewise expressed its "strong indignation that Japanese leaders brutally trample the feelings of the Chinese and other Asian peoples victimized in wars" and urged the Japanese government to reflect on "its history of aggression." The Yasukuni Shrine visit was important because of what the shrine represented politically, but also because it had largely become associated with another aspect of Japan's political landscape—the political apology.[13]

Abe's visit to the shrine occurred almost exactly one year after he had publically questioned whether Japan might repudiate Prime Minister Tomiichi Murayama's 1995 political apology that had become an important moment of rapprochement for relations between Japan and its formerly colonized neighbors. Early in 2013, Abe announced that he was planning to revisit Murayama's apology, which had been made on the fiftieth anniversary of the end of World War II. Looking forward to the seventieth anniversary in 2015, he declared: "I want to make a statement that is forward-facing and appropriate for the 21st century." A month later, he continued to suggest that he would "revisit" the iconic apology and drew criticism from various civil society groups and former Prime Minister Murayama. He faced continued criticism for a position that many maintained would "isolate" Japan from its regional neighbors. As he had done previously in other confrontations, Abe eventually backed down from this position and affirmed that his government would abide by the official apology. Six months later, after initiating a half-year's public debate on the apology, Abe visited Yasukuni Shrine. These two events, the one with which he began the year and the one with which he ended it, were intimately related: His threat to repudiate the apology and his visit to the shrine were two sides of the same coin in Abe's political currency.[14]

Abe's political machinations, his dance with public opinion, his rash public pronouncements made off the cuff and then strategically withdrawn, and his defiant acts meant to alienate foreign leaders while simultaneously heartening his conservative political base reveal the vectors in Japanese politics concerning the memory of World War II. Each of the topics on which

Abe commented or touched in some way—the comfort women, the question of Japan's crimes against humanity in Nanking and Manila, the issue of Japan's motivation in the war, the significance of Yasukuni Shrine, and, most importantly, the question of war responsibility—is a contested point for Japanese politicians. Abe's stand is a nationalist one that is wholly and resolutely unapologetic, and his rhetorical gestures and political acts are meant directly to repudiate and castigate Japan's most important political apology.

While later prime ministers have offered apologies for Japan's wartime acts, Murayama's apology at the fiftieth anniversary of the end of the war, August 15, 1995, stands out as the most significant political apology in Japan's modern history. Prime Minister Junichiro Koizumi, for instance, offered apologies on the fifty-eighth and sixtieth anniversaries of the end of World War II in 2003 and 2005, respectively, but his statements were not as robust as Murayama's. This is not surprising, insofar as Koizumi was, after all, the leader of the LDP, the most fiscally conservative and nationalist political party in Japan, while Murayama was head of the Japan Socialist Party (that became the Social Democratic Party of Japan in 1996). Although a maverick within his own party, Koizumi was no socialist, and his nationalism, while nowhere near as fanatical as Abe's, was nonetheless evident in most of his public pronouncements. His apologies, too, were somewhat uneven in that they consistently shifted from expressing mild remorse to those nations hurt by Japan's aggressions to expressing more heartfelt mourning for the Japanese war dead. He also vitiated his apologies through what were either rhetorical gaffes or political strategies. In his sixtieth anniversary statement, for example, he was forthright at certain points: "Facing these facts of history, I once again express my feelings of deep remorse and heartfelt apology, and also express the feelings of mourning for all victims, both at home and abroad, in the war." But at other points in his speech, he presented a somewhat petulant and self-pitying tone, noting at one point that "Japan's postwar history has indeed been six decades of manifesting its remorse on the war through actions." He additionally felt that this was a good occasion to point out the demographic shift in the nation, noting that the "postwar generations now exceed 70% of Japan's population." The unsubtle point was that the majority of Japan's citizens are now beyond blame for the crimes for which he was putatively apologizing. What most compromised his political apologies, though, were not the statements themselves but the fact that as prime minister he made repeated visits to Yasukuni Shrine, visits, that like Abe's, provoked international criticisms.[15]

Yasukuni Shrine, then, has come to signify the polar opposite of the political apology. Those who refuse to apologize for Japan's war atrocities visit the shrine to express their disdain for the apologists as they affirm their nationalist credentials, while those who do apologize are frequently seen as retracting their apologies with their visits. At least one reason that Prime Minister Murayama's statement of apology has been seen as the most sincere and powerful of the Japanese political apologies may be that it also has not been tainted by any visit to Yasukuni Shrine. We can now turn to Murayama's apology.

The nationally televised speech was delivered from Murayama's home and was given just before he attended the official ceremony commemorating the fiftieth anniversary of the end of World War II. Following his comments on the blessings of peace and the support of those nations that helped Japan in its recovery, Murayama turned to the new initiative his government had just launched for improving relations with its Asian neighbors. Called the Peace, Friendship and Exchange Initiative, this program focused on two areas: an economic one that would promote the "rapid expansion of exchanges with those countries," and a cultural one, in which the initiative would provide "support for historical research into relations in the modern era between Japan and the neighboring countries of Asia and elsewhere." At that point in his speech, he then offered his apology for the events that the "historical research" would obviously substantiate. He spoke as follows:

> During a certain period in the not too distant past, Japan, following a mistaken national policy, advanced along the road to war, only to ensnare the Japanese people in a fateful crisis, and, through its colonial rule and aggression, caused tremendous damage and suffering to the people of many countries, particularly to those of Asian nations. In the hope that no such mistake be made in the future, I regard, in a spirit of humility, these irrefutable facts of history, and express here once again my feelings of deep remorse and state my heartfelt apology. Allow me also to express my feelings of profound mourning for all victims, both at home and abroad, of that history.

Addressing himself to the nation and, perhaps, especially to those members of the Diet who were trying to defy his symbolic acts of rapprochement, he stated that "deep remorse" might help Japan "eliminate self-righteous nationalism" and work toward attitudes more likely to lead to peace and democracy. He concluded by noting that Japan had special cause to work for "the ultimate elimination of nuclear weapons" as the "only country to have experienced the devastation of atomic bombing." Only by assiduously working toward these noble ends, he ended, could "Japan atone for its past and lay to rest the spirits of those who perished."[16]

Predictably, Murayama's apology provoked mixed responses both domestically and in the "Asian nations" to whom the apology was directed, albeit indirectly. The comments from Japanese citizens ran the usual gamut, from those who felt that the apology was long overdue to those who insisted that Japan was not the aggressor in World War II and that there was no evidence that Japan had committed the atrocities for which the apology was offered. Representatives from China and South Korea were cautious in their responses and more forward-looking than forgiving. As the South Korean foreign minister tepidly put it, "We will observe Japan's attitude in the future."[17] This was probably a wise course of action to take, since both the text of Murayama's apology and the context in which it was given contained sufficiently problematic aspects to give pause to the Asian nations. We can see some of these problems by focusing on the *logistics*, the *rhetoric*, and the *representativeness* of Murayama's apology.

The first point to take up is logistics. Political apologies, like private apologies, mean more or less depending on where and when they are offered. In Japan, there was widespread speculation about what it meant for Prime Minister Murayama to deliver the apology *before* and not *at* the fiftieth-anniversary ceremony. For some, it weakened the apology and made it less representative of the nation, while for others its separation from the ritual ceremonial proceedings gave it greater force as a state address. Likewise, it was possible to see the staging of the apology on August 15 as a slight to the Asian nations. After all, one could argue, this is a date more central to Japanese history, more a part of Japan's symbolic universe. Choosing that date, arguably, might be interpreted as making the point that those nations who had been subject to Japan's imperial imperative were at least still subject to its historical calendar. Consider how different an apology would be if it were offered on the anniversary of the date Japan began its colonization rather than had it ended by forces beyond its control. Such an apology might have resonated much more precisely because it would have been offered on a date that was perhaps more symbolic for the victimized people.

In a personal apology, the rhetoric of an apology is obviously important, since what is said and how it is said reveal the degree of sincerity of the person apologizing and also the full realization of the wrong for which the apology is being offered. We all recognize failed apologies when they attempt to exculpate the actor rather than accept responsibility, or when they are not sufficiently cognizant of the wrong for which they are offered. In political apologies, offered from one nation to another, the rhetoric also reveals the degree to which the nation apologizing recognizes the other nation and recognizes it as an equal. The rhetoric of the prime minister's apology was closely scrutinized for the precise language that it used. This was important because Japanese politicians before Murayama had expressed "regret" and some degree of "remorse," but they had never used the words indicating "apology." Yet his apology was rendered less effective by three other rhetorical acts in his speech.

First, the prime minister reminded his audience that Japan was "the only country to have experienced the devastation of atomic bombing," a point that at least hinted at the idea that acts conducted during war are less subject to moral judgment. The reference also makes less stark the difference between those who are aggressors (those apologizing) and those who are victims (those who receive or felt owed an apology). Second, the prime minister was unwilling to affix blame where many felt it belonged. In the question-and-answer period following the apology, Murayama denied that Emperor Hirohito was responsible, stating instead: "It is well known that the Emperor prayed for peace in the world, and made his utmost efforts to avoid the war, and it was the Emperor who decisively judged to end the war."[18] What had been for fifty years an absolute necessity for any Japanese politician—the need to ensure that the royal family not be implicated in the crimes of the state—starkly revealed the difference between how Japan and the nations it colonized viewed the offenses that were the subject of the apology. Finally, the prime minister was remarkably vague in his description of those offenses, neither naming which "Asian nations" he had in mind nor which crimes exactly Japan had committed. Nothing was said of the fact that Japan had colonized Korea from 1910 to 1945, or that the Japanese Imperial Army had made two hundred thousand Korean women into sex slaves. There was no mention of the devastation that the Imperial Army had visited on Nanking when it massacred three hundred thousand civilians and raped eighty thousand women in the so-called "Rape of Nanking."[19]

The media in Japan reported that Murayama had spent the days leading up to August 15 studying West German President Richard von Weizsäcker's famous 1985 apology on the fortieth anniversary of Germany's defeat in World War II.[20] After the Japanese prime minister's apology, newspapers looked at the notable differences between the two speeches and recognized that the Japanese apology was less evocative, less specific, seemingly less able to describe in meaningful detail just what was done that merited an apology.

My third and final point concerns representativeness—that is, the question of how much these apologies actually express the feelings of the people in whose name they are spoken. Some civil society groups were staunchly in favor of the apology. Six weeks before the anniversary, a group of 137 well-known public figures signed and handed to the prime minister a statement of support that urged the government to go further and provide compensation for those to whom it was apologizing. But there was also significant dissent. The fact that the prime minister used the language he did ("apology") raised concerns among some who believed that these words did not represent Japanese citizens' sentiments, or even those of their own representatives. The Japanese House of Representatives earlier that summer had a divisive debate and finally passed a Resolution that used the term *fukai hansei* ("deep remorse") and not *shazai* or *owabi* ("apology"). In addition, half of the 502 members of Parliament did not even vote on the Resolution, expressing their disapproval through abstention. In fact, more members abstained than voted in favor of the resolution (the vote was 230–21–241). (It should be noted that many of these abstentions were because some members of the Diet, especially members of the Socialist and New Frontier Parties, believed the resolution did not offer sufficient remorse.) The former minister of education went so far as to conduct a national campaign and claimed to have collected five million signatures on a petition condemning the resolution.[21]

Let me be clear, though, about just how significant Murayama's apology was, and remains. What Murayama did and how he did it was indeed courageous and groundbreaking. He adopted language that only one premier before him had dared to utter publicly; on August 23, 1993, Prime Minister Morihiro Hosokawa had expressed "deep remorse and apology" (*fukai hansei to owabi*). But Murayama declared this apology to the wider public and the world to which television was broadcast, not only to the Diet as Hosokawa had. And Murayama had arguably transformed what was a day specifically set aside for Japanese mourning into an occasion where he also mourned Japan's victims and acknowledged responsibility for their victimhood. It is telling that those who have offered apologies after Murayama have done so on August 15, and that those who want to display their nationalist credentials do so by threatening to revoke only Murayama's 1995 apology, since it stands well above the perfunctory and ineffective apologies that have been offered by the prime ministers who have followed him. Murayama's apology, then, has become the benchmark for liberal Japanese political sentiments, just as Yasukuni Shrine has become the prime symbol for nationalist ones.

And Yasukuni Shrine played a key role as Murayama expressed the most heartfelt political apology in his nation's history. On the very day of his famous apology, members of Murayama's cabinet and nationalist members of the Diet expressed their dissent by going to Yasukuni Shrine, thereby symbolically rebuking their leader for focusing on other nations' suffering on a day meant to commemorate Japan's war dead. As was appropriate for the occasion, which did mark, after all, the date that Japan officially surrendered to the Allied forces, Murayama mourned the fallen Japanese soldiers, but, significantly, he also included other nations' soldiers and civilians—at least, that is what his opponents understood in his expression of "feelings of profound mourning for all victims, both at home and abroad."[22] Murayama, then, broke at least three precedents in his apology: offering it on the day traditionally reserved for Japan's mourning, mourning the losses of those nations to which he was going to apologize, and offering that apology in language that represented the most heartfelt degree of penitence in Japanese.

I have pointed out some of the problems in the text and political context of Murayama's apology, but these are problems afflicting political apologies more generally. The apology by the executive was one act of several in this performance. His sincerity was not questioned, but the apology itself was clearly affected by the context in which it was offered. The Diet had given it tepid support, and the cabinet ministers had registered their disapprobation by visiting Yasukuni Shrine that very day. In other words, the prime minister's apology resonated less as a national expression, surrounded as it was by other symbolic acts of dissent. The final political context has to do with the *person* offering the apology. The nations to which the prime minister apologized had long expressed their desire to receive an apology from a different office, the one, in fact, that Murayama had to defend in his post-apology interviews—that of the emperor. Both Korea and China have maintained that the person responsible for the crimes of World War II is Emperor Hirohito, and that, therefore, it is only fitting for his son, the current Emperor Akihito, to apologize. During his first visit to China—in fact, the first visit by any Japanese emperor to China—in 1990, shortly after his father's death, Emperor Akihito acknowledged the suffering of China during the war and expressed his "deep sadness." Chinese officials were circumspect and diplomatic, but they also publically noted that they had not received an apology. Almost a quarter century later, South Korean President Lee Myung-Bak said that he was still waiting, and that Emperor Akihito would be welcome in Seoul "if he is willing to apologize from his heart to those who died fighting for independence." Anything less would be unacceptable. Akihito "doesn't need to come if he is coming just to offer his 'deepest regret,'" Myung-Bak pointedly added.[23]

That it was Murayama, the prime minister, and not Akihito, the emperor, who apologized likely vitiated the apology for those nations to whom it was addressed. And Akihito might have exacerbated their frustration by the ambiguity of his own comments on August 15, 1995. At an event later that afternoon, after Murayama's televised apology, Akihito declared: "I, along with all the nation's people, hereby express my deep mourning over those who died." The "nation's people," on whose behalf these words were spoken, wondered aloud just who was being mourned—the Japanese soldiers who perished in the war or all the soldiers and civilian victims killed by Japanese soldiers. In other words, was the emperor adding to or refuting the prime minister's apology? Was his statement the rhetorical equivalent of going to Yasukuni Shrine or repudiating such a visit? In response to media queries about the ambiguity of the emperor's statement, officials at the Imperial Household Agency and the Foreign Ministry claimed not to know what the emperor meant, while the Ministry of Health and Welfare insisted that the emperor was mourning only the Japanese dead.[24]

Here, then, we can appreciate the dynamic of political apologies and the crucial ways they can be understood as *political* statements. Like other declarations, treaties, or legislative acts, political apologies can be revised, renewed, or rejected. When a new executive occupies the office of the one who issued the initial apology—when Abe becomes premier, say—then that new executive can circumscribe or overwrite that apology as he or she sees fit, and the fitness has to do with the politics that the current executive bears and represents. So the most important thing about political apologies, then, the thing that most distinguishes them from interpersonal apologies, is that they are part of a historical record that is subject to the prevailing political winds of later occupants of the apologist's chair. It is usually not the case in interpersonal apologies that those who apologize to us then retract the apology some months later, simply because they have changed their outlook. I am sure it sometimes happens, and when it does, we probably believe that the apology was not sincere from the outset. In other words, we revise our opinion of the apologist, not the apology itself. But when the apologist is a representative of a nation, that revised opinion takes on dramatically different dimensions.

On the whole, the guilted age has not been much marked by such threats as the one Abe made to retract Murayama's political apology. No political leader in Germany has made public statements saying that he or she would like to revisit the statement of remorse made by President von Weizsäcker. No president of France has gone on record to question former President Chirac's political apology for the Vichy regime's complicity with the Third Reich. No later pope has issued a cyclical that urges reconsideration of Pope John Paul II's apology for the Vatican's indifference to the Holocaust. That is not to say that these nations have a fully penitent populace who sees the crimes of the past as indeed being crimes and repudiate the behaviors that led to them; France, Germany, and Austria have all had right-wing, xenophobic political parties, some of which have performed alarmingly well in elections. At least part of their appeal is that they represent nostalgia rather than penitence for precisely the kind of race-thinking that fueled the Third Reich, especially in their urgent calls for halting immigration and their evocation of "purity" in a nation's people and culture. But even the most stridently nationalist and unapologetic politicians in these countries have not dared to question the political apologies their nations extended. Consider the case of Jörg Haider, who led the xenophobic, nationalist Freedom Party of Austria (which eventually split and became the Alliance for the Future of Austria), and who made occasionally supportive comments about the Nazi government (both of his parents belonged to the Austrian Nazi Party). Despite his bombastic rhetoric and sympathy for the Nazi past, he nonetheless signed the important Declaration of Responsibility for Austria in February 2000, a document that explicitly states that "Austria accepts her responsibility" for the "horrendous crimes of the National Socialist regime" and affirms the political apologies that Chancellor Franz Vranitzky and President Thomas Klestil each made in front of the Knesset in 1993 and 1994, respectively.[25]

Japan's, then, is a rare, perhaps unique, situation, both in the amount of public dissent that surrounds the political apology and in the threat made by later premiers to repudiate the one shining example of the nation's political apology. Moreover, in what is assuredly a related fact, Japan has also long been considered the laggard of the Axis in the race to apologize for World War II crimes. The political scientists who have written about Japan have been struck by what they describe as Japan's enduring, multigenerational "reluctance to acknowledge wartime wrongs." Whether it is a product of national "amnesia" or simply an "unapologetic remembrance of its atrocities," Japan "has long been committed to a policy of denial about World War II." If Germany has proven to be the nation most thoroughly committed to atonement in its apologies—the journalist Daniel Vernet describes Germany in *Le Monde* as "unsurpassed both at the crime and at repenting it"—then Japan stands as the polar opposite. If Germany is the "model penitent," as Thomas Berger notes, then Japan has long been considered the "model impenitent."[26] If Japan has long resisted offering a political apology and continues to roil in controversy its most sincere expression of remorse for its prewar and wartime crimes, then the question that must be asked is, why? What makes Japan a "model impenitent" nation?

There are various ways writers have tried to explain this difference between nations that have expressly and repeatedly apologized to the peoples they have wronged and nations that have either resisted apologizing or offered tepid or wholly inadequate apologies—or, more specifically, the difference between Germany and Japan. Some focus on religious differences, arguing that Germany's Lutheran values promote the idea and practice of repentance, while the state-based Shinto practices of Japan and, for some, even Nichiren Buddhism do not. Some focus on what they argue is a fundamental cultural difference between what they identify as Germany's guilt culture and Japan's shame culture. Ruth Benedict is the first to make the case for Japan as a shame culture, and she remains certainly the most influential. Regardless of whether one agrees that Japan is a shame culture, it is clear that shame has certainly played an important part in the ways the Japanese think about their duties and relationships. The Imperial Army's Field Service Code, issued on January 8, 1941, for instance, insists that those "who fear shame are strong" and urges soldiers to kill themselves rather than "shame [themselves] by being taken prisoner alive."[27] Nonetheless, it is one thing to believe in shame as an inspiration for soldiers and quite another to find it the foundation of a culture. Moreover, it is not clear that shame cultures are impenitent, even if they express it differently and to a lesser extent or in a different spirit. After all, as I discuss in the next chapter, the same government that issued pamphlets during the war building on shame as a motive for acting in a particular way also issued pamphlets after the war urging the people to undertake penitence, regularly and collectively.

Those who focus less on cultural and more on historical factors in explaining this difference suggest that Japan differs from Germany in that Japan was not just an aggressor nation but also utterly devastated by the war. Japan felt victimized by the unprecedented bombing of Nagasaki and Hiroshima, by the destruction of its land and starvation of its people in the aftermath of the war, and by the seven years of occupation by the Supreme Commander for the Allied Powers (SCAP) and the transformation of its culture in the course of that occupation. Many Japanese, as John Dower has brilliantly shown, suffered what was called the "*kyodatsu* condition," a collective state of exhaustion and despair brought on in the aftermath of the war. This answer is only somewhat persuasive, though. While Japan is the only nation in history to suffer the unimaginable horrors of the atom bomb, it is not unique in having its land and population devastated in the war, nor in the postwar anomie of its population. Germany suffered the Allied bombings that destroyed its cities, and its population suffered the same kind of hunger as Japan's did. War surveys taken in both countries revealed that the average citizen in each country had been reduced to a diet of 1,200 calories a day in Germany and 1,000 calories a day in Japan.[28]

A more compelling historical reason for the difference is that Japan, unlike Germany, did not have a particular, identifiable leader or political party, like Adolf Hitler or the Nazis, who could be designated as the person and group representing the epoch of terror in the nation. There was in Japan no National Fascist Party as in Italy, or even a Vichy regime, but simply a series of parliaments and prime ministers, as usual, who made the decisions to invade Manchuria, develop an alliance with Germany, and attack Pearl Harbor. The attempt by interested parties to cast General Hideki Tōjō as the equivalent to Hitler was a marked failure, for good reason.

That attention to leadership, though, is precisely where we should focus if we want to note just what distinguishes Japan's experience from Germany's, and it might explain the relative penitence of one and impenitence of the other. It is not a difference in religion or culture but rather a difference in the postwar political history of each nation. In the end, the difference has much to do with the leader who escaped the trials and has attempted to escape historical judgment. Japan's peculiar dynamic involving political apologies has much to do, I argue, with the role the emperor played before the war, the role into which he was cast in the immediate aftermath of the war during the Occupation, and then the role that he has assumed since the war. Officials in China and South Korea, in other words, are right to insist that the only valid political apology should come from the emperor. To understand why, and to examine how Hirohito and those who served as his politicians and his Occupiers created precisely the dynamics that the later political apologies would have to negotiate, we need to return to the date that Prime Minister Murayama commemorated on its fiftieth anniversary.

3

POLITICAL APOLOGIES II

August 15, 1945, just after noon, in the twentieth year of his reign, was the first time his subjects heard the voice of Emperor Hirohito, when he announced over the radio that Japan had officially surrendered to the Allies. The "Imperial Rescript on the Termination of the War" did not use the word "surrender," nor did it sound all that defeated, or even conciliatory. Indeed, it seemed to read more like a lawyer's defense brief. Hirohito declared that the war on America and Britain was purely defensive ("to ensure Japan's self-preservation and the stabilization of East Asia") and that Japan had no intention of infringing on the "sovereignty of other nations" or embarking on any campaign of "territorial aggrandizement." He also hauntingly noted that the dropping of "a new and most cruel bomb" on Hiroshima and Nagasaki augured the potential "total extinction of human civilization," and that Japan's ending the war would prevent that. He then addressed what he acknowledged would be the pain that came with defeat and occupation and told his subjects that they must be noble, act as a family, and take comfort in the fact that the "structure of the Imperial State" was safeguarded and would be maintained. The only statement of remorse to be found in the "Imperial Rescript" was directed to precisely those "Asian nations" Murayama would address exactly fifty years later. Hirohito expressed "the deepest sense of regret to Our Allied nations of East Asia, who have consistently cooperated with the Empire towards the emancipation of East Asia."[1] With that statement, Hirohito seems to have inaugurated the very discourse that nationalist politicians would repeat for the next sixty years (and are likely to continue repeating for many more), especially on the key points of whether Japan had fought a war of aggression and to what extent Japan should be thought of as a victim rather than a victimizer.

At 7:30 that evening, Prime Minister Suzuki Kantarō took to the airwaves to clarify what the emperor had announced—that the war was indeed over—and then spoke on behalf of his country in offering his own expression of remorse: "The nation sincerely apologizes to His Majesty" for the defeat. That same day, the Ministry of Education sent out a message to all local government officials, school principals, and university presidents that "the responsibility for defeat lay with the nation itself," and that these leaders and educators must now "step up indoctrination of the emperor system." After Suzuki stepped down two days after the announcement, the newly appointed Prime Minister Prince Higashikuni Naruhiko repeated his predecessor's message and declared at his first press conference on August 28 that the citizens who bore responsibility for the war would begin national reconstruction first through an act of collective atonement ("the repentance of one hundred million [*ichioku sōzange*]"). He repeated this message to the Diet on September 4, including another version of the national apology to the emperor: "We deeply regret to have caused Him so much anxiety."[2] The tone was set early then, with political leaders and government ministries firmly placing responsibility for the war on the nation rather than on the emperor. Eventually that stance would evolve into placing legal responsibility on the generals and politicians and moral responsibility on the people.

On August 27, the Information Bureau of the central government issued instructions to the public urging them—as the prime minister would suggest the next day—that collective repentance would foster national unity; with such penitence and by fighting against the future use of nuclear weapons, the Japanese could transform themselves from the "losers of war" into the "winners of peace." Civil society groups, such as the East Asia League, a millenarian movement, also urged public repentance. Its leader, Ishiwara Kanji, delivered speeches to the League in August and then to the larger public in September, calling on the entire nation to repent. Some months later, in May 1946, the Ministry of Education added to this push by issuing a tract, *New Educational Guidance*, that claimed that "responsibility for the war must be borne by the entire populace." The people of Japan, it concluded, "must deeply apologize to the world for their crime."[3]

Some were not entirely sure what their crime was. A young woman in Nagano prefecture wondered whether being deceived by the politicians did not exonerate the people: "Are we people who were deceived without crime?" She poignantly answered her own question: "That stupidity, I think, is also a kind of crime." The social critic Abe Shinnosuke echoed her when he noted that the people who were deceived by the military leaders "must bear responsibility for having been stupid." Others came to understand that the crimes in question were not the nebulous ones the government confected and obfuscated but precisely the ones for which the Tokyo Tribunal indicted the military and political leaders—the mass murders and atrocities that went under the names of Rape of Nanking and Rape of Manila, in which civilians were slaughtered and raped and their bodies desecrated. Once the people learned about the extent of the barbarity of the Imperial Army, some, at least, felt a need for the nation to atone. One woman wrote to a newspaper after the revelations became public: "I understood the meaning of collective repentance for the first time when I heard about this." After the execution of seven of those leaders sentenced by the Tokyo Tribunal, one professor in Osaka admitted that the people were manipulated by their leaders, but that nonetheless "all of us must bear responsibility" because the "crime is not that of the leaders alone." At a memorial in March 1946, the Christian president of Tokyo Imperial University, Nanbara Shigeru, spoke of those former students who had died in the war effort as "a sacrifice of atonement for the crimes of the people."[4]

Not all the people thought this apportioning of responsibility for the war all that fair, of course. One newspaper, *Asahi Shimbun*, received a letter from a farmer who candidly claimed that there is "no need to do repentance for something we weren't in on." Those who deceived the people were the ones who should be repenting, he insisted. Another letter thought it was rather "sneaky" for those who conducted the war now to try "to distribute responsibility among the people." It was not the "collective repentance of the hundred million" that was needed, he argued, as much as the acknowledged responsibility of "those in charge of the war." One of Japan's most influential philosophers, Tanabe Hajime, offered a subtler take on how to assign responsibility. In the book *Philosophy as Metanoetics*, which he completed in October 1945 and published in April 1946, Tanabe first accepts his own responsibility for the deaths of those students of his who had perished in a war fueled by blind militarism ("I feel the height of personal responsibility and remorse"). He then notes that the people of Japan must indeed be collectively penitent (to walk "the way of *zange*"). And he concludes by noting that not only Japan but all nations need to atone for such a conflagration as World War II: "*Zange* is a task that world history imposes on all people in our times." In the wake of its surrender, then, Japan was wholly occupied by a feeling of penitence, albeit a penitence that was not uniform and was sometimes directed toward the emperor, sometimes toward the nations the Imperial Army had violated, and sometimes toward the vague idea of loss. The nation had nonetheless become what the influential intellectual Murayama Masao called "a community of remorse."[5]

It seemed to some that the only person who was not a member of this "community of remorse" was its leader, Emperor Hirohito, who was assiduously not assigned and did not accept responsibility for the war. Many of his subjects came to be deeply troubled by this fact. Tanabe states in his book that the emperor too must accept responsibility for the war and likewise demonstrate repentance, a point that others came to accept. At the beginning of the Occupation, Kido Kōichi, Hirohito's closest aide, his mentor, and, officially, the last Lord Keeper of the Privy Seal, told the American-led Supreme Commander for the Allied Powers (SCAP) that the emperor should not be perceived as responsible for the war and that if he did abdicate, it would spell doom for the kinds of political reforms SCAP wished to inaugurate in Japan's fledgling democracy. This, it would turn out, was what SCAP already believed. By the end of the Occupation, though, Kido had reconsidered. He began to urge the emperor to accept responsibility for the war and to demonstrate this sense of responsibility with tangible action. In a message to the emperor, he wrote: "I think it is most proper for you to take responsibility and abdicate for the sake of your imperial ancestors and for the nation." If the emperor chose otherwise, as he did in fact choose, then "the end result will be that the imperial family alone will have failed to take responsibility." That failure, Kido predicted, would create "an unclear mood" and likely leave "an eternal scar."[6]

It was not only those who were closest to him and knew the most about his actions who believed that the emperor was indeed responsible and should show it. At least some, maybe many, ordinary citizens likewise believed the same thing. If Watanabe Kiyoshi's diary entries for the first eight months of the Occupation are any indication of a wider popular sentiment, many Japanese subjects were baffled by the absence of remorse and responsibility in the emperor's "Imperial Rescript." As John Dower notes, this ex-serviceman was "consumed by rage at having been betrayed by his sovereign." Watanabe went through several phases where he assumed that Hirohito would commit suicide before being executed at a military trial, and then, when Hirohito was not indicted, that he would assuredly abdicate, and then, when that did not happen, that Hirohito would at least accept blame. When the emperor did none of these things, Watanabe wondered what kept Hirohito from simply saying to his nation, "I am sorry to have caused you so much difficulty." The failure of offering even an apology, it seemed to Watanabe, was disastrous to public morality. The emperor had set a very low standard and become an exemplar of irresponsibility: When "the emperor gets away without taking responsibility," Watanabe concluded, it becomes clear that "there is no need for us to take responsibility, no matter what we did." At the end of his journal, in April 1945, as Watanabe prepared to leave his village to take a job in Tokyo, he wrote a letter to Emperor Hirohito, giving a detailed account of all that he had been paid in wages and food and clothing while he had been in the Imperial Navy, and then he submitted a check for that total amount of 4,282 yen. "I owe you nothing," he wrote to his emperor.[7] Watanabe, a lowly, uneducated twenty-year-old ex-serviceman, could teach his sovereign how to be responsible, starting with the simplest lesson of how to pay his debts.

Presumably, Hirohito did not receive Watanabe's check, but he likely did receive the direct message from his closest aide and mentor, Kido.[8] At the end of the Occupation in 1952, many people, and not only his closest adviser, expected him to do *something*—abdicate, express remorse, or accept responsibility. A conservative politician, Nakasone Yasuhiro, suggested that since Hirohito bore "responsibility for having degraded the glory of modern Japan," he should acknowledge his responsibility by abdicating. Hajime had suggested that the way for the emperor to show repentance was for him to abdicate. And Hirohito's brothers had also urged him to abdicate to salvage the royal family and ensure the continuity of the Empire. At the end of the Occupation, Hirohito did none of these things—repent, apologize, or abdicate—just as he had done nothing at the end of the Tokyo tribunal trials when, again, many thought he would take the occasion to repent and step down. Indeed, it seems clear in retrospect that Hirohito had decided *before* the surrender that he would reject the idea of accepting responsibility and showing remorse when it was first proposed to him. At a final meeting in the early hours of August 10, 1945, as his closest advisers hashed out how to respond to the surrender terms in the Potsdam Declaration, Hiranuma Kiichirō, an avid ultranationalist and wholehearted believer in the Empire, quietly but pointedly turned to his monarch and spoke: "Your majesty, you also bear responsibility [*sekinin*] for this defeat. What apology [*mōshiwake*] are you going to make to the heroic spirits of the imperial founder of your house and your other imperial ancestors?"[9] If Hirohito answered, it was not recorded by either of the two people who wrote journal accounts of the meeting.

The pattern was set early, then, and the discourse of denial would not change much over the rest of the emperor's reign. As Herbert Bix has expertly shown, Hirohito consistently evaded accepting responsibility when he was asked about it by journalists who interviewed him or by media campaigns urging him to beg forgiveness from the war dead. From the end of the war to the end of his reign, Hirohito maintained the same stolid demeanor when it came to questions about responsibility and remorse. When he visited America, for instance, for the first and only time, in September 1975, he expressed to President Gerald Ford his "profound sadness" (*kanashimi no nen*) that the war had occurred. When he returned to Tokyo, he faced questions from the press about what he meant. When one reporter asked him whether he was finally admitting "war responsibility," his response betrayed precisely the marriage of pretended innocence and cynicism that had marked his career when it came to the question of responsibility: "I can't answer that kind of question because I haven't thoroughly studied the literature in this field, and so don't really appreciate the nuances of your words." A spokesman for the emperor responded in a hardly more helpful way: "I cannot speculate on what the Emperor meant. You must decide for yourself." The same thing would happen in 1995 over Emperor Akihito's expression of condolence for the victims of the war. Perhaps Akihito learned from his father the value of ambiguity in pronouncements of remorse: Say something unclear, and then let your spokespeople admit that they are equally baffled by it. Abstruseness might be the prerogative of monarchy. Indeed, this may have been clear from the beginning of his reign, when Akihito responded to a 1990 question about his father's war responsibility with a remarkably obtuse answer: "My generation has lived for a long time without war, and so I have had no occasion to reflect on the war."[10] He may not have had his father's high-pitched voice, but he spoke in the same tenor.

The question, then, is what to make of this refusal, this intransigence, this inability to accept responsibility. We can consider three alternatives. The first is that Hirohito was simply not responsible because he was not the one making the key decisions—that it was, in fact, the military clique that made all these decisions and imposed them on him. As he put it in a lengthy deposition he gave in March and April 1946 that was transcribed by his aides and submitted to SCAP, "I was virtually a prisoner and powerless." Joseph Grew, who was the U.S. ambassador to Japan at the time, saw it this way also. He believed that Hirohito was a "puppet" of the military faction. That argument is no longer tenable, if it ever was, because the trove of papers that became public after Hirohito's death in 1989 demonstrate that he was much more in control than he appeared and was active in political and military matters much more than previously believed.[11]

The second alternative is that he could not accept responsibility, fundamentally, because he was, in his mind and to his subjects, a divinity. The Meiji Constitution under which Hirohito reigned until 1947, when it was replaced, was founded on the principle of the emperor's divine ancestry. Accordingly, Hirohito traced his ancestry to the sun goddess Amaterasu Ōmikami. This divine ancestry, "unbroken for ages eternal," as Article 1 puts it, rendered him "sacred and inviolable" (Article 3).[12] Most constitutional scholars in Japan interpreted Article 3 to mean that the emperor was "nonaccountable"—that is, he could not be held "responsible." Given that the constitution under which he reigned, according to the constitutional lawyers who interpreted it, rendered him not responsible, it is not surprising that Hirohito should simply be unable to accept whatever responsibility others wanted to impose on him. There are some questions here, too, though, since Shimizu Tōru of the Tokyo Imperial University, the person who taught Hirohito constitutional law, did not hold to the traditional interpretation of Article 3. Likewise, well before SCAP forced Hirohito publicly to deny his divinity in his so-called Declaration of Humanity on January 1, 1946, he had already privately confessed during his European tour in 1921 that he did not believe in the divine descent of his family.[13] There is some doubt, then, that Hirohito believed in either the principle of divine ancestry or the common interpretation of Article 3 as sanctioning the emperor as beyond responsibility.

The third alternative—an extension of the first—is that Hirohito was a pawn in the hands of SCAP, which used him to impose democracy on a conquered nation that would be a bulwark against communism. In this reading, he was willing to accept responsibility, and considered it, but he was swayed by General Douglas MacArthur and his aides not to do so. There is a great deal of incriminating evidence that supports this reading. It would be revealed only later to what extent SCAP, and especially MacArthur himself, stage-managed this assignment and denial of responsibility. At the end of the war, SCAP had toyed with the idea of bringing Hirohito to trial on war crimes. In the end, though, SCAP did not spend much effort investigating Hirohito's role and decided not to prosecute him in the interests of keeping the peace. Prosecuting the emperor for war crimes, General Bonner Fellers wrote in a memo to MacArthur, would have "alienated the Japanese" and made SCAP's job of governing during the Occupation much more difficult. It was better to continue making "good use of the Emperor" for SCAP's own initiatives. Fellers told MacArthur that that there was no "specific and tangible evidence" that Hirohito was responsible for key war decisions; Fellers said that he came to what he called this "definite impression" through "as complete a research as was possible to me." The foremost scholar of Hirohito's war conduct, Bix, has pointed out that there are no official U.S. documents that indicate any such investigation ever took place; just how "complete a research" was involved is in question. Yet in his own memo to General Dwight D. Eisenhower, MacArthur went much further than Feller. This, of course, is no surprise, since MacArthur commanded many things more adequately than he did the truth. MacArthur maintained that indicting and trying Hirohito would "disintegrate" the nation, initiate a "vendetta for revenge" that would cycle for centuries, and likely lead to Japan's going communist after the Occupation. In light of these beliefs, then, it is understandable why SCAP dissuaded Hirohito from acknowledging even moral responsibility for the war.[14]

There is even more shameful evidence of how SCAP managed the question of Hirohito's responsibility in the Tokyo trials. Not only did SCAP not indict and place him on trial; it went so far as to coach the generals on trial to avoid implicating the emperor in their testimony. When such implications happened, intentionally or accidentally, SCAP immediately resorted to forceful tactics to control the situation. When Inukai Takeru, for instance, testified that his father, the former and assassinated Prime Minister Inukai Tsuyoshi, had failed to get the emperor to agree to withdraw the Imperial Army from Manuchuria, the American lawyers quickly got Inukai to issue a partial retraction and make it seem like a conversation about an issue rather than a political request. Likewise, when General Tōjō thought he was defending his sovereign by noting that it would be inconceivable for any of the emperor's subjects to take actions contrary to his wishes, the American lawyers directed the defendant to recant, which the loyal Tōjō happily did.[15]

In addition to controlling court testimony about who was responsible and derailing any attempt by the emperor to assume responsibility, SCAP also wanted to control what it believed to be the focal point for the responsibility it wanted the generals to assume, which had everything to do with just how this war was perceived. During the Tokyo Tribunal trial, U.S. General Headquarters (GHQ) censored any public materials that detracted from Japan's attack on Pearl Harbor. During and after the trial, GHQ censors suppressed accounts that argued that the question of "war responsibility" was primarily a question of Japan's aggressions against China. Those who argued that Tōjō was being given more attention than he deserved as the villain in this story because he was most closely associated with the policies that led to the bombing of Pearl Harbor were likewise censored. This was part of SCAP's efforts to control the memory of the war in Japan. At the very beginning of the Occupation, in autumn 1945, it serialized in all national newspapers the American version of the war; then it aired a radio documentary between December 1945 and February 1946 giving the same version of events, with the unsubtle title *Shinsô wa kô da* ("This is the truth!"). Finally, it even changed the name of the war. The term that Japanese politicians used, "Greater East Asian War" (*diatôa sensô*), was prohibited, and "Pacific War" was made the official term.[16] In court, newspapers, radio, and academic journals—in all venues where history was made and recorded—America was controlling what Japan's history would be.

We are hard-pressed, then, to decide whether Hirohito did not feel responsible or express remorse because he was a god, a puppet, or a pawn. If he was a puppet, then he was one like Pinocchio, if you will, that is not entirely tethered to those who think they are controlling him (there might be a deeper ground for this comparison). And if he was a pawn in American hands, he made moves that belied them. He had his own sources of information about how Tōjō was being coached to testify, for instance, and his own interests deeply at stake in that testimony. He was, in the end, an extremely shrewd politician who knew how to use each role that he was assigned. In his public declarations, he was rarely straightforward. When he surrendered, he made it sound as though he were giving the world the gift of peace. In declaring his "humanity," he did not deny his descent from the sun goddess Amaterasu Ōmikami. In his statement on Japanese democracy, he suggested that it would be native and a continuous development from the Meiji restoration. In each way, then, Hirohito could be said to be responsible for promoting the way he was perceived as being not responsible. However we might emphasize one factor over another, in whatever way we might evaluate the dynamic interplay among SCAP, Hirohito, and the Diet parliaments of the Occupation, it is clear that what we end up with was what Dower calls the "the mystique of nonaccountability symbolized by the sovereign" and what Bix describes as "the Japanese system of irresponsibility designed under Meiji."[17]

Among the very first to diagnose this phenomenon, what he himself first calls Imperial Japan's "massive 'system of irresponsibility,'" is the political theorist Maruyama Masao, who identified this lack of responsibility in 1949 as a key element in Japan's ultranationalism and an ongoing source of problems in postwar Japan. He hinted that it was one of the things that distinguished Japan from other Axis nations, particularly Germany.[18] And it could well be one of the reasons that Japan did not evince the same kind of war guilt that Germany had. I would add to Maruyama's insightful and powerful analysis of Japan's Imperial system one other feature that distinguishes Japan from other Axis nations at the beginning of the guilted age: There was no clean break after the end of World War II that marked a clear transition from one kind of regime to another. In Germany, the Third Reich, as William Shirer puts it, "passed into history" when the German Army surrendered in early May 1945.[19] The constitutional entity of the Weimar Republic likewise ended with the Third Reich when the nation was first partitioned into three and then two German states, and the Federal Republic of Germany (made up of two of those states) approved a new constitution with the passage of the 1949 Basic Law. In Italy, after Benito Mussolini was ousted by the Grand Council of Fascism, and then after the short-lived caretaker government of King Victor Emmanuel III and his son Crown Prince Umberto, a 1946 Italian plebiscite dissolved the monarchy and established a republic. In Germany, then, Adolf Hitler and Heinrich Himmler were dead; in Italy, Mussolini was summarily executed and the monarch deposed. Both the leaders and the constitutions of the nations were new. Even those nations that were occupied by the Third Reich marked the transition in their polity. In France, the Vichy regime immediately gave way to the Fourth Republic, and in Austria, eventually, the Second Republic.

From a distance, it might appear that Japan did undergo such a revolutionary break as its war allies. After all, it was occupied for seven years after the surrender. Its military was completely dismantled. Its constitution was rewritten. Its democracy was transformed in meaningful ways, including granting full franchise to Japanese women. And its leader was demoted from a divinity to a human being. And yet the so-called revolution from above that SCAP imposed on Japan, seen in detail, does not constitute the kind of wholesale change found in the other Axis nations. While accounts differ, the Occupation did not inaugurate an entirely new polity, and the Japanese government seemed to go out of its way to accommodate the occupying army, including recruiting Japanese women to prostitute themselves for the American soldiers under the auspices of the Recreation and Amusement Association. The person making the key decisions about how the occupation would proceed, the Supreme Commander General MacArthur, felt constrained by what he perceived as the larger geopolitical situation as well as other reasons to pursue a less ambitious agenda of national reformation than he might have otherwise. For various reasons, then, there was less of a break than the occupation might have augured or produced. Two important texts of the period demonstrate that.

The first is the constitution of Japan, which took effect on May 3, 1947, and was drafted by Americans in SCAP in the spring of 1946. The American draft was premised on the idea of retaining the emperor but transforming that office into more of a constitutional monarch, akin to the British model. The preamble of the constitution firmly places the nation's sovereignty in the "people," and the section on the emperor begins by reinforcing the point that the emperor is the "symbol of the State and of the unity of the People," who derives his position "from the will of the people with whom resides sovereign power." Prime Minister Shidehara Kijūrō's cabinet ministers were shocked at the transformation of their emperor into a "symbol," and it took some weeks for them to accept these constitutional terms. The emperor too was initially resistant to accepting the constitution. It appears that only the increasing pressure placed on him to abdicate at precisely this moment in late February and early March 1946—pressure placed on him by his younger brothers in privy council meetings and by the reports in Japanese and American media—led him to accept the new terms. In other words, he accepted the constitution because it provided him the opportunity to remain in office, albeit with reduced powers.[20]

The second text is the emperor's Declaration of Humanity. Officially called the "Rescript to Promote the National Destiny," it was printed in newspapers across the country on January 1, 1946. This document, too, was drafted by GHQ in SCAP and then revised by Shidehara and his cabinet. What SCAP wanted was for the emperor to renounce his divinity to reduce at the very top the effect of Shinto on Japan's polity. Two weeks earlier, SCAP had issued its own directive that separated church and state in Japan: The government could no longer fund or support Shinto shrines, nor could it promote Shinto in its educational system, including having school children visit Shinto shrines on field trips. Hirohito's assumption of humanity would be the final nail in the coffin for the ultranationalist Shinto beliefs that America believed were responsible for Japan's entry into the war. There was a profound tension between what SCAP wanted and what the Shidehara cabinet wanted; the former wished Hirohito to deny that he was divine, the latter to maintain that the relationship between the emperor and the people remained the same. The final Rescript, as most of the commentators have revealed, left the emperor somewhere in between—half god, half man?—and did not fulfill SCAP's hopes for the decimation of Shinto. While the Rescript did call the idea of the emperor's being a "living deity" a "false conception," Hirohito in the end did not deny that he was descended from the sun goddess Amaterasu Ōmikami. He put forth a more nuanced statement that suggested that the democracy that would follow constituted not a rupture but a continuity with the Meiji past. The prime minister's accompanying commentary in *Asahi shinbun* emphasized the point: This "new opportunity to start afresh" in the nation's political makeup, he noted, was in fact precisely the very desire of the Meiji emperor and his line, and he traced that trajectory toward postwar Japanese democracy back through the Meiji constitution of 1889, the Imperial Instruction of 1881, and to the founding Charter Oath of Five Articles of 1868.[21] What was "new" was old; what was imposed from without turned out to be the fulfillment of what was germinal in the very founding of modern Japan.

These two texts reveal the larger issues at stake in the battle between the occupiers and the occupied, the most important issue being continuity. It was precisely continuity that mattered to the Shidehara cabinet and to the emperor. He did not deny the continuity of his divine ancestry; the cabinet emphasized the continuity of its constitutional lineage. It is perhaps not surprising, then, that the renunciation of divinity did not signify the kind of clean break that SCAP sought between state and religion or between Japan's past and its future. The emperor and the Shidehara cabinet won this battle. Indeed, a renovation of the Yasukuni Shrine museum exemplifies just how decisively they won. An exhibit put up in 2002 restated just what Shidehara had written in 1946: That in the Declaration of Humanity, "the emperor had done no more than to announce a return to the principles stated in Emperor Meiji's charter oath." A *Guardian* reporter who interviewed one of the Yasukuni priests quotes him as saying: "Within Shinto it is the same as before: his ancestors are from the world of gods so he is a divine being." Unsurprisingly, *The Guardian* concludes its story by noting, "Government spokesmen have refused to comment on the Yasukuni interpretation."[22]

Japan, then, unlike its allies, lost neither its representative leader nor its form of government, and the embodiment of both, the emperor, managed to avoid assuming any responsibility, suffering any serious repercussion, or demonstrating any remorse. It is unclear whether his remorselessness was the result or the cause of his continued power. There is, then, an important continuity in Japan's polity that differs fundamentally from the radical discontinuity in those of its allies. Is that fact relevant to the question of why Germany has been more apologetic for its actions and Japan considerably less? Arguably, it is, but I would add two cautionary notes.

The first is that we should resist the temptation to think of this dynamic between discontinuity and continuity in a nation's polity as if it somehow represented the same process that individuals go through when they acknowledge their wrongs and prepare to atone for them. In other words, at the individual level, in the act of penitence, a person must first recognize that he or she has committed a wrong, understand that this wrong harmed someone, resolve to act in the future in a different manner, and then begin the process of atoning to the person harmed by the wrong. There is a dynamic of continuity and discontinuity in this process. The person who did the wrong and the one who atones for it constitute effectively the same person (sure, there is molecular change and moral transformation, but in the eyes of the law, say, there is only one person). That is the continuity. And yet the person who has come to recognize that the wrong was a wrong and made a resolution to mend his or her ways in that process becomes an ethically different person from the one who did the harm. An apology, as Erving Goffman insightfully notes, is a gesture "in which an individual splits himself into two parts, the part that is guilty of an offense and the part that dissociates itself from" the offense.[23] That "split" constitutes the discontinuity in the process. Some philosophers have focused on this paradoxical situation—that the person who atones for the wrong is not the same person who committed it—to argue that forgiveness is incoherent and impossible.[24] We should resist the temptation to see a parallel between personal penitence and political apology, though, for reasons that I discuss below.

Second, I do not want to suggest that there is a direct correlation between continuity and discontinuity in a national imagination for political apologies to work. By definition, political apologies are fundamentally based on the idea of an *imagined continuity*. Those who apologize are taking responsibility for the events of an earlier regime's actions because they believe themselves to be the rightful inheritors and representatives of the nation's political experience. As a socialist, Murayama could easily have distanced himself from the conservative, right-wing, monarchist and reactionary regimes that had governed Japan through the war, and he could, were he an opportunist, have hinted at the clearly closer connection between their policies and those of the nationalist-conservative LDP that had governed Japan for all but four years between 1955 and the time of this writing (2014). Instead, he affirmed that he was responsible because he was the leader of the nation, and that the nation was responsible because it constituted a continuous community and polity over time. In Japan, of course, that argument is not hard to make, since the nation traces its lineage back three millennia. The point is that political apologies do affirm an imagined continuity, which exists because it is part of the way the nation imagines itself (it is not imagined as in "it is illusory"; it is imagined as in "it is constitutive"). What we also learn from the example of Japan, when compared to the experiences of other nations at the outset of the guilted age, is that the nation might also require an actual discontinuity, a break from the regime for whose actions a political apology can be tendered.

This mystique, then, this "system of irresponsibility," this concerted effort to maintain the deceptive illusion that the person who ended the war was not the one responsible in any way for starting it has had important and enduring effects on Japan's political discourse. As we saw, everyday citizens like Watanabe were distressed at the absence of a moral sensibility in their monarch. Likewise, elites who were unquestionably in support of the emperor, such as Kido and Hiranuma, nonetheless believed that Hirohito's not accepting responsibility or showing remorse would have deleterious effects on the nation. It clearly has. And it is precisely in the context provided by that debate, within the Imperial household and beyond it, within Japan and beyond it, that we can best understand the political stakes at play in the way the war is remembered, recorded, and understood in Japan, and, most significantly, in the way that responsibility for it is apportioned, and atonement for it made or repudiated. In that context, we can best appreciate what Prime Minister Murayama's 1995 apology means to the Japanese who support it and those who reject it, and to the nations to which it was offered. It is that context, likewise, that allows us to appreciate the resonance that Prime Minister Abe's statements hinting at Japan's limited responsibility for the war have with the populace.

This issue—centered on the question of responsibility—remains a vexing and indeed toxic one in Japan. Although subjects are no longer executed, as they had been earlier in the century, when they criticize the emperor—for the crime of *lèse majesté*—it long remained dangerous to do so. A relatively recent episode exemplifies the kinds of danger. When the mayor of Nagasaki, Motoshima Hitoshi, said in a city council meeting in late 1988 that he believed "that the emperor bore responsibility for the war," it created an uproar. The LDP Prefectural Committee demanded a retraction. When he refused, they removed him from his post as committee adviser. Many conservative groups converged on the city in protests, and a member of the right-wing imperialist group *Seikijuku* (Sane Thinkers School) attempted to assassinate him in early 1990. Right-wing party leaders applauded the assassination attempt as "divine punishment."[25] It could well be that this episode simply reflects that this was an especially anxious time in Japan—in late 1988, Hirohito was dying—but it also, more importantly, demonstrates the ways that this issue of war responsibility and remorse are powerfully living issues in the nation's sense of its place.

What the historical analysis of Japan's political apology can teach us is not simply that some apologies fail and some succeed, or that some societies are more sincerely apologetic than others, although it might help us in making some comparisons with other nations in the guilted age. Rather, what it crucially teaches us is that political apologies have a particular discourse and dynamic. So what is distinctive about political apologies? In particular, how do they differ, if they do, from interpersonal apologies? I argue that they do differ, in significant ways.

This distinction, let me note at the outset, is not meant to dispute or dismiss the idea that "the personal is the political." That important statement, which emerged out of political movements demanding the rights of women to control their own bodies, does not deny that there are distinct spheres of human activity—personal life, political action—but rather demands that those who operate in the latter understand the profound effects of their actions on the former. Governments that pass laws denying women the right to reproductive choices, and courts that uphold those laws, are political bodies whose laws and decisions are felt in women's personal lives. That statement does not imply the corollary statement that "the political is the personal," at least not in the sense that all political actions can be only or best understood as personal statements. One of the deepest problems in the study of apology and forgiveness, it seems to me, is precisely that we have not adequately described the differences in these acts when they occur between persons or when they take place between political entities.[26]

Because individuals who apologize to their acquaintances and politicians who apologize to their neighboring countries use the same words, engage in the same ritual discourses, and even assume the same bodily postures appropriate to the occasion, we can be misled into thinking that an apology is an apology, that no matter the level or sphere the speakers of these apologies occupy, they are equally acts governed by the same informal rules and seeking the same kinds of forgiveness. They are not. I would like to conclude this chapter by emphasizing how a political apology differs from an interpersonal apology in three crucial ways: in who speaks them, in how they are spoken, and in what they mean.

I discussed at the beginning of the previous chapter that the case of South Africans who performed acts of gracious forgiveness in the TRC hearings do not fall into the category of political apologies. Those are cases of individuals forgiving individuals who are apologizing for what they did on behalf of the state—that is, as agents of the state and not representatives of it. Likewise, in Japan we see cases where people offer *personal apologies for political acts*, even though they are not even agents of the state. They are simply concerned citizens who believe it their duty to accept responsibility for what the nation does in their name. We can perhaps best see that distinction between *personal apologies for political acts* and political apologies for those acts by turning to an earlier moment in Japan's history that reveals precisely the dynamic that would become manifestly clear in 1945.

When the Japanese Air Force dropped a bomb that sank the American gunboat, the USS *Panay*, on December 12, 1937, President Franklin Roosevelt quickly told Secretary of State Cordell Hull to send a note to Ambassador Grew to tell the Japanese government to make "full expressions of regret and proffer of full compensation." For both the president and the American media that covered the story, the issue revolved around responsibility. Roosevelt took an unusual tack in writing a note directly to the emperor. As the publisher of the *Chicago Tribune*, and a former schoolmate of Roosevelt's, Robert R. McCormick, puts it, it was "an unusual thing" for the president to instruct "the state department to see that his request for apology, indemnity, and guarantees are sent to the Japanese emperor himself." In the end, the apology and the reparations came from the Japanese government, not the emperor, who apparently never responded to Roosevelt's note. At precisely the same moment, Japanese citizens began to send letters of sympathy to the U.S. Embassy in Tokyo and to the Navy Department in Washington. These letters offered condolences and expressed deep remorse. Many came from children. In one particularly moving testimony, thirty-seven Japanese girls attending St. Margaret's School in Tokyo sent letters to the U.S. Embassy. In a representative letter, one of the students writes: "We want to tell you how sorry we are. . . . We want you to forgive us." A young boy attending Shin Kozen Primary School personally brought his letter to the consulate in Nagasaki. The letter reads: "I apologize on behalf of the soldiers. Please forgive. Here is the money I saved. Please hand it to the American soldiers injured." Other letters from older Japanese citizens also included money as well as expressions of remorse, which raised problems for Ambassador Grew, since accepting money might compromise what he in a letter to Hull describes as "the principle of indemnification for which the Japanese Government has assumed liability." This situation—an unapologetic emperor and his eagerly penitent subjects—might have been at least partly what Ambassador Grew had in mind when he called this response to the *Panay* incident a perfect example of the existence of "two Japans."[27]

Fifteen years later, at the end of the Occupation, we find precisely the same dynamic: a penitent populace, who want to atone for the loss, for the war, and for the war crimes about which they learned during the Tokyo trials, and an emperor refusing to accept responsibility or offer remorse. On one side, there were those who expressed their repentance in private and public, in letters to editors, in *waka* poems in newspapers and magazines, in philosophical treatises, and in journals and diaries. In the words of one of these poems, when "the Japanese Army's atrocities are shown," one could feel, collectively, "a sharp gasp." As another poem puts it, the "crimes of Japanese soldiers / who committed unspeakable atrocities / in Nanking and Manila / must be atoned for." And the atonement was not always directed inward. Some of those who were "unaccustomed to writing for the public," as Dower reveals, wrote "letters apologizing to the Chinese people" for the crimes their soldiers committed and asking to make amends. Conceivably, the thirteen-year-old girls attending St. Margaret's in 1937, and others like them and around their age, were precisely the ones who would later write letters of apology and *waka* poems of remorse in the wake of the Tokyo trials. On the other side, there were those who took their emperor's example to heart and claimed no responsibility and felt no remorse. They sought what the president of the chauvinistic Seiyūkai Party, Tsuyoshi, in 1930 called "escape from the diplomacy of apology."[28] The only thing for which they were sorry was the decline in the power of the emperor and the curtailing of his growing empire.

In these cases, Japan's noble citizens were offering personal apologies for political acts. They were not offering political apologies, for they did not have the standing, hold the office, or bear the responsibility to be able to do so. And the one person who did have the standing, hold the office, and bear the responsibility did not offer a political apology.

The second point of difference is in how these types of apologies are spoken. To be effective—in some cases, to be considered an apology at all—an interpersonal apology has to be addressed to the person whose forgiveness is sought. Someone apologizing by proxy or through a mediator is not apologizing. Political apologies, on the other hand, are necessarily offered by a representative, and they are not necessarily presented to the entity whose forgiveness is being sought. In the cases we have been examining here, these political apologies seem often to be overheard by rather than addressed to the harmed entities—in the case of Japan, the nations it colonized. Even the very best of them, Murayama's 1995 apology, did not name the nations, identify the specific crimes, or address the apology to those to whom it was purportedly extended. And yet those nations that were not addressed—namely, China and South Korea—responded favorably, if tepidly, to the overheard apology. In other words, in some political apologies, there is an implied audience in a way that is never the case in interpersonal apologies. This dynamic is at play in exactly the same way when it comes to the case of the politically unapologetic. Those politicians, such as Prime Minister Abe, who want to deny the apology seem to make it a point of pride to say something to the Diet or the Japanese media that they know will be picked up in Seoul or Beijing and alarm those who overhear it.

The final point of distinction is that interpersonal apologies and political ones simply mean different things. It might seem like a bad case of circular reasoning, but what is distinctive about the political apology is that it is *political*. Let me clarify what I suggested at the beginning of the previous chapter. Unlike the interpersonal apology, the political apology is not judged entirely by the manifest quality of its sincerity, nor by the degree of contriteness with which it is performed. If judged that way, all political apologies are compromised, since there is always a part of the represented group that dissents from the apology. Rather, it is to be judged as a political act within a particular and circumscribed discourse between the nation that apologizes and the entities to which it apologizes and, indeed more importantly, the discourse within the apologizing nation itself. It is not an expression of remorse simply addressed to the wronged party; it is also, and in some ways primarily, a statement addressed to the polity for which the apology is offered. As I note above, a snide comment on the willingness of the comfort women, a strategic remark in the Diet on the possibility of reconsidering the future of Murayama's apology—these are all tactics that are meant to be combative for two distinct constituencies. They are meant to alert and antagonize those who overhear them abroad, and they are meant to affirm and celebrate a certain conception of Japanese history at home.

And they do so—for those apologizing, and those contesting the need to apologize at all—by drawing on what we can call the discursive formation around the issue. In the case of Japan, we have seen how in this issue, in this particular historical experience, certain icons, historical markers, and political figures have come to be representative. The emperor stands for irresponsibility—either as a failure of remorse for some or as a sign of his unapologetic divine status for others. Yasukuni Shrine has come to stand for the value of national pride meant to contest what an early Japanese ultranationalist called a national "diplomacy of apology." August 15 has come to represent a time for mourning or guilt, a time for jingoist celebration of one version of history or grieving reflection on another. Given the unfolding of the events of August 15, 1945, then, it is perhaps to be expected that this would constitute the date that Japan's liberal prime ministers would choose to offer apologies to the nations they had attacked and colonized, and it is equally to be expected that the conservative politicians would choose to feel that this date is peculiarly sensitive, since it marked the defeat of the nation, the first time the nation heard the human voice of the emperor they believed descended from the sun goddess Amaterasu, and the date that inaugurated a different tenor in the relationship between the emperor and his subjects. This series of acts—the apology on August 15, the visits to the shrine by the dissenters, and the media questions about whether the emperor is implicated in the apology—constitutes a concerted struggle over a precise discursive formation. The political apology means what it means because it takes place within a particular political script. And like any other drama, we can understand what one role and one speech mean in a political apology only when we examine the full script and the full unfolding of the story of which it is a part.

4

HISTORICAL APOLOGIES I

On May 8, 1985, the president of West Germany addressed the Bundestag in a memorable speech commemorating the fortieth anniversary of the end of World War II in Europe. At one point, he noted that on the date they were commemorating, May 8, 1945, the "vast majority of today's population were either children or had not been born." Ten years later, on April 23, 1995, at the fiftieth-anniversary commemoration of the Russian Army's rescue of 2,500 concentration camp prisoners when their train stalled near Troebitz on its way to the gas chambers of Theresienstadt, the minister of culture for Lower Saxony noted that on the date of that event, April 23, 1945, 85 percent of the German population was five years old or younger. Ten years later, on August 15, 2005, at Japan's commemoration of the sixtieth anniversary of the end of World War II in Asia, Prime Minister Junichiro Koizumi added in passing that the majority of Japanese citizens had not been born during the event he was memorializing. The "postwar generations now exceed 70% of Japan's population," he noted.[1]

What might it mean that the minister of culture for Lower Saxony and the prime minister of Japan should wish to add minister of demographics to their portfolios on these auspicious occasions? For some, it seemed like an attempt for these ministers to evade responsibility. Someone who was less than five years old and a "passenger" on that train near Troebitz when it was rescued, Rabbi Joseph Polak, has responded vigorously by saying that these demographic shifts just did not matter. As "long as people remember history," he concludes, "you are destined to take responsibility for this darkness and never, ever to be forgiven for it."[2] In other words, it is meaningless to count the days until the last survivor of the horrible days of World War II has passed this world and then breathe a sigh of relief, as if the event is now over, the issue of responsibility expired. It does not matter what the makeup of the current population may be, how many were alive in that era, how many conscious agents in that epoch, because responsibility, Polak implies, does not reside in mere existence, agency, capacity, or resolve. Responsibility in this case resides in something else, something frankly more mystical.

What the two ministers were marking, it seems, was the passage of freighted time. Fifty years, sixty years after the events they were commemorating, the people who had participated in them were elderly, if still alive, and the people who were commemorating them had been too young to be conscious, if they were even alive then. This event—the end of the war that Germany and Japan waged against humanity—was fading into history. Soon the only testimonies of that era would be documentary ones, not living ones. There is more than a hint of relief in these ministers' comments. Japan had spent "six decades" manifesting "its remorse" for that war, the prime minister plaintively reflected, and one could almost hear the resentment, the unspoken sense that that was long enough. Only 15 percent of the current population was conscious of what was happening then, the minister of culture bleated, and they, his commentary would seem to imply, could even perhaps be too old to be conscious of it now. Those who remember did not do this, and those who did this might not remember it.

The haunting question, and that might be the best way to put it, is who is the "you" in Rabbi Polak's assertion? Is it the minister of culture who made the remark that inspired his commentary? Is it the people who actively committed the atrocities of the Holocaust? Is it the 15 percent of German people who were older than five in 1945? Or is it all German people who were alive in 1945? Or is it simply all German people from 1933 to eternity? The reason it is worthwhile for us to think about the identity of this "you" is that Polak raises a crucially important point about the nature of collective responsibility but leaves ambiguous just what constitutes this collective. There are at least two ways to understand his comment about who will never be forgiven. In one reading, it is the people who committed the crime. They did what they did, as active agents or complicit collaborators, and they will be eternally remembered as radically evil as long as people remember historical events. In the second reading, it is the people associated with where the crime occurred—namely, Germany. Here, it is not actions that constitute responsibility but belonging. They are who they are because of where they are, and each generation of the people who inhabit the sites of atrocity will be held responsible for what took place there. The first reading identifies criminals who are responsible for their actions; the second identifies inheritors who are responsible for their ancestry. (I later return to these points to examine more closely just what can be said on either side of this issue about collective and inherited responsibility.)

For now, it is enough to recognize that Rabbi Polak is touching on a larger topic about a different kind of commemorative act, one that would take place much later, when no one who commemorates this event will be younger than five or alive, but rather far into the dim recesses of the future, as "long as people remember history," as he puts it. When he uttered his words, in 1995, at the fiftieth anniversary of the World War II event that was being commemorated, that kind of commemoration had begun to gain some traction, and by the time the prime minister of Japan spoke his words at the sixtieth anniversary of the World War II event he was commemorating, that kind of event had become widespread, almost commonplace. That event is the *historical apology*, in which a group of people offer remorse and ask forgiveness for actions that they did not commit but that were committed by their "ancestors." In the act of offering their historical apologies, they express contrition for what their ancestors did, and in doing so, they affirm that very ancestry. And that ancestry can be genetic (by family members biologically descended from the actor), communal (by congregations who see themselves as part of a community whose spiritual descent from previous communities gives it its identity), or political (by citizens who affirm what is an accident of birth into a basis of tribal or national belonging).

Ten years earlier, Richard von Weizsäcker had already anticipated Rabbi Polak's point. Unlike the two ministers who used demographic facts to evade the implications of guilt, he mentions the demographic shifts in Germany to affirm that while the generation who committed those atrocities must bear the guilt for them, the generation who came after "must accept the past," recognize that "their forefathers have left them a grave legacy," and understand that they are "liable" for the consequences of that legacy.[3] It is precisely this sense of accepting and insisting on the continued acceptance of responsibility that has made von Weizsäcker's speech the gold standard for political apologies (even though he actually never apologizes during the speech, a point to which I return in Chapter 7).

Von Weizsäcker concludes his speech by returning to the questions raised by the two key terms it evoked—time and responsibility. It is a speech that marks the time passed since the original event that was being commemorated, but also one that addresses the primary issue in that event—guilt and responsibility. "In the life-span of men and in the destiny of nations," he perorates, "40 years play a great role." This point is especially true for the nation of Israel, which would mark its own fortieth anniversary three years after von Weizsäcker gave this speech. "The Israelites" in the Hebrew Bible, he notes, "were to remain in the desert for 40 years before a new stage in their history began with their arrival in the Promised Land. 40 years were required for a complete transfer of responsibility from the generation of the fathers." Forty years, then, does not end the question of responsibility nor attenuate it, but only complete its transfer. In Germany, von Weizsäcker emphasizes, "A new generation has grown up to assume political responsibility. Our young people are not responsible for what happened over forty years ago. But they are responsible for the historical consequences."[4]

With that speech, rich and soulful, marked throughout with sensitivity and intelligence, von Weizsäcker may be said to have heralded the *historical apology*. What he does, unlike those who wanted to use the passage of time and generations so that they could deny responsibility, is assert that responsibility for events is an enduring, eternal burden; what changes, with the changes of generations, is simply the kind of responsibility that is borne. The generation of the forefathers is criminally responsible; they did what they did. The generations after them are politically responsible; they have inherited what they have inherited.

Let me be likewise responsible here and note that I am not arguing that von Weizsäcker is the one who *invented* the historical apology, that no one before him thought of offering an apology for acts performed by generations long dead, or that people after him cite him as the inspiration for the apologies they offer for acts performed by generations long dead. My argument is not causal; I am frankly unable to determine just who was the first to undertake such an apology. Graham Dodds, the person who has done the most work in cataloguing political and historical apologies, lists the first historical apology in 1986, when the United Church of Canada apologized to the First Nations people for their historic mistreatment by the church (I note some earlier apologies below). The fact that the first listed historical apology occurred the year after von Weizsäcker gave his famous speech is not quite coincidental, but neither is it causal. It is not causal because the two events had nothing to do with each other; it is not entirely coincidental, though, because they are both performances representative of the prevailing sensibility in the guilted age. In any case, my argument is that von Weizsäcker *exemplifies* the discourse of historical apologies, and he is, arguably, the first to suggest how the political apology would evolve into something else, how the passage of time would not relieve the burden of guilt but change it, how the passing of generations would not eliminate the nation's sins but require a different and novel sense of acknowledgment.[5]

The idea that there is such a thing as collective responsibility—and its corollary, that responsibility can pass down through generations—was profoundly contested in those very years between von Weizsäcker's 1985 and Koizumi's 2005 commemorations. As we might imagine, there was a tension between those in the nation (usually conservative) who rejected the idea of apologizing for the past and those (usually liberal) who believed in the idea and pursued the practice. The conservatives held that it was both meaningless and demeaning to reject the actions of the forebears (their reputations should be conserved), while the liberals held that it was meaningful for contemporary social orders to affirm where they stood in relation to those forebears, not to conserve but to progress. These are conflicting ideas of citizenship: One holds that citizenship requires an affirmation of the nation, and the other holds that it requires a critique of it.

Here we might take up again those cases of politicians turning to demography, an act that is curious because of what it granted as much as for what it was trying to deny. What they were asserting, without much subtlety, was that this was a different generation and nation, that these people celebrating and mourning the anniversary of liberation and surrender were epigones, not agents of the acts for which these apologies were made. What they wanted their auditors to hear and believe was that this was not the same nation that had committed the crimes. This is the demographic equivalent of what some see to be the paradox of forgiveness—that the penitence of the person being forgiven had rendered that person different than the one who had committed the wrongdoing being forgiven. Here, demographic changes supplemented national penitence. What is notable, though, is how subtly and perhaps unconsciously these politicians simultaneously acknowledged the idea of collective responsibility. They were not saying that "ordinary" Germans and Japanese were innocent of the crimes of their leaders and generals; they were saying that this was a new generation of Germans and Japanese and implying, thereby, that the older generation *did* bear some responsibility. In denying the responsibility of the contemporary generation, they asserted the responsibility of the entire previous one.

The second issue, concerning inherited responsibility, raises a question about the nature of historical continuity, which could be understood in at least two distinct ways. According to one view, an event can be understood only in terms of its political origins, which are to be traced back to some important trait or development. Those who hold this view believe that the political history of a given nation or people is continuous, that it has evolved according to some germinal feature of their nationhood or peoplehood that led them to do what they eventually did. In the wake of World War II, there were those who saw Japanese war responsibility in the origins of the Meiji restoration of 1868. In the case of Germany, no one represented this position more adamantly than Lord Robert Vansittart, an adviser to the British Foreign Office who saw German war responsibility in the same terms, speaking easily of the continuities "from Bismarck to Hitler."[6] In other words, the seeds of the mid-twentieth-century crisis are implicit in the nineteenth-century development of the Axis nations. A second way is to see that the political history of a given generation has consequences that must be borne by later generations. What a nation does, because of the rippling effects that the act has on the world and on the future, becomes the responsibility of those who inherit the governance of that nation. We can think of one as a germinal theory of historical continuity and the other as a consequential theory. They differ in that one traces the lineaments of a nation backward to discern the origins of its malfeasance, while the other projects forward to see what future generations can do to acknowledge that malfeasance.

These, then, constitute the terms of the debate: What are the continuities that led to the crime, and what are the continuities that follow the crime? The political debate I describe above was implicated in and formed a context for the historical debate about how a nation's past can or should be represented in the wake of an atrocity, and that debate took up precisely those questions about the two meanings of continuity—from the past and to the future. In the nations where the anniversary of the end of World War II was being commemorated most vigorously, Germany and Japan, those debates were particularly sharp and acrimonious.

Beginning a year after von Weizsäcker's speech, Germany engaged in what was called the "historians' quarrel" (*Historikerstreit*). Lining up politically on the right (including scholars Ernst Nolte, Michael Stürmer, Andreas Hillgruber, and Joachim Fest) and on the left (including Jürgen Habermas, Hans-Ulrich Wehler, Eberhard Jäckel, and Hans Mommsen), these philosophers and historians augmented an original debate that began with an undelivered talk by Nolte entitled "The Past That Will Not Pass," published on June 6, 1986, and then a response to it by Habermas on July 11, 1986. These intellectuals wrote letters and polemical essays in the popular press (especially in the national weekly, *Die Zeit*, and the Frankfurt daily newspaper *Frankfurter Allgemeine Zeitung*) to address two questions, especially: what relation the German concentration camps had to Stalin's gulag system, and what relation the Holocaust had to other genocides. Both these questions touched on the sensitive topic of whether Auschwitz, which, as it had before, became the shorthand for all concentration and death camps, was unique. For some, that was the appeal of the debate and seemed its most salient feature. In fact, the subtitle of the English translation of the texts of the debate calls it "The Controversy Concerning the Singularity of the Holocaust." And when von Weizsäcker returned to the podium in October 1988 to declare an end to the debate, he addressed that specific issue: "Auschwitz remains unique. It was perpetrated by Germans in the name of Germany. This truth is immutable and will not be forgotten."[7]

In truth, the debate was about much more than the "singularity" of Auschwitz or whether the Holocaust could be compared to any other genocide. It was about the nature of German historical memory, and it constituted part of the long-term cultural dialogue that began in the late 1940s over what was called *Vergangenheitsbewältigung* (literally, "coming to terms with the past"). While some wanted to reclaim what one described as "a German history that does not have to be read as a prehistory of National Socialism," others saw this as an impossibility. For some it was a matter of politics: "There can be no unbroken, unreflected identity for us." For others, it was also deeply personal, as it involved coming to terms with what one melancholically called "the actions of our parents and grandparents." The debate, then, was between those who sought for Germany a "less guilt-laden identification with its national past" and those who argued that German political identity would always be informed "by a sense of collective shame and grief."[8] The more pressing question behind the ones specifically addressed had to do with the same questions that would arise in Australia and Japan, and, of course, in the United States, during what were called the "culture wars"—namely, whether history should provide a cautionary tale or an inspiring one, should dwell on the salient atrocities of a national past or hold aloft the glorious accomplishments of its cultural heroes.

These ideas would reemerge after the publication of Daniel Jonah Goldhagen's 1996 book, *Hitler's Willing Executioners: Ordinary Germans and the Holocaust*, and especially after his appearance in a televised debate in Berlin later that year. The terms of that debate were centered on the question of complicity and the specific dynamics of anti-Semitism, but the debate itself returned to that same set of questions that had animated the historians' quarrel and, indeed, underwrote "coming to terms with the past": Was Germany destined to be defined exceptionally and only through that one moment of history? Those who wished to open the grounds for comparison (to Stalin or to earlier and later genocides) were implicitly challenging that view: If the Holocaust could be compared to other world historical events, if it was not unique, then it could be emplotted into a larger history, which, in turn, meant that German history would not be defined exclusively as leading up to and leading away from the Holocaust and only the Holocaust.

In Japan, meanwhile, similar debates occurred over the twin issues of "war responsibility" (*sensō sekinin*) and "historical consciousness" (*rekishi ninshiki*). The previous chapter discussed how the war responsibility issue emerged and evolved between the end of the war and the commemoration of the fiftieth anniversary of its ending. By the time the Tokyo Trials ended in 1948, there were two related ways of thinking about responsibility: Some believed that the leaders bore the responsibility (*shidōsha sekininkan*), while others believed themselves to have been duped by the leaders (*damasareta*) and, as I showed, sometimes took responsibility for that. The issue of historical consciousness was, of course, connected to the issue of war guilt, but it also followed its own trajectory in the national debates about the war past. Beginning in the early 1980s, that debate focused on how Japan's textbooks would represent the events of World War II. In 1982, in the first textbook crisis, the Ministry of Education apparently proposed that a textbook author change the wording from "invasion" of China to "advance into" China" (from *shinryaku* to *shinshutsu*). Later debates over textbooks specifically, and the representation of the war more generally, would occur in 1986, 2001, and 2007, involving the representation of the Nanking massacre and the comfort women. Taking the nationalist and conservative position in these later debates was the Japanese Society for History Textbook Reform, which had been formed in 1996. It complained that progressive intellectuals wanted to produce a history that focused solely on the negative events in Japan's past. It criticized what it first named a "masochist view of history" (*Jigyaku-shikan*) but eventually began calling "the Tokyo Trial view of history" (*Tōkyō saiban shikan*). Opposed to this view of the war, it counseled the "Asian liberation" view of the past, which, as shown in the last chapter, was the view held by nationalists before the surrender and made part of the emperor's surrender statement. Fujioka Nobukatsu's controversial 1997 book *What Is the Liberalist View of History?* helps make and publicize these distinctions.[9]

These debates over historical memory in Germany and Japan were about the inaugurating event in the guilted age, World War II, and they were framed by the *political* apologies those nations were offering for the war. Yet the terms of those debates and the questions they raised easily lent themselves to debates in other nations about the nature of responsibility for events in the distant past and about a different kind of apology that was starting to emerge—the *historical* apology.

In Australia, just to take one example, what took place at the same time as the debates in Germany and Japan came to be called the "History Wars," but the "war" that was central to the debate in the other two nations had nothing to do with the debate in Australia. The debate there was about the white colonizers' relationships with the Aboriginal peoples they displaced and oppressed. While some of the practices for which Australia was seeking atonement were recent—the forced integration of the Aboriginal and Torres Strait Islanders by separating the children from their families continued to the late 1960s—the debate was ultimately about the larger history of colonization and oppression on which that practice and others were based. What Australia was debating was its very origins. And the two positions identifying the poles of that debate were what the historian Geoffrey Blainey terms the "the black armband view of history" and the "Three Cheers" view of Australian history, one mourning and one celebrating the past. The first term quickly made its way into Australian political discourse and was used by Prime Minister John Howard to decry those who were, in his view, focused exclusively or excessively on white colonizers' "imperialism, exploitation, racism, sexism, and other forms of discrimination."[10] Although he held that neither view of history was accurate, he tended to use the "black armband" tag to identify those who were demanding that the government apologize for its oppressive history, which he refused to do. That apology came in 2007 when the Labor Party won the elections and Prime Minister Kevin Rudd delivered it.

That shift in the terms of the debate over what acts a nation or church or other group ought to apologize for—from the recent to the distant past—is important, for it marks the emergence of the historical apology as a form. The best place to investigate that debate about the dynamic and politics of historical apologies is in a very small and specialized nation, Vatican City, to which we can also trace what is arguably the inaugural historical apology of the guilted age.

No one person has offered more historical apologies than Pope John Paul II, and his accession to the papacy was one of the most important developments in the emergence of the historical apology as a discursive form. A book published in 1997 collects "ninety-four quotations in which Pope John Paul II admits the past faults of the Church or asks pardon for them."[11] That was three years *before* the Jubilee year of 2000, and the pope arguably issued even more apologies after 1997 than he had in the previous nineteen years of his papacy. Some of those apologies were political apologies that sought forgiveness for events connected to World War II, especially the Vatican's failures regarding the Holocaust, but most of them were historical apologies that addressed events in the Church's history that date back to the end of the first millennium. The pope apologized to other religious leaders: to Muslims for the Crusades, to Jews for the Church's anti-Semitism, and to Protestants for the Inquisition and other Counter-Reformation terrorisms. He also apologized to groups of people whom the Church had hurt through its actions, inactions, or attitudes, such as Africans and women. In other words, these were events or behaviors that dated anywhere from five hundred to a thousand years ago. What were these apologies supposed to address?

First, I need to note that popes historically had not apologized (this, perhaps, is one of the prerogatives of infallibility). The last pope to apologize before Second Vatican in 1963 was Pope Adrian VI. He was pontiff for twenty months in 1522–1523, and he openly admitted what he called the "abominable things" done by previous popes and Curias. In September 1963, 440 years later, Pope Paul VI opened the second session of the Second Vatican Council with an explicit request for forgiveness. Pope Paul VI may well have inaugurated the form of the historical apology when he and Patriarch Athenagoras of Constantinople lifted the excommunications that had been mutually issued in 1054. That took place on December 5, 1965, and was attended with the publication of a statement that expressed mutual "regret" and committed the "excommunications to oblivion." On that same day, the Catholic bishops of Germany and of Poland met and begged forgiveness of each other for the crimes of their nations to mark the millennial anniversary of the introduction of Christianity to Poland. One of the leaders of that meeting, who later defended the act when Poland's communist government criticized it, was Archbishop Karol Wojtyla. He was later to become Pope John Paul II.[12]

John Paul II followed in that tradition of assessing and apologizing for the Church's sins set by Paul VI during Second Vatican (significantly, he was also the first non-Italian pope since Adrian VI). Soon after his accession, he began to urge the Church to "examine the dark places of its history" and then to ask forgiveness for them. In 1994, he presented a memorandum that does just that in a consistent and concerted way. That memorandum, entitled "Reflections on the Great Jubilee of the Year Two Thousand," urges the Church to reconsider the past thousand years and admit its errors, its faults, and the violence it exerted in pursuing those errors. He called a Consistory to consider the memorandum and at the opening of that Consistory stated explicitly that "the Church needs a *metanoia*." There was some debate at the

Consistory over what it would mean for the Church to ask forgiveness—not much of a debate, admittedly, but what little there was followed the pattern of the debates in Germany, Japan, and Australia: that acknowledging the sins of the past weakens the loyalty of the citizens (or congregations). There was likewise the question of "responsibility." Cardinal Giacomo Biffi most insistently raised this point, noting that "we are no longer responsible" for those acts and concluding that it was best left to a different authority to judge them. "Therefore, as regards the sins of history," he asked, "would it not be better for all of us to wait for the Last Judgment?" Undeterred, John Paul II published an Apostolic Letter, *Tertio Millennio Adveniente*, in November 1994 that states the course of atonement the Church would follow leading up to the millennium.[13]

This debate in the Vatican raised the same set of questions that had already arisen in earlier, and would again arise in later, debates about national responsibility for the past. The issues were clear and stark. Some felt a strong imperative to address and acknowledge some kind of responsibility for past crimes that their forebears had committed and held that this kind of acknowledgment, especially in the form of an apology to the descendants of the aggrieved group, performed a particular kind of work—usually called reconciliation or healing. Others believed that such expressions of responsibility for what no living agent had done betrayed some of the most important Enlightenment ideals about the legal categories of agency, subjectivity, and responsibility. Those who claim responsibility for things they did not do may feel good about themselves, but they do incalculable damage to the very ideas of innocence and guilt on which most systems of law and justice depend. On the one hand, then, some held that accepting responsibility for their ancestors' acts helped consolidate and unify the citizenry and improve relations in the world; on the other, some believed that doing so betrayed the ancestors (by judging them by ahistorical standards) and misconstrued the very notion of responsibility.

These, then, were the terms of the debates that surrounded the emergence of the historical apology as it evolved from the political apology into something more encompassing and something that raised quite different conceptions of responsibility and belonging. We can turn now to a specific case to see how these ideas played out in a particular dynamic: the apology for slavery of African people. This case allows us to explore the apologies that have been offered by three kinds of apologists: (1) the *collective* body representing the nation or church, (2) the *executives* who represent the nation or church, and (3) the *familial* individuals who represent their families.[14]

On July 29, 2008, the 110th Congress of the United States passed House Resolution 194, entitled "Apologizing for the Enslavement and Racial Segregation of African-Americans." It had 120 co-sponsors, was introduced on February 27, 2007, and was agreed to a year and a half later as a "Simple Resolution" (that is, it was passed only by the House, did not go forward to the president, and had no force of law). The Senate passed its own Senate Concurrent Resolution 26, with the same title, on June 18, 2009. The Senate's version differs in its ending from Congress's version on three grounds: First, the Senate took out the resolution that passed in the House version acknowledging "that slavery is incompatible with the basic founding principles recognized in the Declaration of Independence that all men are created equal." (No doubt, the Senate objected to Jefferson's denying the rights of women.) The second change was the addition of a "Disclaimer" at the end of the Resolution stating that "Nothing in this resolution (A) authorizes or supports any claim against the United States; or (B) serves as a settlement of any claim against the United States." Lest there be any misunderstanding, the Senate wanted to clarify that this was an apology, not an offer of reparation; an expression of responsibility, not guilt; about sorrow, not money. The final change involved what this apology was supposed to accomplish. For the House, "an apology for centuries of brutal dehumanization and injustices cannot erase the past, but confession of the wrongs committed can speed racial healing and reconciliation and help Americans confront the ghosts of their past." The Senate took out the "ghosts of their past" and replaced it with "help the people of the United States understand the past and honor the history of all people in the United States."[15] The Senate version was clearly milder, more an expression of multiculturalism than an acknowledgment of the particular horrors of slavery, and it was also less focused on the historical hypocrisy of America's founding and haunted more by imagined lawsuits than by ghosts of the past.

Some media attention was given to these congressional resolutions, but considerably less than had been given a decade earlier when, on June 12, 1997, Representative Tony Hall, the Democratic congressman from Dayton, Ohio, introduced a bill that would have Congress apologize to the descendants of slaves for the nation's treatment of their ancestors. That bill contained a single sentence: "Resolved by the House of Representatives (the Senate concurring), That the Congress apologizes to African-Americans whose ancestors suffered as slaves under the Constitution and laws of the United States until 1865." The bill began with twelve co-sponsors, six Democrats and six Republicans, and was referred to the House Committee on the Judiciary. In presenting his resolution, Hall noted that he was "stunned to learn" from the Congressional Research Service that "we have never apologized" for slavery. His resolution was not intended to "fix the lingering injustice resulting from slavery," but he did believe that all "reconciliation begins with an apology," which in this case would provide a "start of a new healing between the races." He noted that though "no one alive today is responsible for slavery, all Americans share" in its "shameful heritage," and "all suffer from the consequences of a divided Nation." He concluded his brief speech in Congress with his belief that while this "apology is long overdue," it "is never too late to admit we were wrong and ask for forgiveness."[16]

Between the time it was introduced in mid-June and the time it died in committee in the first week of August, the resolution and the idea of apologizing for slavery inspired an enormous amount of energetic debate in the form of congressional speeches, editorial commentaries, op-ed columns, popular opinion polls, letters to editors, and website commentaries.[17] Partly, the resolution aroused interest because it was presented to Congress two days before President Bill Clinton called for a "national dialogue on race." Hall's proposal essentially became the first, spontaneous issue in the newly inaugurated national dialogue. But the idea of apologizing for slavery provoked profound interest and lively debate because it fundamentally struck a resonant chord in America, since it was about what had long been called America's original sin. The debate over slavery in the United States resembled the debate over the Holocaust in Germany's *Historikerstreit*, because these two events represented the ineradicable institutions in each nation's past.

The majority of the civil society groups supporting Hall's 1997 bill were Christian: the National Association of Evangelicals, the Christian Life Commission of the Southern Baptist Convention, the Traditional Values Coalition, and the Christian Coalition.[18] This was fitting not only because of the spiritual value that churches place on penitence and forgiveness but also because it had largely been Christian institutions that had attempted earlier to offer an apology for slavery.

In 1995, the Southern Baptist Convention celebrated its 150th anniversary and used the occasion of this anniversary to address its blighted racist history. The "Declaration of Repentance and Rededication" reads in part: "We lament and repudiate historic acts of evil such as slavery from which we continue to reap a bitter harvest. . . . We apologize to all African-Americans for condoning and/or perpetuating individual and systematic racism. . . . We ask for forgiveness from our African-American brothers and sisters. . . . We hereby commit ourselves to eradicate racism in all its forms from Southern Baptist life and ministry."[19] It was auspicious that the apology was made at this particular celebration, since it was 150 years earlier in 1845 that the Northern and Southern Baptist organizations had severed their relationship over the issue of slavery.

And it was significant because the Southern Baptist Convention had been so committed to white supremacy that it had been nicknamed "the chaplaincy arm of the Ku Klux Klan."[20]

While it is significant that a group that was formed out of its founders' defense of slavery should finally apologize for that sin, the Southern Baptist Convention also had other, more practical motivations to issue that public apology. First, between 1990 and 1995, several Southern-based denominations apologized for slavery or held symbolic foot-washing rituals as atonement for racist sins of the past. The National Association of Evangelicals and the Promise Keepers had both held such rituals, and two groups of moderate Baptists that had broken away from the Southern Baptist Convention apologized for slavery in 1990 and 1992. Second, the Southern Baptist Convention was in a competition with other denominations for the recruitment of black Baptist congregations. Virtually all the growth in the Convention since 1980 had been among ethnic minority groups, and the Convention in 1990 had set a goal of bringing four hundred new black congregations into its organization each year. Whatever sincere motivations there might have been for the 1995 apology, then, there also appear to have been practical reasons for the Southern Baptist Convention to issue some kind of symbolic gesture to attract membership from the ethnic community that was the most sought after by other denominations and the most important for its continued growth.

The final issue worth noting about the Convention's 1995 apology concerns the staging of it—who would give and who would accept the apology. Following a twelve-minute debate—and only three delegates spoke against the resolution—the twenty thousand Southern Baptists voted overwhelmingly in favor of the apology. The white president of the Convention, James B. Henry, embraced the black second vice president, Gary Frost, who spoke in acceptance of the apology: "On behalf of my black brothers and sisters, we accept your apology and we extend to you our forgiveness in the name of Jesus Christ. We pray that the genuineness of your repentance will be demonstrated in your attitude and your action."[21] Frost then led the congregation in prayer, asking God to forgive "white racism and black racism."[22] Drawing back from his all-encompassing act of forgiveness, Pastor Frost noted that he could not speak for all black people in America, but that he did "speak on behalf of . . . African-American believers in our Lord Jesus Christ, who are committed to be obedient to the word of God and long to see healing and unity in the Body of Christ."[23] Later, in response to media questions of reparations, Frost emphasized that the Southern Baptists were "not confessing for all whites, and I'm not receiving [that apology] for all blacks. This is a family matter. So the issue of restitution would be in terms of this family."[24]

These cases of collective apologies—from Congress and from a convention of churches—show some of the particular conditions that operate when an apology is made after a vote. The same dynamic operates in these historical apologies as operates in political ones, as demonstrated in the case of Japan's Diet. These apologies offer opportunities for dissent, and the apology must appear compromised as a result. These cases included less dissent than in Japan's Diet, but that was likely because the dissent was already rife outside the chambers of Congress. Media outlets conducted polls to determine what percentage of the population supported or repudiated the congressional apology proposed by Representative Hall, and letters to editors and web commentaries expressed the opinions those polls tabulated. These apologies, also like the political apologies, were also offered to *no one*. When Congress passed its resolutions, there was no body or representative group to receive the apologies they embodied. And, apparently, there are good reasons to avoid that scenario, as the Southern Baptist Convention learned the hard way that a staged act of forgiveness can cause more problems than it solves.

With executive apologies, some of the problems that plague collective apologies are alleviated. We can begin with Pope John Paul II, who made the apology to people of African descent a crucial part of his project of atoning for the sins of the Church before the Jubilee. Indeed, his earliest apologies, before he penned his 1994 memorandum and Apostolic Letter and before he designed a program of premillennial penitence, were apologies for the Vatican's involvement in the slave trade. During his 1985 trip to Cameroon, he asked "pardon from our African brothers who suffered so much because of the trade in blacks."[25] In 1989, the Vatican issued a document entitled "The Church and Racism: Towards a More Fraternal Society," in which the Church acknowledges how it had insufficiently tried to offset the practices of colonization and slavery.[26] John Paul II made his most powerful and repeated statements about the Vatican's complicity in the African slave trade in 1992. He began in February by praying for forgiveness on Gorée Island in Senegal—"From this African sanctuary of black pain, we implore forgiveness from heaven."[27] A month later, he urged his listeners at St. Peter's to approach Lent "in a spirit of penance [for] all the crimes which in that long period were perpetrated against the people of Africa by that shameful trade." In June, he addressed again during a visit to Sao Tomé what he called "this cruel offense against the dignity of the African people." In October, he visited Santo Domingo—on the fifth centenary of the arrival of Columbus and Christianity—and he continued to apologize for what slavery did to the New

World. A week later in a general audience at St. Peter's, he stated: "We do not cease asking these people for 'forgiveness.'"[28] Nor did he cease. He apologized again during his visit to Jamaica the following year.[29]

It took longer for a political executive to apologize for slavery than it did for a church executive, and there are good reasons for that. In the spring of 1998, President Clinton took a trip to Africa during which he expressed remorse at American involvement in the slave trade. Speaking at the Kisowera Primary School, just outside the capital of Uganda, President Clinton commented: "I think it is worth pointing out that the United States has not always done the right thing by Africa . . . going back to the time before we were even a nation. European Americans received the fruits of the slave trade. And we were wrong."[30] Most of the media commentators immediately noted that Clinton had not offered a formal apology but had rather expressed regret. The distinction was important, according to some editorials, because a formal apology would have "legal implications" and could have increased "legal, as well as moral, pressure for reparations."[31] The stop in Uganda was early in Clinton's tour of Africa. Senegal was the last stop, and the place many people thought or hoped that Clinton might apologize for slavery. During his visit to the slave factories on Gorée Island, Clinton saw the steel ball and chain used to restrain captives, he walked into a three-foot-high slave cell, and he looked pensively at the slave port known as the "door of no return." His comments were moving, but again he steered far from anything resembling an apology. The trip ended, then, with many believing that there had been no apology offered for slavery, amid much debate in America about what such an apology would have meant and much speculation about what form it might have taken—speculation that his staff, notably his Under-Secretary of State for Africa Susan Rice, had attempted to quell with little success.

Five years later, on July 8, 2003, President George W. Bush stood on the same grounds of the slave factory at Gorée Island, Senegal, looking at the expansive ocean on an unending horizon on which human beings had been transported to the New World. He mourned what he described as "one of the greatest crimes of history," in which people of African descent were "delivered, sorted, weighed, branded with marks of commercial enterprises and loaded as cargo on a voyage without return." He noted that the "stolen sons and daughters of Africa helped to awaken the conscience of America" and to show her that slavery was a "sin."[32] These presidential apologies and expressions of regret were important and inspired Congress, which incorporated them into its resolutions, noting that both presidents "acknowledged" the crime of slavery as literally a pretext for their own resolution to apologize.

The final kind of historical apology for slavery to consider here is that performed by an individual on behalf of a family. Will Hairston's is a representative familial apology. In January 2006, Hairston attended a retreat at Eastern Mennonite University in Harrisburg, Virginia, under the auspices of Coming to the Table, an organization he and Susan Hutchison founded to permit dialogue about the legacies of slavery between those descended from slave owners and those descended from enslaved people. Hairston is descended from one of the largest slave-owning empires in the South, while Hutchison is the six-times great-granddaughter of Thomas Jefferson and his legal wife, Martha. At that inaugural event in the formation of Coming to the Table, Hairston stood up, faced descendants of people his ancestors had owned, and spoke: "I am not sure if you want or need an apology, but I know I need to give one. I am not sure if this will be a blessing to you but I know I need to do this. I apologize and ask your forgiveness for my ancestors' involvement in slavery that deprived your ancestors of their liberty." The people to whom he was addressing this apology were not strangers; he had known them and developed a relationship with them for the past ten years. At the end of his speech, many of them embraced him. One of them, eighty-three-year-old Joe Henry Hairston, responded: "For the part of me that is part of your ancestry, I join in your apology. For the part of me that is not part of your ancestry, I accept your apology."[33]

Joe Henry Hairston's response is remarkable for a number of reasons. By attesting to the fact that his descent is mixed, he affirms that he is a Hairston by blood as well as deed. His acceptance of responsibility combined with his simultaneous acceptance of his status as the harmed person complicate the apology considerably. It is an exposé of the need for an apology, since he is revealing just what kinds of crimes are being apologized for—namely, rape—at the same time as it blurs the lines about what descent means and therefore who should or needs to apologize. Meanwhile, Will Hairston's apology is a gracious act, especially in acknowledging that it is more necessary for him than it might be for those to whom it is addressed. That kind of honesty in recognizing not the duty but the psychological need to apologize is rare. Hairston's is one of a number of such apologies.

Some of these apologies have been for acts of empire against Africa more generally. In 1993, for example, a noted British advocate for reparations, Lord Anthony Gifford, sought an audience with Asantehemaa, the Queen Mother of the Ashanti, and apologized for his ancestor, the third Lord Gifford, who had, as Gifford put it, "played a role in the destruction of Africa" as an officer in the British campaign against the Ashanti people in Ghana in 1873–1874.

Most apologies, though, have been for the acts of those who participated specifically in the slave trade and enslavement. In 1998, Edward Ball wrote an account of his coming to know and apologize to the descendants of his Charleston, South Carolina, slave-owning family. And in 2008, Thomas Norman DeWolf wrote about the ways he and his family have come to terms with their descent from "the largest slave-trading dynasty in U.S. History."[34]

These familial apologies reveal many things. They show, as Joe Henry Hairston's comment demonstrates, that family, descent, and responsibility are complicated categories. He had to split himself to apologize and to accept the apology. In doing so, he was not mocking the apology or saying that it was unnecessary, but rather demonstrating the depth of the crime as well as the hidden intimacy of the divided people on both sides of it. Commenting on the cultural inheritance of America, Ralph Ellison has said that whatever else America is, it is insistently mulatto because African Americans have constitutively created its culture (not "contributed to," but co-created). Joe Henry Hairston's comment reveals that the same could be said of American families. It points out the pretense of whiteness and the imposition of blackness as arbitrary. In speaking to this group, Will Hairston addresses relatives, white and black—and, if she were to have spoken to a gathering of all the children who traced their lineage back to her ancestor Thomas Jefferson, so too would Susan Hutchison. But that fact, of course, does not mean that there is no wrong or that all share equally in it. Descent is not equal; there are those who profit by it and those who must bear it as a burden. Will Hairston believes he profited, and that is why he apologizes. Joe Henry Hairston bears it as a burden, and that is why he feels divided. Perhaps Will Hairston's apology reveals another kind of burden that inheritance can give—not one of being divided genetically but of being responsible for those ancestors who imposed that burden on those they owned and raped and stole and oppressed. Given the centuries of laws that made slavery an inheritable condition, there is perhaps some justice in thinking likewise of mastery.

The historical apology for slavery and the slave trade, then, reveals a few important things. It reveals how large and how personal the institution was—large enough that several nations' governments and global religious bodies are implicated in it, yet intimate enough that it involved what are effectively paternity cases of two centuries' duration. Congress and the presidents wanted to express contrition to fellow citizens whom they represented, while Joe Henry Hairston wanted to make it clear that the ties were considerably deeper, biological, and less a matter of elective affinities. This was about wrongs done to family; these were ties of cousins as much as citizens. Likewise, it reveals how pervasive the institution was, as it involved governments, churches, and families in overlapping ways. Slavery, nations belatedly realized, was a crime that their governments had made legal; it was a sin, churches now acknowledged, that had been accepted and hidden; it was a violation and a denial of familial ties that were still difficult to affirm. Had only Congress apologized, or only the pope, this crime would look considerably different, and considerably narrower in focus. It is only when we hear the apologies offered by differently situated groups and individuals that we learn just how encompassing the crime was for which they are apologizing. That is a lesson that we can apply to other historical apologies. It is only by looking at the variety of sites at which a historical apology is offered—and the variety of positions held by the agents who offer it—that we can appreciate just what range of wrongs are addressed in that apology. The crimes of the past require a more detailed accounting, a more searching analysis, and, in the end, a more attentive apology for the event and its consequences. When an apology is long in coming, as historical apologies inevitably are, it has to assume a stance in relation to not only the specific wrong committed against a people but also the enduring effects of that long unaddressed wrong. A historical apology, in the end, is about history—not an isolated event, but a series of interconnected ones.

5

HISTORICAL APOLOGIES II

Religious organizations, as I have shown, first employed the historical apology as a means of reconciliation with groups that their predecessors had oppressed. And these apologies were first offered to other religious bodies, whether it was the Vatican and the Patriarchate of Constantinople apologizing to each other for animosities dating to the tenth century or the bishoprics of Germany and Poland for events from the ninth. Although popes were not given to apologizing for the acts of the Vatican before Paul VI, it was a practice of course, like confession of sins more generally, that had an august tradition, and in all the Abrahamic faiths it was the presumed rite connected to the religious duty to forgive. So, when a pope, patriarch, and bishop spoke words of contrition for events of the distant past, they were participating in a religious ritual, and participating in it with other corporate bodies that would understand it as such. It is important, of course, that these were rituals that received renewed energy and assumed a distinctly new status in the guilted age. In the mid-1960s, in the very years in which Germany and Japan were rediscovering a second generational guilt for World War II, and when France and America were confronting anew their relationships to Vietnam (and then, through that, their relationships to the Vichy and slave regimes of their past), the churches began to apologize. What is perhaps most striking in retrospect is that they chose to offer historical apologies instead of political ones. After all, in 1963, what must have seemed more pertinent in the relations between Germany and Poland was less likely the introduction of Christianity a millennium earlier and more likely the introduction of concentration camps as part of the Third Reich's own millennial aspirations.

What began as a practice within religious bodies, though, eventually became a practice between different kinds of corporate bodies, and that shift changed the meaning of the practice itself. When the Vatican apologized to the Patriarchate, they both understood the terms of that exchange, and they both understood that the confession of sins, while spoken by and to earthly representatives of the church, was ultimately an address to God, whose divine forgiveness was sought. That was obviously not the case when, for instance, in 1986 the United Church of Canada apologized to Canada's First Nations people for past wrongs. What might have made sense to the United Church leadership and laity—a confession of sins for which they felt responsible to a God to whom they felt accountable—might not necessarily have made sense to the First Nations people who had different faith traditions, and who might have understood the expression of contrition as directed to them and not to a divine arbiter. A practice that had traditional meanings in the religious sphere did not necessarily carry those meanings into the political. And soon the religious practice was entirely subsumed within the political sphere, as it was no longer only religious bodies that offered apologies but political ones. So when nations began to apologize to subnational groups or other nations they had historically oppressed, there was understandable puzzlement at just what these acts meant. Some saw them as deeply problematic and an attempt to escape the kinds of justice that more recognizable forms of politics pursued—financial reparations, trials, sanctions, and so on—while others saw them as promising because they provided something that people believed those more recognizable political forms lacked.

The most common objection to the phenomenon of church and national leaders apologizing for grievances they did not commit, events that happened a hundred or five hundred years ago, and atrocities for which nothing more is offered than contrition is that these historical apologies are nothing more than a spectacle. Some call it a form of "cheap grace," atonement without the rigor of remorse and restitution. Others see as audacious those leaders' assumption that they can speak on behalf of a dead past. Critics of historical apologies usually fall into two groups: those who believe that apologies are not enough and those who believe that apologies are unnecessary. Those in the first group argue that such symbolic acts should be accompanied with material reparations, or that it cheapens a tragic historical experience to believe that it can be forgiven. Those in the second group resist the idea that guilt can be collective or responsibility transmitted, believing that only those culpable of committing the crime can apologize and that only those actually and directly victimized can forgive.

Those who do see in historical apologies some promise emphasize that symbolic acts do have deep meanings. They believe that such gestures are less important in redressing the actual victimization of the past and more important in establishing a shared truth about the crime and expressing a future commitment to the shared and equal humanity of the victims and the offenders.[1] They believe that such historical apologies can prevent a cycle of retributive violence, lead to collective healing, and promote reconciliation.

Here I return to the case study of apologies for slavery to weigh these benefits against these problems.

First of all, the apology-forgiveness dynamic sometimes lends itself not to reconciliation but to the *division* of those who apologize from those to whom an apology is offered. Let us consider again the congressional apology for slavery. In one way, Congress's attempts to apologize inspired some racist Americans to express their not-so-hidden belief that Americans of African descent were really not Americans. One thoughtless but sadly representative letter writer puts it crudely: "Those seeking an apology should appreciate the freedom and opportunity this country gave them, and be thankful they are not victims of slavery, AIDS and tribal genocide sweeping across most of sub-Sahara Africa."[2] That division—between people who believe they belong and that others, who have been here for more than four hundred years, are interlopers—is also manifest if we take seriously the idea of representation. One informative editorial points out the illogic of the apology, which would endorse the belief that "Congress is the Congress of white people, not all the people," since the apology would presumably not be made by African Americans or African American representatives.[3] Even the most thoughtful attempts to work through this question sometimes go astray or reveal an underlying pattern of thinking about race in America. In attempting to accept responsibility for slavery, Professor Solomon Schimmel accepts that he is responsible for his political as well as his biological ancestors. As a member of what he calls "an American family," he does not attempt to "dissociate [him]self from the history of [his] family." He states: "I am ashamed of what some of my American family did to African Americans (and to Native Americans and other groups as well)."[4] As generous as this gesture is, and as much as Schimmel is to be applauded for exhibiting a deep sense of comprehensive responsibility, he is also implicitly defining who are *not* members of that family. (I do not think that this is Schimmel's intent at all, but it is a danger that resides in the historical apology modality.)

Another danger that these apologies for slavery reveal is that they can also *level* in the sense that all sins somehow become equally forgivable or at least can be equated in some way that makes them almost fungible. When President Bill Clinton was struggling to express remorse for the American participation in the slave trade, the president of Uganda, Yoweri Museveni, responded by effortlessly demanding an apology not from America but rather from the "African chiefs" he claimed were responsible for capturing and selling their own people into slavery.[5] When Tony Hall "had the Library of Congress investigate slavery's aftermath," the researchers discovered that "the only apology had come from tribal chiefs in Ghana, who a few years ago acknowledged their ancestors' complicity in the slave trade."[6] When Edward Ball wanted to apologize for his family's role in the slave trade, he traveled to Sierra Leone and told Chief Alkali Modu III that the Ball and Modu "families have a shared responsibility" for the slave trade.[7] Were these two families really equal partners? Likewise, in accepting the apology from the white members of the Southern Baptist Convention, Pastor Gary Frost prayed for forgiveness of "white racism and black racism." How much are these racisms the same, or how much have they had the same historical force? How much was the African slave trade an equal opportunity employer? Apologies, as we know from our daily practices, are interactive processes that often become mutual acts of penitence; they are a way to acknowledge that no one is sinless. What is good for interpersonal apologies, though, is dangerous for an understanding of history, where the force of power is a more important fact than the question of morality.

The final point I would like to make about the historical apologies for slavery is that they can *racialize* those whose forgiveness is being sought. On the whole, in these spectacles of historical apologies, little thought seems to be given to the possibility that the apologies might not be accepted. Why is that? Why is the assumption that these apologies would matter, and be acceptable to, the people to whom they are offered? Is it because these are groups of people who are considered weaker? They have, after all, suffered at the hands of those stronger groups that are now offering apologies. And is that weakness seen in a particular way—namely, is the weakness of the formerly colonized, formerly enslaved, formerly oppressed marked in the apologists' minds as "forgiving"? Is there an unspoken belief that there is a race of forgiving people and, perhaps the corollary, that forgiving people have a race? This idea has been both contested and affirmed by writers of African descent. For instance, in his poem on the lynching of Emmett Till, the Congolese poet Tchicaya U Tam'si claims: "I forget to be Negro to forgive the world for this."[8] U Tam'si uses "Negro" here as a new political identity—postcolonial and pan-

African—to describe those who challenge the racist world order. Faced with another racist crime, another atrocity, U Tam'si notes that to forgive, he has to forget his newly forged identity as a black man (a Negro) and return to an earlier colonized identity associated with accepting and accommodating such crimes. Blackness, in other words, is not associated with forgiving; colonization is. Others have maintained just the opposite: That it is very much the attribute of blackness, or a fundamental feature of black cultural values, to forgive. *Ubuntu*, writes Archbishop Desmond Tutu, is a central feature of the African worldview, and a central feature of *ubuntu* is the ethic of forgiveness.[9] The danger, then, is that forgiveness can be perceived as a racial attribute, a special gift in a particular group of people. Those who were oppressed in the past become those who forgive in the present; those who used to be held to have one kind of racial characteristic (submissive and malleable) that permitted them to be enslaved now have another characteristic that seems almost indistinguishable that permits them to forgive. Historical apologies can *racialize*, then, in the sense of creating widespread beliefs that a certain kind of people are more contrite and another more accepting.

There are occasions when the act of apologizing sometimes reiterates the dynamics of the crime for which it is offered; in this case, apologies for slavery make assumptions about race and power. Let me give one final example. When Lord Anthony Gifford, a person of Caribbean origin, addressed the British House of Lords and suggested the propriety of reparations for slavery and the slave trade, the white Viscount of Falklands objected on the following grounds: "I have worked for a long time in central and eastern Africa. . . . In my experience, the African people are immensely forgiving. They have forgiven the indignities that they suffered in recent times. To encourage the kind of attitude of fervent desire for reparation suggested here would go against the grain, certainly among Africans, *because it is not in their nature*" (my emphasis). This is the danger, then, of the apology dynamic—it makes assumptions that, more often than not, build on precisely the kind of assumptions used to justify the oppressions to which those who are receiving apologies have been subjected. The assumptions in this case are racial. As Wole Soyinka puts it in more mordant terms, "To err is human, to forgive, African."[10]

These, then, are the perceived benefits and the perceived costs of the historical apology for slavery. As a general point, we can notice that the apologies offered by religious bodies are more successful than the ones offered by political entities, because they largely avoid the issues of vicarious representation on which politics depends. The virtue of a religious historical apology is that it usually is not directed to the victim but to a higher being whose forgiveness is sought. When the appeal is made for God's forgiveness, the historical apology becomes less taxing and less presumptuous than when the appeal is made to the descendants of the victimized group, on whom is implicitly placed a moral burden to accept the apology or be perceived as filled with *ressentiment.* Pope John Paul II's apologies strike me as most effective precisely when he did not implicate people of African descent into his acts of contrition. Aside from the apology he made in 1985 in Cameroon when he asked forgiveness directly from "our African brothers," John Paul II thereafter requested forgiveness directly from God. The example of the Southern Baptist Convention shows very clearly the problems with trying to stage a human exchange of apology and forgiveness, where one cannot avoid the issue of vicarious representation. In the end, the Southern Baptists had to confess that their apology was completely an in-house affair; the "family" they meant was the Southern Baptist family, whose black membership, while growing, was still minimal. While staged apologies have their problems, so too do those where the apologists go out of their away to avoid the staging of forgiveness. The apologies of Congress and the presidents were compromised precisely because they could not be staged and because there is no higher order of appeal in the political world. The resolution was recorded, no one received it, and it had no binding power. It was the political equivalent of the unsent letter that some therapists advise their patients to write as a practice to forgive those who wronged them, or the empty chair to which they are urged to speak. These, one is tempted to say, are sorry displays rather than displays of sorrow.

Having now provided a sense of what is at stake in the historical apology, and a case study of historical apologies for one particular crime, I can address a couple of key questions. First, what distinguishes historical apologies from other forms of apology and forgiveness I have been discussing in this book? Second, what work is it that these historical apologies do?

The first question, then: Is there any difference between a political apology and a historical one? Or are they both effectively contested political statements expressing an attitude toward the past? The only real difference is the longer time frame, where the crimes are not forty but four hundred years old. Otherwise, do these two penitential discursive forms do the same work?

In one way of thinking, they are the same and do largely the same work. They are both political statements that are meant to solicit and recruit a constituency, formulate a particular program, and sometimes justify certain political strategies and courses. It is no surprise that historical apologies are a prominent part of the politics of those nations where affirmative-action programs are debated, where the violation of former treaties with aboriginal groups are topics of discussion and legislation, and where reparations are demanded. These historical accounts serve as the backdrop for why these programs of redress are necessary.

By another way of thinking, though, political and historical apologies are not quite the same. Historical apologies demand more, because they require those who hold to them to claim a different kind of belonging. A citizen of Germany in 1985 or of Japan in 1995 might sympathize with, or resent, the apologies that the president and the prime minister respectively delivered for crimes committed by their nations; they either agree or disagree with the account (was it a war of aggression or a war against colonization?), but they do not generally question the continuity from one regime to the next. The Third Reich no longer exists, but Germans do not pretend that it was a separate nation in a different time that had nothing to do with Germany after the Basic Law. Japan might have undergone a revolution after the Occupation, but Japanese citizens do not pretend that they live in a land whose history started in 1952. And so they affirm or dissent from the political apologies in political terms, as either expressing or denying the facts of the political history that is contested.

The historical apology, though, implicitly affirms a different sense of belonging. Many of the respondents who wrote letters during the 1997 debate over Congress's apology for slavery, wishing to disclaim responsibility for America's slave past, did not argue that slavery was benign or that there should not be collective, inherited responsibility for it; they argued that their ancestors arrived on American shores after the end of the Civil War, and that therefore they should not be expected to be held responsible for it. Those who should be responsible, they implied, are those who arrived earlier. In other words, they claimed a familial inheritance, not a national (or at least not to the nation to which they immigrated). Those who respond to this kind of statement argue that it is not familial inheritance that is at issue, but national. To be a citizen in 1997 is not to think of oneself as someone whose family arrived in 1890 and therefore as responsible only for American history since then, but to think of oneself as someone whose national identity is staked on acknowledging the full history of the nation (or church) to which one belongs. What distinguishes the historical apology from the political, then, is that it demands a more rigorous sense of belonging—tied not to actual experience (I was there when it happened) or to familial descent (my ancestors were here when it happened) but strictly to political identification (I belong to where it happened).

The second question, then, is: What work do these historical apologies do? What work they do, of course, depends on what they are, and what they are is not simple to state. We can probably best approach it by identifying the key question about the nature of belonging—that is, *responsibility*. The question raised in the debates over historical apologies has to do crucially with historical responsibility, which really involves two separate questions, one having to do with *collective* responsibility (to what extent can a population be responsible for the decisions and acts of its leaders), and the other with *inherited* responsibility (to what extent can a population be held responsible for what its political forebears did).

Let us take up the question of collective responsibility first. One can imagine a wide spectrum for the ascription of responsibility, at one pole a strong individualist position (one is responsible solely for acts that he or she committed) and at the other a strong collectivist position (one inhabits roles as a citizen or congregant and therefore assumes responsibility for the actions of those who had earlier held those roles). Somewhere in the mid-range of that spectrum, we will likely find people insisting on distinctions among a complex of terms that include, especially, *responsibility*, *guilt*, and *liability*. For the sake of simplicity, we can identify the spheres where these terms operate: *Responsibility* is a moral term concerning ethical choices, *guilt* a legal one concerning punishment, and *liability* a moral and economic one concerning restitution. These are, by no means, universally agreed on definitions or ascriptions, but I think that they are reasonable approximations that most people would intuitively accept, even when they use other terms. Karl Jaspers, to take one famous example, talks about "guilt" to identify four different levels of responsibility. There is *criminal* guilt, which involves a violation of the law; *political* guilt, which involves citizens' responsibility for the acts of their states; *moral* guilt, which involves the choices we make about our personal conduct; and *metaphysical* guilt, which involves our shared responsibility for all injustice in the world.[11] Even though Jaspers calls each of these forms of responsibility "guilt," he means and also uses the term "responsibility" as his guiding concept (other than for criminal guilt, by which he means just that). We can see the same contestation over terms in Richard von Weizsäcker's speech, in which he maintained two distinct kinds of responsibility: The generation that lived through the Third Reich holds actual responsibility, while the generations since are held to political, or inherited, responsibility (and "liability").

For my purpose at this point in the argument, I am really not concerned with that specific meaning of "guilt" in a legal context, about acts done or commissioned to be done by an agent who would be held criminally responsible for doing or commissioning them. I am concerned with *responsibility* and *liability*, which are moral concepts about acts done in the name of the polity with which one claims identification. Some, though, continue to hold to a largely legalistic framework when they describe the nature of collective responsibility. Joel Feinberg, for instance, argues that a necessary condition for "collective responsibility" is "opportunity for control."[12] If an agent can control a situation, either directly or indirectly, then that agent is liable and responsible. The issue is not control, but the *opportunity* to control. Culpability requires ability. If someone does not vote, say, but is repelled by the legislative actions of his or her government, one is responsible by virtue of having an "opportunity to control" the outcome of the election (as statistically marginal as that opportunity is in actuality). This way of thinking strikes me as legalistic, since it is drawing on the model of what can constitute guilt or innocence in an action and not necessarily responsibility and liability, which are more flexible concepts that are unhelpfully hampered by being restricted to legalistic frameworks.

We can turn now to the question of inherited responsibility. When we look back at the three forms of historical apologies for slavery, we see that each of the forms expresses a different kind of belonging: biological, by birth into a family; political, by birth or naturalization into a nation; and social, by birth into or conversion to a religion. It is notable—and either disturbing or comforting, depending on one's outlook—that the accident of birth plays so significant a role in our placement. We are born into families, polities, and, for some of us, congregations. Might it be that one of the imperatives that drives some people to apologize for the past is precisely the wish for a stronger sense of free will, of their own choices for affiliation? Consider two different ways of thinking about the accidents of birth.

The first is resignation: We are born into the conditions into which we are born, and that position largely determines our sense of ourselves as historical agents. Chancellor Helmut Kohl, for instance, famously expressed his gratitude for what he called the "blessing of a late birth" (*Gnade der späten Geburt*).[13] Kohl was born in 1930, and he was therefore too young to have been recruited into the army of the Third Reich (his older brother was killed in action during World War II, and Kohl was drafted shortly after his fifteenth birthday in the last weeks of the war). Was the blessing being born too late to have his life endangered by the war? Or was it something more—that by virtue of being underage at the time of the Third Reich, he had less responsibility for it, that he was too young to have been caught up in whatever frenzy produced it? If so—and I am not sure, but I suspect that since he noted this fact during a 1984 visit to Israel, he did mean something more—then what is he saying about our capacity for making political choices? Is the blessing or accident of birth a sufficient excuse for the choice of politics?

The other way is resistant: We are born into certain conditions, but we make choices that determine the kinds of historical agents we are going to be. One way of exercising that freedom of choice is by apologizing for the past events of one's family, church, or nation. That choice to apologize makes one's birth less determinate, since one is expressing dissent about the events of the past and acknowledging a sense of belonging by choice, not accident: "I choose to take responsibility for what my nation did, and that is what makes me the kind of citizen I am." The accident of birth—being born into a particular epoch and social class—comes with responsibilities, not just privileges, and a key responsibility is to acknowledge the ways in which the past has formed the "blessings" of that birth. And apologizing for the crimes that produced some of the privileges is a way of seeing them for what they are, not fate but political acts.

If, then, the historical apology can be thought of as a strategy for accepting collective, inherited responsibility for what a nation or church did in the past, what work does that apology do? For most commentators, that work is reparative—that is, it is a moral or symbolic reparation for past crimes. It is, admittedly, the least tangible form of reparation. In 2001, the International Law Commission (ILC) completed its Articles on State Responsibility, which address the ways that states can respond to past injustices. The ILC identified three forms of reparative work: *restitution*, which attempts "to re-establish the situation which existed before the wrongful act was committed"; *compensation*, in which money is given "to compensate for the damage caused thereby, insofar as such damage is not made good by restitution"; and *satisfaction*, in which discursive means are meant to "give satisfaction for the injury caused by that act insofar as it cannot be made good by restitution or compensation." The ILC lists "acknowledgment of the breach, an expression of regret, a formal apology or another appropriate modality" as forms of satisfaction.[14] The historical apology, then, does reparative work of a symbolic sort, usually described in language that ranges from the cognitive (acknowledgment) to the therapeutic (reconciliation, healing).

Do historical apologies accomplish that reparative work? Do they promote reconciliation or the healing of ruptured relationships? As shown in my earlier discussion of political apologies, the answer is not simple. We can begin with a statement of the key problems of identification involved.

Consider Feinberg's comment on the different ways differently situated populations *feel* the effects of the past. Looking at American race relations in the late 1960s, he notes the difference between a sense of solidarity among all people of African descent and a complete absence of that sense among white people. He understands how African Americans can imagine, and build a politics based on, the connections among all black people. It is just not an option for him. "I, for one," he writes, "am quite incapable of feeling the same kind of solidarity with all white men." He is implying, I think, that oppression had produced a communal feeling, while freedom from oppression had not. But it is also possible that he is commenting on the nature of an individual's having or not having a choice. Independence is a luxury, and not one enjoyed by those who must strive for their human rights and the recognition of their humanity. That "incapacity" for feeling that sense of solidarity is also a form of power. Feinberg then reflects on how this sensibility of solidarity is connected to two distinct ways of perceiving the past. Again writing personally, he comments: "I certainly feel no bonds to seventeenth-century slave traders analogous to those ties of identification an American Negro must naturally feel with the captured slaves." What Feinberg is describing here is a condition central to the guilted age and worth exploring in some detail.

He does not say so, but part of the reason he does not feel those "bonds" with slave traders is that such a connection induces guilt. As I show above, those feelings come more naturally, or are more easily imposed, on those who trace their *biological and genealogical* descent to the slave traders and masters. Familial identification trumps national when it comes to accepting or rejecting responsibility for historical events and crimes. Feinberg notes that without feeling those "bonds" with the slave traders, he "can feel no shame on *their* behalf." Feinberg implies that this incapacity to feel solidarity, this inability to feel the bonds with the past, is problematic. A sense of "vicarious shame" might be personally distressing, but it is also a mark of more profound attachment. One "cannot be intensely ashamed of one's country," he writes, "unless one also loves it." In other words, the incapacity to accept those bonds and feel that vicarious shame is a symptom of a deeper malaise. Solidarity, a feeling of oneness with another person or being or nation, "is a necessary condition of the vicarious emotion, which is in turn an index to the solidarity." What Feinberg describes here is a condition of fragmentation, of diffusion; in other words, the absence of a solidarity that would give strength. Feinberg tellingly calls it "a failure of imagination."[15]

It is precisely this failure that historical apologies seem to wish to correct. What those who make them, and those who demand them, declare is that it is only by accepting a sense of civic kinship as readily as we accept a biological one that we can feel and benefit from an enlarged feeling of solidarity.

We can find the most robust debate over that choice—whether to deny or embrace the "vicarious shame" for a national past—in Australia. These debates took place in multiple sites in Australia: in politics and parliament, in courts, in the public sphere, and in philosophical colloquia. The issue of whether the nation ought to apologize for the treatment of Aborigines was a political debate and lightning rod. The Labor Party made Prime Minister John Howard's Liberal Party's refusal to apologize a central feature in the 2001 elections (unsuccessfully, as it turned out), and the party made its pronounced parliamentary apology in 2007, when it finally assumed power, part of its symbolic platform. It was one political promise these party members kept. In court cases, too, the issue of a historical apology arose. In a case involving Australia's child-removal policy, *Cubillo v. Commonwealth*, the presiding judge, Maurice O'Loughlin, noted that an apology "would be covered by absolute parliamentary privilege." These debates did not just occupy politicians and jurists; they involved citizens directly, who responded directly. A grassroots effort led to the striking of a National Sorry Day Committee, which proposed a National Sorry Day to be held on May 26, 1998, as a "day when all Australians can express their sorrow for the whole tragic episode, and celebrate the beginning of a new understanding."[16] In the interim, Australians signed what were called "Sorry Books" to record their personal sense of remorse for the nation's past treatment of its Aborigines. It was a symbolic act, and a deeply meaningful one. With their personal signatures, they acknowledged and recognized what crimes had been committed *in their name.*

The issues at stake in these political pronouncements, judicial decisions, and acts of an aroused citizenry had long been the domain of philosophers of ethics: the nature and meaning of responsibility, justice, and identification. And Australian philosophers hastened to contribute to the debate. In an article in the *Australasian Journal of Philosophy*, Robert Sparrow focuses on what is presupposed by those who wish to apologize—that by "profiting from past injustices," current generations may be said to be "complicit" and "'accessories after the fact' to injustices committed in the past"—and then describes just what work a historical apology does: "An apology . . . reaches back to the original events and changes their significance by placing them in a historical context which includes the later recognition of the wrong which has been committed." Janna Thompson examines how historical apologies could be justified in the same way that "posterity-binding" treaties could be—that is, each imposes "moral obligations on future members of a society." On that basis, then, contemporary citizens have what she calls "historical obligations" to provide restitution for the past. Sparrow implicitly and Thompson explicitly have taken up an argument that Jeremy Waldron had presented some years earlier in which he denies the basis of such restitution. There are circumstances, Waldron claims, in which past injustices, because of demographic and ecological changes, become "superseded"—that is, no longer compelling to claims of restitution. Although his argument is primarily aimed at Robert Nozick's philosophical "principle of rectification," Waldron uses historic cases of Aboriginal land claims to give substance to his argument. His conclusion, like that of many liberal critics of historical apologies, is that these symbolic measures do not address the problems of contemporary society. If contemporary poverty is the problem, then we should focus our attention on establishing a fair redistribution of resources, not on offering "reparation for something whose wrongness is understood primarily in relation to conditions that no longer obtain."[17]

There are three things especially that distinguish the position held by Waldron from that held by Sparrow and Thompson. First, Waldron focuses on land and properties, whereas Sparrow and Thompson imply that the more important losses have been cultural and political. Second, they disagree on whether the "conditions" do or do not still pertain. For Sparrow and Thompson, the conditions caused by the violations of treaties, by the oppression of the populations, by the crimes committed against their families and their cultural integrity do pertain; they endure and explain the inequities of contemporary Australian society. Finally, they focus on different agents in this exchange; Waldron is interested in seeing what kinds of rectification of the past are possible, and implicitly he is looking at the kinds of claims that the injured polity—the Aboriginal people, in this case—can or cannot make. Sparrow and Thompson focus on the white Australians who are held responsible for the injuries and on what rectification of the past may do for that population that will enhance its sense of responsibility, its feelings of solidarity with all the people who share the land, and the political programs it might establish to create a more equitable union.

I would return now to the question with which I begin my analysis of historical apologies—namely, what, if anything, distinguishes them from political apologies—and add one more element to my earlier answer. Although not universally the case, political apologies tend to be from one nation to another, while historical apologies tend to be from the nation to a group within its borders. There are many exceptions to this very loose rule—so many exceptions, actually, that it probably does not deserve to be thought of as a rule at all. Vatican City, a curious nation at that, has been offering historical apologies to groups that are not nations at all—Muslims, Jews, Protestants, women. And in other cases, groups within nations have offered historical apologies to other groups within nations. When Polish and German bishops held a reconciliation ceremony, their mutual apologies addressed not only the atrocities of World War II but also the longer history of a thousand-year relationship. And nations sometimes do offer historical apologies to other nations, and sometimes just *in* other nations. Both President Clinton and President George W. Bush offered their historical expressions of remorse for the slave trade in Senegal, although neither the Senegalese people nor its head of state was presumably the intended primary auditor. And, in some cases, what one nation thinks of as the extended nation, the other nation thinks of as two distinct nations. Britain's apology to Ireland for English indifference to the potato famine can be seen as an intranational apology, if Great Britain is the point of reference, or an international apology, if England and Ireland are thought of as separate nations, one attempting to occupy the other.

Other examples of historical apologies are not nearly so convoluted: those cases where the government in a settler nation apologizes to its Aboriginal or First Nations population—examples include Canada, Australia, New Zealand, the United States—or cases where a nation apologizes for the enslavement and oppression of a specific population. What this distinction suggests, then, is that historical apologies play a significantly different role than do political apologies. They are primarily statements about what kind of polity the nation has been, and what kind it repents of having been. Just as political apologies are political statements, so too we can think of historical apologies as *historical* statements. They record what the apologist hopes will be recognized and accepted as a shared history and a shared understanding of that history.

The terms of that history are exactly what are under dispute, of course, as demonstrated in the examples above. In his comments on the work of truth commissions, Michael Ignatieff famously writes that what these commissions do is "narrow the range of permissible lies" that can be told about a nation's past.[18] In the face of the Truth and Reconciliation Commission (TRC) Report, no rational South African can deny that apartheid operated through the violence it did, or that the state-sanctioned violence took the particular forms it took. This work is similar to that done by the Nuremberg and Tokyo tribunals. There are, of course, irrational people who deny the Holocaust and apartheid and American slavery; like the poor, the crazies we will always have among us. But the trial records, the commission reports, the tribunal findings—these establish just what cannot thereafter be denied. It might be naïve for us to hope that historical apologies could do more than Ignatieff sees possible for truth commissions. Perhaps the best that they can do is simply limit which lies can be told.

But the historical apologies seem to strive for more. When Congress apologizes to African Americans for American slavery, for example, it describes the full gamut of horrors of that enduring and formative institution in American life: "Africans forced into slavery were brutalized, humiliated, dehumanized, and subjected to the indignity of being stripped of their names and heritage." In a nation where the historical profession had long trafficked in, produced, and promoted the "permissible lies" that slavery was benign and good for those who were enslaved—and did so, in American textbooks, history seminars, and public discourse until the 1960s—this statement seems to be straining to alter not only the description of what is being apologized for but the very foundation of the nation offering that apology. The House version resolves that slavery was "incompatible with the basic founding principles in the Declaration of Independence." The Senate version insists: "The system of slavery and the visceral racism against people of African descent upon which it depended became enmeshed in the social fabric of the United States."[19] In one case, the origins of the nation are questioned; in the other, its civil relations. These, then, are not tepid statements of what is no longer permissible to say (slavery was good for the Africans) but rather affirmations that slavery was truly formative to the nation. It was there at the compromised beginning of the national endeavor, and it was and remains part of the very fabric of the society we inherited.

What such a historical apology does, then, is promote a particular version of history that is intended to recruit or persuade citizens to accept a specific kind of citizenship. What drives an individual or group to make a historical apology is clearly that it expresses a sense of belonging. There is a certain portion of the citizenry and congregation who seeks a more historically burdened sense of corporate identity, one in which their membership or citizenship is rooted in the national and congregational actions of the past, one that establishes them most emphatically as not autonomous beings. Belonging for them is about responsibility, not just benefits. Political philosopher Michael Sandel refers to what he calls "thickly constituted, encumbered selves," by which he means those members of whatever institution or nation who believe that the obligations of membership "presuppose that we are capable of moral ties antecedent to choice." This philosophical model takes issue with a strain of thinking about justice from Immanuel Kant to John Rawls that holds that "we are free and independent selves, unbound by antecedent moral ties." There is much to be said, and much has been said, about this Enlightenment model of the autonomous subject. But there is much to be questioned about it, too. We are clearly not equally free and independent, and we are also clearly not equally bound or unbound by the past. Some of us bear the burden of history more than others, or, more accurately, some of us choose to remember the burden of our past more than some of us choose to forget the blessings of our past. And, indeed, the debates over those who want and those who resist historical apologies can sometimes be mapped onto precisely those who want to believe in that unbounded subjectivity and those who feel held to be "conscientiously encumbered selves"—those, in other words, who accept "the obligations of solidarity" as the duties of membership.[20]

The groups offering historical apologies for what their nations and churches did in the past clearly uphold a sense of membership that is premised on their accepting a tacit responsibility of things done in the name of the group with which they are affiliated. Instead of clinging to a limited and limiting definition of responsibility, these are people who accept that we are responsible for membership in a country or a church, and that we are accountable not only for the limited range of what we do but also for the more significant practices of where we belong. People who accept that being citizens and congregants of particular polities and churches means being accountable for the church and nation with which we identify are people who respect history as a force that has made our present what it is instead of denying it.[21]

We can perhaps extend this insight and argue that an encumbered sense of selfhood presupposes an embodied sense of history. Continuity matters for the collective in a moral way, just as courts hold it to matter for the individual in a legal way. We may each personally feel remorse at having committed a crime, and that remorse might well make us a new person, but in the eyes of the law we remain the same embodied legal person who committed the original crime. Certain congregations and certain groups of passionate citizens in nations across the globe grasp onto that sense of being responsible for an embodied history. What these citizens and congregations seek, additionally, is an emotionally freighted sense of belonging. It is for this reason, I think, that we see these ritual acts of *emotional* expression. When a national head of state presents himself or herself as contrite, he or she is assuming a posture we think of as belonging to a personality, not an abstraction like the state or the church. These are acts that belong not to the procedural republic of politics but to a different realm of claiming belonging to a polity, what some call an "intergenerational community."[22]

The issue, then, is continuity. Are we willing to consider ourselves citizens of a nation in a thick or a thin way, in a way that we limit by our biological claims (our familial descent) or that we expand by our civic ones? Most white Americans share in what Feinberg calls that "failure of imagination" that would permit them to think of the solidarity they share with slave-traders or masters. And that probably is not what a historical apology asks of them, in any case. It is not asking them to claim a solidarity with a past that is at odds with their personal, familial experience, nor is it asking them to see themselves reflected in that experience of what was, after all, a minority of Americans who owned slaves. It is asking them to recognize and acknowledge that the nation to which they claim allegiance has a particular history, and that that history was formative for the nation and therefore constitutive of the society we now form. It is asking them to accept the principle of continuity as a basis for belonging.

For some, that concept seems to go against the American grain, against American ways of thinking. It might even be the basis of the one philosophical tradition that has its origins entirely in American soil. American Pragmatism is a subtle, multifaceted school of thought that deals with several realms of philosophy, but I want to note here one specific strain in it, exemplified by William James, which states that we can make a world by willing it. James encapsulates it most succinctly when he declares that we can choose our ideas, and that these ideas we will ourselves to choose create our attitudes and therefore our world. He makes the point in pithy statements that first appeared in graceful essays and now sometimes grace disposable paper napkins: "Act as if what you do makes a difference. It does." "Begin to be now what you will be hereafter." "Believe that life is worth living, and your belief will help create the fact." And, a final homely version: "We don't laugh because we're happy, we're happy because we laugh."[23] The principle that belief is willed and that willed belief is transformative helps us understand the imperative behind that American sensibility that values discontinuity, holds that we are unbound by the past, and clings to the hope of the possibility to start anew ("Begin to be now"). It is, frankly and literally, an enchanting idea. As the British philosopher R. G. Collingwood notes in his *Essay on Metaphysics*, in a statement that might be a summation or an indictment of American Pragmatism: "As long as you believe in a world of magic, that is the kind of world in which you live."[24]

So what then might be concluded about these historical apologies? I concluded that political apologies register as political statements; they are not emotional expressions, and the emotion is important only in their *performance*. Whoever apologizes must *appear* to be sincere, because that is what is expected of people who apologize in interpersonal cases. Their impetus and effect are as political statements, and they work by invoking a particular local past that is either atoned for or recast in another way. Historical apologies are different, since these apologies occur in diverse sites and occupy a range of contexts. Unsurprisingly, these historical apologies embody the practices and ideals of the spheres where they take place. When a congregation or church leader apologizes, those apologies are governed by the rules operating in the religious sphere. When a political body or executive apologizes, those historical apologies are political statements. And when an individual apologizes for his or her biological ancestor's actions, that apology is governed by the rules of the interpersonal sphere. What these historical apologies all share, however, is a deeply felt sense that historical continuities matter to a given person, nation, or church. They exemplify and advocate a thick, encumbered, narrative sensibility of what makes us who we are.

There are, as I have shown above, both dangers and benefits to the historical apology when it does this kind of work. The undeniable benefit is that it inspires in a citizenry a more robust and powerful sense of belonging, one that makes the accident of birth into something more meaningful. The possible dangers are the ones I have highlighted above—the danger of division, disunion, and reinscription of the differences that the apology tries to address. There lurk also other dangers, having to do with the existential status of an event for which an apology is offered, which I address in Chapter 6. I can end here, though, by noting that these historical apologies, especially our case study of the historical apology for American slavery, are not simple discursive statements. They are heavily burdened with meanings and implications. In the guilted age in which we live, they have become more routine and therefore less meaningful, as numerous pundits have pointed out. But, as with political apologies, these historical apologies are not to be assessed simply by whether they seem sincere. They are to be understood by what specific historical and political work they do. As I have been at pains to point out, that is not one kind of work but many kinds, depending on the context and the role of the person who is apologizing. But what they all share, of course, is that they are apologizing for one thing—slavery. The question that is begged when forgiveness for slavery is begged by politicians, popes, and presidents, by families, nations, and churches, is that the kind of reconciliation, healing, and sense of belonging that the apology might produce implicitly involves a person, a population, a community that has often been asked to bear precisely the costs of that healing and sense of citizenship.

I end with the admonitory words of someone who wrote well before the guilted age but addresses precisely the conditions of it. Pauline Hopkins was an African American writer whose main period of publishing activity coincided with the crucial moment of reconciliation between the white South and the white North in the 1890s. David Blight has expertly shown how that reconciliation was premised on the denial, absence, and proscription of African Americans. Indeed, the main "article of faith" of that moment and of the Lost Cause mythology that defined it was "the disclaimer against slavery as the cause of the war." For reconciliation to happen, those who had fought over the bodies of enslaved Africans had to deny that that was the reason they had fought. Hopkins was troubled by what she saw in this moment of fervent reconciliation and the necessary denial on which it depended. She understood, of course, that slavery was precisely the cause of the Civil War, and she understood, moreover, that slavery continued to have profound effects. It was and remained what she calls "the cankering sore which is eating into the heart of republican principles and stamping the lie upon the Constitution." The healing of that sore required more than what the nation was doing at that time to reconcile in that way. "We may right a wrong, but cannot restore our victim to his primeval state of happiness," she writes. "Something is lost that can never be regained. The wages of sin is death. Innocent or guilty, the laws of nature are immutable. So with shoulders bent and misshapen with heavy burdens, the Negro plods along bearing his cross—carrying *the sins of others*" (emphasis original).[25] Hopkins is not simply dismissing the possibility for forgiveness, the presumed righting of a wrong; she is noting how such forgiveness, when it takes the form of self-forgiveness, when the sections of the nation can forgive each other and be reconciled by making absent the people who have borne the suffering of slavery and must now bear the burden of this forgiveness, can replicate the very thing it forgives and therefore continue to haunt the nation. It does not have to be that way, but it has been that way. In a land whose native philosophical traditions affirm willful discontinuities, this burden has been the historical continuity.

6

THE METAPHYSICS OF UNDOING

At the end of his 1748 sermon preached at the London Infirmary, Joseph Butler comments that all his auditors should be aware of their sins and be stimulated by that awareness to perform good deeds. He urges them to remember how in "many instances we have all left undone those things which we ought to have done, and done those things which we ought not to have done." This interplay of the *done* and *undone*—the evil done, the good undone—ends with an exhortation about the making of amends. When he describes what is involved in that process, he uses precisely the same phrases: To make amends is for each person to "undo the evil which he has done."[1] The word *done* means effectively the same thing in both cases, referring to the wrongs, sins, or evil that we have performed. But the word *undone* is *not* the same in both cases. In the first case, it means a failure of obligation (we have not done what we ought to have done), while in the second it means a reversal of conditions or time (we undo now what we had previously done). That curious idea—that making amends or apology or forgiveness can *undo* the wrongdoing—has assumed an important place in the discourse of the apology-forgiveness dynamic, especially during the guilted age. It is important, I think, to see what it might mean and, indeed, to see the different things it seems to have meant to those who employ it.

While philosophers since Heraclitus have debated whether it is possible to undo something probably for as long as they have debated about the physics of cause and effect and the properties of time itself, it is in the guilted age that I think we can see a more concerted effort to define the ways it is possible to say that apology or forgiveness perform this work of undoing. After examining how some writers from an earlier epoch identify the key factors in the problem of undoing, we can discern three distinct ways that writers during the guilted age have argued that we can understand undoing—as a psychological, a political, or a mystical phenomenon. We can then return to the historical apology for slavery to see how this concept of undoing operates in it.

When we talk about undoing, we talk about an act (to undo) and the medium within which it can take place (time). The key concept is "difference." When we undo something, is the something different? Let me offer some simple examples to help us get clarity. We generally think of undoing in terms of material objects that we manipulate. I can tie or untie a shoelace, for instance, because it is material. A shoelace I have untied is not different from the one I have tied. I have successfully undone what I had earlier done. Someone could object that with each untying the friction reduces the shoelace so that the untied shoelace is, in fact, different from the one I tied; it has lost mass and elasticity. And while I might dismiss this as the quibbling of a too-enthusiastic physicist, I cannot deny its truth. Strictly speaking, each action *does* alter the world in some miniscule way, so I cannot say there is *no* difference. Instead, I might say there is no *appreciable* difference and continue to believe just that until my shoelace snaps. In any case, my concern here is with events, not material objects, and events, for most of us, can patently not be undone.

What is at issue here is a philosophical question: What can happen to something that has happened? Deeper philosophical questions can be posed about what we mean by "has happened"—that is, what constitutes an event. Likewise, there are deeper philosophical questions about what we mean when we pose two different times in the life of an event (what has happened, what can happen), a question in this case about the nature of temporality. These are questions that can be posed in different ways according to different interests. In the case of time, for instance, the philosopher Gottfried Wilhelm von Leibniz contested Isaac Newton's theory on whether time was or was not an absolute in one way, while the theoretical physicist Albert Einstein contested Newton from a different perspective. For our purposes, we simply note that in a world where time is flexible, where it can bend and is not unidirectional, where time travel is possible, forgiveness will come to have a vastly different meaning. We will not withhold forgiveness from those who do us a wrong, but only those who refuse to go back in time and undo it. Until that day comes—at which point, I will go back and revise this section—we still largely abide in a Newtonian world and take for granted that there are events that happen in the world, and that they occur in sequence.

The first question, then, is: Can some later event wholly reverse an earlier one? Jeremy Bentham puzzles over this problem in terms of the law. Can a judicial decision alter the past? He examines cases of judicial sentences that involve "forfeiture of condition," such as those, say, where a magistrate pronounces that a negligent father has lost the right to claim a son. A decision of that sort, Bentham notes, is supposed to alter both the "paternal and filial condition." Bentham writes that such power in a magistrate appears extraordinary precisely because it seems to be a power over reversing time. How "can it be in the power of any human tribunal to cause that which has taken place, not to have taken place?" When Bentham examines how this alteration can be understood, he largely focuses on acts of propaganda—in other words, how the court can make a wider public believe that the relationship never existed, no matter what the father and the son might still maintain. In some nations, the court endeavors "to cause it to be believed" that the relation is null, sometimes by a mystical statement that "the blood of the person in question undergoes some real alteration, which is a part of the punishment." In other nations, less mystical means are used; in France and Portugal, "all trace" of the "fact of parentage" is "abolished" by obliging the father to change his name.[2]

Bentham returns to this philosophical question when he takes on his *bête noir*, the benefit of clergy (a term now used almost exclusively in its negative form to refer to people who cohabit "without benefit of clergy," but which used to mean the right of clergymen to be tried in ecclesiastical rather than civil courts). What distinguishes the "benefit of clergy" for Bentham is that it permits clergy found guilty of a crime not to lose their reputation. The reason is that "the benefit of clergy operates as a pardon." When a clergyman has committed a crime, that crime cannot be ascribed to him, whereas for nonclergy it can. Let's say a mother with a hungry daughter steals a loaf of bread and is not punished; anyone is now free to call her a thief. If she is caught and punished, whoever afterward calls her a thief can now be convicted of "verbal defamation." One must use a term that puts her crime in the past, such as "ex-felon." In the case of clergy, however, the statute that operates as a pardon performs a magical feat: "It has the virtue to make that not to have been done which has been done." There is no past event, and so even calling the clergyman an "ex-felon" is libelous. Bentham is skeptical, for good reason, because he despises the "benefit of clergy," but also because he feels that expressing the law in such a way damages its authority. For the law to affirm what is physically impossible—that something did not happen that happened—is for the law to "bear marks of its own falsehood."[3]

Modern commentators have seen that the problem of undoing is especially relevant to questions involving free will and determinism. In an article combatively titled "Free Will as Involving Determination and Inconceivable without It," R. E. Hobart notes that we respond to our own wrongdoing with reproach precisely because we do not have the power of English magistrates or the benefit of clergy, the power to make something that happened not have happened. We "wish we could undo what we did in the past, and, helpless to do that, feel a peculiar thwarted poignant anger and shame at ourselves that we *had it in us* to perpetrate the thing we now condemn" (emphasis original). Hobart's larger point, as his title indicates, is to affirm that the debate between free will and determinism is based on a false antithesis and, in the history of philosophy, constitutes "a huge waste in the region of reasoning itself," one he hopes "should end" with his article (it did not).[4] His point about the wish for people to "undo" what harm they have done reveals the motives some have to affirm determinism and escape the judgment of blame (it was done) or to affirm free will and accept that judgment (I did it).

Of course, the basis of that remorse and contrition—the belief that the person who is contrite is different from the one who committed the wrong—is, as Daniel Dennett points out, just as incoherent as the desire to "undo." One desires to transform the events of the past, the other to transform a person of the present. There is a difference, of course, in that one desires something that is impossible according to a Newtonian conception of time, while the other desires something that is not. It desires simply to characterize the past agent as embodying beliefs that the present one no longer does. Dennett suspects that this frustrated desire "to undo what I did" might be the motivation for those philosophers who hold to "'radical freedom' or 'contra-causal' freedom of choice." Such a belief runs as follows: "I can't change the past (dammit), but I'd feel better about myself if I thought I could *almost* change it, *or*, I'd feel better about myself if I learned that it was a sort of cosmic slip for which I was *not* responsible."[5]

These, then, are the important concepts that animate and lie at the core of this debate about undoing: time, event, difference, effect. The concept of "undoing," as both Hobart and Dennett imply, has much to do with remorse, with the desire to alter the past act for which one feels penitent. I turn now to the problem of undoing as it is found in the specific topic of forgiveness—that is, the belief that to forgive is to undo the deed forgiven.

Understandably, most writers believe that forgiveness does not actually alter the past. In the words of someone opposed to forgiveness in general, Friedrich

Nietzsche, "Forgiveness does not extinguish, what is done is not undone."[6] What he means, I suspect, is that the event really happened and it remains in place, no matter what happens later. The event does not disappear, nor, in his mind, does forgiveness necessarily eradicate the *ressentiment* that the original event inspired. His is an insistence founded on the principle of the endurance of events. If something happens, it stays happened, no matter what may come after. It is the second part of his argument that contemporary writers challenge—that forgiveness does not eradicate the *ressentiment*; that is, forgiveness does not undo what happened but rather what we feel about what happened.

Here, then, we can see the two distinct modes of thinking about undoing: Either the *event* itself is changed or the *effects* of the event are changed. From these two modes, we can identify the three ways that contemporary thinkers have argued that forgiveness may perform the work of undoing. Those who believe that forgiveness can undo by changing the event itself—that is, by returning the world to the anterior condition before the wrong was committed—see undoing as *mystical*; I examine this argument shortly. Those who believe that forgiveness can undo by repairing the world—that is, by using reparations or restitution in a way that makes reconciliation and social life possible—see undoing as *political*; I explore this argument in the next section. Those who believe that forgiveness can undo by changing our attitude toward the wrongdoer—that is, by returning our mind-set to what we felt previous to the wrongdoing—see undoing as *psychological*, and I take up that argument here.

In a 2008 study, for example, Lucy Allais comments that there are situations where "the perpetrator has undone the harm, through apology, repentance, penance, and restitution," and other cases where "the harm cannot be undone." She does not explain what it means to be or not to be "undone," largely because the discourse has unquestioningly accepted that term as descriptive of a particular kind of psychological action. As Christopher Bennett puts it, apologizing is an effort by the penitent "to undo the material, emotional and moral damage caused."[7] It is, in other words, the wrongdoer's means of eradicating the *effects* of the harm through restitution, both material and symbolic. But it is not apology only that performs the work of undoing. Forgiveness, too, is cast as doing precisely the same thing. Joanna North, for instance, uses Immanuel Kant to make that point. She first presents Kant's theory of forgiveness, which for him requires "making undone what has been done." Kant concludes that forgiveness is therefore impossible, since not even God can "undo" what has been done. North counters that when we say that forgiveness can "undo," we mean that it can lessen or remove the *ramifications* of the deed. "What is annulled in the act of forgiveness," she writes, "is not the crime itself but the distorting effect that this wrong has upon one's relations with the wrongdoer and perhaps with others."[8] Forgiveness undoes by eradicating the effects of the wrongdoing from our perceptual apparatus so that we can see the wrongdoer with new eyes and not as someone entirely defined by the wrongdoing. It is, in this case, the harmed person's means of eradicating the effects of the harm. Forgiveness, then, is a *psychological* act.

Let us take a simple example to explore this idea: A stranger steps on my shoe and walks away. There is no way for him or her to unstep on my shoe. An apology, in this case, is meant to express that the event was an accident and not meant maliciously, and it thereby fades from my memory. But say that the event were not an accident but an intentional action. A formerly trusted colleague angrily accuses me of an impropriety and then discovers that I am innocent of it. She apologizes, sincerely, and I accept her apology and forgive her. For the advocates of undoing, her apologizing is, as Andrew Schaap puts it, "intended to undo the meaning of a wrong by withdrawing endorsement of the insulting message" her act communicated. By apologizing, she tells me not only that she was wrong but also that it was wrong of her to think of me as the kind of person who could be guilty of that impropriety. When I forgive her, I endorse her attempt to undo. For Schaap, this happens by my seeking a particular kind of narrative closure. Forgiveness, he maintains, "undoes the meaning of a wrong by bringing to an end the story that continues to implicate the other in an original transgression."[9]

My forgiveness completes undoing the event that her apology had begun to undo; my colleague and I are now back to where we started—there is no difference in our relationship. Because apology and forgiveness have what Nicholas Tavuchis describes as the "capacity to effectively eradicate the consequences of the offense," an apology, he writes, can be said to "*undo* what has been done" (emphasis original). And by this he means that the apology has managed to "resolve conflicts and somehow restore an antecedent moral order by expunging or eradicating the harmful effects of past actions."[10] My colleague and I do not now have a more acrimonious relationship, precisely because the apology began and the forgiveness completed our return to the original terms of our relationship. There is no difference; we have returned to the same place, the same "antecedent moral order."

Here is where the critics of the concept of undoing attack. Of course there is a difference, they insist. What my colleague implied is that I am the kind of person who could have committed that impropriety, and I now know that she could think such a thing about me. How could this knowledge—that she has in fact accused me of a wrong and thought me capable of that wrong—*not* affect the terms of our relationship? By forgiving, I might not act resentful at having my character impugned, but have I entirely renounced what amounted to a character assassination, or do I act cautiously around my colleague because I know that she has doubted my moral integrity? And does she now act differently toward me, both more diffidently because she knows that she has bruised my feelings and more cautiously because she believes she had good reason at one time to think me capable of the kind of impropriety of which she accused me? This scenario of a relationship based on dancing around the obvious reminds us of the two lovers in William Shakespeare's sonnet 138 who both pretend to be something they are not; she is a liar, but he pretends to believe her so that she thinks he is naïve, which he hopes will lead her to think that he is not as old as he is. She is a liar, he is old, and neither wants that fact published. In that case, Shakespeare sympathetically reveals the frailties of human desires but also cynically exposes the more general idea that "love's best habit is in seeming trust."[11] "Seeming trust" might be the best way to describe the post-forgiveness relationship with my colleague, which was previously based on *real* trust. It is, in other words, not the same relationship; it is different, even if it appears to be the same.

Let us imagine a different case where the wrong is more tangible. I have stolen something from my colleague's desk. I repent, I apologize, and she forgives me. I will likely notice obvious differences in her behavior—my colleague no longer leaves spare change around the office—but perhaps not the more subtle one: that my colleague is hurt not as much by the crime as by the fact that I had considered her the kind of person against whom I *could* commit the crime. Even in this more tangible case, there is a residue of resentment at what amounts to *disrespect*. This is a point that Jeffrie Murphy has preeminently made in his critique of forgiveness that is too easy: That what remains after forgiveness is granted is a residue of resentment at what appears to be the most unforgivable aspect of the crime—that it was premised on the belief that the victim could with impunity be disrespected. And disrespect, according to some, cannot be undone. Gerald Gaus makes the point that no act of reparation or compensation can address that fundamental fact of disrespect. As Janna Thompson puts it, wrongdoers "cannot undo a failure of respect any more than they can undo murder."[12]

Here, then, is where we hit the impasse. One side argues that this residue remains, and that forgiveness may bring reconciliation but cannot restore the antecedent moral order or return us to precisely the same relationship. The other side argues that these are not then acts of genuine or sincere forgiveness, which would truly restore the original relationship. The argument cannot go further, since neither side can prove the presence or absence of what is genuine or sincere; these are not empirical or measurable qualities. The argument also takes another form between what we can call enchanted pragmatists and realist absolutists.

American pragmatism holds that we can make a world by willing it. As discussed in the previous chapter, William James encapsulates that belief most succinctly when he declares that we can choose our ideas, and that the ideas we will ourselves to choose create our attitudes and therefore our world. The world of the pragmatist is enchanted by this belief, and for the enchanted pragmatist, forgiveness is fundamentally the art of *acting as if* in order to *make it be*. Margaret Walker describes what takes place in the practice of restorative justice in just these terms. People who were wronged and the people who wronged them engage with each other, for one to apologize and the other to forgive, in a way that permits them to "begin to *act out* the more morally adequate relationships at which they aim" (emphasis original).[13] Acting as if, in other words, is not insincerity; it is practice. We undo the effects to undo the damage. The realist absolutists disagree, probably on every possible ground, from the premises to the conclusions. What was done was done, and all the king's men and all the king's horses cannot undo it.

The writers we have looked at so far hold that undoing through forgiving is a psychological practice, which they then argue is either possible or impossible. Neither camp believes that what is done can actually, really, physically be undone. I turn now to two writers who have a more subtle understanding of what it means to undo: one who shares the belief that what is done can be undone only psychologically but adds to the discussion an important philosophical and political context, and one who might not believe that undoing is physically impossible.

Hannah Arendt is the first modern thinker to argue that the special and most significant attribute of forgiveness is its capacity to "undo" the effects of the wrong. Arendt most forcefully makes that argument in her 1958 book *The Human Condition*. In the most oft-quoted sentence of her study, she writes: "Forgiveness" serves "to undo the deeds of the past."[14] Her larger argument in this section of the book is that there are two human predicaments involving time: irreversibility and unpredictability. We can neither return in time to remedy what has happened nor go forward in time to ascertain what will happen. Forgiveness provides a means of dealing with irreversibility, just as promising provides a remedy for unpredictability. What, then, does it mean for forgiveness to "undo the deeds of the past"?[15]

Arendt makes five important points in her argument about what forgiveness does. First, she describes why we would wish for the faculty of forgiveness to have that ability to undo the past. If we were never forgiven, she writes, we could never be "released from the consequences of what we have done." One wrong deed would have eternal consequences, for all our future actions, and those of others affected by our deed, would become effectively reactive. Our "capacity to act would, as it were, be confined to one single deed from which we could never recover." Second, she then traces the genealogy of forgiveness to its origins, when she argues that the "discoverer of the role of forgiveness in the realm of human affairs was Jesus of Nazareth." She argues that this capacity that Jesus discovered is not entirely bound to the religious sphere nor entirely a power that only God possesses, and, in fact, that what is most revolutionary in Jesus's insistence on the power of forgiveness is that he firmly places it in human hands, something that "must be mobilized by men toward each other." In other words, forgiveness as Jesus articulates it is an operative capacity in human affairs; it is precisely part of the public realm. Arendt's first two points establish the political motivation for forgiveness (to be able to act) and its political genealogy (Jesus establishes it as something that happens in the public realm).[16]

The third and fourth points Arendt makes are about opposites and alternatives to forgiveness. When an act is not "undone" through forgiveness, it simply produces the conditions for a reaction. Vengeance produces a "chain reaction," in which the one act provokes a reaction, which in turn provokes another, and so on. What vengeance leads to is "the relentless automatism of the action process," which can "never come to an end." The alternative to forgiveness is punishment, which, like forgiveness, can produce an "end" because it creates protocols for *one* organized reaction that breaks that chain of automatic reactions. The punishment, presumably inflicted by a community, puts an end to the reaction by determining what constitutes an equivalent and joint reaction appropriate to answer the original act. So, both justice and mercy can put an end to the dangerous cycles that threaten a world of irreversibility. What that act of mercy—forgiveness—does is, for Arendt, more meaningful because its equivalency is based not on retribution but on grace.

Arendt's final point is that forgiveness as an act of grace is ultimately based on an emotion opposed to vengeance: *respect*. Respect is in the public realm what love might be said to be in the private, although the effect of each is quite different. Whereas love, in its passion, has the effect of destroying "the in-between which relates us to and separates us from others," respect is precisely the kind of regard that constitutes "the distance which the space of the world puts between us." And that distance, that recognition that in the public realm each of us lives not *in* another but in the "surrounding presence of others," is what gives the world its political character. We need distance from others to speak and act, and we need others to forgive. If love destroys the distance, if it produces the illusion that two are one, then it makes it impossible for forgiveness to happen, since, as Arendt insists, "Nobody can forgive himself."[17] What makes forgiveness possible and desirable is that we live in a world surrounded by others. We cannot forgive ourselves, which is why we need others, and we cannot live among others if we do not forgive.

Arendt's analysis raises three crucial questions: (1) What conception of time does she posit? (2) What kind of action is forgiveness in relation to that conception of time? (3) In what sphere of activity is that kind of forgiveness relevant?

Arendt raises the first question about time earlier in the book when she discusses what distinguishes the "human condition" from that of other animals. She posits a crucial distinction between the movement involved in biological existence (where time assumes the shape of "the biological life cycle") and the trajectory of human existence (what she calls "human life in its unique and unlinear movement"). This spatio-temporal tension between circles and straight lines, between cyclical movement and rectilinear motion, between a time governed by necessity and a time marked by freedom, defines the human condition.[18] When she turns to the evolution of the human condition, she finds that two earlier forebears that precede the human condition in modern times—what she calls *animals laborans* and *homo faber*—are bound to the temporal *cycles* of biology. Forgiveness is precisely what offers an opportunity to escape the biological cycle and emerge into a human condition. Without "the faculty to undo what we have done and to control at least partially the processes we have set loose," she writes, we would be "doomed to swing forever in the ever-recurring cycle of becoming."[19]

Second, having posited two conceptions of time in a tense relationship to each other, Arendt then considers forgiveness as a form of activity that permits escape from oppressive biological time into a freer human time. What makes forgiving a particularly important faculty, then, is that it is a genuine action. Indeed, Arendt goes so far as to call it "the only reaction which does not merely re-act, but acts anew and unexpectedly." All other responses follow Newton's third law of motion: Every action has an equal and opposite reaction. Only forgiveness is wholly "unconditioned by the act which provoked it."[20] Forgiveness, then, allows us to escape the cycle of biological time, which in turn allows us to escape the corollary cycle of reactive vengeance. In escaping both, we become more fully human, which, for Arendt, means more fully social.

Third, Arendt argues that, given this conception of time (cyclical or linear) and the promise that forgiveness holds for escaping the cyclical by making it possible to act "anew," we have to think of forgiveness as emphatically a *political* act. Its proper sphere is not religion but politics; its proper emotion is not love but respect. It is emphatically about how we can be social beings in "the surrounding presence of others."

To appreciate how political an act it is, and to comprehend the profound importance that Arendt ascribes to this idea of beginning anew, we need to understand what Arendt assumes about the nature of *responsibility*. In *The Origins of Totalitarianism*, and elsewhere, Arendt proposes an extremely stringent sense of collective, political responsibility. She describes it in the original conclusion to the first edition of *The Origins of Totalitarianism* as "our consequent responsibility for all deeds and misdeeds committed by people different from ourselves." Like Karl Jaspers's model of "metaphysical guilt," this is a sense of responsibility that takes seriously the idea of "humanity." It is precisely this sense of radical responsibility that she raises in the one reference to "undoing" that she makes in *The Origins of Totalitarianism*. She writes that man who "has not been granted the gift of undoing" is therefore "always an unconsulted heir of other men's deeds," always "burdened with a responsibility that appears to be the consequence of an unending chain of events rather than conscious acts." In other words, we are mired in the world, caught up in an endless cycle or chain of events that seems to permit only reactive and responsive acts.[21] If, then, we cannot undo the deeds of the past, we are therefore bound to the world, and its cycles, in a particular way.

In the final section of that book, on the dynamics and operation of totalitarian regimes, Arendt develops what is implied in this point about undoing. She argues that what is distinctive about totalitarianism—as a movement, more than as a state formation—is that it destroys individuality, which is to say that it destroys spontaneity. Without that capacity, she notes, the victims and executioners of totalitarianism are equally "ghastly marionettes with human faces." Arendt emphasizes the power of spontaneity, which she defines as "man's power to begin something new out of his own resources." A spontaneous act is humane because it is creative; it commences a new train of thought or action. Instead of being always reactive, a spontaneous human being can develop a novel course of beliefs, actions, thoughts, and deeds. Spontaneity, then, produces something, writes Arendt, that "cannot be explained on the basis of reaction to environment and events." Spontaneity does not react; it *begins*. And the reason that totalitarianism cannot tolerate spontaneity and exerts every effort to eviscerate it is because spontaneity can effect a beginning, and beginning constitutes freedom. As an "inner capacity of man," writes Arendt, freedom is "identical with the capacity to begin." As she puts it in the final paragraph of the conclusion to the revised edition of *The Origins of Totalitarianism*, beginning is "the supreme capacity of man." To begin or not to begin—that is the question that defines a free man or an unfree one, a person or a marionette, a victim of or a refugee from totalitarianism.[22]

We can see, then, in her study of the negative conditions of life under totalitarianism how Arendt affirms the value of spontaneity precisely because it grants exactly the same capacity that forgiveness grants in less oppressive conditions—that is, the capacity to begin anew and not be bound in a reactive cycle of events from which there is no escape. These, then, are the contexts in which we can understand Arendt's commentary on the power of forgiveness: how it is related to the human power of acting, how it is related to the human desire to escape a certain kind of temporal order, how it is related to human political systems.[23]

To Arendt, then, undoing is not a mystical, metaphysical, or spiritual thing. She does not mean "undo" in a literal sense, and when she speaks about forgiving as miraculous, she is talking about a terrestrial miracle, not a supernatural one. It is miraculous in the same way freedom is. It is a miracle because it permits us to be released from a binding chain of reaction, not because the past event is annihilated through some supernatural agency. We can say that Arendt means undoing in two separate senses. Partly, what she means is that undoing means to undo the psychic *effects* of wrongdoing.

But her more important point about forgiving as undoing is that it is not a mystical nor, in the end, only a psychic event but a political one. Arendt's account of forgiving as undoing, cast in the midst of a subtle, layered, and deep analysis of the evolution of the human condition, the origins of our relationship to time, and the dynamic of our relationship to others, emphasizes that the effects are *political*. When we forgive, we undo the coils that bind us to a regressive past and affirm the kinds of freedom that alone can keep us from becoming subject to an oppressive political regime. Not forgiving preempts spontaneity and reduces freedom. Forgiving permits spontaneity, which ensures freedom. One leads to and is the product of totalitarian regimes; the other keeps them at bay. In the end, we can say that, in Arendt, what forgiveness can undo is not only the past but also the future.

Arendt, then, represents one way of thinking about forgiving as undoing, presenting the miracle of forgiveness as a terrestrial phenomenon, as a moral and political act. I turn now to those who are more intent on making the case that it is an actual, supernatural miracle that has less to do with politics and more to do with faith. Many of those thinkers, understandably, write about forgiveness in the religious sphere. These are writers who do not believe in the limitations imposed by Newtonian time, nor, I suspect, are they all that committed to the terms of time in Einstein's theory. They hold to a mystical notion of time in which, according to some, an event that took place in the past really can be undone. Emmanuel Levinas, for instance, writing as a scholar of the Talmud, holds that forgiveness has "the power to efface, to absolve, to undo history."[24] This is the mystical language of the religious sphere, and these are terms we most often find in Christian theologians' writings. Virgilio Elizondo, a Roman Catholic, argues that since "to forgive means to uncreate," and since "only God . . . can uncreate, it is only God who can truly forgive." John Chryssavgis, writing from a Greek Orthodox position, argues that through the power of repentance and the grace of Christian forgiveness, "the past can be undone."[25] As we might expect, the mystical writers on forgiveness are the ones who are most drawn to the discourse of undoing, and the one who has most thoroughly, and ambivalently, examined that mystical notion of forgiving as undoing is Vladimir Jankélévitch.

The issue at the heart of undoing, as we have seen, is the nature of time, since the question is whether something that happened at one moment can somehow be made to unhappen at a later moment. Can time itself be reversed, or even the actions that take place in time? Is time, to employ the metaphors that Stephen Jay Gould uses in his exploration of the deep time of geology, an *arrow* or a *cycle*, something that moves in one direction only or something that returns? That such a question concerning the dynamic of time would engage someone like Jankélévitch, who studied under Henri Bergson and who wrote his first book on, and with a preface by, Bergson, is not surprising. And throughout *Forgiveness*, Jankélévitch articulates a sense of time that is, like Bergson's, not uniform and not straightforwardly flowing. In one particularly salient section in which he talks about "naked time" as not having moral significance, he describes temporality in at least seven different ways, distinguishing among "the time of expiation and penitence," "empty time," "inert time," "a dead time," "biological time," "a fecund time," and "an invincible time." Jankélévitch is clearly someone with a lot of time on his hands, and it is not a simple homogenous time. In some cases, he suggests that time is an arrow, always moving ahead. What he finds objectionable in "the man of *ressentiment*" is the delusiveness of someone who believes that planting oneself into one particular emotional moment can somehow stall temporal movement. At other places, though, he seems to suggest that time is not an arrow, and, if not quite a cycle, it at least has some properties of discontinuity. The "instant of a decision," he writes, "that arbitrarily cuts the temporal continuation is alone definitive." Whereas *ressentiment* cannot stall time, an act of will can; presumably, it is the difference between an ill will and a good one.[26]

That tension between different conceptions of time has long occupied Jankélévitch. In a letter dated October 8, 1929, Jankélévitch maintains that the idea of temporal irreversibility is central to the problems of philosophy and, indeed, of spiritual life more generally.[27] Is time irreversible? Jankélévitch is ambivalent and seems at different points in his career to hold different opinions on the topic. In his 1966 book, *La Mort*, for instance, he writes, "The fact of having done is undoable." This is an appropriate comment, one supposes, in a book on the subject of death, but it is not the final thought Jankélévitch has in that book. According to Joëlle Hansel, he makes a distinction between "the irreversible, which, being inherent to our condition of being temporal, has a 'destinary and objective' character," and "the irrevocable," which "insofar as it has not been fulfilled, is always revocable." At another point in his life, in his 1974 book, *L'irreversible et la nostalgie*, Jankélévitch writes, "Once an event has happened it becomes eternal: not eternally eternal like truths, but at least immortal."[28] We might be wary of someone who makes a distinction between "eternally eternal" and some other kind of eternal. And, likewise, the distinction between the irreversible and the irrevocable might, like other tensions in Jankélévitch, prove irresolvable.

The problem of the irreversibility of time, then, is central to Jankélévitch's commentary on the work of forgiveness. What is most exemplary about genuine forgiveness, he writes, and not the facsimiles of it we find in acts of forgetting, integrating, excusing, or acting with self-interest, is that it can *undo*. This is a concept that has occupied Jankélévitch almost as long as has the concept of time. In another letter to Louis Beauduc dated January 31, 1931, Jankélévitch writes, "The will can do everything—except one thing; to undo what it has done" (*La volonté peut tout—sauf une seule chose; défaire ce qu'elle a fait*). He does not dismiss the possibility that things can be undone—just not by will. "The power of undoing," he continues, "is of another order: of the order of grace, if you like. It is a miracle." Three-and-a-half decades later, in *Le Pardon*, that miracle gets a name: forgiveness. Forgiveness, he writes, constitutes that "very sudden miracle, this miraculous coincidence of position and negation."[29]

What, then, does Jankélévitch mean when he says that forgiveness can undo? He offers two conflicting answers to that question. We can call one answer the *psychological*, since that is where the miracle happens. He affirms in that case that time cannot undo an event: "Time cannot make it so that what came to pass did not come to pass." Holding to the belief that time is irreversible, that what is done cannot be undone, he argues that forgiveness can operate in the psyche. When we forgive, "we can *make as if*, but we cannot *make it that*, we can make it as if that which happened did not happen, but not that what happened did not happen" (emphasis original). As discussed earlier, this is the most common understanding of the "miracle" of forgiveness—that what is undone, as Jankélévitch writes, are the "*effects* of the misdeed" (emphasis original). The tension here seems to be between semblance and reality (something really happened, but we act as if it did not). At other places in *Forgiveness*, Jankélévitch articulates this distinction as a difference between how we act or what we say and what we know. Forgiveness "declares the sin null and as not having come to pass although it knows that it did come to pass."[30] In either case, the miracle of forgiveness takes place in the psyche, where we act as if an event has not happened to rid ourselves of the effects of that event. So when he says that forgiveness "undoes" an event, he is talking metaphorically and referring to the psychic effects.

The other answer we can call the *mystical*, because the miracle of undoing is not psychic or intellectual but supernatural. Here, Jankélévitch waxes eloquent about the work of forgiveness, which, he says, "converts the sinners whom it pardons to innocence." Forgiveness "initiates a change *of all into all*" (emphasis original). In "one fell swoop and in a single, indivisible *élan*," it "pardons undividedly; in a single, radical, and incomprehensible movement, forgiveness effaces all, sweeps away all, and forgets all." Here, it is more than the rhythms of the prose that are Pauline; it is the very mysticism of the sentiments. Likewise jettisoned is that earlier sense that time is irreversible. Forgiveness, Jankélévitch argues, alters time because it is immediate and eternal. To forgive once is to forgive for all time. "Forgiveness forgives one time, and this time is literally *one time for all*!" (emphasis original). What this means, of course, is that forgiveness has now exceeded the basic tenet of forgiveness, which is that we cannot forgive what has not happened. Preemptive forgiveness is not forgiveness in any meaningful sense; it is license. And yet that is just what Jankélévitch is arguing constitutes forgiveness, which, he maintains, "forgives all of the misdeeds that this guilty person would be able to commit or still will commit." Both time and events, then, are transformed by forgiveness. The decision to forgive, writes Jankélévitch, "cuts the temporal continuation." What happens, he writes, is that the "*misdeed* vanishes as if by magic!" (emphasis original).[31] What was done is undone, not in the mind but in the world. These two answers are irreconcilable. In one, *undoing* is used literally, or almost literally, to mean that the event "vanishes," while in the other, *undoing* is used metaphorically to describe the semblance one can perform in the face of an unaltered past.[32]

To see how seriously irreconcilable these two positions are, let us examine two moments in his book, one in which he argues the *psychological* position, and the other the *mystical*. When he assumes the psychological position and writes that forgiveness permits us to act "as if" the event were changed, although we know very well that it has not, he puts it in the following terms: "To claim to make a tabula rasa of what was is very close to being an absurdity." One suspects that he uses "tabula rasa" as an echo of John Locke, who, of course, uses that term to describe the state of the human mind at birth; Jankélévitch is implying that we can no more undo an event that has transpired than we can reverse our age. When he argues the mystical position, though, he writes, "Forgiveness makes a tabula rasa of the past." What was close to being absurd is now logic; what was impossible is now what happens. Jankélévitch uses that same phrase in a sense that cannot indicate a mental state but an existential one. In the end, he makes precisely the argument that he has earlier repudiated: That the event can really be undone, not in semblance but in fact.[33]

These tensions in Jankélévitch's thinking about the nature of time, event, and forgiveness are informative. And, in the case of forgiveness, the very subject of Jankélévitch's meditations, these tensions reveal a more profound problem. The question for us is: What is the source of that tension, and what does the expression of tension in these terms indicate? What I think is the most promising argument is that this ambivalence expresses the tension between Jankélévitch's religious affiliations and affinities—that is, between Judaism and Christianity.[34] Jonathan Judaken has argued that Jankélévitch "articulates his position on forgiveness in a philosophical idiom that is Greco-Christian in its filiations, but that he bends this tradition toward a set of Jewish thematics." Earlier commentators have noted the same tension in Jankélévitch and resolved it in different ways. Levinas, for instance, argues that Jankélévitch is a Jewish thinker. Although Levinas knows that Jankélévitch is uninterested in Jewish "rites," Jewish forms of worship, or the Hebrew language, and that what "ethics of Judaism" he does know come from "Christian and lay texts," he yet, according to Levinas, is "able to divine the words of the Talmud." For Judaken, this tension comes down to a form of practice. He concludes that we can understand and resolve the tensions in Jankélévitch's writings by seeing them as indicative of a personal struggle with the practice of forgiveness. He writes, "We might think of Jankélévitch's texts as prayers (*tellihim*), as self-reflexive exercises in order to consider the terms upon which his own forgiveness might come about."[35] It is worth examining how the historical tension in the shifts from the Hebrew Bible to the New Testament, from Jewish to Christian ways of thinking about forgiveness, might inform the philosophical tensions found in Jankélévitch. I differ from Judaken, with whom I largely agree, in two ways: First, I think the tension is ultimately not resolved in Jankélévitch; and, second, I do not think the tension is entirely about his practice or struggle to forgive, but equally about what he deems to be the inherent contradictions in the philosophical concept of forgiving.

When we see Jankélévitch affirming that forgiveness is largely a psychological phenomenon, we can perhaps intuit that he is echoing the tradition of forgiveness that emerges from the Judaic tradition. This conception of forgiveness is not uniquely a Judaic inheritance, but it is, I think, in that tradition that we first see it formulated and promoted as a way of resolving particular kinds of tensions in human affairs. That form of repentance and forgiveness has formulae and rules guiding its expression and acceptance and a calendar scheduling its performance, and, while attuned to the divine presence in all its human practices, it is nonetheless largely focused on the human dimension in which it takes place. While religious, it is terrestrial. When we see Jankélévitch affirming that forgiveness is a mystical phenomenon, we can see the Christian elements in his lyrical descriptions. Here, forgiveness is a cosmic performance that is very much about undoing—namely, undoing the Fall through Redemption, transforming law into love, and believing that this moment constitutes the most important temporal break in human history. This is supernatural forgiveness, which does not traffic in the terrestrial details of time, space, and sequence. What I am suggesting, then, is that there is at least a resemblance between the tensions in conceptions of forgiveness in these two Abrahamic faiths and the tensions in Jankélévitch, not necessarily that he is drawing on one or the other.

If I am correct in seeing a meaningful echo between the tension in Jankélévitch's ideas about what it means for forgiveness to "undo" and the tension between these two conceptions of forgiveness, then we might perhaps read differently the concluding thoughts to his book as expressing precisely that tension between a Judaic and a Christian understanding of forgiveness. In his concluding paragraph, he argues first that forgiveness simply cannot "make it so that the action that occurred did not occur." But he argues in the next sentence, "in another truly pneumatic and incomprehensible sense," that by the "grace of forgiveness, the thing that has been done has not been done." It is precisely on this mystical note that Jankélévitch ends his book: "The mystery of irreducible and inconceivable wickedness is, at the same time, stronger and weaker, weaker and stronger, than love." Forgiveness, Jankélévitch utters in the final sentence, "is strong like wickedness, but it is not stronger than it."[36] This is a perfect expression of precisely the kind of irresolution that Jankélévitch exhibits when it comes to each deep problem he poses in the book: Can there be an unforgivable, or can something done be undone? He ends in a state of tense equilibrium, which might well be indicative of what he believes forgiveness can be in our world—neither the kind of euphoric, exuberant act that he applauds and devoutly wishes it to be nor the kind of malicious, impure facsimile of it that attempts to deny and revise historical atrocities like the Holocaust.

Some mystics have complained that Jankélévitch is insufficiently mystical. John Milbank, for instance, holds that Jankélévitch is "wrong in supposing that the past is entirely unalterable and that past suffering must in justice be left unatoned." As we have seen, this is a misreading. Jankélévitch holds to that belief when he is being psychological, but not when he is being mystical. In any case, Milbank holds to a more robust notion of the power of forgiveness to undo. In the act of penance and forgiveness, he writes, one "has to recall the past; allow with Augustine that as the past is abidingly real as a trace, the past is still *really there* insofar as it is there in my memory" (emphasis original). That "really there" trace of the past, though, seems to have more than a mental existence in Milbank's conception; it seems to have a noumenal one. When Milbank claims that "it is possible to revise what has already occurred even with respect to its occurrence," he is treading on the threshold of the mystical—changing what exists in memory into what exists outside memory—and, then, when he insists that in "a certain way we can go back in time and redo the things that still darkly echo in the present," he has fully crossed that threshold (but, of course, in this conception of time, he can always return).[37]

Mystics, by my account, tend to extremes (it would be their failing were it not their whole point). So it is not surprising to find them engaged in debates among themselves over whether forgiveness undoes the past psychologically or actually, metaphorically or really. These discussions might well remind some readers of debates over the status of the bread and wine in the Eucharist. In that debate, the question is whether the bread and wine of the sacrament are changed literally into the body and blood of Christ or whether they symbolize them. Most church doctrines hold that there is a literal change, and they differ only with respect to the technicalities—that is, whether the change is a case of transubstantiation, consubstantiation, pneumatic presence, or sacramental union. Those opposed to this doctrine are called memorialists, and they believe, as the 1647 Westminster Confession of Faith phrases it, that although they are "called by the name of the things they represent, to wit, the Body and Blood of Christ," they "still remain, truly, and onely Bread and Wine." The writers of the Westminster Confession of Faith reject transubstantiation as "repugnant, not to scripture alone, but even to common Sense and Reason."[38]

These questions of real or symbolic presence, of irreversible or reversible time, of psychological or actual undoing might strike us as engaging for philosophy, theology, or any other branch of theoretical knowledge, but not so much for the practical or political ideas I have been presenting about the meaning of apology and forgiveness. With the exception of the mystics, people who make personal apologies to those they hurt do not believe that they are undoing the actual performance of the hurt; no politician who is offering a political apology for his or her nation's war crimes is maintaining that the crimes are now effaced; and no head of church or state who is apologizing for the historical atrocities of that church or state believes that those events are now dissolved. If there is any undoing, it is symbolic and psychological. In this world of what it means to apologize and forgive, we are all memorialists (except for the mystics, of course).

And the mystics confuse those of us who are not mystics, perhaps because they conflate two distinct models of forgiving, both evident in the Abrahamic faiths. The Hebrew Bible uses the word *salakh* to describe the power of divine forgiveness. This verb is ascribed only to God in the Hebrew Bible, and it implies a power of blotting out entirely, of rendering undone what had been done.[39] The term for human forgiveness in the Hebrew Bible is *nasa*, which implies bearing or carrying one's sins. In the New Testament, the terms shift somewhat, with the Greek word *aphiema* implying the forgiveness of debts ("Forgive us our trespasses as we forgive those who trespass against us") and *charizomai* implying to show grace and also "a favor that *cancels*" (emphasis original).[40] In other words, in these two Abrahamic faiths, we see a distinction between the power carried by a divine attribute (the capacity to undo) and a human capacity (to bear with others, to forebear their trespasses). This distinction, when it is not noted in those who write on forgiveness and apology, has created a great deal of confusion. What is symbolic appears real.

Sometimes, of course, the language employed seems to indicate *more* than symbolic behavior. Mark Amstutz, for example, argues that forms of collective forgiveness require "a moral reformation of memory." He is consciously echoing Pope John Paul II, who stated that the Church needed to approach the jubilee year of the millennium by asking for forgiveness in a spirit of what he called "the purification of memory." For a pope, or any other religious figure, this is the discourse of religion, and "memory" means something else. The New Testament uses such phrases to indicate what God can do: "I will be merciful to their unrighteousness, and their sins and their iniquities will I remember no more" (Hebrews 8:12). So, too, does the Hebrew Bible, which Paul is referencing here: "I, even I, am He that blotteth out thy transgressions for Mine own sake; And thy sins I will not remember" (Isaiah 43:25). On the human level, or at the level of the church, to purify memory means to alter the ways we behave toward others; it is to unfix the residual prejudices that keep us from accepting others.[41] Yet it does not register in the same way when a political scientist uses it in a book on political forgiveness. In our age, that has quite different implications. When a nation undergoes a "moral reformation of memory," that phrase resonates as revisionist, as an attempt to rewrite history so that the atrocities, now forgiven, disappear, so that the crimes, now atoned for, are eviscerated. That, of course, is not Amstutz's meaning. It is, nonetheless, the danger that attends us if we are not careful in distinguishing what altering a memory can mean for a divinity, a person, or a nation.

So, to be clear, it is not my argument that those who offer political or historical apologies are attempting to "undo" the past events for which they are apologizing. What happens when known history is revised, photographs airbrushed, and propaganda published in totalitarian societies are different and nefarious things. The good-willed people who are addressing the national and historical atrocities for which they wish to claim some responsibility and effect some positive change in human relations between groups are doing something different—not debasing a history in those stark revisionist ways of undoing it, but rather grappling with a history that they find intolerable. In the case of the historical apologies, especially, we see genuinely concerned individuals, congregations, and populations undertaking a difficult self-examination of the terms of their belonging to atone for what their biological and political ancestors did. And yet there are implications for those historical apologies. Let us return to our case study for historical apologies—the apologies offered for American slavery—to tease out the implications of what these apologies might be doing that is at odds with the intentions of those who are offering them. I take up two moments and two discourses of American slavery, one from the eighteenth century and one from the twenty-first century.

The first comes from 1705, when the General Assembly of Virginia gathered in Williamsburg on the twenty-third day of October, in the fourth year of the reign of Queen Anne, and revised the laws of Virginia for the fifth time since the settlement of the colony. The relevant chapter is the forty-ninth, "An act concerning Servants and Slaves," and the relevant law is found in the thirty-fourth paragraph of that act, which reads as follows: "And if any slave resist his master, or owner, or other person, by his or her order, correcting such slave, and shall happen to be killed in such correction, it shall not be accounted felony; but the master, owner, and every such other person so giving correction, shall be free and acquit of all punishment and accusation for the same, as if such accident never happened."[42]

I choose to focus on this law in particular for obvious reasons, given my concern with strategies of undoing, but also because it is about punishment—that is, the most important power of the law. When social contract theorists, such as Thomas Hobbes and Locke, argue that society provides protections that the "state of nature" cannot, what they mean is precisely the power of a society to enforce established laws and punish those who break them. It is by concentrating the forces of violence within its solitary authority that a state gains its legitimacy. Moreover, this is not an isolated moment in the formulation of the slave laws that Virginia produced, and which were adopted by other states, but part of a trajectory that defined who was and was not a citizen or a person, who had and did not have certain rights that defined citizenship and personhood.

Because it is a law, it is a statement emphatically based on retributive principles. What this law should do, as every law does, is propose fitness of punishment for the particular crime. But that is *not* what this law does. Instead of stating what punishment is fit for this crime, it states that this is a forgivable crime. As writers from Cesare Beccaria to modern theorists of restorative justice have recognized, punishment is precisely the opposite of mercy, the basis of forgiveness, in most religious and secular traditions. What a law does is tell us what will inevitably happen if we do something; what forgiveness does is tell us that what would have happened is stayed or pardoned in an act of extraordinary mercy. So, like all laws, this one is representative and retributive. It is what political sociologists call a script for a society, defining what is appropriate, what is acceptable, and what measure of justice can be meted out to those who violate these mores. But, unlike all laws, this law is emphatically exculpatory in a way that I suggest constitutes an act of forgiveness.

What makes it exculpatory is that this law states and defines what makes for responsibility in this given situation. In modern legal statutes, what is exculpatory is based almost exclusively on the status and condition of the *agent*: Does she or he have *mens rea*; does he or she have some special status, some disability, some reason for not being liable at all or not fully responsible? In this case, extraordinarily, what makes an act exculpatory is not so much the agent's status, which is covered entirely by whether the act is intentional or accidental, but primarily the victim's status and condition. That, of course, makes sense, because this is, after all, a law about slavery. But we should not forget what is exceptional in that act of the law's focusing on the victim, nor can we ignore just what it says about the victim's status. This particular law follows on and augments the earlier Virginia laws that deny the right of enslaved peoples to bear arms, to raise their own physical arms in self-defense against a white person, to testify in court against a white person, or to own property. In this law, then, we find added to the denial of the right to testify, own, protect, or be free the culminating law of being denied existence. We might be tempted to think that this law makes literal the metaphor of "social death," which Orlando Patterson has so vividly shown to be a fundamental feature of every slaveholding society. But this law is not about death, per se. Rather, this law denies the right of existence. To be killed in the course of correction is to have one's death marked as not only an "accident" but also, what must confound us, an "accident that never happened"! I have written elsewhere about this law that can change something that happened (an event) into something that "never happened" (a nonevent). That law defines who is a slave: It is someone to whom something does not happen.[43] That is what I mean when I say that this law denies the right to existence: This is a body whose existence, whose absence of life, cannot be explained, because it is the result of something that never happened.

So far, then, we see two paradoxes: A statement of retribution becomes an expression of forgiveness, and the declaration of exculpation is based on the claim that what happened did not happen. We can see, I think, where I am going. Here is a case where we can see precisely that dynamic celebrated by those writers who argue that forgiveness can "undo." This law works on that very premise of forgiveness that I have been investigating—the magic of undoing. What it says, in effect, is that the murder of the enslaved being who is accidentally killed while being whipped and tortured is not a murder. It is, in fact, not even a death. It is something that "never happened." It is undone. And, I suppose, the logical next step for me to take would be to deplore the apologies for slavery since they replicate precisely what was the very basis of slavery—the undoing of the right to existence. Enslaved people who were accidentally killed suffered their existence to be undone by this law; the descendants of people of African descent would suffer that part of their history of injustice and oppression to be undone by those beseeching forgiveness for American slavery. That, however, is not the point I wish to make. The point I wish to make is more subtle, I hope, and considerably less concerned with what are, in the end, merely apparent similarities between an offensive slave law and good-willed efforts by honest people who wish to address the damages of the past.

Before I get to that point, though, let us make sure that these terms work. Is that what this law is doing: *forgiving*? Most legal analysts would immediately object, believing as they reasonably do, that laws cannot forgive. The only thing a legal setting, if not a law, might do that resembles, and barely resembles, it, is *pardon*. Most studies that distinguish forgiveness from pardon note that the salient difference is that pardoning is a legal act with visible power (only an executive, such as a judge, governor, president, or king, pardons), while forgiving is a moral act with invisible power (anyone can forgive). Pardoning, then, is a performative utterance (the words "I pardon" when spoken by the appropriately empowered person must mean what they say), while forgiving is not (to say "I forgive" randomly does not constitute forgiveness). Finally, while the act of pardoning overrides what was done, the act of forgiving, for most writers, does something much more mystical, as we have seen. A pardon as "an official act that removes the consequences of a criminal conviction," as Kathleen Moore puts it, does not erase the legal record of what was performed that deserved punishment but was pardoned. As Elliot Dorff phrases it, what is pardoned "does not go away." But what is forgiven, he continues, does, because, in the mystical way we have been tracing in this chapter, in the act of forgiveness the "original violation itself is removed."[44]

Let us now return to that Virginia law. One might be pardoned because the act was an "accident"—that is, the individual would be pardoned because of exculpatory circumstances that indicate no *mens rea*, no ill will, no intention to harm to the degree that occurred. It was an "accident." And the legal record will show that a crime was committed, but that the circumstances under which it was committed led the executive officer to exonerate the person who committed it. Legal pardons cannot meaningfully say that the court should act "as if such accident never happened." Their logic is that the act was an "accident," that the accident is precisely what did happen, and that is why the act is not being punished. And so a law that claims "such accident never happened" is doing something more than pardoning or stipulating under which conditions an executive may grant a pardon. What that law is doing, I argue, is *forgiving*, precisely in the sense that the writers we have been discussing talk about forgiving, by removing from the record, in Dorff's terms, or undoing, in the language of those who have borrowed from Arendt. So this law not only states what makes an agent exculpatory, what can exonerate a particular act, or under which conditions a person who commits such an act may be pardoned; this law forgives.

And now the final paradox of this law: It preemptively forgives what it itself makes unforgivable. We have seen that it forgives, not pardons. And we have seen that it forgives *before* the fact—it is a law that states that when such a thing happens in the future, no one will be punished for it. So, it forgives preemptively, which is, of course, itself a paradox, as we have seen in our discussion of Jankélévitch. The final part of this paradox is that it forgives what it *makes* unforgivable. While there are rich and important disagreements in the debates about the moral and existential category of the "unforgivable," those debates all agree on one point: For something to be forgivable or unforgivable, it had to happen. What is categorically unforgivable is something that did not happen. In no meaningful way can we say that we forgive something that just did not happen. This murder, because ownership permits accidents, because ownership transforms the existential status of what is owned, did not happen. It is forgiven ("free of punishment"), but what is forgiven is nonexistent ("as if it never happened"). If forgiveness is about undoing, as so many say, one wonders what we can make of an undoing of an undoing of what had never been done.

That, then, is the original discourse on American slavery. Now let me turn to a more recent example. In 1990, mainstream political commentator Charles Krauthammer offered a solution to America's ongoing racial dilemmas in the post–civil rights era: reparations. Reparations, he notes, would be just because they would "honor our obligation to right ancient wrongs." The ancient wrong, of course, is slavery, what he calls "America's sin." "There is no wrong in American history to compare with slavery," he writes, and reparations are the only way to "repay some of the bondsman's 250 years of unrequited toil." So far, then, we might see some promise in this way of thinking, but, like other efforts at thinking through the race problem as a problem of market allocations, Krauthammer flounders on two grounds. The first is logistical. He argues that the reparations must not be "symbolic" but substantial. He suggests a payment of $100,000 to each family of four. In 1990 dollars, in an economy of $6 trillion, that is not a particularly generous offer. At the rate of $25,000 per person, it is only $5,000 more per person than the amount President George H. W. Bush gave earlier that year to every survivor of the American World War II Japanese internment camps. It is always disheartening to compare oppressions of different peoples, but if we take seriously the premise that Krauthammer suggests, it seems odd to give only $5,000 more for a crime that endured 250 years, or around 247 years longer, than the internment, especially when Krauthammer claims that the crime is comparable to no other national sin.

Perhaps even more egregious than the pittance of remuneration he offers as reparations for that crime, though, are the conditions he places on the reparations package. Here are the terms of what he unblushingly describes as "a historic compromise: a monetary reparation to blacks for centuries of oppression *in return for* total abolition of all programs of racial preference, a one-time cash payment *in return for* an era of irrevocable color blindness" (my emphasis). A decade later, after David Horowitz had made reparations for slavery a salient topic in American political discourse, Krauthammer revisited the topic and reconsidered his earlier offer. Perhaps thinking his earlier offer too generous, he lowered his offer to $50,000 per family of four in 2001 dollars, when the GDP of the nation was $10 trillion. And he continued to call reparations the "cornerstone of a Grand Compromise," tellingly describing it as the only strategy that would "cleanly—and fairly—cut the Gordian knot."[45]

On one point, Krauthammer is right: This package would indeed be akin to other political compromises in American history—the 1787 compromise on the Constitution that granted representation to three-fifths of enslaved people, the 1820 Missouri compromise that established the geography of slavery in the young republic, the 1850 Fugitive Slave Law compromise that protected property in slaves throughout the fragile Union, and the 1877 Reconstruction compromise that placed Rutherford Hayes in the White House and removed federal troops from Southern states. On another point, though, Krauthammer is wrong: He calls it a "historic compromise." We can more accurately call it a compromise of history.

We cannot mistake the terms that Krauthammer proposes: In exchange for money, there would be silence. What would be abolished alongside affirmative action programs is the understanding of how profoundly slavery created the American society we inhabit. What would be revoked in an era of "irrevocable color blindness" are the guilt, shame, and sense of responsibility for the history of the previous eras. What Krauthammer represents here—and he is representative of much unspoken sentiment—is that there are symbolic gestures (reparations for him, historical apologies for others) that, in his terms, cut the Gordian knot that connects the present society to the ones from which it evolved. To be fair, he does not advocate "undoing" as in thinking that the slave past is now abolished, but he does advocate a program of political action that assuredly lessens the pressing importance of thinking historically about the present conditions of American life and culture. Reparations offered with conditions are not reparations; they are "blood money" or "hush money," an exchange of money for silence. What Krauthammer is attempting to buy is the political discourse that promotes certain programs of restitution as a form of historical redress—say, the kind of political discourse that advocates that a government has an obligation to address the lives of those whose ancestors were robbed for 250 years to provide its unjust enrichment. What he is attempting to buy is silence; what he is attempting to buy is history.

What, then, might we conclude about these two discursive moments, these two acts of atonement for American slavery? One forgives the perpetrator prior to the crime, and the other silences the victim after it. One literally undoes the event by having the law act "as if it never happened," and the other metaphorically undoes the event by having us act as if what happened does not matter. Now Krauthammer is not apologizing for American slavery, although his offer of reparation is obviously part of the same discursive realm and practical politics as that of the historical apology. And so it is somewhat unfair to compare his obnoxious offer of a compromise with those of the good-willed presidents, pope, and politicians who offer more sincere apologies for American slavery. Unlike Krauthammer, they are not counseling anyone to forget the horrors of that historical institution, nor are they suggesting that the work of atoning for it "undoes" the harms caused by it. So why am I suggesting any connection? Because all these historical apologies do a particular kind of work and operate within a specific set of discursive rules that share something with Krauthammer's offer of reparations. I note two points about those discursive rules: First, the apologies frame the event for which they apologize; and second, they establish a temporal framework for it.

To understand how they frame the event for which they apologize, let us take an example from the practice of interpersonal apologies. Say someone has stolen money from a colleague's desk. The event when it is cast in the discourse of historical fact is simple: "I stole the money from the desk." Once the person apologizes, he or she narrates the event not in the neutral discourse of historical fact but in the encompassing discourse of apology. When the event is recast into an apologetic discourse, it changes meaning: "I am sorry that I stole the money from the desk." The event is exactly the same, and it is described in precisely the same words. Yet it does not mean the same thing, because the apology framing it has rendered it not a historical fact but a historical fact for which someone is penitent. It is not only a crime now but also an antecedent event for which someone is seeking atonement. Whether we think of that event as subject to a reduction in value (it is not so bad, because it is something for which he is sorry) or as subject to a surplus in value (he did a wrong, but he is also sorry for it), the event is changed, its meaning now determined by the language of atonement in which it is represented. That, in a sense, is also an undoing: Our focus is transferred from the event of the crime to the event of the apology.

My second point is that historical apologies establish a temporal framework as well as a discursive one. The moment an apology is made alters the past event, even if it does not undo it. People who use the language of medicine in talking about the value of apology and forgiveness demonstrate this temporal framing most clearly. What was a wound when it went without atonement has now begun healing because of the act of apology. The apology marks a clear chronological break. Part of what we imply when we apologize for personal harms we have done is that we will not do them again, because we are not that kind of person anymore. The moment we apologize is the moment that marks us as someone different than the one who committed the crime. By virtue of being penitent, we become less of a wrongdoer.

The question whose answer I will imply rather than articulate is: In historical apologies, do we do the same thing? Are our historical accounts of past atrocities changed by being framed within the discourse of apology? Is our sense of ourselves as a nation altered by virtue of an apology that establishes a temporal break between what we were (a slave society) and what we now are (a penitent one)? If so, and if these turn out be more subtle forms of undoing, we need to be just as vigilant of the implications of historical apologies as we are of laws that preemptively forgive or offers of reparation that would silence.

Let me end by noting the findings from a relevant scientific experiment. In a 2006 study published in *Science*, researchers Chen-Bo Zhong and Katie Liljenquist set out to demonstrate how "physical cleansing alleviates the upsetting consequences of unethical behavior and reduces threats to one's moral self-image." The major point of their study was to show the connection between physical and moral behaviors—were it a different journal, one would be tempted to say the connection between body and soul. Through a series of intriguing experiments, they demonstrated that exposure to moral indiscretions "poses a moral threat and stimulates a need for physical cleansing." People who felt morally compromised were twice as likely to express a desire to wash their hands. The researchers called this phenomenon the "Macbeth effect."[46]

This conclusion is probably not startling for those who study religion and recognize the deep connection between ablution and absolution, or for those who study psychology and recognize how some prohibited desires manifest themselves in psychosomatic symptoms. The rest of us, I suspect, might recognize some hints of the "Macbeth effect" in our more conventional alternatives to hand-washing for acts that are offensive to morality—that is, apologizing. There is a similar hope in both acts—the actual or metaphorical cleansing of self through a ritual performance. Indeed, when theologians write about it, they often invoke precisely the ways that apology can cleanse the soul, but even when more secular scholars write about it, as we have seen, they invoke the ways that it can cleanse either the effects of the past or the past itself.

The final experiment the scientists conducted among a sample of students was to see what effect the cleansing had on them. One group was permitted to use an antiseptic wipe to wash their hands after describing an unethical deed from their past, and one group was not. They were then asked whether they would volunteer to help in another study for a graduate student who was in desperate need of experimental subjects. Of those who washed their hands, 41 percent volunteered; of those who did not, 74 percent did. The Bible, especially in the book of Psalms and Job, makes an equation between those who are clean of hand and pure of heart (Psalms 24:4; Job 17:9).[47] It turns out, apparently, that clean hands might not lead to purer hearts, that what is good for the body might not be great for the soul.

There might be an important lesson here related to the cases we have been examining—that is, the cases of those who have sought absolution for what their ancestors, churches, or states have done in the past, those who have attempted to offer apologies for the ways their congregations and nations have enslaved or permitted the enslavement of peoples. The language that is usually used to describe the desired outcomes of these moments of symbolic reparation, of collective atonement, of historical apologies is the language of therapy. These moments will lead to healing. Perhaps the lesson, though, is that corporate or collective self-forgiveness can also lead to other kinds of self-satisfaction. Maybe we need our dirty hands to remind us of our dirty deeds. Maybe our desire for undoing will, in fact, undo us.

7

THE CONCRETE PAST

Memorials

American philosophers have recently turned to stone—shiny black granite, actually, and they are particularly interested in discerning the emotional content of it to make, as it were, the mute stones speak, to determine just what they hold deep in their density. The stones to which many have turned their attention are the blocks of black granite of the Vietnam Veterans Memorial, which was designed by Maya Ying Lin and dedicated in November 1982. The memorial contains three parts: the Memorial Wall, made of highly reflective stone on which are etched the names of fifty-eight thousand veterans who were killed or are missing in action; the Three Soldiers statue, which was commissioned afterward to appease those veterans who believed the wall alone was too abstract and missing the usual heroic signs of more traditional memorials; and the Women's Memorial, a statue of three women, named Faith, Hope, and Charity, tending to a wounded male soldier. (It is worth noting that the designer of the Women's Memorial originally also had a standing nurse holding a Vietnamese baby, which she was asked to remove, and which she replaced with a kneeling nurse holding an empty helmet.) The philosophers focus on the Memorial Wall, which was the winning design and the solitary original plan for the memorial, to which the other elements of the piece were later added.

Shortly after the dedication of the Vietnam Veterans Memorial, Arthur Danto wrote a piece on it for *The Nation* that focuses on the ways that the memorial speaks to people in different registers. Writing at the moment in the mid-1980s when American academies were coming to terms with "theory"—that is, the "linguistic turn" that philosophy took before the "turn to stone"—Danto argues that everything about the memorial "is part of a text." Indeed, the memorial itself seems to resemble a primary form of text—a book. He echoes the point that the *New Yorker* had made in its review of the memorial—that the hinge connecting the two walls makes it look like "a huge open book with black pages," a "book of the dead," as Danto poignantly adds. It is a book, though, with the capacity to express more than is inscribed into it. Danto argues that even the "determination to say nothing political is inscribed by the absence of a political statement." Here, then, is a text (literally, metaphorically) filled with absent signifiers. How could one not feel invited to use the terms of modern French theory? Moreover, the shiny black walls with the names etched in them act as a kind of mirror, since they reflect the face of the reader in the very act of reading the etched names. Consider the possible meanings in this mirror effect between the living and the dead, this interplay between those who read and those whose names are read. In less sensitive hands, this might provide an opportunity to do more theorizing about the reflected relationship between the reader and the text. To his credit, Danto does not. The memorial represents a disjuncture that inspires Danto to resort to older, Platonic terms. Soberly, he notes that "the living are in it only as appearances. Only the names of the dead, on the surface, are real." In this text, there is something real.

Danto ends on two points that are implicit in his gorgeous opening distinction of the different ways stones speak to us: "We erect monuments so that we shall always remember, and build memorials so that we shall never forget." The first point he makes is that the memorial is profoundly an emotional work. "Be prepared to weep," he instructs his audience. "Tears are the universal experience even if you don't know any of the dead." His second point is that this memorial, like a book, will change over time. Someday, it will be like every other war memorial whose loved ones are no longer living, where the names remain "powerful as names, and there will only be the idea of death to be moved by." As it stands now, though, "we are all moved by the reality of death, or moved by the fact that many who stand beside us are moved by its reality."[1] It is, in other words, a living memorial, in that those who see their faces reflected in the shiny black rock have a lived experience with those who names are hewn in it. What are reflected are their tearful faces, and perhaps their torn relationships.

In a piece published the following year, Charles Griswold takes up some of the points that Danto raises. He too sees the memorial's resemblance to a book, but he sees it rather as an open book whose "openness indicates that further chapters have yet to be written, and read." In other words, the memorial invites the viewer to see the Vietnam War as but one "chapter in the book of American history." Likewise, Griswold comments on how the polished black granite, which was imported from Bangalore, India, especially for its reflective quality, acts as a mirror for the viewer, who is forced to see a reflection of himself or herself as well as the reflections of the Lincoln Memorial and Washington Monument in the stone. This, in turn, makes the viewer reflective, as one is forced to ask what it means for the names to be etched on the stone, what role one has played in supporting or criticizing this war, and what role one might play in a future war. The character of the memorial, concludes Griswold, is "fundamentally interrogative." And in the questions it poses and the repose it inspires, Griswold argues, the memorial is both therapeutic and yet disquieting. Its "therapy depends on an understanding of certain overreaching values," while it is disquieting because it does not necessarily affirm those values.[2]

Griswold spends a fair portion of his essay situating the memorial in its immediate context, showing how it physically comments on and refracts the other monuments on the Mall, how it alters the ways we can read more traditional statuary of war heroism, and how it enhances and raises questions about the war veterans whose lives it is memorializing. He concludes that there is an informative tension between the "overreaching values" on which the memorial's "therapeutic potential" rests and the places where we might find those values. In the end, like the viewer, the values turn out to be reflected on the surface of the granite—as are the Washington Monument and the Lincoln Memorial—but they are perhaps only reflected, not etched like the names of those who sacrificed themselves for those values. Griswold, like Danto, notes that the memorial is "an extraordinarily moving monument," but one, he adds, that "demands the detachment of thought from emotions."[3]

Martha Nussbaum is the most recent American philosopher to comment on the Vietnam Veterans Memorial. Given her book's focus on "political emotions," it is not surprising that Nussbaum picks up on the emotional content that Danto observes and is troubled by what she sees as Griswold's insistence that the contemplative interrogation the memorial inspires is "fundamentally detached and unemotional." For her, it is profoundly emotional. Nussbaum approaches the Vietnam Veterans Memorial as what she calls a "Socratic work"—that is, a work of public art that invites "deliberative" responses, including "calm critical conversation" and "ambivalent emotions." These are public works of art that are not meant to rouse uncritical patriotic emotions or embody tenaciously held but cool principles like, say, justice. Instead, a Socratic work of public art expresses the complexity, and invites viewers to appreciate the complexity, of the people or events it memorializes.

Nussbaum notes that the Vietnam Veterans Memorial does just that, bringing people together in an act of communal mourning in a "contemplative space." It is unlike a church or a temple, because it is not a sectarian place for mourning but a truly ecumenical and communal one in which the "community" is constituted of any and all who wish to enter. She concludes that the best analogy to the memorial is an Athenian tragedy, because the memorial, like a play by Euripides, say, summons "powerful emotions" and at the same time poses "questions about the events connected to these emotions." So the memorial, then, does the serial work of appealing to "personal grief and detached critical reflection," and then, working through those, it "leads people toward an experience of reconciliation and shared grief."[4]

Almost a quarter century after he first wrote about it, Griswold returns to the Vietnam Veterans Memorial at the end of his book *Forgiveness*. He takes up and revises his earlier reading of the memorial, this time to see in which ways the "Memorial seeks to bring about civic reconciliation by correcting the record and through public recognition." He then pointedly asks whether it accomplishes that goal. In other words, can the Memorial do what political apology is supposed to do—make reconciliation possible? Is it, in his phrase, a monument affirming "reconciliation without apology"? That it is meant to be and has proven therapeutic is without doubt. Almost everyone associated with the memorial expressed this focus on healing, and healing in many different ways—on the idea that this work in stone would generate comfort for individuals, produce reconciliation for communities, and promote acceptance in a nation. The designer Lin said in an interview that her hope for the memorial was that it would "bring out in people the realization of loss and a cathartic healing process." The book authored by the founder of the Vietnam Veterans Memorial, which gives an account of how it came to be, is entitled *To Heal a Nation*. The National Parks Service refers to the memorial as "The Wall That Heals." And so Griswold does not doubt that it inspires what he calls "reconciliatory therapy."[5]

His point is whether it should. Should it do the work of political apology, without actually doing the *work*? He points out the pregnant silences in the memorial. The Vietnam Veterans Memorial Fund had explicitly set rules that the memorial must contain no political content. Griswold notes that there is, for instance, no mention of the millions of Vietnamese killed in the war. (Here, one can see the implications that would have been involved in the statue of the Vietnamese baby in the Women's Memorial: It would either have warmed the viewer's heart to see an American caring for the innocent baby or alerted the viewer to how America orphaned a nation.) What is also absent in the memorial, Griswold continues, are the questions about responsibility and justice. This is a work that placates through evasion. The "therapeutic reconciliation" it strives for is "built on a blend of truth, minimal assertion," an "invitation to reflection, and deliberative silence." What is needed, he concludes, is something else: a political apology that addresses precisely those questions that the memorial inspires: about responsibility, justice, and wrong. The memorial cannot replace that more discursive and explicit acknowledgment. When the powerful "apologize when apology is due," concludes Griswold, there is a possibility for genuine reconciliation and authentic healing; "without apology for injuries done," there is "no future worth hoping for."[6] The memorial for Griswold raises problems that it cannot resolve.

We have, then, what appear to be two irreconcilable readings—one arguing that the memorial is trying to do something that another kind of work can better undertake (the political apology), the other arguing that it does precisely the kind of work that is called for (reconciliation through shared grieving). I do not believe that these two readings are, in fact, incommensurable. Indeed, there does seem to be an intimate connection between stone memorials and efforts at establishing reconciliation through the apology-forgiveness dynamic. When Archbishop Desmond Tutu addressed the first National Conference on Forgiveness in 1995, he implied that there was an important connection between what the conference was doing—exploring the "ramifications of forgiveness for personal life, for community life, for national life"—and the memorial that the Japanese erected to commemorate Hiroshima.[7] Presumably, forgiveness can do the work in our hearts that a memorial does for a national space—attest to something's having happened without allowing it to stall the emotional life of people or nations.

Likewise, in *Gather at the Table*, an account of a journey of reconciliation undertaken by what the title calls "a daughter of slavery and a son of the slave trade," Thomas Norman DeWolf and Sharon Leslie Morgan conclude their journey in the shadow of the Reconciliation Triangle memorial statue in Richmond, Virginia. It is one of three identical statues situated at each corner of the triangular transatlantic slave trade: The other two are in Liverpool, England, and Benin. As they sit under the fifteen-foot-tall bronze sculpture that depicts "two people embracing," which they read as "symbolizing apology and reconciliation for slavery," DeWolf and Morgan follow suit and apologize to each other for whatever pain their harsh words during the journey have caused. And it would appear that it is precisely this sense of atonement that some people seek in memorials. The point of Berlin's Memorial to the Murdered Jews of Europe, writes the philosopher Avishai Margalit, "should be an effort by the German people to reestablish themselves as an ethical community, encumbered with painful shared memories." Such a memorial, he concludes, might be capable of transforming historical "cruelty" into "repentance."[8] And so it would seem that there is some connection between memorials and heartfelt forgiveness, between the stones that do not weep and the people who do. To see that connection more clearly and deeply, let us return to two key moments in German postwar history.

President Richard von Weizsäcker's May 8, 1985, speech to the Bundestag has been hailed as one of the landmark statements of a nation's taking account of its history, of a state's taking responsibility for its past. It is even more remarkable when we consider the immediate historical context in which it was delivered and the longer, familial past of the person who delivered it. It was delivered three days after President Ronald Reagan and Chancellor Helmut Kohl had visited the Kolmeshöhe cemetery near Bitburg, Germany. What had originally been arranged as a ceremony of two national leaders demonstrating reconciliation between former war foes turned instead into a large-scale international debate once it was discovered that forty-nine members of the Waffen-SS were buried in the cemetery. A majority of the House and of the Senate signed a letter urging Chancellor Kohl to withdraw his invitation, and many advocates, most notably Elie Wiesel in a White House ceremony, exhorted the president not to visit the cemetery. Meanwhile, Chancellor Kohl became more truculent, stating in a *New York Times* interview that the German people would be deeply offended if the ceremony were cancelled. In the end, a compromise plan was arranged: Reagan and Kohl would visit the concentration camp site at Bergen-Belsen as well as the Kolmeshöhe cemetery in Bitburg. (Reagan had originally ruled out a visit to a concentration camp site because he feared it would "reawaken the passions of the time.")[9] After an acrimonious, tumultuous, international debate that revealed just how awake those passions already were, and three days after the much-anticipated visit to Bitburg on May 5, von Weizsäcker delivered his speech.

At the time he delivered his speech, von Weizsäcker had been president of the Federal Republic of Germany for less than a year, and prior to that he had been governing mayor of West Berlin for three years. His political genealogy, then, was fairly standard. What gave his speech more authority was his actual genealogy. Von Weizsäcker was the son of Ernest von Weizsäcker, who had been in the German diplomatic corps, rising to become ambassador to Bern and then ambassador to the Vatican during the National Socialist era. After the war, the elder von Weizsäcker was arrested and tried at Nuremberg as part of the Ministries Trials. He was found guilty, sentenced to seven years' imprisonment, and served eighteen months before being granted amnesty. His son, Richard, then in law school in Göttingen, came to Nuremberg and joined his father's defense team as an assistant. Nuremberg gave the younger von Weizsäcker what he considered a thorough education in "contemporary history." What he learned about the happenings in the Germany for which his father was an ambassador, and he a young soldier in the Russian front, haunted him. After his May 8, 1985, speech, he said he received a lot of rebuke from German people who claimed that they did not deserve the responsibility he placed on them because they had not known what was being done in their name. What he learned during his father's trial at Nuremberg made him skeptical and revealed to him just how easy it was for citizens to look the other way, to be silent and unquestioning, and, in a memorable phrase of his, "to let a pliable conscience be distracted."[10] What von Weizsäcker learned at Nuremberg, what he saw in the spectacle around Bitburg, informed his attitude toward the history that he addressed in his May 8 speech.

The May 8 speech was a resounding success in Germany and around the world. The president's office received sixty thousand mostly laudatory letters and telegrams. The Israeli ambassador to Bonn called it a "moment of glory" in German-Israeli relations. A government agency produced an initial print run of 250,000 copies of the speech to distribute to schools.[11] The speech exemplified just what made a French journalist comment in *Le Monde* that the Germans were "unsurpassed both at the crime and at repenting it." What made that speech possible, though, in some ways, was something that had happened fifteen years earlier, when another governing mayor of West Berlin had performed a similar act of penitence that had likewise broken new ground in the postwar world.

On December 7, 1970, Chancellor Willy Brandt visited Warsaw, Poland, to sign a treaty that would supplement the treaty he had just signed with Moscow. The Treaty of Warsaw was deeply important because it acknowledged the Allied-imposed Oder-Neisse Line as defining the western border of Poland and the eastern border of the Federal Republic of Germany. In effect, in this treaty the Federal Republic of Germany accepted the loss of what had traditionally been German territory prior to World War II; this loss, and the acceptance of it, constituted an extremely sore point in German politics. In his speech at the signing ceremony, Brandt stated: "My government accepts the lessons of history." He saw this treaty as ending one particular course history had taken and commemorating it: "The Warsaw Agreement," he concluded, "shall be the symbolic end of sufferings and sacrifices of an evil past." In addition to signing the treaty on that day, Brandt had two wreath-laying ceremonies scheduled for his official visit. The first was at the grave of the Unknown German Soldier, and the second was at the Monument to the Ghetto Heroes, a structure built to commemorate the Jewish victims of the Warsaw Ghetto uprising in 1943. During the whole trip through Poland, he had been haunted by thoughts of the "victims of violence and treachery," and especially of the "fight to the death of the Warsaw Ghetto" that he had followed as a journalist in Stockholm during the war. As the leader of the nation that, under Adolf Hitler, had imposed such enormous suffering on Warsaw, on Poland, on what he called "six million murder victims," Brandt bore an enormous burden.[12] As he approached the Monument to the Ghetto Heroes, he suddenly and unexpectedly fell to his knees in front of it. He stayed kneeling, humbled in posture and attitude before the memorial that represented one part of the crimes the country he represented had committed more than a quarter century before.

What came to be called the *kniefall* represented a crucial moment in European history and politics, and attitudes toward that history and politics. One historian calls this episode the "beginning of the contemporary German attitude to the Holocaust" as well as the "first rupture in the Cold War." Another writer, a political scientist, refers to it as "not only a turning point in the transformation of German-Polish relations after the War, but a catalyst in reshaping Eastern European politics more generally."[13] It was indeed a defining moment in Brandt's *Ostpolitik*, his approach to détente with the East that changed the course of West German politics that had reigned under Konrad Adenauer's long, conservative rule. The gesture was initially met with somewhat mixed reactions. The next week, the German magazine *Der Spiegel* ran the photograph of the kneeling Brandt on its cover and reported from a poll of five hundred German citizens that 48 percent had felt it exaggerated (*übertrieben*), and 41 percent appropriate (*angemessen*). Nonetheless, it quickly became and remained a defining moment in European political culture. The following year, the Norwegian Nobel Committee awarded Brandt the Nobel Peace Prize for his work at reconciliation, and the presenter highlighted that moment when Brandt "knelt at the foot of the Jewish monument" as a symbol of his sincere attempt to "bury hatred" and "seek reconciliation across the mass graves of war."[14]

Here, then, were two iconic moments in the careers of two important German politicians, each at one time governing mayor of West Berlin—Brandt when Nikita Khrushchev erected the Berlin Wall in 1961, and von Weizsäcker shortly before that wall came down. These two men had quite different war experiences, each of which nonetheless gave him a distinctive claim to authority for expressing responsibility. Brandt had fled Germany as a nineteen-year-old and spent the war years as a journalist in Sweden. He was stripped of his German citizenship and regained it only in 1948. During the war, he traveled to Germany at great personal risk and reported what was happening. He was, then, part of the European Resistance movement. Von Weizsäcker served seven years in the German Army, watching as his brother was shot and died in his arms, learning to hate the leader in whose army he served, and participating, finally, in a covert way in one of the failed plots to assassinate Hitler. One had the authority of distance, the other the authority of proximity. One could be penitent because he was not personally guilty, the other because he was in some uneasy way associated with those who had been found guilty.

What, then, can we make of these two gestures—one a speech, the other an act? Most careful readers of von Weizsäcker's speech have noted that he does not apologize nor ask for forgiveness, and some have pointed out how inappropriate it would have been for him to have done so. At an event four years later at the Union Theological Seminary in New York, Donald Shriver asked him whether forgiveness had any place in politics. Von Weizsäcker was skeptical, believing, as he put it, that it would be pretentious "to think that we can ask forgiveness for the sins of nations." Shriver did not fully agree. He argued that if "the von Weizsäcker speech is not a demonstration of the relevance of forgiveness to politics, it is nonetheless a powerful example of the relevance of public *repentance* to politics" (emphasis original).[15] It was a speech, Shriver believed, that exemplified and contained all the necessary elements of a political *apology*. And that is what many commentators, including Aaron Lazare in his book *On Apology* and Alexis Dudden in her book *Troubled Apologies*, call it: von Weizsäcker's apology.[16]

Brandt's gesture has also been widely recognized as an act of apology. Writers everywhere have hailed it as unassailably an apology, and indeed, for some, arguably the founding event in the emergence of the political apology. I think it is worth citing some of these commentaries, since they come from all over the world, which suggests to me, anyway, that this symbolic act registered in the same way across a range of different cultural traditions. One German commentator calls it the moment when "morality became a political force." An Australian notes that this "simple gesture of repentance" provided a model for later "political apologies," while an American calls it "perhaps the most famous act of contrition in the world, then or since." An Ethiopian calls Brandt's "bold and unprecedented" *kniefall* an "apologetic gesture" that remains a "lasting image of public contrition in modern times." A Canadian comments that Brandt's act had a "cathartic effect by officially associating the German state with the process of atonement." And, finally, a Dutch writer states that Brandt's *kniefall* was intended "to apologize for what the Nazis had done." It is, perhaps, worth adding that von Weizsäcker also thought of it as an act of atonement, referring to it as Brandt's "public apology at the Warsaw Ghetto" that was effective precisely because Brandt "removed any contradictions between power and morality."[17]

Each of these gestures, then, has been understood as an apology—although one does not contain the word "apologize," and the other contains no words at all. This is a curious thing that might reveal more about the intellectual predilections of our guilted age than it reveals about what precisely those two gestures might be and mean. Let us take up von Weizsäcker's speech first. It holds the place it holds and is understood in the terms in which it is cast—that is, as a political apology—I think precisely because of the context in which it was delivered: three days after the visits of Reagan and Kohl to Bitburg and Bergen-Belsen, and in the midst of a rancorous debate about what it means to remember or forget the past. That context is crucial, and we need briefly to see how the events around "Bitburg" unfolded.

The White House added the Bergen-Belsen visit to the president's itinerary because of the uproar about his visiting a cemetery with SS soldiers buried in it. The thinking, I imagine, was that the visit to a site more sacred to victims would put to right the visit to a site now associated with the victimizers. Of course, it unfortunately reminded many people of the already profoundly problematic connection the president had made in his earlier press conference, defending his decision to visit the cemetery near Bitburg where German soldiers were buried. In a question-and-answer session with the press about three weeks before the visit, Reagan stated that he believed that "there's nothing wrong with visiting that cemetery where those young men" are buried since they are "victims of Nazism also," he concluded, "just as surely as the victims in the concentration camps."[18] As numerous commentators noted, this was not just a sign of the president's frail grasp of history; it was profoundly an affront to the meanings of responsibility and of politics. But now the connections were in place. Reagan would visit two places associated with death—one where the soldiers were supposed to rest in peace under their individual gravestones, and one where the victims were mercilessly killed and buried in mass piles.

The White House, in other words, wanted to make an equation between how Reagan would honor both the Germans and the Jews, but that equation was precisely the problem. How could someone visit a concentration camp and then the gravesite of SS soldiers on the same day? asked Wiesel. That was a journey, he thought, that should take centuries. And so the association was made between the two sites that were otherwise dissimilar in every way.

That association affected the symbolism that the original visit was supposed to accomplish—that is, to represent the reconciliation between the United States and Germany forty years after the war. But the visit to Bergen-Belsen, of course, could not be part of that moral itinerary; it had to symbolize a very different kind of thing—namely, remembrance—which, in this case, was at odds with reconciliation. The one visit, then, was to commemorate, the other to reconcile. But what that second visit to Bitburg, the visit intended to reconcile, came to mean to many people was something else: It came to signify forgiveness.

In a *Time* editorial entitled "Forgiveness to the Injured Doth Belong," Lance Morrow makes the point that Reagan's visit to Bitburg "left an impression that the President of the U.S. was conferring a sort of official forgiveness upon the German army that did Hitler's work." And that is how the visit registered for many who protested it. A man who had survived the war by fleeing to Amsterdam wore a sandwich board outside the cemetery that read: "God, do not forgive them. They knew what they were doing." His daughter wore an identical one, with the same phrase Abe Rosenthal had made famous in a 1965 article on the twenty-fifth anniversary of the creation of the Warsaw Ghetto. The terms "them" and "they" clearly referred to the soldiers who committed the crimes, but they probably also included the chancellor and the president whose visit—giving the impression of forgiveness—in the face of outrage was also an act of those who knew "what they were doing." A concentration camp survivor wrote to Reagan to register her resistance to his visit to Bitburg: "Mr. President, you have no right to forgive in our names." An editorial in the *Jerusalem Post* made the same point about Reagan's visit to the Bergen-Belsen concentration camp: "Do not drag our dead into your reconciliation with Kohl's Germany."[19]

It is in this immediate context, I believe, that we can best appreciate just why von Weizsäcker's speech came to mean what it does. It is widely thought to represent a political apology, I think, *because* the Bitburg visit was perceived to be an act of political forgiveness. Let us now return to that speech and see what it might reveal. As I have noted, the words of apology appear nowhere in the text. And, for many, that lack is a big part of what makes the speech effective. We can compare it with one that does and see the difference. On the same day that von Weizsäcker spoke to the Bundestag, Joseph Höffner, the cardinal of Cologne, delivered a radio broadcast sermon to commemorate the fortieth anniversary of May 8, 1945. Like von Weizsäcker, Höffner enumerates the Nazi crimes in detail, but unlike the president, the cardinal concludes his sermon with a call for forgiveness: "We should not, again and again, exhume past guilt and mutually committed injustices, in constant self-torment. We should not constantly weigh guilt against guilt and use it as a weapon, one against the other. All guilt is abolished in the mercy of Jesus Christ, who taught us the prayer: 'Forgive us our sins, as we forgive those who sin against us.'"[20] The speech accepts responsibility with clarity and commitment; the sermon is unclear about what is buried (exhumed) or not, and, more troubling, just what "mutually committed injustices" he might be talking about. What "guilt," "what injustices" are being equated between those who sinned and those who were sinned against? As discussed in Chapter 4, one of the dynamic features of apologies and forgiveness in the interpersonal sphere is that they often work by this kind of exchange: "I am sorry for what I did." "Yes, that is okay; I was not entirely guiltless myself." That works fine for individuals; it does not work at all when the subject of forgiveness is the Holocaust or slavery. And so von Weizsäcker showed supreme wisdom in restraining himself and focusing on the issue of responsibility rather than on resolution.

That is not to say that von Weizsäcker did not wish for resolution. He did, but he did not want it to come in the form of cheap grace. He realized that it was a process that would emerge from a series of different kinds of acts, beginning, as he recognized, with acknowledgment of responsibility. We can turn to a telling comment he made about the ceremony at Bitburg. Before it was botched by the White House's poor research and then poorer public relations work, von Weizsäcker believed that the ceremony provided just that sort of possibility, precisely because of the setting in which it would occur: "A cemetery is surely a suitable site for marking an end to discord and persecution," he noted.[21] What makes it suitable, of course, is that it is a place to bury—in this case, to bury past grievances and enmities. But what I think von Weizsäcker had even more in mind was that cemeteries are also places to *mourn*. And that, I believe, is the key to understanding his speech.

While von Weizsäcker's May 8 speech is especially notable for its accounting and apportioning of responsibility, and its acceptance of the sins of the fathers, it is also a speech that focuses intently on particular acts of emotional remembrance. The speech opens by noting that the meaning of May 8 differs for different nations. Most celebrate it as a day of liberation, which it is also for Germans, but it is additionally for Germans a day of reflection. That reflection takes two forms in particular. One recognizes the continuity of history. He notes: "We must not separate 8 May 1945 from 30 January 1933." We cannot celebrate the end without seeing the beginning of the war in the rise of Hitler and National Socialism. He likewise punctuates his speech with two key terms in German war memory to recast them. He claims at one point, "It is not a case of coming to terms with the past. That is not possible."

And then, at another point, he states: "There was no 'zero hour.'" These two phrases—"coming to terms with the past" (*Vergangenheitsbewältigung*) and "zero hour" (*Stunde Null*)—are crucial parts of the German lexicon on the war. One connotes healing, and the other starting over. Indeed, "zero hour," which used to be a military term to designate the beginning of a campaign before it assumed its current meaning of the moment of German surrender at midnight on May 8, 1945, connotes a forgetting of the past, a wiping clean of the slate, an act something like forgiveness.[22] And so what von Weizsäcker is doing, specifically, is challenging both forms of disengaging from history. He dispels the desire for discontinuity in the German imaginary. There is no moment when history begins anew, and there is no simple healing of the historical wounds. This insistence on the continuity of history is an important point on which von Weizsäcker's bases his concluding comments about the legacy of responsibility for the generations who came after the war.

The second form that the reflection takes is to remember—which, of course, is the opposite course of action of thinking discontinuity possible. "May 8 is a day of remembrance," he intones. "Remembering means recalling an occurrence honestly and undistortedly so that it becomes a part of our very beings." And throughout that section near the beginning of his speech, he repeatedly employs a sequence of four verbs that are meant to become interchangeable: "Today we mourn. . . . [W]e commemorate. . . . We commemorate. . . . [W]e mourn. . . . We recall. . . . [W]e pay homage." It is especially that opening sequence of "mourn" and "commemorate" that alerts us to von Weizsäcker's strategy of making recollection an act of mourning and mourning an act of recollection. "Today," he says at the end of a litany of war crimes, "we sorrowfully recall all this human suffering." And that sorrow is not penitence, although there is obviously a hint of that involved, but primarily grief. Once he has made that intimate connection between the act of commemorating and the act of mourning, the rest of the speech assumes the quality of an elegy. It expresses and embodies mourning. He not only expresses grief as well as guilt but also notes that this act of remembering so powerful and honest that the memory "becomes part of our very beings" is a monumental, memorial act. As he concludes one especially moving section in his speech: "We must erect a memorial to thoughts and feelings in our own hearts."[23]

What von Weizsäcker is doing, then, is memorializing the events and people and suffering, but not necessarily and certainly not explicitly expressing penitence for them, at least not in the sense of addressing that penitence directly to those victims. There is penitence, no doubt, but it is not directed to those harmed by the atrocities. Unlike Cardinal Höffner, President von Weizsäcker does not mention forgiveness. He sees it as a possibility, certainly, and he mentions how it occurs in different spheres governed by religious principles and conducted at levels well below the national. He mentions one act only in his speech about such penitence when he refers to the "*Aktion Sühnezeichen*"—that is, a "campaign in which young people carry out atonement activity in Poland and Israel"—as a way of promoting "reconciliation" and "understanding." It is individual citizens who do it, under the auspices of their churches, and it is the "young," not those who committed the crimes but those who remain in some way responsible for them, who express that penitence. So von Weizsäcker hints at apology and forgiveness far in the distant horizon and by differently situated generations. We can compare this sensibility with a comment Chancellor Kohl had made two weeks earlier at an event commemorating the fortieth anniversary of the liberation of Bergen-Belsen. We are summoned to this event, he said, "to mourn, to remember, to seek reconciliation."[24] Here, too, is the profound connection between remembering and mourning, but also we see the unseemly haste with which Kohl seeks immediate "reconciliation." Wisely, von Weizsäcker prophesies reconciliation while focusing primarily on *mourning*.

And in this, I think, he was most emphatically following the example of his fellow governing mayor of West Berlin, Brandt, whose *kniefall*, long considered the founding act of the political apology, seems to indicate something more than penitence. Undoubtedly, in that moment before the Monument to the Ghetto Heroes, Brandt was contrite and penitent. He had already begun the process of reassessing German responsibility for the war when he had addressed the Bundestag in uncompromising terms and stated plainly that German suffering during the war was a result of German aggression. Germany, Brandt stated, had committed "criminal activities for which there is no parallel in modern history" and "had disgraced the German name in all the world."[25] But was this moment in Warsaw an apology for those criminal activities? Standing in front of a memorial that attested to the truth of his earlier words, Brandt did not attempt to apologize for the crimes he had already acknowledged. Instead, he performed, apparently unscripted, an act of grief in the face of unspeakable horror. In his 1992 autobiography, he quotes a contemporary newspaper account that describes the event: "Then he knelt, he who had no need to do so, for all those who should have knelt, but did not do so—either because they did not dare to, or could not, or could not dare to." In his own words, Brandt says that faced with the "burden of millions of victims of murder," he "did what human beings do when speech fails them." In his memoirs, he does not call it an apology. In interviews following the publication of his memoirs, he begins to describe it in fuller terms and moves toward the language of apology. In 1993, *The Guardian* quotes him:

"I wanted on behalf of our people to ask for pardon for the terrible crime that was carried out in Germany's misused name." In a documentary that aired around the same time, he is even more explicit: "All I could do was give a sign to ask for forgiveness for my people and pray that we might be forgiven."[26]

It may have been an apology, a silent apology, but was it *only* that? We can be misled, I think, if we do not look at it in the range of contexts within which it took place. We have already noted the political context: It was part of Brandt's *Ostpolitik*, his attempt to achieve reconciliation with Eastern Europe, even as West Germany retained its NATO ties to the West. It was a symbol of acceptance of Germany's war crimes and also an acceptance of the consequences of those war crimes—that is, what the Warsaw Treaty had just ratified, the loss of formerly German territory. But the most important context, I suggest, is just where it took place: at a ceremony commemorating the *war dead*, and not those who died fighting for their country (the grave of the Unknown Soldier), but those who died fighting for their lives and their people, those who were the victims of the known and unknown soldiers. After the flower wreath was laid at the base of the memorial, Brandt bent down, straightened out the ribbons on the wreath, stood back up, and then knelt. Having laid down and ensured the proper presentation of the traditional symbol of mourning—the wreath—he knelt in the traditional symbol of mourning: humility before death.

What I am suggesting, then, is that what Brandt in 1970 and von Weizsäcker in 1985 did is not so much *apologize* for the crimes of their nation (again, one did not use the word at all, and the other was silent) as *mourn* for the loss of those against whom those crimes were committed. Or, perhaps, we can better say that what has been received as an apology was expressed as an act of mourning. And that is significant, I think, for what it reveals about these leaders as representatives of Germany. Brandt's and von Weizsäcker's acts of mourning served to represent to their nations, of which they were respectively the political and symbolic representatives as chancellor and president, what they considered the appropriate response to the histories embodied in their polity. In mourning, they performed what they urged the nation to do. And that is important in the case of Germany, especially, since their actions countered another German condition associated with "coming to terms with the past" and the concept of "zero hour"—what was diagnosed as a national incapacity to grieve.

Ian Buruma tells a wonderful story about Oskar Matzerath, who had formed a jazz band shortly after World War II. In 1949, he and his band landed a gig at a nightclub near Düsseldorf called the Onion Cellar. As the band began its repertoire by playing ragtime, each patron of the nightclub was given an onion, a chopping board, and a paring knife. As Matzerath tells it, the point was for the patrons to chop the onions as they listened to the music. The onion "brought forth a round human tear. It made them cry. At last they were able to cry again. To cry properly, without restraint, to cry like mad." The onion permitted them to grieve, to do what Matzerath says "the world and the sorrows of the world could not do"—to heal them temporarily of their inability to mourn. In 1967, the German psychoanalyst husband-and-wife team Alexander and Margarete Mitscherlich published what Tony Judt calls a "hugely influential" book that diagnoses that very condition, entitled *The Inability to Mourn* (*Die Unfähigkeit zu trauen*). The book became a bestseller in Germany, with one hundred thousand copies sold almost immediately and passages from it incorporated into school textbooks.[27]

The Mitscherlichs' argument is that the fall of Hitler and National Socialism had incapacitated the nation's emotional resources for two generations. And what they diagnose as the nation's "inability to mourn" is accompanied by, and a result of, the nation's inability to accept and process its sense of guilt. The older generation continued to ward off "real guilt," while the younger proved unwilling "to get caught up in the guilt problems of their parents." The nation's eagerness to place all responsibility on Hitler and assume none that came with following him amounted to an extreme case of denial, upon which followed a repressed feeling of guilt, which, because it went unexpressed, eventually led to the inability to mourn properly. Following Sigmund Freud, the Mitscherlichs distinguish between mourning—which is a process of healing—and melancholia, which is not because it involves "an extraordinary diminution in [the melancholic's] self-regard, an impoverishment of his ego on a grand scale." They do not go so far as to say that Germany has become melancholic, but they do insist that the failure to accept responsibility and acknowledge "our collective guilt" has produced stagnation and rendered impossible any "genuinely felt reconciliation with our former enemies." As A. Roy Eckardt puts it, the "inability to mourn" is "dialectically-existentially linked with the inability to repent."[28]

Had Germany accepted responsibility and guilt and expressed penitence, and then been able to mourn, the Mitscherlichs argue, there would have been a process of healing: "It is in the nature of mourning that in the course of time it fades and one learns to bear the loss one has suffered without forgetting it." That did not happen, however, and therefore "in Germany the impression remains that remembrance of the German war dead is kept alive less out of reverence than as a means of apportioning blame."[29] In other words, the war dead become simply another weapon in the ongoing war of memory. If so, then that would certainly explain some of the dynamic of the

Bitburg controversy, where the battle was literally over the apportioning of blame right over their remains. What could have been a moment of penitence and reconciliation became instead a fight over the meaning of the war dead.

The Mitscherlichs published their book in 1967, and so Brandt's *kniefall* is not part of their original study of atonement and mourning. They do mention him in the text once: They note that during the 1965 Bundestag elections, vicious rumors circulated that after leaving Germany, Brandt had served in the Norwegian Army and "perhaps even fired on his fellow Germans." Even though it was untrue, and recognized immediately as being libelous, the rumor went relatively undisputed. Even members of Brandt's own party did not dare to "show it up for the scurrility it was." Part of the reason, the Mitscherlichs argue, is that, if true, Brandt's actions would have shown the nation that there was an alternative political course of action—that resistance to Hitler was possible. Instead, German politicians and voters denied this possibility and then felt "resentful of Brandt's greater guiltlessness."[30]

When the English translation of their book came out in an American edition in 1975, the Mitscherlichs did not revise the text, but they did add several footnotes that address the developments since the first German edition was published eight years earlier. In these new footnotes, the Mitscherlichs comment on Brandt's 1970 *kniefall*, which they describe in three different ways. They see it first as an act of humility: "This act provided an ineradicable counterweight to centuries of German arrogance in its encounters with a neighboring people." In bowing down before another nation's memorial, Brandt humbled himself and the nation he represented. They also see it as an acknowledgment of a particular history. In their psychoanalytic terms, Brandt "recalled" the war crimes to "consciousness by falling on his knees in Warsaw" and therefore "made impossible" the "*denial* of the past" (emphasis original). With humility comes the ability to see clearly what has been repressed, and with acknowledgment of what has previously been denied comes the strength of mind and purpose to accept responsibility and guilt. That is their third point: "Brandt showed that he no longer intended to deny the suffering which for generations the policies of Germany had inflicted on her Eastern neighbor; with this symbolic gesture he accepted the guilt."[31] What they do not say is that Brandt does all this in one act of mourning, and I think they do not say it because it is obvious to them, in a book entitled *The Inability to Mourn*, that what Brandt has exemplified is just that—the ability to mourn. And the ability to mourn comes from, and with, the capacity to accept responsibility and guilt and to express remorse and contrition. What Brandt first, and von Weizsäcker later, accomplished, then, in the act of mourning was considerable because it represented for the nation they represented a new ability, a new attitude toward a past for which they accepted responsibility and expressed grief.

There is, obviously, some connection between mourning and apology. We see that fairly clearly in the English terms they share ("sorry" and "sorrow"); we see it too in the French *désolé*, which implies grief and desolation as well as contrition. And clearly what I am suggesting here is that acts of mourning *have been* read as acts of apology because they do express contrition, albeit expressing it in what I think is the appropriately indirect way that proved most successful. And perhaps that is what the guilted age has also demanded—an acceptance of responsibility that involves acknowledging the past and a form of atonement that shares in the grief of the loss for which that atonement is offered. Not any kind of mourning succeeds, though, both in practice and in theory. I conclude by looking at one of each type—a case of aggressive mourning in practice and a cautionary tale about excessive mourning in theory—before ending with some comments on what might be seen as the special propriety of this kind of contrite mourning.

As discussed in Chapter 3, Japan's Yasukuni Shrine has come to represent the absence of contrition. When politicians visit it, it is seen by the neighboring nations as an affront, either a repudiation of the apologies they have made or an additional sneer to their refusal to make an apology. The reason is that Yasukuni Shrine houses some of Japan's Class A war criminals, and because it represents the particular kind of Shintō practices associated with Japan's earlier ultranationalist militarism. But Yasukuni Shrine is also, of course, the place where Japan honors and mourns its war dead, its fallen soldiers, in the same way that such memorials as the Vietnam Veterans Memorial does in the United States, as the Kolmeshöhe cemetery does in Germany, and as the memorial to the Unknown Soldier does in most nations. As Philip Seaton has argued, the term *sanpai*, which is often translated as "worship" in reference to politicians' visits to Yasukuni, can be better translated as "paying one's respects to the dead."[32] It is, in other words, a site of mourning.

It is also politically contested, since it profoundly represents the Occupation and stalled process of mourning in Japan. If Germany had "an inability to mourn" because of denial, Japan had the same inability because it was denied the opportunity. Just four days after the end of the Allied-led Occupation, on May 2, 1952, the prime minister of Japan, Yoshida Shigeru, and his government organized a national memorial service to honor the war dead. Six months later, on October 16, Emperor Hirohito worshipped at Yasukuni Shrine, the second time he had done so since his visit on November

20, 1945. Less than a month after that 1945 visit, Supreme Commander for the Allied Powers (SCAP) had issued the Shintō directive that separated church and state. What both events had in common is that they marked the beginning of a new phase in post-Occupation Japan, and that phase involved mourning. On August 15, 1963, Japan celebrated the first National Ceremony for the Commemoration of the War Dead. It was at later iterations of this event that Prime Minister Morihiro Hosokawa and Prime Minister Tomiichi Murayama, in 1993 and 1995, respectively, offered their condolences for the dead of Japan's victims as well as Japan's soldiers[33] by making this commemoration about not solely Japan's dead but the war dead throughout Asia. What they did, in other words, is make the mourning more comprehensive by framing it in an act of atonement. That succeeded, to an extent, but acts by previous and future premiers of Japan have reinvested Yasukuni Shrine with the earlier militarist meaning that it had somewhat shed in those crucial political apologies. What those other prime ministers have done, I think, is mourned aggressively. They have flaunted their theatrical grieving in a way that, frankly, seems intended to antagonize rather than to express acceptance in the face of loss.

And, perhaps, that is another distinguishing feature between political apologies in Japan and Germany. In Japan, the acts of public mourning have been largely seen as pugnacious. The Japanese politicians who visit Yasukuni Shrine do so defiantly, and this act of mourning, if that is what it is, is wholly lost in the announced and recorded visits. The German politicians who grieve publicly in places as different as Warsaw and Bitburg—the former with considerably more success than the latter—do so mournfully and with what is read as an intent to appease those to whom they *offer their mourning as their apology*. That, I believe, is what makes Brandt's *kniefall* and von Weizsäcker's speech so powerful and celebrated. It is not that they are just political apologies; it is that they are also something more. They are acts of grief.

Acts of mourning can also be vague, sometimes meaningfully so, and sometimes dangerously so. For instance, three presidents of France—Charles de Gaulle, Valéry Giscard d'Estaing, and François Mitterand—each ordered the prefect of the Vendée to place flowers on the grave of Marshal Philippe Pétain on the Isle of Yeu. De Gaulle had ordered it on November 11, 1968; d'Estaing on November 11, 1978; and Mitterand on September 22, 1984. The first two acts were commemorations on the sixtieth and seventieth anniversaries of the signing of the armistice, and they were intended to place Pétain firmly in the public mind as the hero of World War I and not as the leader of the Vichy regime and a collaborator. These were clearly acts of reclamation, of leaders who wanted very much to maintain the myth of France as a nation that had largely resisted instead of capitulated to the Third Reich. Even those who clearly had capitulated, who had created Vichy, had been heroic in an earlier era, and it was that earlier era and heroism that these commemorative acts of symbolic mourning were meant to invoke. Mitterand's act was not so simple. It was ordered on the same day that he stood holding hands with Chancellor Kohl, first at Verdun and then at two Verdun-area cemeteries at Douaumont Ossuary and Consenvoye. All of these sites and tributes were meant to remind the world of World War I: Verdun as a battle site, and the two cemeteries, one German on French soil and one where French and German soldiers from the Great War were buried together. Yet this whole ceremony, as the world also knew, was clearly a sop offered to Kohl, who had been unhappy at not being invited to the fortieth-anniversary celebrations of the Allied landings in Normandy. It was the wrong place and the wrong war, and by bringing Pétain's grave into it, Mitterand seemed to be making a strategic error. Here was the grave of a French leader who had stood with instead of up to Germany; here was a French leader standing with a German one at a grave. I suspect that for most who saw this spectacle, they remembered not Pétain, the "Lion of Verdun," but Pétain of Vichy, which is just what Mitterand was trying to avoid. It was not the first nor would it be the last time Mitterand would be haunted by the ghosts of Vichy.[34]

Of course, mourning, like the inability to mourn, can take on pathological features when it becomes indulgent and excessive. Let me offer the theoretical example to which I alluded earlier. In the lectures he delivered at Clark University in 1909, which became *Five Lectures on Psycho-Analysis*, Freud imagines two different scenarios of such excess. What should we think, he asks, of a modern Londoner "who paused today in deep melancholy before the memorial of Queen Eleanor's funeral instead of going about his business in the hurry that modern working conditions demand or instead of feeling joy over the youthful queen of his own heart?" What, in other words, can we make of someone who forgoes the present (his own living queen) because of a morose attachment to the distant past (the queen who has been buried six hundred years)? In the second scenario, Freud asks: "What should we think of a Londoner who shed tears before the Monument that commemorates the reduction of his beloved metropolis to ashes although it has long since risen again in far greater brilliance?" What can we make of what Freud calls these "two impractical Londoners"? In the distinction that Danto usefully makes, is the one before the memorial doomed never to forget and the one at the foot of the monument condemned always to remember? So it would appear, and in Freud's diagnosis that makes them hysterics and neurotics: "Not only do they remember painful experiences of the remote past, but they still cling to them emotionally." This inability to "get free of the past" is pathological. Of course, as Freud most emphatically insists, what is pathological is a difference in degree, not kind, from what is healthy. And so a proper "display of mourning" is a "normal emotional process."[35]

Freud raises an interesting question for us, then, as we attempt to understand just what these displays of mourning, these practices of political and historical apology, can mean about what I am calling the guilted age. We have witnessed the uneasiness displayed by some of the people who have offered what they now took to be rote political apologies for the crimes of World War II; we have heard them comment, in the middle of the apologies, that what they are doing might be unseemly, given the passage of time, the change of generations. It has been fifty years, already, sixty, seventy. . . . When can we be "free of the past"? And when the political apology evolved into the historical apology, when people began to consider their responsibility for events that are coeval with the Great Fire of London (1666) and the death of Queen Eleanor (1290), does that holding onto the traumatic events of the distant past imply something unhealthy? Is the guilted age perhaps better described as the hysterical one? The answer, as one might imagine, depends on one's outlook. Political and historical apologies, as we have seen, have had their critics, their naysayers, their scoffers, and their parodists. And what is implied in those jocular dismissals is that the past is dead and buried. But people who otherwise differ in religion, citizenship, and political beliefs are also drawn to these practices, and they have been increasingly drawn to them since the end of World War II. Those who offer them do so because they believe that they serve a particularly acute purpose, and those who witness and sometimes accept them do so because they, too, believe that the apologies address something they need. The question raised in this chapter is whether what they need to express or hear is solely an apology, or whether it might not be something else, something more like contrite mourning.

Finally, what does this act of mourning provide for those to whom it is directed, those who witness it and understand it as an act of penitence? In the cases of Brandt and von Weizsäcker, their acts of mourning have been celebrated and acknowledged as just what was necessary, of hitting the right tone and expressing the right things in just the right conditions. And my argument is that they have been so received because they have implicitly been acts of mourning, which do a kind of work that apology by itself cannot. First, grief does not repudiate or deny responsibility, one's own as complicit or acknowledgment of an ancestor's as actual. We have seen how apology can sometimes—too often—slide into excuse, exculpation, or some other form of justification. Mourning simply does not permit that; to mourn is to accept implicitly that what is mourned was done and that the person mourning has some relationship to it.

Second, grief seeks atonement rather than forgiveness. It expresses a sorrow that reaches out for the sake of humanity rather than with the expectation of a response. As we have seen, political and historical apologies are events that are freighted and burdened with excessive anxiety precisely because they raise the question of response. And here is the dilemma: They are equally fraught whether they demand or do not demand a response of forgiveness—in the one case because they place a moral burden on the previously victimized, and in the other because they seem to be ignoring the previously victimized. By removing the question of whether forgiveness is forthcoming, by instead affirming that the only issue is an emotional expression of grief for what was lost, these acts of mourning completely bypass the question of response and often inspire it. Consider this case: On July 2, 1995, Pope John Paul II, in an unscheduled act, walked through the rain in Prešov, Slovakia, and stood silently praying in front of a monument honoring the Calvinist martyrs killed by the Catholics in the city in 1687. Later, in a general audience, John Paul II simply referred to it as a prayer, and in context it was clearly an act of mourning before the memorial. But for those present, it registered as an act of atonement. The Lutheran bishop of Prešov, Ján Midriak, told journalists, "[I am] truly grateful for this gesture; we never thought that anything like this would ever happen."[36] Ironically, then, mourning in some cases can inspire the forgiveness that historical and political apologies sometimes fail to do.

Finally, and most importantly, mourning implicitly acknowledges that what is grieved is beyond recovery. This acknowledgment constitutes a challenge to a basic premise of the apology-forgiveness dynamic, which we have seen forcefully expressed by those who hold that forgiving "serves to undo the deeds of the past." When a nation or a church offers an apology, then, it seeks to recover something, to redress in some symbolic way, the deeds of the past, to return to an older time before the damage—a "zero hour," as it were. The ultimate logic of the apology-forgiveness dynamic, then, is *undoing*. That is the most extreme manifestation of that dynamic, admittedly, but even the colloquial wisdom of "forgive and forget" urges us to put what is forgiven out of our mind. Grief, on the other hand, openly and tacitly understands the fact of irreversibility and accepts or learns to accept that some things are not recoverable and cannot be recuperated. The ultimate logic of mourning is the opposite of undoing—that is, it is remembrance. The "painful work of mourning," as Michael Roth notes in an elegant and moving essay on the ritual of shibah, expresses and represents "a way of living with the dead as the past in the present." Mourning is not "a reparation," he writes; "it is not replacing the dead but making a place for something else to be in relation to the past."[37]

Those who have been participating in the apology-forgiveness dynamic in the guilted age have clearly sought some kind of relationship to the past. In some cases, these connections to the past are more palpable than in others. Some trace their genealogy, some their congregational feeling of belonging, some their sense of citizenship to a past for which they feel responsible enough to apologize. Some likewise feel they are owed an apology because of the genealogical ties they have, and the intergenerational trauma they see helically intertwined with their DNA. In other cases, the connections are more diffuse, and the claims are admittedly more elective affinities. But the imperative is the same: to see oneself in relation to the past, not as an alien from it but as integrally an engaged product of it. And the acts of contrite mourning discussed in this chapter suggest that this particular strategy seems to work for both those who seek to apologize and those who hope to forgive.

Mourning is an act of bowing down and kneeling to the inescapable, the ineluctable, accepting what has to happen to all; in the cases of contrite mourning, it is also a way of bearing witness to the past and simply feeling the pain of a human history filled, as it is, with hurt, suffering, anguish, and horror. But mourning is also an affirmative act, a remembrance, and a quiet celebration of our ability to feel at one with those we lost; in the cases of contrite mourning, it is a testament to our capacity for being historical beings, for belonging to the past in a way that demonstrates our grief at it as past, which simultaneously and silently expresses a resolve that we will not relive that past. We have seen that the apology-forgiveness dynamic contains many divisions. To apologize is to recognize the past self that committed a wrong and the present self now able to recognize it as wrong. To forgive is to recognize a division between the person who hurt us, and the person who is penitent about hurting us. Mourning also expresses an implicit division. What is mourned is dead and buried, not in its importance and legacy but in fact. What is mourned is also alive in our memory, and therefore alive in fact.

CONCLUSION

What I have argued throughout this book is that our postwar epoch can in meaningful ways be described as a guilted age. Guilt seems to be the appropriate emotion to describe a world emerging from two global wars and a series of atrocities that required new categories of crime that recognized our barbarity (genocide, crimes against humanity) at the same time as they recognized our potential (humanity). That sense of guilt also followed a particular trajectory, both spatially and temporally. What began as specific criminal guilt among particular governments became manifest as guilt among nations and then a larger and more expansive kind of species-wide guilt, what Karl Jaspers famously calls "metaphysical guilt." At the same time, as this sense of guilt was expanding spatially from particular nations to the larger world, it began to expand temporally as it addressed and encompassed the longer past, from the political crimes that existing regimes and institutions committed in the past decades to the historical crimes past polities committed in the distant centuries. That, then, has been the trajectory of the guilted age in terms of its accounting of the past.

In response to the conditions at the dawn of the postwar world, intellectuals in the guilted age struggled to identify what struck them as an order of guilt for which we had no legal or moral precedent. The only account that seemed comparable was Adam and Eve's Fall, but the idea of casting a half century of genocide and world wars as a product of original sin seemed wholly inappropriate. What was required was not theology but political philosophy, and many intellectuals, especially Jaspers and Hannah Arendt, began to formulate conceptions of human responsibility that would describe what we as a species owed to each other, and ideas of guilt that would identify what we felt when we failed to meet those obligations. Even those who could claim no guilt at all, those who were, in fact, victims of the guilty regimes, felt implicated in the spreading guilt of the epoch. Primo Levi, for example, who was a prisoner in Auschwitz, writes that he felt "guilty at being a man, because men had built Auschwitz." The victim felt guilty at what he shared with the criminals—humanity. Elsewhere, Levi refers to what he calls the "feeling of guilt" that "the just man experiences at another man's crime." He is describing the emotions of those Russian soldiers who rescued him and the few survivors from Auschwitz. It is telling that both the heroes and the victims should feel "guilt that such a crime should exist, that it should have been introduced irrevocably into the world of things that exist."[1] Here is metaphysical guilt exemplified, and it demonstrates the dynamic of the guilted age, in which we began to assume responsibility for what others did—our immediate others and then our distant ones, our contemporaries and then our forebears.

As we approach what one suspects is the final generation of the guilted age, what might we make of the developments I have been tracing? What do these practices mean—the political apologies by nations and churches who suffer pangs of guilt for what they did and did not do during World War II, these historical apologies by individuals, congregations, parliaments, and world leaders who feel remorse for things their families, churches, and nations have done in the distant past? Each of the cases I have presented teaches us something different, I think.

In the scenes of political apology I have examined, these apologies resonate in very particular ways within a national discourse. To appreciate what a given apology by a nation atoning for its prewar colonizing of its neighbors and its wartime conduct means, we need to return to not only the events for which the apology is offered but also the larger social setting where all the terms, linguistic and cultural, are in play. An apology is part of a larger discursive universe where religious, nationalist, and cultural values are expressed, debated, and contested. In the case of Japan, that means not only the specific terms that are employed ("I regret" or "I am deeply sorry") but also the setting in which the apology is made, the historical calendar it implicitly endorses, and the political background, immediate and enduring, in which it takes place. What complicates the apologies in the case of Japan is that ultimately those to whom they have been offered believe that they can come from only one office, because the recipients have determined where responsibility lay. That case is profoundly complicated by all the politics in which it is saturated: Japan's imperial politics with its principle of divine irresponsibility,

Supreme Commander for the Allied Powers's (SCAP's) politics of how best to effect the goals of the Occupation, and the emperor's own containment politics for maintaining the empire. What we learn from that complex case, though, is that political apologies must be understood as being in dialogue with an array of other political statements in an ongoing conversation. In the model case scenario of interpersonal apology, forgiveness is granted and life goes on. In the case of political apologies, this does not happen; the apology becomes one more contestable statement in the discourse that governs relations within and beyond the nation.

In the scenes of historical apology I have presented, these apologies are offered from a range of differently situated people: executives of nations and churches, legislative bodies of states, congregants and individuals who feel connected through membership or biological descent to a church or family, and individuals who simply wish to claim and proclaim a richer, deeper, more committed sense of civic belonging. It is worth probing a little more just what is involved in that desire and how it is manifest. When citizens accept responsibility for their nation's past, I think, what they are doing is affirming that the past matters for the kind of encumbered, historically meaningful citizenship they desire. Membership, for them, requires responsibility as well as conferring privileges, and the responsibility they seek is full and not anemic in its ethics, encompassing and not constrained in its burden, capacious and not narrow in its focus. To belong somewhere is to be responsible for what happened *there*. What these historical apologies express, in the end, is precisely the kind of political and moral guilt that Jaspers identifies at the dawn of the guilted age—that is, for each of us to be responsible for what was done where we are and in our name. More, though, these historical apologies express what Jaspers calls metaphysical guilt, and what Arendt defines as "our consequent responsibility for all deeds and misdeeds committed by people different from ourselves."[2] What it bespeaks, I suggest, is not only a different conception of citizenship or congregational belonging but, even more so, a redefinition of the meaning of being in the world. What the guilted age has proposed, and what historical apologies have taken as their challenge, is how to accept a notion of guilt that requires a very different conception of identity.

When Arendt surveys that world in 1946, she sees two competing notions. One is the tradition of existentialism, which posits a Self that is inhuman. The "concept of Self," she writes, "is a concept of man that leaves the individual existing independent of humanity and representative of no one but himself." The other is the tradition of Humanity. It is expressed by Immanuel Kant, who holds that "the essence of man consisted in every human being representing all of humanity," and in the rallying call of the

French Revolution's Declaration of the Rights of Man that holds "that all of humanity could be debased or exalted in every individual." Here are two options facing the world in the wake of World War II, one in which the Self seeks "nothing but his own nothingness" and one in which Humanity actively seeks and accepts the rigorous terms of belonging. Arendt is clear; this is not a choice of accepting or denying that one is guilty because one has or has not performed the deed. The guilt is palpable and there; it is a matter of how one deals with it and how one defines one's relation to the world in that choice. The existentialist Self would make one choice: It would insist on a conception of identity premised on "the destruction in every individual of the presence of all humanity," and it would therefore devolve into what Arendt calls "the experience of guilty nothingness." The other choice, the one Arendt holds to be the true tradition of Enlightenment, would be to accept "that every human act had to bear responsibility for all of humanity."[3]

That was a hard thing to claim in 1946, after four decades of global carnage and unprecedented inhumanity. It was easier to focus, as does her teacher, Jaspers, on *The Question of German Guilt*—the question, in other words, of the more circumscribed body of one nation than the diffuse one of all of humanity. Using Arendt's terms, then, we might say that the guilted age had a choice between the guilt of nothingness and the responsibility of humanity, between retreating to a conception of limited liability or moving boldly toward a conception of expansive responsibility. What the political and historical apologies of the guilted age have accomplished, at their best, is the latter, precisely because they have insisted on a notion of responsibility that challenges the model of limited liability, precisely because they have aspired to see how we are all responsible for what was done to define what *here* was prior to our being here. "German guilt" is a good place to start, but Jaspers's point is that it is not the place to conclude, because, in the end, the guilted age that he and Arendt began to identify is also the beginning of the end for the nation-state. In an age of "crimes against humanity," in the wake of two wars that involved and wracked a whole world, the nation's borders could no longer define and contain the conception of belonging and citizenship.

It is worth exploring the profound connection between these practices of the guilted age and the fact that we are also living in a post-national era.[4] Consider the case of France. When the French Parliament passed the law belatedly identifying slavery and the slave trade as crimes against humanity, for instance, and when President Jacques Chirac apologized for the roundup at Vel d'Hiv, these statements were not meant for a French audience only. The apology for the slave trade was, in fact, meant to prepare for the Durban, South Africa, conference later that summer, an explicitly international gathering. France intended for these apologies to be overheard by other nations. In an earlier era, these kinds of commemorative events used to consist entirely of an internal dialogue within the nation where they took place—a commemoration of a French historical event on French soil, a French law passed by French legislative bodies. But in the guilted age, we see a different dynamic in which such domestic issues are being aired for a wider, global audience. Likewise, we have seen nations apologizing to other nations, in itself an international event, obviously, but these strategic apologies are also meant to be overheard by other nations. And when apologies and acknowledgments are not forthcoming within or between nations, we have seen international pressure applied to the nations involved. When Japan refused to apologize for the Korean comfort women, for example, the U.S. Congress introduced a bill that stated that it was "the sense of Congress that the Government of Japan should formally issue a clear and unambiguous apology for the sexual enslavement of young women during colonial occupation of Asia and World War II."[5] Turkey has come to represent precisely that kind of impenitence, and it has come to feel pressure from several other nations for its government to acknowledge responsibility for the Armenian genocide. Nations' consciences are no longer their own business.

Again, I would go back to 1945 to see the inauguration of the institutions that implied the possibility of an international moral order and established institutions to make it real. Both the United Nations and the International Military Tribunal were created in 1945, and both were specifically meant to address sites—international relations, law, human rights, and so on—where national sovereignty should not matter as much. There were limits to what the United Nations could do, obviously, because it was established by governments that wanted very much to guard their own sovereignty, even if it meant granting that status to nations they believed did not deserve it. It was, nonetheless, a step away from the isolationist policies of the past and toward a more global order. The guilted age has been marked precisely by even more such shifts toward making national borders immaterial. This is most marked in Europe, where the formation of the European Economic Community in 1958 eventually led to the mature European Union in 1992, and then the Schengen Agreement in 1995, through which a coalition of twenty-six countries have effectively stopped policing their territorial borders. Other parts of the world followed suit with regional economic and cultural organizations, but none with the same freedom of movement across borders as the European Union. With this development of institutions that are meant to govern nations beyond their borders, the creation of tribunals, economic organizations, and other strategies of globalization, national sovereignty has been accordingly attenuated.

The strategies of political and historical apologies, it seems to me, do not just coincide with these international developments. They seem to express something deeper. A utopic thinker might think they indicate a new social order and new global conscience that betokens the end of nationalism itself. At the dawn of the guilted age, George Orwell contemplates the dangers of nationalism in an essay he wrote in May 1945. One of the hallmarks of nationalism, writes Orwell in "Notes on Nationalism," is that it relies on denial and dishonesty about the nation's past, or what he calls "indifference to reality." "The nationalist," he notes, "not only does not disapprove of atrocities committed by his own side, but he has a remarkable capacity for not even hearing about them." They are denied, evaded, or, where necessary, simply revised. "Every nationalist believes that the past can be altered" so that the historical crimes of the nation disappear. Part of what makes this possible, he notes, is isolationism: "Indifference to objective truth is encouraged by the sealing-off of one part of the world from another." It is now possible to be more attentive to the information from the rest of the world, and it is possible, and necessary, he concludes, to struggle against "nationalism," and the way to do that is through what he calls "a *moral* effort" (emphasis original).[6] Orwell does not explicitly say that the counterweight to nationalism is internationalism, although he certainly implies it, and he also does not suggest that the "moral" strategy will be anything like the political and historical apologies of the guilted age. But, again, he seems to imply it.

If a nationalist is someone unable to disapprove of or see or hear about his or her nation's atrocities, then presumably someone who struggled to know about and disapprove of his or her nation's crimes would be an anti-nationalist. An anti-nationalist is capable of seeing a different world, unblinkered by borders of the mind, and able to see his or her nation as one among equal others. In other words, if nationalism is, as Ernest Renan suggests at the end of the nineteenth century, always premised on a collective amnesia in which the origins and atrocities of the nation are conveniently forgotten, might not the very act of remembrance in a political or historical apology represent a positive act against such amnesia, and therefore against the nationalism premised on it? And might the fact that nations apologize to each other, and overhear each other's apologies, and sometimes demand apologies for other nations suggest a new international order? Might that be the utopic "moral" effort that the author of the century's most memorable dystopias has in mind?

If so, if borders have come to mean nothing in some places and to mean less everywhere in the world's communications systems, perhaps we can see these political and historical apologies as part of that dismantling of the old ideas of national sovereignty. Let me return to that group of people I mentioned in the Preface who literally crossed national borders as they retraced the steps of the original Crusaders in their Reconciliation Walk. In his book *States of Denial*, Stanley Cohen mocks this group and the atonement practices they represent. His sardonic comment—"They should have been treated with total derision and told to pack their crosses and go back home"—expresses what is likely a widely shared sentiment. The whole idea of what he calls "collective apologies for the past" is, he says, "preposterous." It is, however, unclear just what precisely Cohen finds particularly disagreeable about the practice. The subject of his book, after all, is denial—that is, the ways in which we individually and collectively manage to evade evidence of atrocities and suffering. And he is attentive to denial of all sorts. He wants to understand what makes us toss aside the Oxfam pamphlets we get in the mail that contain horrifying images and information about suffering in other places. He wants to know what to make of the psychic strategy of denial and the therapeutic practice of healing by forcing the psyche to confront what it has previously denied. And he wants to examine what it means when a nation passes a law making it illegal publicly to deny an event like the Holocaust. Given his subject matter, it is curious that he so vigorously dismisses what is, after all, an acute effort to avoid denial, to accept the past and attempt to atone for it. Since he makes the claim that to "deny past horrors is immoral," why is he so hard on those attempts by people who want to be moral by remembering them, even if this is the best way they can devise for doing that? If that is the only choice we have, is it better to be immoral in our denial or preposterous in our apology? Moreover, it would seem that the modern Crusader apologists are following Cohen's final advice about how we might respond to past atrocities—and prevent future ones—by looking for "some cosmopolitan identity" instead of remaining "locked in the very loyalties that caused the suffering" in the first place.[7]

Is that perhaps not what the modern Crusaders who walk in the footsteps of history, the modern white Australians who affirm what was done in their name by signing a Sorry Book, the modern white Americans who sanctify a site by remembering the souls of those who were killed there for their "manifest destiny" are doing—affirming an identity that is indeed cosmopolitan because it based on a recognition of the crimes that made our world what it is? The "apology" in cases like these might seem "preposterous," and, in some ways, it is still slightly discordant, but it is also something more, and I think we are unfair to those who practice it by denying just what it means to them and what it could mean to all of us as we approach what might be the end of the guilted age. A sense of guilt can be allayed or assuaged in many different ways—including some very socially destructive ways. I have outlined what I think are pressing dangers and liabilities in some of the practices we have been examining here. Some of these political and historical apologies can replicate the dynamics of the offense for which they are offered, often deny what they should affirm, and frequently misunderstand what is most offensive about the events they attempt to address. Apologizing is a strategy that has serious pitfalls. What these apologies do nonetheless reveal is a deep desire, felt by many people in many different cultures and countries, for some kind of fuller, more robust, and emotional engagement.

In some cases, assuredly, an apology is meant to allay guilt, achieve easy resolution, and end a particular kind of encounter. Those kinds of apologies are as bad as denials because they are dismissive. But in other cases, an apology is the beginning of something, the establishing of new ground rules for behavior and a sincere reaching out for the sake of genuine encounter. Those kinds of apologies are attempts to discover and promote a cosmopolitan identity based on a powerful encounter with what we are taught to think of as the Other, through a robust encounter with what we are taught to think of as the Past. What is "denied" in those kinds of apologies is that there is an Other that is other and a Past that is past. And that strikes me as a promising if preposterous act precisely because it questions the borders that make possible a parochial nationalism and an equally parochial sense of identity, unmoored from the past and responsible for a limited gambit.

Let me end this book by returning to where we began: Africa. For many people, the Rwandan genocide in 1994 was a chilling reminder of what they learned about in 1945. In a hundred days, eight hundred thousand people were killed. Philip Gourevitch gives us the desperate mathematics of that mortality: 333 people were killed every hour, 5.5 every minute. And the world stood by. Later, in the wake of the latest genocide of a genocidal century, we saw again precisely the same questions raised that we have been discussing throughout this book—questions about responsibility, guilt, reconciliation, atonement, and mourning. Leaders of nations and of international agencies expressed their guilt and responsibility and apologized for their inaction. An international tribunal was created to try the *génocidaires*, and while it found guilt, it failed to accomplish anything resembling justice. It was historic in one way: When Jean-Paul Akayesu was pronounced to be guilty of genocide, he became the first person ever convicted for that crime. What history is likely to judge to be the tribunal's most important accomplishment, however, is that it established rape as a crime against humanity and a component of genocide.[8]

This combination of justice and apology was striking, sometimes startlingly so. On March 25, 1998, President Bill Clinton gave his famous apology speech in front of the survivors of the genocide at the Kigali airport, in which he accepted responsibility for the world's inaction: "The international community, together with nations in Africa, must bear its share of responsibility for this tragedy, as well. We did not act quickly enough after the killing began. We should not have allowed the refugee camps to become safe haven for the killers. We did not immediately call these crimes by their rightful name: genocide. We cannot change the past. But we can and must do everything in our power to help you build a future without fear, and full of hope." He then announced his full support for the International Criminal Tribunal for Rwanda and for the pursuit of justice of those who committed the crime the international community did not name. One month later, though, when twenty-two people were scheduled for execution, Clinton, along with Pope John Paul II and some human rights groups, expressed concern about the fairness of the trials. The twenty-two were executed in the sports stadium in Kigali in front of twenty thousand exuberant witnesses.[9]

That same dizzying connection between apology and punishment was to be found in the law Rwanda's Parliament had passed two years earlier, entitled "The Organization of Prosecutions for Offences Constituting the Crime of Genocide or Crimes against Humanity." This law creates categories of *génocidaires*, ranging from Category 1, those who planned the genocide and would be subject to the death penalty when found guilty, to Category 4, those who committed crimes against property during the genocide. The law stipulates that those who confessed and pled guilty had not only to provide a detailed description of the offenses committed and name the accomplices with whom they were committed but also offer "an apology for the offences committed by the applicant." Those guilty of Category 3 (serious assault, but not murder) and Category 4 crimes could be offered plea bargains; those in Categories 1 and 2 would be sentenced.[10] Here, encased in a law, one legislating how to punish genocide, no less, is the practice of *apology*.

And where there is apology, forgiveness, in theory if not in practice, is sure to follow. When it became clear that the international tribunal created to try the *génocidaires* was miserably failing to bring the cases to trial in a reasonable time, it was proposed to permit the *Gacaca* courts to try some cases. These are local village courts that are meant to settle family squabbles or community disputes over such issues as property or domestic relations. In the ten years that the *Gacaca* courts dealt with *génocidaires*, until they closed in June 2012, they were clearly charged with more strictly apportioning retribution rather than trying to coordinate reconciliation. Nonetheless, according to Rwandan President Paul Kagame's assessment in his formal closing of them, the *Gacaca* courts also promoted reconciliation and prepared the grounds for the "restoration of social harmony" precisely because they provided a communal opportunity for people "to genuinely seek and be granted forgiveness."[11]

Was this possible? As in South Africa, which was proceeding with its Truth and Reconciliation Commission (TRC) on apartheid as the genocide in Rwanda unfolded, some thought it was, while others vehemently disagreed. Some believed that the only way that Rwanda could move forward was for survivors to forgive and learn to live with the *génocidaires*, but others were appalled at the very thought. When Edmond Mrugama had identified his brother's killer, who remained free in Kigali, he had conflicting desires about what he wished: "I want him to explain to me what this thing was, how he could do this thing." After all, he thought, what "good is prison, if he doesn't feel what I feel?" For punishment to be effective, Mrugama thought, it required conscience, and he was not sure this *génocidaire* had that. He resolved that one day he would confront his brother's murderer: "When the time is right, I want to make him understand that I'm not asking for his arrest, but for him to live forever with what he has done. I'm asking for him to think about it for the rest of his life." It would be a kind of "psychological torture," Mrugama claimed, as he spoke from his own tortured position. To talk of "reconciliation" now, Mrugama concluded, is offensive.[12]

What Mrugama was doing, even as he was fantasizing about the confrontation with his brother's killer, was mourning. It was what all the survivors were doing. There were mass reburial ceremonies held all over the country. At one representative one, in Gisenyi in the summer of 1995, the mass grave was opened, and the village leaders told the locals to see and "smell the death smell." Then the villagers, conscripted by the army and given plastic gloves, took out the mutilated bodies within the grave and laid them out. Some pieces were placed in coffins, some in green plastic sheets. After politicians gave speeches about the need for accountability and reconciliation, and after a benediction, the dead were placed in new mass graves. Those who had been unceremoniously killed were ceremonially reburied. It was unclear, though, just what these reburial services were meant to accomplish. Was it to have some *génocidaires* confront their handiwork? Was that the point of having the villagers smell and handle the corpses? Or was it some kind of psychological rejuvenation, not to distinguish one corpse from another but to separate the living from the dead? Rwandans coined a phrase for the nation's people after the genocide: *bapfuye buhagazi*. As one Rwandan put it, "It means the walking dead. This is the land of the walking dead."[13] Was this ritual the opposite of Jesus's injunction to "let the dead bury their dead"? Was it meant to inform those who performed the burial that they were, in fact, alive? Or was it simply an act of mourning, a handling of the dead by those who lost them? It is hard to say.

The language of mourning seemed endemic, and appropriately so. When the leader of the United Nations Assistance Mission for Rwanda (UNAMIR), Canadian Lieutenant-General Roméo Dallaire, testified on Canadian television, he asked pointed questions about the failure of the international community. People talk, he noted, but what good is that? "Who is grieving for Rwanda and really living it and living with the consequences?" he asked. Those who earlier failed to be accountable were now failing to express the requisite grief for the losses caused by their irresponsibility. Dallaire might have been suggesting something even more when he used that same language to talk not about the people who were lost but about the ideals. My "real mourning," he pronounced, is for the "the apathy and the absolute detachment of the international community, and particularly of the Western world."[14] He was grieving for lost souls and mourning lost principles. It seemed the right tenor in the wake of an atrocity that required a more conventional wake.

What was being mourned, in the end, were more than just the people who had been brutally killed and the principles of international solidarity that had been betrayed while they were being killed—it was truth. Would the International Criminal Tribunal for Rwanda discover what happened and why? Would the *Gacaca* courts? Would Mrugama when he confronted his brother's killer? The truth is a rare commodity anytime, but especially in the aftermath of an atrocity or during a political transition. The function of "truth commissions," famously writes Michael Ignatieff, is "to narrow the range of permissible lies." There is something bracing and edifying in Ignatieff's skepticism. He has reported widely on a world in turmoil and written with genuine insight about what he calls the "modern conscience" and "political ethics" in "an age of terror." He recognizes that in cases like Rwanda, South Africa, the former Yugoslavia, and in every other quarter of the world, there is a tension because the crimes committed in those places—contemporary, recent, ancient—cannot "safely be fixed in the historical past; they remain locked in the eternal present, crying out for vengeance." The past, he notes, "continues to torment because it is not the past." He gently reproves those who seek a balm in the truth, which they hope will set them free from pain, at least. It is "putting too much faith in the truth to believe that it can heal," Ignatieff notes. But there are practices that can help produce healing. What he calls "public rituals of atonement" can help individuals "to heal and to reconcile" with other individuals. Such rituals serve another purpose, which does have to do with the truth that is impossible to arrive at—they make the search for it possible. We need "guilt, shame, and remorse," he writes, because those are "the emotions necessary for any sustained encounter with the truth."[15]

As we have seen, that has been an abiding belief of the guilted age, even before intellectuals as eloquent as Ignatieff could articulate it. Guilt, remorse, contrition, a desire for atonement—these are the preconditions for understanding and striving for the truth. The one other belief that seems hidden in his account and misunderstood in so many others, and that those who suffer these atrocities seem intuitively to recognize, is that the encounter with the truth also requires pious mourning. A popular T-shirt in Rwanda seemed to capture perfectly the spirit of the times: "Genocide. Bury the dead, not the truth."[16] It was a hopeful statement in what seemed a hopeless situation. This T-shirt did just what the international community had failed to do: It named the crime, *genocide*. And then it posited two acts together, intimately connected—one of burial and one of testimony, one putting to rest and commemorating those whose lives were tragically cut short and one urging us to struggle for the life of the truth. And in the act of mourning, of burying those who were lost forever, it saw an opportunity for atonement in the truth, which need not be lost forever.

NOTES

PREFACE

1. James Ojera Latigo, "Northern Uganda: Traditional-Based Practices in the Acholi Region," in *Traditional Justice and Reconciliation after Violent Conflict: Learning from African Experiences* (Stockholm: International Institute for Democracy and Electoral Assistance, 2008), 85–120, esp. 105–107; and Marc Lacey, "Atrocity Victims in Uganda Choose to Forgive," *New York Times*, April 18, 2005.

2. Pope John Paul II's statement quoted in Nick Smith, *I Was Wrong: The Meanings of Apologies* (Cambridge: Cambridge University Press, 2008), 219–220. See also Luigi Accattoli, *When a Pope Asks Forgiveness: The Mea Culpa's of John Paul II*, trans. Jordan Aumann (New York: Alba House, 1998), 83–86; and Thomas Dixon, "Jerusalem: Reconciliation Walk Reaches Pinnacle: Western Christians Ask Forgiveness for Crusader Atrocities," *Christianity Today*, September 6, 1999.

3. John Dawson, *Healing America's Wounds* (Ventura, CA: Regal Books, 1994), 148–149.

4. Danielle Celermajer, *The Sins of the Nation and the Ritual of Apologies* (Cambridge: Cambridge University Press, 2009).

5. Here is just a sampling of the hundreds of editorials and thousands of letters to the editors that I have read in my research: Jeffery L. Sheler, "The Era of Collective Repentance," *U.S. News and World Report*, July 13, 1995; Kenneth L. Woodward, "Who's Sorry Now?" *Newsweek*, July 17, 1995; J. M. Lawrence, "1995 Was Year of the Apology: Nations, Individuals Said 'I'm Sorry,'" *Boston Herald*, December 31, 1995; Jonathan Petre and Jo Knowsley, "Church Leaders: Let's Say Sorry for Our Evil History," *The Telegraph*, March 16, 1997; Jeff Jacoby, "All the President's Apologies," *Times-Picayune*, May 27, 1997; John Anders, "All of a Sudden, Everyone Has the Contrite Stuff," *Dallas Morning News*, June 6, 1997; John Leo, "Group Apologies Are Not in Order," *Tampa Tribune*, June 24, 1997; Nina Planck, "The Limits of Apology," *Time*, December 8, 1997; Peter Dizikes, "When Apologizing Means Never Saying You're Sorry," *Newsday*, December 28, 1997; Joe Blundo,

"It's Been a Great Year for Apologies, Most of Them Bogus," *Columbus Dispatch*, December 30, 1997; David Hinckley, "The Sorry State of Redemption from Broadway to the Beltway, Absolution Is Posing a Dilemma," *Daily News*, February 8, 1998; David Nyhan, "The Folly of Apologies That Go Unappreciated," *Boston Globe*, March 29, 1998; P. J. O'Rourke, "I Apologize," *Weekly Standard*, April 20, 1998; "Who's Sorry Now? Institutional Apologies," *Commonweal*, April 24, 1998; and Jacob Weisberg, "Sorry Excuse: Rules for National Apologies," *Slate*, April 4, 1998.

6. Jay Rayner, *Eating Crow* (New York: Simon and Schuster, 2004). Jonathan Dee, *A Thousand Pardons* (New York: Random House, 2013).

7. See Jacques Derrida, "To Forgive: The Unforgivable and the Imprescriptible," in *Questioning God*, ed. John D. Caputo, Mark Dooley, and Michael J. Scanlon (Bloomington: Indiana University Press, 2001), 21–51; Jacques Derrida "Le siècle et le pardon," *Le Monde des debats*, December 1999, available at http://hydra.humanities.uci.edu/derrida/siecle.html; and Jacques Derrida, "On Forgiveness," trans. Michael Hughes, in *On Cosmopolitanism and Forgiveness* (London: Routledge, 2001), 27–60. Pascal Bruckner, *La tyrannie de la pénitence: Essai sur le masochisme occidental* (Paris: Édition Grasset et Fasquelle, 2006); and Pascal Bruckner, *The Tyranny of Guilt: An Essay on Western Masochism*, trans. Steven Rendall (Princeton, NJ: Princeton University Press, 2010). Neither Derrida nor Bruckner calls it a "guilted age." Derrida refers to it as "an immense scene of confession in progress, thus a virtually Christian convulsion-conversion-confession" (*"une immense scene de confession en cours, donc a une convulsion-conversion-confession virtuellement chretienne"*; "On Forgiveness," 31), while Bruckner calls it a form of "masochism" of a world gripped by "torments of repentance" (*"les tourments du repentir"*; *Tyranny of Guilt*, 6).

8. In *The Sins of the Nation and the Ritual of Apologies*, Celermajer makes a distinction between what she calls "inter-temporal or historical apologies" and "transitional apologies" (15).

INTRODUCTION

1. I have drawn on the list of apologies created and revised by Graham G. Dodds, who created an original list that he appended to his "Political Apologies and Public Discourse" for the Penn National Commission on Society, Culture, and Community meeting in October 1999 and then revised and updated for the Penn National Commission website, available at www.upenn.edu/pnc/politicalapologies.html.

2. Chris McGreal, "Britain Blocks EU Apology for Slave Trade," *The Guardian*, September 3, 2001.

3. Martha C. Nussbaum, *Political Emotions: Why Love Matters for Justice* (Cambridge, MA: Belknap Press of Harvard University Press, 2013).

4. See Eric Hobsbawm, *The Age of Extremes: A History of the World, 1914–1991* (New York: Pantheon, 1994); and Pierre Nora, "The Era of Commemoration," in *Realms of Memory: The Construction of the French Past, Volume 3: Symbols*, trans. Arthur Goldhammer, ed. Lawrence D. Kritzman (New York: Columbia University Press, 1998), 609–637, esp. 626.

5. Albert Camus, *The Rebel: An Essay on Man in Revolt*, trans. Anthony Bower (1951; repr., New York: Vintage, 1991), 103, 225, 184.

6. Gitta Sereny, "Generation without a Past," reprinted in *The Healing Wound: Experiences and Reflections on Germany, 1938–2001* (New York: Norton, 2001), 53–86, esp. 71, 82–83, 85.

7. Gitta Sereny, "Beginnings," in *The Healing Wound*, 1–14. Gitta Sereny, "Stolen Children," in *The Healing Wound*, 25–53 (Himmler is quoted on 38–41). Sereny, "Generation without a Past," 62.

8. Sereny, "Generation without a Past," 61.

9. Primo Levi, "Letters from Germans," in *The Drowned and the Saved*, trans. Raymond Rosenthal (New York: Summit Books, 1998), 167–197, esp. 181, 178. Levi received forty letters between 1961 and 1964.

10. We need to acknowledge that there are profoundly complicating factors in assessing the existence and meaning of German postwar guilt. For one thing, polls reveal profound ambivalence. A survey taken in December 1951 showed that only 5 percent of West Germans admitted feeling "guilty" toward Jews. On the question of reparations, implicitly the idea of repairing that for which guilt is felt, 29 percent responded that the nation should pay reparations to Israel, 40 percent thought that only those "who really committed something" should pay, and 21 percent believed that Jews "were partly responsible for what happened." See Tony Judt, *Postwar: A History of Europe since 1945* (New York: Penguin, 2005), 271–272. As well, there is the question of how the guilt came to be felt, even by the minority who claimed it. Under the rubric of de-Nazification, the Allies undertook a broad campaign to induce a feeling of collective guilt. Controlling the media in postwar Germany, they issued radio broadcasts, produced films, and used print media to reinforce the sense of collective guilt. In some cases, this was done at a distance—for example, the posters that placed pictures of the Dachau and Belsen concentration camps above the caption "YOU ARE GUILTY OF THIS!"—while in other cases it was done by forcing German civilians to tour the camps and exhume the bodies from the mass graves. See Harold Marcuse, *Legacies of Dachau: The Uses and Abuses of a Concentration Camp, 1933–2001* (Cambridge: Cambridge University Press, 2001), 61, 128. My point is that guilt remains the salient issue—even when it is claimed by a small minority, and even if it is the result of a media campaign—because it becomes the crucial focus of debate, for those who express it as well as for those who deny it. My sense of a "guilted age," then, as I argue more fully in the next chapter, depends on what I describe as a diffuse sensibility that cannot be captured by surveys or polls but can be hinted at in anecdotal evidence of the sort on which I draw.

11. Telford Taylor, *The Anatomy of the Nuremberg Trials: A Personal Memoir* (1993; repr., New York: Skyhorse Publishing, 2013), 368, 539, 453. Sereny, "Children of the Reich," 286–308, esp. 303.

12. Alfonso A. Narvaez, "Gen. Curtis LeMay, an Architect of Strategic Air Power, Dies at 83," *New York Times*, October 2, 1990. For an account of LeMay's unauthorized strategy for firebombing Tokyo, see John Toland, *The Rising Sun: The Decline and Fall of the Japanese Empire, 1936–1945* (New York: Random House, 1970), 671–677. For an account of the campaign and its effects, see John W. Dower, *War without Mercy: Race and Power in the Pacific War* (New York: Pantheon, 1986), 40–41; I quote Dower's description of the conflagration. The account of LeMay's receiving the Japanese honor and the quotations from the Ministry are taken from Herbert P. Bix, "The Showa Emperor's 'Monologue' and the Problem of War Responsibility," *Journal of Japanese Studies* 18, no. 2 (Summer 1992): 295–363, esp. 363.

13. Itami Mansaku, quoted in Ian Buruma, *Wages of Guilt: Memories of War in Germany and Japan* (London: Jonathan Cape, 1994), 260.

The terms "responsibility" and "guilt" do not mean the same thing, but they are sometimes used by the writers I cite here—and sometimes, in particular cases, by me—to mean the same thing. In places in the text where the distinction is not that important for the argument, I do not make it; when it is, I do try to identify the precise terms of the distinction—that is, when it is important to distinguish either as a moral or juridical term, or as something a court finds rather than something a subject feels, for instance.

14. Gitta Sereny, "The Hitler Wave," in *The Healing Wound*, 147–161, esp. 160; this essay was published in 1978. Watanabe Kazuo, quoted in John W. Dower, "'An Aptitude for Being Unloved': War and Memory in Japan," in *Ways of Forgetting, Ways of Remembering: Japan in the Modern World* (New York: New Press, 2012), 105–135, esp. 107.

15. For surveys of the range of institutional mechanisms used in transitions from a criminal to a democratic regime, see Carlos Santiago Nino, *Radical Evil on Trial* (New Haven, CT: Yale University Press, 1996), 3–40; Martha Minow, *Between Vengeance and Forgiveness: Facing History after Genocide and Mass Violence* (Boston: Beacon Press, 1998); Lawrence Weschler, *A Miracle, a Universe: Settling Accounts with Torturers* (1990; repr., Chicago: University of Chicago Press, 1998); and Lawrence Weschler, *Calamities of Exile: Three Nonfiction Novellas* (Chicago: University of Chicago Press, 1998), 63–135.

16. Tina Rosenberg, *The Haunted Land: Facing Europe's Ghosts after Communism* (New York: Vintage, 1996), 243, 385–393. For a particularly good-humored account of someone confronting the people who spied on him, see Timothy Garton Ash, *The File: A Personal History* (New York: Vintage, 1998).

Popular entertainment also played a role in producing the climate of the guilted age. Many historians have noted the importance of the airing of the miniseries *The Holocaust* in Germany (akin to the airing of *Roots* in the United States). In Japan, too, the popular media played an important role. In the years leading up to Prime Minister Tomiichi Murayama's iconic 1995 apology, Japanese television produced numerous documentaries and fictionalized dramas focusing on the war. In 1993, it aired the extremely important NHK six-part documentary, *The Documentary: The Pacific War*. In 1994, three channels (NHK, Asahi Television, and Nihon Telebi) aired at least eight documentaries on the war. In 1995, Japanese television aired twenty-six documentaries and six fictionalized dramas on World War II. See Naoko Shimazu, "Popular Representations of the Past: The Case of Postwar Japan," *Journal of Contemporary History* 38, no. 1 (2003): 101–116, esp. 107.

17. See *Transitional Justice: How Emerging Democracies Reckon with Former Regimes*, ed. Neil J. Kritz, 3 vols. (Washington, DC: United States Institutes of Peace Press, 1995); Ruti Teitel, *Transitional Justice* (New York: Oxford University Press, 2000); and Priscilla B. Hayner, *Unspeakable Truths: Confronting State Terror and Atrocity* (New York: Routledge, 2001).

18. That debate was particularly acute in South Africa, as it developed its own reconciliation commission that departed in some key ways from the Latin American truth commissions. See Antjie Krog, *Country of My Skull: Guilt, Sorrow, and the Limits of Forgiveness in the New South Africa* (New York: Three Rivers Press, 2000), 21–22; and Kader Asmal, Louise Asmal, and Ronald Suresh Roberts, *Reconciliation through Truth: A Reckoning of Apartheid's Criminal Governance*, 2nd ed. (New York: St. Martin's, 1997). See the essays in *Truth v. Justice: The Morality of Truth Commissions*, ed. Robert I. Rotberg and Dennis Thompson (Princeton, NJ: Princeton University Press, 2000), for discussions of this debate in other nations, but also focusing on South Africa. The Chilean human rights activist José Zalaquett put a possible compromise nicely: "The whole truth, and as much justice as possible."

19. Hobsbawm, *The Age of Extremes*, 22, 52.

20. Richard von Weizsäcker, *From Weimar to the Wall: My Life in German Politics*, trans. Ruth Hein (New York: Broadway Books, 1999), 127.

21. For acts of revenge in postwar Europe, see Judt, *Postwar*, 41–62; Ian Buruma, *Year Zero: A History of 1945* (New York: Penguin, 2013), 75–127; and Keith Lowe, *Savage Continent: Europe in the Aftermath of World War II* (New York: St. Martin's, 2012), 75–93.

Andrew Kelley, "Translator's Introduction," to Vladimir Jankélévitch, *Forgiveness*, trans. Kelley (Chicago: University of Chicago Press, 2005), vii–xxvii, esp. xix.

22. Both Camus and Mauriac are quoted in Anne Sa'adah, "Forgiving without Forgetting: Political Reconciliation and Democratic Citizenship," *French Politics and Society* 10, no. 3 (1992): 94–113, esp. 106–108.

23. For Mauriac, see Sa'adah, "Forgiving without Forgetting," 107. Camus, *The Rebel*, 124–125. See also Camus, "Reflections on the Guillotine," in *Resistance, Rebellion, and Death: Essays*, trans. Justin O'Brien (New York: Vintage International, 1988), 175–234.

CHAPTER 1

1. Eric Hobsbawm, *The Age of Extremes: A History of the World, 1914–1991* (New York: Pantheon, 1994), 52. He also calls it the "thirty-one years' world war" (22).

2. Gary Jonathan Bass, *Stay the Hand of Vengeance: The Politics of War Crimes Tribunals* (Princeton, NJ: Princeton University Press, 2000), 68, 116, 122, 131.

3. "Charter of the International Military Tribunal," reprinted in Telford Taylor, *The Anatomy of the Nuremberg Trials: A Personal Memoir* (1993; repr., New York: Skyhorse Publishing, 2013), 645–653, esp. 648.

4. Desmond Tutu, *No Future without Forgiveness* (New York: Doubleday, 1999), 19. Bass, *Stay the Hand of Vengeance*, 232. Lake was weighing options not dismissing the idea of an international tribunal.

5. Taylor, *The Anatomy of the Nuremberg Trials*, 29–32. For acts of revenge in postwar Europe, see Tony Judt, *Postwar: A History of Europe since 1945* (New York: Penguin, 2005), 41–62; Ian Buruma, *Year Zero: A History of 1945* (New York: Penguin, 2013), 75–127; and Keith Lowe, *Savage Continent: Europe in the Aftermath of World War II* (New York: St. Martin's, 2012), 75–93.

6. Cf. Ruti Teitel, *Transitional Justice* (New York: Oxford University Press, 2000), 45, where she refers to "the Nuremberg principle that the defense of due obedience must yield to the principle of individual responsibility."

7. Karl Jaspers, *The Question of German Guilt*, trans. E. B. Ashton (Westport, CT: Greenwood Press, 1978), 31–32, 40. The book was first published in 1948.

8. Ibid., 31, 62, 61, 73–74, 61, 102, 66.

9. Ibid., 32, 71, 72.

10. Ibid., 60.

11. "Dabru Emet," *New York Times*, September 10, 2000. Michael Signer, quoted in Victoria Barnett, "Provocative Reconciliation: A Jewish Statement on Christianity," *Christian Century*, September 27–October 4, 2000.

12. Herbert Anderson and Edward Foley, *Mighty Stories, Dangerous Rituals: Weaving Together the Human and the Divine* (San Francisco: Jossey-Bass, 1998), 171. See John Dawson, *Healing America's Wounds* (Ventura, CA: Regal Books, 1994), 15, 241, on "identificational repentance."

13. George Steiner, *Language and Silence: Essays on Language, Literature, and the Inhuman* (New York: Atheneum, 1967), 163. Theodor Adorno, *Can One Live after Auschwitz? A Philosophical Reader*, ed. Rolf Tiedemann (Stanford, CA: Stanford University Press, 2003). Steiner, *Language and Silence*, 158.

14. Willy Brandt, *My Life in Politics*, trans. Anthea Bell (New York: Viking, 1992), 200. Steiner, *Language and Silence*, 163. Hannah Arendt, *The Human Condition* (Chicago: University of Chicago Press, 1957), 241.

15. Jaspers, *The Question of German Guilt*, 100, 118–119, 120.

16. Ibid., 118–120, 122.

17. Konrad Adenauer, Deutscher Bundestag: *Stenographische Beritchte, erste Wahlperiode*, September 27, 1951, 6697–6698, quoted and translated in Stefan Engert, "A Case Study in 'Atonement': Adenauer's Holocaust Apology," *Israel Journal of Foreign Affairs* 4, no. 3 (2010): 111–122, esp. 116. Elazar Barkan, *The Guilt of Nations: Restitution and Negotiating Historical Injustices* (New York: Norton, 2000), 12–13, is skeptical of whether Adenauer did in fact apologize. On the political context of Germany during the Adenauer years, see David Art, *The Politics of the Nazi Past in Germany and Austria* (Cambridge: Cambridge University Press, 2006), 49–56.

18. Adenauer, quoted in Jeffrey K. Olick, *The Politics of Regret: On Collective Memory and Historical Responsibility* (New York: Routledge, 2007), 141–142.

19. "Honesty, Not Apology," *The Economist*, no. 328 (August 21, 1993): 17. Matthew D. LaPlante, "MacArthur Aide: U.S. Must Learn from Errors," *Salt Lake Tribune*, December 7, 2006. None of the biographies of Hirohito I consulted mention this incident. See Edward Behr, *Hirohito: Behind the Myth* (New York: Villard Books, 1989); Stephen S. Large, *Emperor Hirohito and Shōwa Japan* (New York: Routledge, 1992); Peter Wetzler, *Hirohito and War: Imperial Tradition and Military Decision Making in Prewar Japan* (Honolulu: University of Hawai'i Press, 1998); John W. Dower, *Embracing Defeat: Japan in the Wake of World War II* (New York: Norton, 1999); and Herbert P. Bix, *Hirohito and the Making of Modern Japan* (New York: HarperCollins, 2000).

20. Henry Rousso, "Did the Purge Achieve Its Goals?" in *Memory, the Holocaust, and French Justice: The Bousquet and Touvier Affairs*, ed. Richard J. Golsan (Hanover, NH: University Press of New England, 1996), 100–104, esp. 100. See Rousso, *The Vichy Syndrome: History and Memory in France since 1944*, trans. Arthur Goldhammer (Cambridge, MA: Harvard University Press, 1991). When President Georges Pompidou had pardoned Bousquet in 1972, he justified it by saying that he wanted to "draw a veil over the past" (quoted in *Memory, the Holocaust, and French Justice*, xxv). On the Touvier case, see the newspaper articles and essays collected in *Memory, the Holocaust, and French Justice*, 126–198. Annette Lévy-Willard, "Trémolet de Villers Prefers Forgiveness to Remembrance: An Interview with Touvier's Lawyer," in *Memory, the Holocaust, and French Justice*, 126–128, esp. 128.

21. Both Jacques Chirac and François Mitterrand are quoted in Marlise Simons, "Chirac Affirms France's Guilt in Fate of Jews," *New York Times*, July 17, 1995. The 2001 French law is quoted in Leonard Jamfa, "Germany Faces Colonial History in Namibia: A Very Ambiguous 'I Am Sorry,'" in *The Age of Apology: Facing Up to the Past*, ed. Mark Gibney, Rhoda E. Howard-Hassmann, Jean-Marc Coicaud, and Nicklaus Steiner (Philadelphia: University of Pennsylvania Press, 2008), 202–215, esp. 210. Some have also argued that the French law does not constitute an apology, since it acknowledges but does not offer any remorse for the events recognized, and, moreover, its use of the present tense (*"reconnait"*) "suggests an unwillingness to take responsibility for the past." See Rhoda E. Howard-Hassman and Anthony P. Lombardo, "Words Require Actions: African Elite Opinions about Apologies from the 'West,'" in *The Age of Apology*, 216–228, esp. 217.

CHAPTER 2

1. Martha C. Nussbaum, *Political Emotions: Why Love Matters for Justice* (Cambridge, MA: Belknap Press of Harvard University Press, 2013), 261, 320–338, 339–359, 381, 15.

2. Ernest Verdeja, *Unchopping a Tree: Reconciliation in the Aftermath of Political Violence* (Philadelphia: Temple University Press, 2009), 19.

3. P. E. Digeser, *Political Forgiveness* (Ithaca, NY: Cornell University Press, 2001), 4, 3; cf. 207.

4. Liz Sly, "De Klerk Apologizes For Apartheid's Abuses," *Chicago Tribune*, April 30, 1993.

5. For de Kock's testimony, see "Truth and Reconciliation Commission Amnesty Hearings" (at Port Elizabeth, October 1, 1997, Case No. 0066/96), available at www.justice.gov.za/trc/amntrans%5Cpe/mother3.htm. For the appeal and apology to the Motherwell widows, see Pumla Gobodo-Madikizela, *A Human Being Died That Night: A South African Story of Forgiveness* (Boston: Houghton Mifflin, 2003), 14–15, 97.

6. Brian A. Weiner, *Sins of the Parents: The Politics of National Apologies in the United States* (Philadelphia: Temple University Press, 2005), 5. Ruti Teitel, *Transitional Justice* (New York: Oxford University Press, 2000), 84, makes the case for one kind of political apology, what she calls the "transitional apology," which, she argues, "allows for the continuity of state responsibility, even as it also affords discontinuity—a letting go of the past." Cf. Nancy L. Rosenblum, "Justice and the Experience of Injustice," in *Breaking the Cycles of Hatred: Memory, Law, and Repair*, ed. Martha Minow (Princeton, NJ: Princeton University Press, 2002), 77–106, esp. 98–99, on the work that is done by public apologies.

7. "Remarks by the President in Apology for Study Done in Tuskegee," Office of the Press Secretary of the White House, May 16, 1997.

8. Jennifer Lind, *Sorry States: Apologies in International Politics* (Ithaca, NY: Cornell University Press, 2008), 4, 180–181.

9. For the testimony of the comfort women and their movement for reparations and acknowledgment, see *When Sorry Isn't Enough: The Controversy over Apologies and Reparations for Human Injustice*, ed. Roy L. Brooks (New York: New York University Press, 1999), 87–151.

10. Colin Joyce, "Anger at Claim That 'Comfort Women Were Smiling Volunteers,'" *The Telegraph*, March 18, 2001. "No Comfort," *New York Times*, March 6, 2007. "Shinzo Abe's Double Talk," *Washington Post*, March 24, 2007.

Kobayashi also wrote a like-minded commentary on the war debate, *The New Special Statement 'Gōmanizumu': The War Debate*, that sold 650,000 copies when it was published in the late 1990s. He was also on the educational advocacy Committee to Produce New History Textbooks. See Naoko Shimazu, "Popular Representations of the Past: The Case of Postwar Japan," *Journal of Contemporary History* 38, no. 1 (2003): 101–116, esp. 113–114.

11. David McNeill, "History Redux: Japan's Textbook Battle Reignites," *Japan Policy Research Institute Working Paper* no. 107, June 2005. Shuko Ogawa, "The Difficulty of Apology," *Harvard International Review* 22, no. 3 (2000): 42. Simon Tisdall, "Shinzo Abe: Is Japan's PM a Dangerous Militarist or Modernising Reformer?" *The Guardian*, December 16, 2013. "Japan's Difficult Drive to Be a 'Beautiful Country,'" *Hankyoreh*, September 2, 2006.

12. Nick Renaud-Komiya, "Japanese Prime Minister Shinzo Abe Skips Visit to World War Two Shrine in Order to Ease China Tensions," *The Independent*, August 15, 2103. For a fuller history of Yasukuni Shrine, see essays in John Breen, *Yasukuni, the War Dead, and the Struggle for Japan's Past* (New York: Columbia University Press, 2008). For a brief description of its history, see Ben Kiernan, *Blood and Soil: A World History of Genocide and Extermination from Sparta to Darfur* (New Haven, CT: Yale University Press, 2007), 457.

13. "Japan Marks 'Return of Sovereignty Day," BBC News, April 28, 2013. Hiroko Tabuchi, "Japanese Premier Visits Contentious War Shrine," *New York Times*, December 26, 2013. Reuters, "Japanese Minister Follows Abe in Visit to War Shrine," *New York Times*, January 1, 2014.

14. Julian Littler, "Japan's Nationalist Prime Minister Wants to Revise War Apology," *The Telegraph*, January 1, 2013. "Japan 'May Revisit Second World War Statement,'" *The Telegraph*, February 1, 2013. "Former PM Murayama Cautions Japan on Reviewing 1995 War Apology," *Japan Daily Press*, July 2, 2013. Martin Fackler, "Japan Says It Will Abide by Apologies over Actions in World War II," *New York Times*, May 7, 2013.

15. "Statement by Prime Minister Junichiro Koizumi," available at www.kantei.go.jp/foreign/koizumispeech/2005/08/15danwa_e.html. Anthony Faiola, "Koizumi Stirs Anger with War Shrine Visit," *Washington Post*, August 15, 2006.

16. "Statement by Prime Minister Tomiichi Murayama 'On the Occasion of the 50th Anniversary of the War's End (15 August 1995),'" available at www.mofa.go.jp/announce/press/pm/murayama/9508.html.

17. Sheryl WuDunn, "Japanese Apology for War Is Welcomed and Criticized," *New York Times*, August 16, 1995.

18. Sheryl WuDunn, "Premier of Japan Offers 'Apology' for Its War Acts," *New York Times*, August 15, 1995.

19. See *When Sorry Isn't Enough: The Controversy over Apologies and Reparations for Human Injustice*, ed. Roy Brooks (New York: New York University Press, 1999), 80, 104. Also see Laurence Rees, *Horror in the East: Japan and the Atrocities of World War II* (Cambridge, MA: Da Capo Press, 2001); and Iris Chang, *The Rape of Nanking: The Forgotten Holocaust of World War II* (New York: Basic Books, 1997).

20. It is worth noting that von Weizsäcker's speech had been translated into Japanese and had gone through twenty-nine editions within twelve years. It would, in other words, have been also familiar to Maruyama's audience. See Sebastian Conrad, "Entangled Memories: Versions of the Past in Germany and Japan," *Journal of Contemporary History* 38, no. 1 (2003): 85–99, esp. 96.

21. "60 Years after Defeat: Has Japan Addressed Its War Responsibility?" available at http://asiangazette.blogspot.com/2005_02_13_archive.html. John W. Dower, "Japan Addresses Its War Responsibility," *Journal of the International Institute* 3, no. 1 (1995), available at http://quod.lib.umich.edu/j/jii/4750978.0003.103/--japan-addresses-its-war-responsibility?rgn=main;view=fulltext. Dower appends several important documents relating to the Diet debate and the prime minister's apology, including the signed statement by the 137 public figures. On Japan's political apologies more generally, see Ogawa, "The Difficulty of Apology," 42; and Michael Cunningham, "Prisoners of the Japanese and the Politics of Apology: A Battle over History and Memory," *Journal of Contemporary History* 39, no. 4 (2004): 561–574.

22. WuDunn, "Premier of Japan Offers 'Apology' for Its War Acts." "Statement by Prime Minister Tomiichi Murayama 'On the Occasion of the 50th Anniversary of the War's End."

23. David E. Sanger, "Japan's Emperor Tells China Only of His 'Sadness' on War," *New York Times*, October 24, 1992. "Japanese Emperor Must Apologize for Colonial Rule: S. Korean President," *Japan Times*, August 15, 2012.

24. WuDunn, "Premier of Japan Offers 'Apology' for Its War Acts." Emperor Hirohito had boycotted Yasukuni Shrine after 1978 when he discovered that the Class A war criminals had been secretly enshrined in it; after his accession, his son Emperor Akihito has continued that boycott.

25. Thomas U. Berger, *War, Guilt, and World Politics after World War II* (Cambridge: Cambridge University Press, 2012), 112–116. The Declaration of Responsibility for Austria is available at http://oe-journal.at/0300/06_030300_e.htm.

26. Girma Negash, *Apologia Politica: States and Their Apologies by Proxy* (Lanham, MD: Lexington Books, 2006), 57. Lind, *Sorry States*, 99. Mark F. Amstutz, *The Healing of Nations: The Promise and Pitfalls of Political Forgiveness* (Lanham, MD: Rowman and Littlefield, 2005), 20. Berger, *War, Guilt, and World Politics after World War II*, 123. Cf. Daniel Philpott, *Just and Unjust Peace: An Ethics of Political Reconciliation* (New York: Oxford University Press, 2012), 11. The Daniel Vernet quotation is taken from Lind, *Sorry States*, 101. Berger is challenging just how apt these "model" categories are. Lind, *Sorry States*, 26–100, is arguing that these apologies often created more tensions than they resolved in international relations between Japan and its neighbors.

27. Herbert P. Bix, *Hirohito and the Making of Modern Japan* (New York: HarperCollins, 2000), 281. Ruth Benedict, *The Chrysanthemum and the Sword: Patterns of Japanese Culture* (1946; repr., New York: Houghton Mifflin, 1989).

28. John W. Dower, *Embracing Defeat: Japan in the Wake of World War II* (New York: Norton, 1999), 87–167. Berger, *War, Guilt, and World Politics after World War II*, 41, 132.

CHAPTER 3

1. Emperor Hirohito, "Imperial Rescript," Transmitted by Domei and Recorded by the Federal Communications Commission, available at www.mtholyoke.edu/acad/intrel/hirohito.htm. Hirohito does make one other statement of atonement—"to atone ourselves before the hallowed spirits of our imperial ancestors"—but it is not directed toward anyone harmed by the war. For an account of the composition and responses to the "Imperial Rescript," see John W. Dower, *Embracing Defeat: Japan in the Wake of World War II* (New York: Norton, 1999), 33–64; and Herbert P. Bix, *Hirohito and the Making of Modern Japan* (New York: HarperCollins, 2000), 525–530.

2. Suzuki Kantarō and Prince Higashikuni Naruhiko quoted and the Ministry of Education message paraphrased in Bix, "The Showa Emperor's 'Monologue' and the Problem of War Responsibility," *Journal of Japanese Studies* 18, no. 2 (1993): 295–363, esp. 302–303.

3. Dower, *Embracing Defeat*, 493–494. Bix, *Hirohito and the Making of Modern Japan*, 540–541.

4. Dower, *Embracing Defeat*, 248, 505, 506, 505, 489.

5. Ibid., 496, 498, 501, 234.

6. Bix, "The Showa Emperor's 'Monologue' and the Problem of War Responsibility," 315–316.

7. Watanbe Kiyoshi, quoted in Dower, *Embracing Defeat*, 339, 343, 344, 345.

8. Kido asked his son to send to the grand master of ceremonies at the Imperial household the message he recorded in his diary, who would presumably give the message to the emperor.

9. Bix, *Hirohito and the Making of Modern Japan*, 649, 605–607, 516–517.

10. Ibid., 676. Jane Yamazaki, *Japanese Apologies for World War II: A Rhetorical Study* (New York: Routledge, 2006), 36, 163. Bix, *Hirohito and the Making of Modern Japan*, 687.

11. Bix, *Hirohito and the Making of Modern Japan*, 3. Joseph C. Grew, *Turbulent Era: A Diplomatic Record of Forty Years, 1904–1945*, vol. 2 (Boston: Houghton Mifflin, 1952), 1435. Cf. Bix, *Hirohito and the Making of Modern Japan*, 498; Bix, "The Showa Emperor's 'Monologue' and the Problem of War Responsibility"; and Herbert Bix, "War Responsibility and Historical Memory: Hirohito's Apparition," *Japan Focus* (posted May 6, 2008), all available at http://japanfocus.org/-Herbert_P_-Bix/2741.

12. "The Constitution of the Empire of Japan," trans. Ito Miyoji, in National Diet Library, available at www.ndl.go.jp/constitution/e/etc/c02.html.

13. Bix, *Hirohito and the Making of Modern Japan*, 291, 79. Dower, *Embracing Defeat*, 308–317. Bix, *Hirohito and the Making of Modern Japan*, 560–563, 119–120. The account of Hirohito's 1921 acknowledgment is taken from the unpublished memoirs of his military aide, Nara Takeji, who completed this memoir in 1956. See Peter Wetzler, *Hirohito and War: Imperial Tradition and Military Decision Making in Prewar Japan* (Honolulu: University of Hawai'i Press, 1998), 32, 201. Wetzler was one of the first to make the case for Hirohito's responsibility in making the decisions that led to expansion and war and concluded that Hirohito was "a party to the decisions, and responsible for them." For an assessment of Hirohito that claims he is not responsible, see Stephen S. Large, *Emperor Hirohito and Shōwa Japan: A Political Biography* (New York: Routledge, 1992).

14. Dower, *Embracing Defeat*, 497–499, 278. Bix, *Hirohito and the Making of Modern Japan*, 567. Dower, *Embracing Defeat*, 324. Also see William Manchester, *American Caesar: Douglas MacArthur 1880–1964* (Boston: Little, Brown, 1978). SCAP received many letters from Japanese citizens, some urging that the emperor be tried as a war criminal and others stating that indicting the emperor would cause the "complete annihilation" of the Japanese people. See Ian Buruma, *Year Zero: A History of 1945* (New York: Penguin Press, 2013), 174.

15. Bix, *Hirohito and the Making of Modern Japan*, 599–600. Dower, *Embracing Defeat*, 468, 325.

16. Dower, *Embracing Defeat*, 510–511. Sebastian Conrad, "Entangled Memories: Versions of the Past in Germany and Japan," *Journal of Contemporary History* 38, no. 1 (2003): 85–99, esp. 91, 89.

17. Bix, *Hirohito and the Making of Modern Japan*, 586, 560–563. Dower, *Embracing Defeat*, 561. Bix, *Hirohito and the Making of Modern Japan*, 436.

18. Maruyama Masao, "Thought and Behavior Patterns of Japan's Wartime Leaders," in *Thought and Behavior in Modern Japanese Politics*, ed. Ivan Morris (Oxford: Oxford University Press, 1963), 84–134, esp. 128 (this essay was originally published in May 1949). Also see Murayama, "Theory and Psychology of Ultra-Nationalism," in *Thought and Behavior*, 1–24, which was originally published in May 1946.

19. William L. Shirer, *The Rise and Fall of the Third Reich: A History of Nazi Germany* (1990; repr., New York: Simon and Schuster, 2011), 1140.

20. Bix, *Hirohito and the Making of Modern Japan*, 571–572. Also see Dower, *Embracing Defeat*, 346–404. Miyoshi Tatsuji wrote an article in the spring 1946 issue of the popular magazine *Shinchō* stating the reasons the emperor should abdicate. See Bix, "The Showa Emperor's 'Monologue' and the Problem of War Responsibility," 314. The text of the new constitution is available at www.kantei.go.jp/foreign/constitution_and_government_of_japan/constitution_e.html.

21. Bix, *Hirohito and the Making of Modern Japan*, 560–563. Also see Dower, *Embracing Defeat*, 308–317. SCAP's Directive for the Disestablishment of State Shinto is available at www.trinity.edu/rnadeau/Asian%20Religions/Lecture%20Notes/Shinto%20and%20Zen/Shinto%20state.htm.

22. Jonathan Watts, "Japan's Revisionists Turn Emperor into a God Once More," *The Guardian*, August 20, 2002.

23. Erving Goffman, *Relations in Public: Microstudies of the Public Order* (New York: Basic Books, 1971), 113.

24. See Aurel Kolnai, "Forgiveness," *Proceedings of the Aristotelean Society*, New Series, 74 (1973): 91–106; Jacques Derrida, "To Forgive: The Unforgivable and the

Imprescriptible," in *Questioning God*, ed. John D. Caputo, Mark Dooley, and Michael J. Scanlon (Bloomington: Indiana University Press, 2001), 21–51; Jacques Derrida, "Le siècle et le pardon," *Le Monde des debats* (December 1999), available at http://hydra.humanities.uci.edu/derrida/siecle.html; and Jacques Derrida, "On Forgiveness," trans. Michael Hughes, in *On Cosmopolitanism and Forgiveness* (London: Routledge, 2001), 27–60.

25. Buruma, *The Wages of Guilt: Memories of War in Germany and Japan* (London: Jonathan Cape, 1994), 249–250. Cf. Bix, "The Showa Emperor's 'Monologue' and the Problem of War Responsibility," 355.

26. Brian A. Weiner, *Sins of the Parents: The Politics of National Apologies in the United States* (Philadelphia: Temple University Press, 2005), 146–159, offers a good example of someone who examines in a serious way the possibilities of moving from interpersonal to collective acts of apology.

27. Arthur Scherr, "Presidential Power, the Panay Incident, and the Defeat of the Ludlow Amendment," *International History Review* 32, no. 3 (2010): 455–500, esp. 463–464, 473. Trevor K. Plante, "Two Japans: Japanese Expressions of Sympathy and Regret in the Wake of the '*Panay*' Incident," *Prologue* 33, no. 2 (2001): 108–120. Also see Bix, *Hirohito and the Making of Modern Japan*, 340–342.

28. Dower, *Embracing Defeat*, 507. Bix, *Hirohito and the Making of Modern Japan*, 245.

CHAPTER 4

1. Richard von Weizsäcker, "Speech in the Bundestag on 8 May 1985 during the Ceremony Commemorating the 40th Anniversary of the End of War in Europe and of National-Socialist Tyranny," trans. Auswärtiges Amt Germany, Office of the Budespräsident. The Minister of Culture for Lower Saxony, quoted in Joseph A. Polak, "The Lost Transport," *Commentary*, September 1995, 24–27, esp. 26. "Statement by Prime Minister Junichiro Koizumi," available at www.kantei.go.jp/foreign/koizumispeech/2005/08/15danwa_e.html. Anthony Faiola, "Koizumi Stirs Anger with War Shrine Visit," *Washington Post*, August 15, 2006.

2. Polak, "The Lost Transport," 26.

3. Von Weizsäcker, "Speech in the Bundestag on 8 May 1985."

4. Ibid.

5. Graham G. Dodds compiled the list originally as a supplement to the document for the Penn National Commission on Society, Culture, and Community entitled "Political Apologies and Public Discourse," October 21, 1999. He then revised the list for the Penn National Commission website on January 23, 2003. On both lists, the United Church of Canada is the first historical apology. This distinction—between political and historical apologies, one for crimes in which the victims are living and one for which they are not—is mine, and I am applying it to Dodds's list. The United Church of Canada's apology is available at www.united-church.ca/beliefs/policies/1986/a651.

One can also see the mid-1980s as a key moment in the development of the historical apology by comparing Pascal Bruckner's 2006 book, *The Tyranny of Guilt*, to his 1983 book, *The Tears of the White Man*, which are both screeds against what he identifies as a leftist sensibility of political correctness in criticizing the West. Whereas the 2006 book focuses on public apologies as the primary expression of that anti-Western sentiment, his 1983 book does not mention apologies at all (although he does refer to the kind of individual penitence, guilt, and remorse that he finds and indicts in leftist Western writers who embrace the Third World). In that earlier book, he identifies Western intellectuals' solidarity, compassion, and imitation as the primary manifestations of Western masochism—that sense that comes from feeling metaphysically guilty for European and American history. In the later book, he identifies what he calls "the culture of apologies" as the primary manifestation of that sensibility. See Pascal Bruckner, *La tyrannie de la pénitence: Essai sur le masochisme occidental* (Paris: Édition Grasset et Fasquelle, 2006); Pascal Bruckner, *The Tyranny of Guilt: An Essay on Western Masochism*, trans. Steven Rendall (Princeton, NJ: Princeton University Press, 2010); Pascal Bruckner, *La sanglot de l'homme blanc: Tiers-monde, culpabilité, haine de soi* (Paris: Editions du Seuil, 1983); and Pascal Bruckner, *The Tears of the White Man: Compassion as Contempt*, trans. William R. Beer (New York: Free Press, 1986). The term "culture of apologies" is taken from *The Tyranny of Guilt*, 42.

6. Lord Vansittart, quoted in Sebastian Conrad, "Entangled Memories: Versions of the Past in Germany and Japan," *Journal of Contemporary History* 38, no. 1 (2003): 85–99, esp. 90. Vansittart articulates his position on the dangerous continuities in Germany most famously in his *Black Record: Germans Past and Present* (London: Hamish Hamilton, 1941).

7. The texts are in *Forever in the Shadow of Hitler? Original Documents of the Historikerstreit, the Controversy Concerning the Singularity of the Holocaust*, trans. James Knowlton and Truett Cates (Atlantic Highlands, NJ: Humanities Press, 1993). Von Weizsäcker, quoted in Serge Schmemann, "Bonn Journal: Facing the Mirror of German History," *New York Times*, October 22, 1988. Cf. von Weizsäcker, *From Weimar to the Wall: My Life in German Politics*, trans. Ruth Hein (New York: Broadway Books, 1999), 290–291.

8. Hanno Helbling, "A Searching Image of the Past: What Is Expected from German History Books," in *Forever in the Shadow of Hitler?* 98–100, esp. 99. Robert Leicht, "Only by Facing the Past Can We Be Free: We Are Our Own Past: German History Should Not Be Retouched," in *Forever in the Shadow of Hitler?* 244–248, esp. 245. Christian Meier, "Keynote Address on the Occasion of the Opening of the Thirty-Sixth Conference of German Historians in Trier, October 8, 1986," in *Forever in the Shadow of Hitler?* 135–142, esp. 141. Wolfgang M. Mommsen, "Neither Denial nor Forgetfulness Will Free Us from the Past: Harmonizing Our Understanding of History Endangers Freedom," in *Forever in the Shadow of Hitler?* 202–215, esp. 210. Walter Euchner, "The Nazi Reign—A Case of Normal Tyranny? On the Misuse of Philosophical Interpretations," in *Forever in the Shadow of Hitler?* 237–242, esp. 237.

9. Philip A. Seaton, *Japan's Contested War Memories: The "Memory Rifts" in Historical Consciousness of World War II* (London: Routledge, 2007), 18, 40, 101, 51, 59. Madoka Futamura, "Japanese Societal Attitudes towards the Tokyo Trial: A Contemporary Perspective," *Asia-Pacific Journal* 9, issue 29, no. 5 (2011), available at www.japanfocus.org/-Madoka-Futamura/3569/article.html. Seaton, *Japan's Contested War Memories*, 141–143.

10. Geoffrey Blainey, "Drawing Up a Balance Sheet of Our History," *Quadrant* 37 (July/August 1993): 7–8. Blainey first delivered this talk as the 1993 Sir John Latham Memorial Lecture. John Howard, "The Liberal Tradition: The Beliefs and Values Which Guide the Federal Government," Sir Robert Menzies Lecture Trust, November 18, 1996. Like Blainey, Howard believed that both views of history (black armband and three cheers) were misrepresentative. His lecture is available at www.menzieslecture.org/1996.html. The government document detailing the crimes is entitled *Bringing Them Home: Report of the National Inquiry into the Separation of Aboriginal and Torres Strait Islander Children from Their Families* (Commonwealth of Australia, 1997).

11. Luigi Accattoli, *When a Pope Asks Forgiveness: The Mea Culpa's of John Paul II*, trans. Jordan Aumann (New York: Alba House, 1998), xv.

12. Ibid., 5–6, 6, 26, 49–51.

13. Ibid., 57, 58, 65, 68–69.

14. For a full range of attempted apologies and what they might mean, see the documents and essays in *When Sorry Isn't Enough: The Controversy over Apologies and Reparations for Human Injustice*, ed. Roy L. Brooks (New York: New York University Press, 1999), 309–390. Also see Roy L. Brooks, *Atonement and Forgiveness: A New Model for Black Reparations* (Berkeley: University of California Press, 2004).

15. H. Res. 194—Apologizing for the enslavement and racial segregation of African-Americans (110th Congress, 2007–2008). S. Con. Res. 26—Apologizing for the enslavement and racial segregation of African-Americans (111th Congress, 1st Session). Several state legislatures had already passed resolutions apologizing for slavery in 2007, including Virginia (February), Maryland (March), North Carolina (April), and Alabama (June).

16. 1997 H. Con. Res. 96; 105 H. Con. Res. 96. U.S. Congress, Report to Membership on Flood Aid Negotiations (House of Representatives—June 12, 1997) *Congressional Record*, 105th Cong., 1st sess., H3722. Sabrina Eaton, "Rep. Hall Proposes an Apology for Slavery," *Cleveland Plain Dealer*, June 13, 1997. "Capital Briefly," *Orange County Register*, June 13, 1997. Scott Montgomery, "Congress Ponders Apologizing for Slavery," *Atlanta Journal and Constitution*, June 13, 1997.

17. U.S. Congress, Resolution Apologizing for Slavery (House of Representatives—June 18, 1997) *Congressional Record*, 105th Cong., 1st sess., H3890. "Apology for Slavery Dormant, Sponsor Agrees," *San Diego Union-Tribune*, August 6, 1997. Scott Montgomery, "Proposal to Apologize for U.S. Slavery Put on Hold Indefinitely," *Atlanta Journal and Constitution*, August 7, 1997.

18. Jonathan Tilove, "A Question of an Apology: Ohio Lawmaker Redefines Racial Debate with Focus on Slavery," *Cleveland Plain Dealer*, June 25, 1997.

19. Jeannine Lee, "Southern Baptists Offer an Apology," *USA Today*, June 21, 1995.

20. Gayle White, "Echoes of the Past: Southern Baptists Face an Old Shame," *Atlanta Journal and Constitution*, June 18, 1995.

21. "SBC Renounces Racist Past. Southern Baptist Convention," *Christian Century*, July 5, 1995, 671.

22. Bruce Nolan, "Baptists Repent Roots in Racism: Church Leaders Accept Apology," *Times Picayune*, June 21, 1995.

23. Judith Lynn Howard, "Baptists Apologize for Racism: Resolution Says Funding of SBC Rooted in Slavery," *Dallas Morning News*, June 21, 1995.

24. Judith Lynn Howard, "Black Scholars Question Baptists: Some Say Convention's Apology Must Include Remedy for Racism," *Dallas Morning News*, June 22, 1995.

25. E. J. Dionne Jr., "Pope Apologizes to Africans for Slavery," *New York Times*, August 14, 1985; cf. Accattoli, *When a Pope Asks Forgiveness*, 240.

26. James L. Franklin, "Vatican Traces the Roots of Racism: Calls Holocaust Worst Example, Cites South Africa," *Boston Globe*, February 10, 1989.

27. "Pontiff Recalls Horror of Slave Depot in Senegal," *Los Angeles Times*, February 23, 1992; cf. Accattoli, *When a Pope Asks Forgiveness*, 240–242.

28. Accattoli, *When a Pope Asks Forgiveness*, 244–245.

29. "Pontiff Apologizes in Jamaica for Catholic Support of Slavery," *Fort Lauderdale Sun-Sentinel*, August 10, 1993.

30. Bryna L. Bates, "Clinton's African Triumph," *Ebony*, June 1998: 43.

31. Douglas Stanglin et al., "Jesse Jackson to the Rescue," *U.S. News and World Report*, April 6, 1998: 7.

32. See http://georgewbush-whitehouse.archives.gov/news/releases/2003/07/20030708-1.html# (accessed November 19, 2012).

33. Thomas Norman DeWolf, *Inheriting the Trade: A Northern Family Confronts Its Legacy as the Largest Slave-Trading Dynasty in U.S. History* (Boston: Beacon, 2008), 228–229. Thomas Norman DeWolf and Sharon Leslie Morgan, *Gather at the Table: The Healing Journey of a Daughter of Slavery and a Son of the Slave Trade* (Boston: Beacon, 2012), 6–7. For the Hairston family story, see Henry Wiencek, *The Hairstons: An American Family in Black and White* (New York: St. Martin's Press, 1999). Joe Henry Hairston's response—taking into account the parts of his ancestry that are descended from owner and owned—is highly unusual. In all other accounts of descendants of formerly enslaved people responding to apologies by the descendants of plantation owners, there is no mention of any kind of joint responsibility. As well, I think that Joe Henry Hairston's comment is not meant to indicate anything like a shared responsibility but rather to reveal the kinds of crimes in slavery that produced shared ancestry.

34. Anthony Gifford, *The Passionate Advocate* (Kingston, Jamaica: Arawak, 2007), 245. Edward Ball, *Slaves in the Family* (New York: Farrar, Strauss, and Giroux, 1998). DeWolf, *Inheriting the Trade.* I have written about Ball and others elsewhere. See Ashraf H. A. Rushdy, "Seeking Family, Seeking Forgiveness: The Memoirs of Slaveholders' Great-Grandsons," *Southern Review* 35, no. 4 (1999): 789–805.

Another recent addition to this literature is Chris Tomlinson, *Tomlinson Hill: The Remarkable Story of Two Families Who Share the Tomlinson Name—One White, One Black* (New York: St. Martin's, 2014). Tomlinson does not apologize but recognizes the necessity of confronting the past to acknowledge the truth and commence the healing of the nation's slave past (378–379). He is particularly insightful when he describes the kinds of informal and formal education he received that taught him to see slavery and prejudice as wrong but also to ignore the question of "responsibility" for those historical forces and institutions. "That allowed me to hold on to the love of my ancestry while embracing equality for all," he writes (294).

CHAPTER 5

1. Brian Weiner, *Sins of the Parents: The Politics of National Apologies in the United States* (Philadelphia: Temple University Press, 2005), 151–152, especially makes the case for how the apology-forgiveness dynamic can reestablish equality between antagonists.

2. Letters, *Detroit News*, June 28, 1997.

3. Eric Chevlen, "Apologies Are Due—From Tony Hall," *Cleveland Plain Dealer*, July 2, 1997.

4. Solomon Schimmel, *Wounds Not Healed by Time: The Power of Repentance and Forgiveness* (New York: Oxford University Press, 2002), 216.

5. Reuters, "Uganda Says Tribal Chiefs Should Apologize for Slave Trade," *Buffalo News*, March 23, 1998. Susan Rice, an African American woman who was then the assistant secretary of State for African Affairs, had said the same thing, only to be criticized by newspapers in Uganda. See John F. Harris, "Clinton Says U.S. Wronged Africa; President Cites Slavery, 'Neglect,'" *Washington Post*, March 25, 1998. When Clinton spoke at Gorée Island, the president of Senegal, Abdou Diouf, indicated that an apology was not important: "We have already forgiven, but we will not forget," he said. See George E. Condon, Jr., "Out of Africa: Clinton Ends Trip with Visit to Slave Port," *San Diego Union-Tribune*, April 3, 1998. For leaders of African nations who have apologized for the slave trade, see

Charles P. Henry, *Long Overdue: The Politics of Racial Reparations* (New York: New York University Press, 2007), 5, 126.

6. Matthew Rees, "Birth of an Apology," *Weekly Standard*, June 30, 1997.

7. Edward Ball, *Slaves in the Family* (New York: Farrar, Strauss, and Giroux, 1998), 442.

8. See *The Negritude Poets*, ed. Ellen Conroy Kennedy (1975; repr., New York: Thunder's Mouth Press, 1989), 210–215.

9. Desmond Tutu, *No Future without Forgiveness* (New York: Random House, 1999), 31.

10. "The Official Record from Hansard of the Debate Initiated by Lord Gifford, QC in the House of Lords of the British Parliament on 14th March 1996 Concerning the African Reparations," in *Reparations for Slavery: A Reader*, ed. Ronald P. Salzberger and Mary C. Turck (Lanham, MD: Rowman and Littlefield, 2004), 96–115, esp. 106. Wole Soyinka, *The Burden of Memory, the Muse of Forgiveness* (New York: Oxford University Press, 1999), 21. For Lord Gifford's statements on reparations, see Anthony Gifford, *The Passionate Advocate* (Kingston, Jamaica: Arawak, 2007), 243–268; and Hilary McD. Beckles, *Britain's Black Debt: Reparations for Caribbean Slavery and Native Genocide* (Kingston, Jamaica: University of the West Indies Press, 2013), 177–182.

Sometimes the staging of these apologies—since they are large-scale political theater—can also replicate the events for which the apologies are offered. During President George W. Bush's visit to Gorée Island, for instance, the island's Senegal residents were rounded up and placed in holding pens as a security measure during his speech. In effect, then, as the president apologized for African enslavement, American security forces held Africans involuntarily in what some might consider modern-day barracoons. It was not enslavement, obviously, but it was a sign of the kind of values regarding human worth (who needed to be protected, and from what) that were used to justify enslavement. See Susan Neiman, *Moral Clarity: A Guide for Grown-Up Idealists* (Princeton, NJ: Princeton University Press, 2009), 359–362.

11. Karl Jaspers, *The Question of German Guilt*, trans. E. B. Ashton (Westport, CT: Greenwood Publishers, 1978), 31–32. This book was originally published in 1947.

12. Joel Feinberg, "Collective Responsibility," *Journal of Philosophy* 65, no. 21 (1968): 674–688, esp. 687. Cf. Janna Thompson, *Taking Responsibility for the Past: Reparation and Historical Injustice* (Cambridge, UK: Polity Press, 2002), 8–12.

13. Hans Mommsen, "Search for a 'Lost History'? Observations on the Historical Self-Evidence of the Federal Republic," in *Forever in the Shadow of Hitler? Original Documents of the Historikerstreit, the Controversy concerning the Singularity of the Holocaust*, trans. James Knowlton and Truett Cates (Atlantic Highlands, NJ: Humanities Press, 1993), 101–113, esp. 107. Wulf Kansteiner, *In Pursuit of German Memory: History, Television, and Politics after Auschwitz* (Athens: Ohio University Press, 2006), 252.

14. James Crawford, *The International Law Commission's Articles on State Responsibility: Introduction, Text, and Commentaries* (Cambridge: Cambridge University Press, 2002), Article 35, Article 36 (1), Article 37 (1), Article 37 (2). Cf. Max du Plessis, "Historical Injustice and International Law: An Exploratory Discussion of Reparation for Slavery," *Human Rights Quarterly* 25, no. 3 (2003): 624–659, esp. 630–631.

15. Feinberg, "Collective Responsibility," 679, 678, 679.

16. Melissa Nobles, *The Politics of Official Apologies* (Cambridge: Cambridge University Press, 2008), 24–25. Eleanor Bright Fleming, "When Sorry Is Enough: The Possibility of a National Apology for Slavery," in *The Age of Apology: Facing Up to the Past*, ed. Mark Gibney, Rhoda E. Howard-Hassman, Jean-Marc Coicaud, and Niklaus Steiner (Philadelphia: University of Pennsylvania Press, 2008), 95–108, esp. 102.

17. Robert Sparrow, "History and Collective Responsibility," *Australasian Journal of Philosophy* 78, no. 3 (2000): 346–359, esp. 355, 359. Janna Thompson, "Historical Obligations," *Australasian Journal of Philosophy* 78, no. 3 (2000): 334–345, esp. 336, 339–340. Jeremy Waldron, "Superseding Historic Injustice," *Ethics* 103, no. 1 (1992): 4–28, esp. 27. Robert Nozick, *Anarchy, State, and Utopia* (New York: Basic Books, 1974). A later contribution to this debate about collective and continuous responsibility can be found in Danielle Celermajer, *The Sins of the Nation and the Ritual of Apologies* (Cambridge: Cambridge University Press, 2009), 215–246.

18. Michael Ignatieff, *The Warrior's Honor: Ethnic War and the Modern Conscience* (New York: Henry Holt, 1997), 174.

19. The House version uses "entrenched" rather than "enmeshed." It is also worth noting that the Senate version adds two paragraphs as a prologue to the House version, which read, "Whereas during the history of the Nation, the United States has grown into a symbol of democracy and freedom around the world; Whereas the legacy of African-Americans is interwoven with the very fabric of the democracy and freedom of the United States." Why is the Senate insisting, twice, that what is at stake is the "very fabric" of the United States and the principles for which it stands? These are somewhat contradictory statements: One declares that African Americans are part of the warp and woof of the nation's principles (freedom), and the other states that slavery and racism are the woven strands of that fabric. The House version has a tidy answer that the Senate version removed—that is, it declares that slavery was a hypocritical betrayal of the principles of the Declaration of Independence on which the nation is based. The Senate seems to be trying to have it both ways; rather than seeing that the fabric was rent at the outset, it sees two different, conflicting ways in which it was woven and remained whole cloth. In doing so, I think, the Senate follows another American intellectual tradition—the failed metaphor for slavery. Just to give two brief examples of that tradition: First, American Revolutionary slaveholders consistently called themselves "slaves" insofar as they were subject to "taxation without representation." Second, in writing about early American history, Henry Adams calls slavery a "cancer" in an otherwise healthy body. These were intelligent people who simply could not understand just what slavery was or, apparently, what cancer does to a body. I discuss that idea of failed metaphors for slavery in Ashraf H. A. Rushdy, *Remembering Generations: Race and Family in Contemporary African American Fiction* (Chapel Hill: University of North Carolina Press, 2001).

20. Michael J. Sandel, *Democracy's Discontent: America in Search of a Public Philosophy* (Cambridge, MA: Harvard University Press, 1996), 15–16. Michael J. Sandel, *Public Philosophy: Essays on Morality in Politics* (Cambridge, MA: Harvard University Press, 2005), 214, 256. Michael J. Sandel, *Justice: What's the Right Thing to Do?* (New York: Farrar, Straus, and Giroux, 2009), 225.

21. Weiner, *Sins of the Parents*, 4, calls it a desire for ascertaining membership in "an intergenerational polity." Cf. Nobles, *The Politics of Official Apologies*, x–xi, 2–3.

22. Thompson, *Taking Responsibility for the Past*, xviii; and Celermajer, *The Sins of the Nation and the Ritual of Apologies*, 247–263.

23. See www.goodreads.com/author/quotes/15865.William_James.

24. R. G. Collingwood, *Essay on Metaphysics* (1940; repr., Oxford: Oxford University Press, 1998), 194. Cf. Bernard Williams, "An Essay on Collingwood," in *The Sense of the Past: Essays in the History of Philosophy*, ed. Myles Burnyeat (Princeton, NJ: Princeton University Press, 2006), 341–358, esp. 356.

25. David W. Blight, *Race and Reunion: The Civil War in American Memory* (Cambridge, MA: Harvard University Press, 2001), 282. Pauline E. Hopkins, *Contending Forces: A*

Romance Illustrative of Negro Life North and South (New York: Oxford University Press, 1988), 202, 332.

CHAPTER 6

1. Joseph Butler, "Sermon VI: Preached before His Grace Charles Duke of Richmond, President, and the Governors of the London Infirmary," in *The Works of Joseph Butler*, ed. W. E. Gladstone (Oxford: Clarendon Press, 1896), II: 375–396, esp. 395.

2. Jeremy Bentham, *The Rationale of Punishment* (London: Robert Heward, 1830), 269–271.

3. Ibid., 393, 269.

4. R. E. Hobart, "Free Will as Involving Determination and as Inconceivable without It," *Mind* 43 (1934): 1–27, esp. 4, 27.

5. Daniel C. Dennett, *Elbow Room: The Varieties of Free Will Worth Wanting* (Cambridge: MIT Press, 1984), 166, 142.

6. Friedrich Nietzsche, *The Will to Power*, trans. Walter Kaufmann and R. J. Hollingdale, ed. Walter Kaufman (New York: Vintage, 1968), 212.

7. Lucy Allais, "Wiping the Slate Clean: The Heart of Forgiveness," *Philosophy and Public Affairs* 36, no. 1 (2008): 33–68, esp. 38. Christopher Bennett, "Is Amnesty a Collective Act of Forgiveness?" *Contemporary Political Theory* 2, no. 1 (2003): 67–76, esp. 70.

8. Joanna North, "Wrongdoing and Forgiveness," *Philosophy* 62 (October 1987): 499–508, esp. 499–500.

9. Andrew Schaap, "Political Grounds for Forgiveness," *Contemporary Political Theory* 2, no. 1 (2003): 77–87, esp. 82.

10. Nicholas Tavuchis, *Mea Culpa: A Sociology of Apology and Reconciliation* (Stanford, CA: Stanford University Press, 1991), viii, 5.

11. William Shakespeare, Sonnet 138, in *The Complete Sonnets and Poems*, ed. Colin Burrow (Oxford: Oxford University Press, 2002), 655.

12. Gerald F. Gaus, "Does Compensation Restore Equality?" in *NO-MOS XXXIII: Compensatory Justice*, ed. John W. Chapman (New York: New York University Press, 1991), 45–81. Janna Thompson, *Taking Responsibility for the Past: Reparation and Historical Injustice* (Cambridge, UK: Polity Press, 2002), 48. Thompson does see more room for how acts of atonement, apology, and forgiveness can repair the relationship, even in cases where the act of disrespect cannot be undone (49).

13. Margaret Walker, *Moral Repair: Reconstructing Moral Relations after Wrongdoing* (Cambridge: Cambridge University Press, 2006), 212.

14. Hannah Arendt, *The Human Condition* (Chicago: University of Chicago Press, 1958), 237. The book is partly based on a set of lectures Arendt had delivered two years earlier at the University of Chicago. Throughout this section, I am going to retain Arendt's use of "man" to refer to humanity and make the necessary accommodations in my own prose, because altering it in each case simply disrupts the elegance of her prose. In every usage I quote, she intends all human beings when she uses the term.

15. Note that Arendt is *not* saying undoing is possible, but desirable. When we return to the oft-quoted sentence and look at it more closely, we see the distinction she makes between promising and forgiving. Promising is the "remedy for unpredictability." As a remedy, something that applies, it will heal. Forgiving, on the other hand, is only the "possible redemption from the predicament of irreversibility." This is not an affirmation of fact but a

hope, and it is doubly hopeful (it is *possible*, that is not assured, and it is a possible *redemption*, not a healing, which places it in a different realm that is not medical but religious). Arendt is always careful with this distinction and always makes it clear that, like all things that are possible, undoing requires an attempt. When she published parts of this book in earlier form, as she did, for instance, in a 1954 essay, she maintains that same distinction between possibility and assurance. Forgiving, she writes there, is "certainly one of the greatest human capacities and perhaps the boldest of human actions" precisely because "it tries the seemingly impossible, to undo what has been done, and succeeds in making a new beginning where everything seemed to have come to an end." It *attempts* a certain act (to undo), but its *success* is something else (to begin anew). It would appear, then, that Arendt consistently deemphasizes the *fact* of undoing at the same time that she insists on the political benefits of the *effects* of undoing. See Hannah Arendt, "Understanding and Politics (The Difficulties of Understanding)," in *Essays in Understanding, 1930–1954: Formation, Exile, and Totalitarianism*, ed. Jerome Kohn (New York: Schocken Books, 1994), 307–327, esp. 308. This same idea is repeated in Hannah Arendt, *The Promise of Politics*, ed. Jerome Kohn (New York: Schocken Books, 2005), 57–60.

16. Arendt, *The Human Condition*, 237, 238. There is probably a hint of Christian eschatology in Arendt's analysis, since in that belief the one act that arguably has eternal repercussions is the Fall of Adam, and the one that redeems that Fall through a sacrificial, forgiving act is Christ's crucifixion, but Arendt in this section actually never mentions the Fall, and she never talks about the divine Christ, only Jesus, and only about Jesus as a political thinker. It is only once, in the concluding section, that Arendt mentions Adam's Fall and Christ's Passion, and it is in her discussion of immortality, not forgiveness (315).

17. Ibid., 240–241, 243, 242, 183, 243.

18. Ibid., 19, 18, 120.

19. Ibid., 246.

20. Ibid., 241, 237.

21. Hannah Arendt, *The Origins of Totalitarianism* (1948; repr., New York: Schocken Books, 2004), 631, 270. On this point, also see Hannah Arendt, "What Is Existential Philosophy?" in *Essays in Understanding, 1930–1954*, 163–187, esp. 181.

22. Arendt, *The Origins of Totalitarianism*, 586, 610, 616.

23. To get one final sense of what Arendt might mean by this strategy of basing a desirable political goal (spontaneity, freedom) on an impossible physical fact (irreversibility of time), we can turn to the final book she wrote, *The Life of the Mind*. In the second volume, *Willing*, she returns to this question about undoing in a brief discussion of Nietzsche (although she does not use the term). "Nietzsche's discovery that the Will cannot 'will backwards,'" she writes, led to precisely those aggressive emotions we associate with him: "not only frustration and resentment, but also the positive, active will to annihilate what was." I take "will[ing] backwards" to be equivalent to "undoing" what has happened, or at least similar enough to permit insight into Arendt's meaning for the latter. Not being able to undo can lead to either of two possibilities: Nietzschean *ressentiment* (the opposite of forgiveness) or forgiveness (which involves foregoing resentment). The Nietzschean path is treacherous and predetermined; to change metaphors, it is constituted of only reactions. The forgiveness path opens up new vistas and permits us to act anew. We can discover that we cannot undo the past and react with fury and destructiveness, or we can attempt to undo the past and act toward freedom. See Hannah Arendt, *The Life of the Mind* (San Diego: Harcourt, 1978), 176. This is the one-volume edition of the two books, *One: Thinking* and *Two: Willing*. The passage is in *Willing*; the pagination is discontinuous. These are the two volumes of the projected three that Arendt was writing when she passed away in 1976.

24. Emmanuel Levinas, *Totality and Infinity*, trans. Alphonso Lingis (Pittsburgh: Duquesne University Press, 1969), 231. Emmanuel Levinas, *Totalité et infini* (The Hague: Nijhoff, 1961), 207. One certainly sometimes wishes to undo history, as Levinas recognizes. He notes in one of his lectures on Talmudic readings that "one can forgive many Germans, but there are some Germans it is difficult to forgive." For him, it was "difficult to forgive Heidegger," whom he had met while he was a student and whose work he introduced to French readers. See Emmanuel Levinas, *Nine Talmudic Readings*, trans. Annette Aronowicz (Bloomington: Indiana University Press, 1994), 25. For more on Levinas, see Robert Bernasconi, "Travelling Light: The Conditions of Unconditional Forgiveness in Levinas and Jankélévitch," in *Vladimir Jankélévitch and the Question of Forgiveness*, ed. Alan Udoff (Lanham, MD: Lexington Books, 2013), 85–96.

25. Virgilio Elizondo, "I Forgive but I Do Not Forget," in *Forgiveness*, ed. Casiano Floristán and Christian Duquoc (Edinburgh: T. and T. Clark, 1986), 69–79, esp. 72. John Chryssavgis, *Repentance and Confession in the Orthodox Church* (Brookline, MA: Holy Cross Orthodox Press, 1990), 4. I am indebted to David Konstans, whose book *Before Forgiving: The Origins of a Moral Idea* (Cambridge: Cambridge University Press, 2010) alerted me to these two writers.

26. Vladimir Jankélévitch, *Forgiveness*, trans. Andrew Kelley (Chicago: University of Chicago Press, 2005), 39–40, 19, 154. See Stephen Jay Gould, *Time's Arrow, Time's Cycle: Myth and Metaphor in the Discovery of Geological Time* (Cambridge, MA: Harvard University Press, 1988). Henri Bergson, *Time and Free Will: An Essay on the Immediate Data of Consciousness*, trans. F. L. Pogson (1910; repr., Mineola, NY: Dover, 2001). In the first chapter, Jankélévitch begins in a Bergsonian vein and commences his lyrical analysis of the "natural dimensions of becoming"—that is, of the movement of time. He begins by defining the differential experiences of time that forgiveness or its failure produces. The "man of *ressentiment*," for instance, struggles against the inexorable march of time, struggling to keep alive a sentiment that is based on the past, and keeps the man of *ressentiment* mired in the past. In other words, he is static and fights against *becoming*. Foregoing *ressentiment*, though, forgiveness, in other words, alters the flow of time in that retarded life. Forgiving, as Jankélévitch puts it in his characteristically abstract metaphysical way, "helps becoming to become, while becoming helps forgiveness to forgive." See Jankélévitch, *Forgiveness*, 13, 15.

27. Jankélévitch, *Une vie en toutes lettres (Lettres à Louis Beauduc, 1923–1980)*, ed. Françoise Schwab (Paris: Liana Levi, 1995), 172: "Je crois que c'est un problème central et qui se rattache, par l'intermédiare du problème de la Douleur, au fait primitif de la vie spirituelle: 'l'Irréversibilitité.'"

28. Joëlle Hansel, "Forgiveness and 'Should We Pardon Them?': The Pardon and the Imprescriptible," in *Vladimir Jankélévitch and the Question of Forgiveness*, 111–125, esp. 119. Jankélévitch, *L'irreversible et la nostalgie* (1974; repr., Paris: Flammarion, 1983), quoted in Kevin Hart, "Guilty Forgiveness," in *Vladimir Jankélévitch and the Question of Forgiveness*, 49–66, esp. 56.

29. Jankélévitch, *Une vie en toutes lettres*, 195; *"Le pouvoir de défaire est d'un autre ordre: De l'ordre de la grâce, is tu veux. C'est un miracle."* I am indebted to Hart, "Guilty Forgiveness," 53, for drawing my attention to this passage. Jankélévitch, *Forgiveness*, 48.

30. Jankélévitch, *Forgiveness*, 48, 99.

31. Ibid., 145, 153, 154, 153. One might discern a similar position about preemptive forgiving in Georg Wilhelm Friedrich Hegel: "A heart thus lifted above the ties of rights, disentangled from everything objective, has nothing to forgive the offender, for it sacrificed its right as soon as the object over which it had a right was assailed, and thus the offender has done no injury to any right at all." The difference is that Hegel is working from a

position in which forgiveness does not need to be extended since rights are renounced prior to the offense, while Jankélévitch sees the act of forgiveness as hereafter renouncing the rights. Hegel also claims that "what happened cannot be undone." Georg Wilhelm Friedrich Hegel, *The Spirit of Christianity and Its Fate*, in *Early Theological Writings*, trans. T. M. Knox (Chicago: University of Chicago Press, 1948), 236, 227.

32. Jankélévitch makes some mild efforts to suggest that, perhaps, they are reconcilable. Just before he embarks on his final lyrical descriptions of forgiveness as a supernatural miracle that erases the past, for instance, he offers a tepid and somewhat bewildering attempt to suggest that the change is not really to time and event but to something in the forgiver's mind. He writes, "The supernaturality of forgiveness consists in this, that my opinion on the subject of the guilty person precisely has not changed; but against this immutable background it is the whole lighting of my relations with the guilty person that is modified, it is the whole orientation of our relations that finds itself inverted, overturned, and overwhelmed!" The terminology here is of stagecraft—the lighting changes, the orientation is reset—and later Jankélévitch refers to the "dramatic and so strongly contrasted antithesis of dark regions and light." And so it is not surprising that Jankélévitch refers to the "coup de théâtre that we call forgiveness." But what he describes is more like a *deus ex machina*; it is a supernatural intervention that alters the events and makes some of them disappear. It is not the lighting that changes how the event appears, nor how we are situated in relation to it—what he is saying is that what changes is the event itself. See Jankélévitch, *Forgiveness*, 152.

33. Ibid., 48, 153.

34. Another possibility is based on the tensions in the distinct kinds of philosophies that Jankélévitch practiced. Andrew Kelley, for instance, argues that "for Jankélévitch forgiving is both an ethical and a metaphysical gesture." We might then think of the tensions between what I have called the *psychological* and *mystical* approaches in Jankélévitch as expressing these two modes: on the one hand, forgiving as an ethical act, something that is performed and has moral meaning among human beings; on the other, as a metaphysical manifestation of something wondrous and beyond comprehension, something that exceeds meaning in the physical and human worlds. See Andrew Kelley, "Jankélévitch and the Metaphysics of Forgiveness," in *Vladimir Jankélévitch and the Question of Forgiveness*, 27–46, esp. 27.

35. Jonathan Judaken, "Vladimir Jankélévitch at the *Colloques des intellectuels juifs de langue française*," in *Vladimir Jankélévitch and the Question of Forgiveness*, 3–26, esp. 6. Emmanuel Levinas, *Outside the Subject*, trans. Michael B. Smith (Stanford, CA: Stanford University Press, 1994), 87, 89, 87; cf. Emmanuel Levinas, *Hors sujet* (Paris: Fata Morgana, 1987), 131, 133, 131. Judaken, "Vladimir Jankélévitch at the *Colloques des intellectuels juifs de langue française*," 18.

36. Jankélévitch, *Forgiveness*, 164, 165.

37. John Milbank, "The Ethics of Honor and the Possibility of Promise," in *Vladimir Jankélévitch and the Question of Forgiveness*, 161–190, esp. 171. Others who write from an avowedly Christian perspective do challenge the idea that forgiveness means to undo, although they are not necessarily less mystical in doing so. Cf. Stephen Cherry, *Healing Agony: Re-Imagining Forgiveness* (New York: Continuum, 2012), 175, 189, who calls Arendt's commentary on forgiveness as a means of escaping irreversibility "overstated." He sees forgiveness as "not a zero-sum reversal of the apparently irreversible" but rather "a matter of transcendence, a true resurrection."

38. *The Humble Advice of the Assembly of Divines by Authority of Parliament Sitting at Westminster: Concerning a Confession of Faith* (London, 1647), 51.

39. Cf. Avishai Margalit, *The Ethics of Memory* (Cambridge, MA: Harvard University Press, 2002), 185–189, 197–199.

40. Anthony Bash, *Just Forgiveness: Exploring the Bible, Weighing the Issues* (London: Society for Promoting Christian Knowledge, 2011), 41, 43–49. V. Norskov Olsen, "Forgiveness in the New Testament," *Ministry Magazine*, July 1963. The word *apoluo* is also translated as "forgive" (it is usually rendered as "let go," "put away," or "dismiss"), but it is used only twice in the New Testament. As well, *aspondia* is used twice as "unforgiving" (Bash, *Just Forgiveness*, 53).

41. Mark R. Amstutz, *The Healing of Nations: The Promise and Limits of Political Forgiveness* (Lanham, MD: Rowman and Littlefield, 2005), ix. Luigi Accattoli, *When a Pope Asks Forgiveness: The Mea Culpa's of John Paul II*, trans. Jordan Aumann (New York: Alba House, 1998), xxi; cf. xiii on "revision of memory."

42. William Waller Hening, *The Statutes at Large: Being a Collection of All the Laws of Virginia, from the First Session of the Legislature in the Year 1619*, vol. 3 (Philadelphia, 1823), 459. The 1688 British law in the Barbados held that a master who murdered a slave "willfully" would be subject to a fine of £15, while one who killed his slave while punishing the enslaved person would be compensated at market value. Richard Hall, *Acts Passed in the Island of Barbados, 1643–1762* (London, 1764), no. 42, quoted in Hilary McD. Beckles, *Britain's Black Debt: Reparations for Caribbean Slavery and Native Genocide* (Kingston, Jamaica: University of the West Indies Press, 2013), 61.

43. Ashraf H. A. Rushdy, *American Lynching* (New Haven, CT: Yale University Press, 2012), 153. For a beautiful meditation on the variety of meanings of "undoing" and an insightful commentary on the existential meaning of enslavement, see Saidiya Hartman, *Lose Your Mother: A Journey along the Atlantic Slave Route* (New York: Farrar, Strauss, and Giroux, 2007), 6–8. Hartman posits three kinds of undoing, all intimately connected. The first is the undoing of enslavement—that is, what slavery itself produced. She notes that she went to Ghana "desperate to reclaim the dead—that is, to reckon with the lives undone and obliterated in the making of human commodities." The second is the undoing of the effects of slavery—in other words, the continuing and ongoing traumas flowing from the past. Slavery, she writes, "had established a measure of man and a ranking of life and worth that has yet to be undone." The third is the undoing of the contemporary descendent of enslavement, the person who wishes to be a fugitive from that past and from the effects of that past. "Unwilling to accept the pain of this," she writes, "I had tried to undo the past and reinvent myself." The first undoing is a crime, the second an indictment, and the third a strategy (one that Hartman reveals throughout her powerful memoir that is as impossible as it is necessary).

44. Kathleen Dean Moore, *Pardons: Justice, Mercy, and the Public Interest* (New York: Oxford University Press, 1989), 182–188; the quotation is taken from 182. Elliot N. Dorff, "The Elements of Forgiveness: A Jewish Approach," in *Dimensions of Forgiveness: Psychological Research and Theological Perspectives*, ed. Everett L. Worthington Jr. (Philadelphia: Templeton Foundation Press, 1998), 29–53, esp. 37.

45. Charles Krauthammer, "Reparations for Black Americans," *Time*, December 31, 1990. Charles Krauthammer, "David Horowitz and Reparations," *Pittsburgh Post-Gazette*, April 7, 2001.

46. Chen-Bo Zhong and Katie Liljenquist, "Washing Away Your Sins: Threatened Morality and Physical Cleansing," *Science* 313 (September 8, 2006): 1451–1452. Cf. Linda Radzik, *Making Amends: Atonement in Morality, Law, and Politics* (New York: Oxford University Press, 2009), 6.

47. Zhong and Liljenquist, "Washing Away Your Sins," 1452.

CHAPTER 7

1. Arthur C. Danto, "The Vietnam Veterans Memorial," *The Nation*, August 31, 1985: 152–155, esp. 153, 154, 152, 155, 152.

2. Charles Griswold, "The Vietnam Veterans Memorial and the Washington Mall: Philosophical Thoughts on Political Iconography," *Critical Inquiry* 12, no. 4 (1986): 688–719, esp. 708, 711, 713.

3. Ibid., 713, 711.

4. Martha C. Nussbaum, *Political Emotions: Why Love Matters for Justice* (Cambridge, MA: Belknap Press, 2013), 428n49, 284–288, 381.

5. Charles Griswold, *Forgiveness: A Philosophical Exploration* (Cambridge: University of Cambridge Press, 2007), 204, 206. Lin quoted in *U.S. News and World Report*, November 21, 1983, 68; Lin quoted in Griswold, "The Vietnam Veterans Memorial and the Washington Mall," 718n17. Jan C. Scruggs and Joel L. Swerdlow, *To Heal a Nation: The Vietnam Veterans Memorial* (New York: HarperCollins, 1985). See the National Parks Service website: www.nps.gov/vive/index.htm. Griswold, *Forgiveness*, 207. Griswold, *Forgiveness*, 201n11 notes that the discussion in this book "departs in a significant way" from his earlier essay. In the earlier essay, Griswold deals at length with the physical context of the Vietnam Veterans Memorial, especially its relationship to other memorials and monuments on the Mall (691–704). He then makes the same observations he repeats in *Forgiveness* on how the memorial functions as a national gravestone (707), as a reflective mirror calling forth certain reflections in the spectator (711), and as a book that remains unfinished (708). He also notes that it works as a therapeutic device, although he there argues that the "therapy depends on an understanding of certain overreaching values" (713). He does not at all address the question of whether the memorial can bespeak or represent forgiveness, nor does he raise the question of how the memorial raises questions it cannot answer about the politics of the war.

6. Griswold, *Forgiveness*, 207, 208, 210, 209.

7. Archbishop Desmond Tutu, "Foreword: Without Forgiveness There Is No Future," in *Exploring Forgiveness*, ed. Robert D. Enright and Joanna North (Madison: University of Wisconsin Press, 1998), xiii–xiv, esp. xiv.

8. Thomas Norman DeWolf and Sharon Leslie Morgan, *Gather at the Table: The Healing Journey of a Daughter of Slavery and a Son of the Slave Trade* (Boston: Beacon, 2012), 185–186. For the background story of the DeWolf family and their efforts to apologize, see Thomas Norman DeWolf, *Inheriting the Trade: A Northern Family Confronts Its Legacy as the Largest Slave-Trading Dynasty in U.S. History* (Boston: Beacon, 2008). Avishai Margalit, *The Ethics of Memory* (Cambridge, MA: Harvard University Press, 2002), 81.

9. See the "Chronology," in *Bitburg in Moral and Political Perspective*, ed. Geoffrey H. Hartman (Bloomington: Indiana University Press, 1986), xiii–xvi.

10. Richard von Weizsäcker, *From Weimar to the Wall: My Life in German Politics*, trans. Ruth Hein (New York: Broadway Books, 1999), 87–101, esp. 89, 94.

11. James M. Markham, "Facing Up to Germany's Past," *New York Times*, June 23, 1985.

12. Willy Brandt, *My Life in Politics*, trans. Anthea Ball (New York: Viking, 1992), 199. The second passage from the Warsaw Treaty speech is quoted in Aase Lionæs, "Award Ceremony Speech" for Brandt's 1971 Nobel Peace Prize, in *Nobel Lectures in Peace, 1971–1980*, ed. Irwin Abrams (Singapore: World Scientific, 1997), 7–16, esp. 13.

13. Elazar Barkan, *The Guilt of Nations: Restitution and Negotiating Historical Injustices* (New York: Norton, 2000), 11. Danielle Celermajer, *The Sins of the Nation and the Ritual of Apologies* (Cambridge: Cambridge University Press, 2009), 18.

14. "Kniefall Angemessen Oder Übertrieben?" *Der Spiegel* 51 (December 14, 1970). Lionæs, "Award Ceremony Speech," 13.

15. Donald W. Shriver Jr., *An Ethic for Enemies: Forgiveness in Politics* (New York: Oxford University Press, 1995), 112, 252n95.

16. Aaron Lazare, *On Apology* (New York: Oxford University Press, 2004), 84, 253. Alexis Dudden, *Troubled Apologies among Japan, Korea, and the United States* (New York: Columbia University Press, 2008), 32.

17. Peter Bender, *Die Neue Ostpolitik und ihre Folgen: Vom Mauerbau bis zur Vereinigung*, 4th rev. ed. (Munich: Deutsche Taschenbuch Verlag, 1996), 182, quoted in Celermajer, *The Sins of the Nation*, 17. Celermajer, *The Sins of the Nation*, 17. Jennifer Lind, *Sorry States: Apologies in International Politics* (Ithaca, NY: Cornell University Press, 2008), 128. Girma Negash, *Apologia Politica: States and Their Apologies by Proxy* (Lanham, MD: Lexington Books, 2006), 1. Michael Ignatieff, *The Warrior's Honor: Ethnic War and the Modern Conscience* (New York: Henry and Holt, 1997), 187. Ian Buruma, *Wages of Guilt: Memories of War in Germany and Japan* (London: Jonathan Cape, 1994), 243; Buruma also describes it as an attempt "to apologize for historical crimes" (9). Von Weizsäcker, *From Weimar to the Wall*, 366–367. Cf. Thomas U. Berger, *War, Guilt, and World Politics after World War II* (Cambridge: Cambridge University Press, 2012), 35, 63, in which Berger says Brandt's *kniefall* "begged for forgiveness" and calls it "the most powerful and enduring symbol of German penance."

The image itself, in the form of the famous photograph of Brandt grimly kneeling at the foot of the memorial, has been used to grace the cover of at least two recent books on political state apologies, Lind's *Sorry States* and Negash's *Apologia Politica*. Here, then, are writers from all over the world, representing four continents, noting the influential and lasting importance of Brandt's apology.

18. "Remarks of President Reagan to Regional Editors, White House, April 18, 1985," in *Bitburg in Moral and Political Perspective*, 239.

19. Elie Weisel quoted in Mark Krupnick, "'Walking in Our Sleep': Bitburg and the Post-1939 Generation," in *Bitburg in Moral and Political Perspective*, 187–190, esp. 188. Lance Morrow, "Forgiveness to the Injured Doth Belong," in *Bitburg in Moral and Political Perspective*, 179–181, esp. 180. James M. Markham, "For Bitburg, Day of Anger Ends Quietly," in *Bitburg in Moral and Political Perspective*, 150–152, esp. 152. Krupnick, "'Walking in Our Sleep,'" 188. Meir Merhav, "Honouring Evil," in *Bitburg in Moral and Political Perspective*, 194–198, esp. 198. See A. M. Rosenthal, "On My Mind: Forgive Them Not," *New York Times*, September 14, 1990.

20. "Sermon of Cardinal Joseph Höffner at the Ecumenical Service in the Köln Cathedral, 8 May 1985, Broadcast by West German Radio WDR," quoted in Saul Friedländer, "Some German Struggles with Memory," in *Bitburg in Moral and Political Perspective*, 27–42, esp. 35.

21. Von Weizsäcker, *From Weimar to the Wall*, 266–267.

22. Richard von Weizsäcker, "Speech in the Bundestag on 8 May 1985 during the Ceremony Commemorating the 40th Anniversary of the End of War in Europe and of National-Socialist Tyranny," trans. Auswärtiges Amt Germany, Office of the Budespräsident. For the connotations of "Zero Hour," see Keith Lowe, *Savage Continent: Europe in the Aftermath of World War II* (New York: St. Martin's, 2012), xiv.

23. Von Weizsäcker, "Speech in the Bundestag on 8 May 1985." Cf. Buruma, *Wages of Guilt*, 243: von Weizsäcker's "speech was drenched in *Trauer*" (sorrow or mourning).

24. "Address by Helmut Kohl, Chancellor of the Federal Republic of Germany, dur-

ing the Ceremony Marking the 40th Anniversary of the Liberation of the Concentration Camps at the Site of the Former Bergen-Belsen Concentration Camp, April 21, 1985," in *Bitburg in Moral and Political Perspective*, 244–250, esp. 244.

25. Brandt quoted in Lind, *Sorry States*, 127.

26. Brandt, *My Life in Politics*, 200. "The Leaders' Apologies," *The Guardian*, October 13, 1993, 25, quoted in Melissa Nobles, *The Politics of Official Apologies* (Cambridge: Cambridge University Press, 2008), 156. The video of the documentary is available at

www.dailymotion.com/video/xyhgpb_pure-history-moments-1970-willy-brandt-in-warsaw_shortfilms. Cf. Celermajer, *The Sins of the Nation*, 17–18; and Lind, *Sorry States*, 127–128.

27. Buruma, *Wages of Guilt*, 303. Tony Judt, *Postwar: A History of Europe since 1945* (New York: Penguin Press, 2005), 416. Alexander and Margarete Mitscherlich, *The Inability to Mourn: Principles of Collective Behavior*, trans. Beverley R. Placzek (New York: Grove Press, 1975). Robert Jay Clifton, "Preface," to Mitscherlich, *The Inability to Mourn*, x.

28. Mitscherlich, *The Inability to Mourn*, xx, 26, 44; they hint at the possibility of German melancholia later in the book (55, 62–63). A. Roy Eckardt, "The Christian World Goes to Bitburg," in *Bitburg in Moral and Political Perspective*, 80–89, esp. 85.

29. Mitscherlich, *The Inability to Mourn*, 31.

30. Ibid., 51–53.

31. Ibid., 7n 14n, xix.

32. Philip A. Seaton, *Japan's Contested War Memories: The "Memory Rifts" in Historical Consciousness of World War II* (London: Routledge, 2007), 78.

33. Ibid., 42. Hirohito had visited the shrine in October 1948 in a "private act of worship." See Stephen S. Large, *Emperor Hirohito and Shōwa Japan: A Political Biography* (New York: Routledge, 1992), 159. Seaton, *Japan's Contested War Memories*, 47.

34. Henry Rousso, *The Vichy Syndrome: History and Memory in France since 1944*, trans. Arthur Goldhammer (Cambridge, MA: Harvard University Press, 1991), 171. "Mitterand and Kohl Honor Dead of Verdun," *New York Times*, September 23, 1984. Mitterand had earlier responded to attacks on his reputation by visiting the tombs of Resistance heroes, Jean Moulin and Victor Schoelcher in the Pantheon, a week and a half after his election in 1981. See Rousso, *The Vichy Syndrome*, 184, 315.

35. Sigmund Freud, *Five Lectures on Psycho-Analysis*, in *The Standard Edition of the Complete Psychological Works of Sigmund Freud*, trans. and ed. James Strachey, vol. 11 (London: Hogarth Press, 1953–1974), 16–17.

36. Luigi Accattoli, *When a Pope Asks Forgiveness: The Mea Culpa's of John Paul II*, trans. Jordan Aumann (New York: Alba House, 1998), 147–148.

37. Michael S. Roth, "*Shoah* as Shivah," in *The Ironist's Cage: Memory, Trauma, and the Construction of History* (New York: Columbia University Press, 1995), 214–227, esp. 226, 225. Throughout the essays in this collection, and in his next collection, Roth develops the concept of "piety" as a stance toward the past, comparable to what I am calling "mourning" here. For him it is, implicitly, a way to escape the "ironist's cage." See Michael Roth, *Memory, Trauma, and History: Essays on Living with the Past* (New York: Columbia University Press, 2012), xxxiii, 85–86, 93–97.

Katrina Browne's documentary *Traces of the Trade: A Story from the Deep North* (California Newsreel, 2008) likewise concludes with an emphasis on mourning as an apt response to the transatlantic slave trade. As Browne puts it in her address to the Episcopal Church convention considering the case of the church's complicity in the slave trade, "It becomes very natural to want to make things right, not out of personal guilt, but out of grief." I would like to thank my friend Christina Sharpe for directing me to this documentary and to her own important work on mourning in thinking about contemporary conditions in and out of the academy. See Christina Sharpe, "Black Studies: In the Wake," *Black Scholar* 44, no. 2 (2014): 59–69.

CONCLUSION

1. Primo Levi, *The Periodic Table*, trans. Raymond Rosenthal (New York: Everyman's Library, 1995), 157. Primo Levi, *The Reawakening*, trans. Stuart Wolf (New York: Simon and Schuster, 1995), 16. Cf. Primo Levi, *The Drowned and the Saved*, trans. Raymond Rosenthal (New York: Summit Books, 1988), 70–87.

2. Hannah Arendt, *The Origins of Totalitarianism* (1948; repr., New York: Schocken Books, 2004), 631.

3. Hannah Arendt, "What Is Existential Philosophy," in *Essays in Understanding, 1930–1954: Formation, Exile, and Totalitarianism*, ed. Jerome Kohn (New York: Schocken Books, 1994), 163–187, esp. 181.

4. Pascal Bruckner, *The Tyranny of Guilt: An Essay on Western Masochism*, trans. Steven Rendall (Princeton, NJ: Princeton University Press, 2010), suggests that these public apologies do spell the end of nationalism, although he deplores this prospect. "Universal repentance," he writes, "is contemporary with the final stage of the state, that of its collapse" (108). His anti-cosmopolitan sentiment is most clearly expressed in his paean to borders: "The border is not only an obstacle, it is the condition for the exercise of democracy, it establishes a durable link between those sheltered within it and gives them the feeling of belonging to a common world" (190).

5. H. Con. Res. 195, 107th Congress, 1st Session (July 24, 2001).

6. George Orwell, "Notes on Nationalism," *Polemic: A Magazine of Philosophy, Psychology, and Aesthetics* 1 (October 1945), reprinted in George Orwell, *Essays* (New York: Everyman's Library, 2002), 865–884, esp. 872–873, 874, 883–884.

7. Stanley Cohen, *States of Denial: Knowing about Atrocities and Suffering* (Cambridge, UK: Polity, 2001), 248.

8. Philip Gourevitch, *We Wish to Inform You That Tomorrow We Will Be Killed with Our Families: Stories from Rwanda* (New York: Farrar, Straus and Giroux, 1998), 133; cf. Ben Kiernan, *Blood and Soil: A World History of Genocide and Extermination from Sparta to Darfur* (New Haven, CT: Yale University Press, 2007), 559. Elizabeth Neuffer, *The Key to My Neighbor's House: Seeking Justice in Bosnia and Rwanda* (New York: Picador, 2001), 272. Bill Berkeley, *The Graves Are Not Yet Full: Race, Tribe, and Power in the Heart of Africa* (New York: Basic Books, 2001), 252–253.

9. "Text of Clinton's Rwanda Speech," available at www.cbsnews.com/news/text-of-clintons-rwanda-speech/. Neuffer, *The Key to My Neighbor's House*, 337–338. Samantha Power, *"A Problem from Hell": America and the Age of Genocide* (New York: Basic Books, 2002), 386, slyly notes that Clinton spoke "with the grace of one grown practiced at public remorse." For a discussion of how the United States backtracked on calling what happened in Rwanda "genocide," see Girma Negash, *Apologia Politica: States and Their Apologies by Proxy* (Lanham, MD: Lexington Books, 2006), 77–108.

10. Rwanda Organic Law No. 08/96 on the Organization of Prosecutions for Offences Constituting the Crime of Genocide or Crimes against Humanity Committed since October 1, 1990 (passed August 30, 1996). Neuffer, *The Key to My Neighbor's House*, 258–259.

11. For the debates over whether to empower the *Gacaca* courts with trying *génocidaires*, see Neuffer, *The Key to My Neighbor's House*, 397–399. On the variety of Rwandan

responses to the genocide, see Alex Boraine, *A Country Unmasked: Inside South Africa's Truth and Reconciliation Commission* (New York: Oxford University Press, 2000), 404–409. Paul Kagame's speech is available at www.paulkagame.com/2010/index.php?option=com_content&view=article&id=691%3Aspeech-by-he-paul-kagame-president-of-the-republic-of-rwanda-at-the-official-closing-of-gacaca-courts&catid=34%3Aspeeches&Itemid=56&lang=en (accessed January 10, 2014).

12. Gourevitch, *We Wish to Inform You That Tomorrow We Will Be Killed with Our Families*, 240–241.

13. Ibid., 250–251. Neuffer, *The Key to My Neighbor's House*, 251. In postwar Germany also, civilians were forced to visit the concentration camps and perform exactly these same ritual actions—that is, to exhume mass graves and bury decomposing corpses. See Harold Marcuse, *Legacies of Dachau: The Uses and Abuses of a Concentration Camp, 1933–2001* (Cambridge: Cambridge University Press, 2001), 128.

14. Gourevitch, *We Wish to Inform You That Tomorrow We Will Be Killed with Our Families*, 168–169.

15. Michael Ignatieff, *The Warrior's Honor: Ethnic War and the Modern Conscience* (New York: Henry Holt, 1997), 174. Michael Ignatieff, *The Lesser Evil: Political Ethics in an Age of Terror* (Princeton, NJ: Princeton University Press, 2004). Michael Ignatieff, "Articles of Faith, Index on Censorship," *Harper's*, September/October 1997: 15–17. Ignatieff, *The Warrior's Honor*, 186–187, 177.

16. Gourevitch, *We Wish to Inform You That Tomorrow We Will Be Killed with Our Families*, 196.

INDEX

Ashraf H. A. Rushdy is the Benjamin Waite Professor of the English Language, a Professor of African American Studies, and the Academic Secretary at Wesleyan University. He is the author of *The Empty Garden: The Subject of Late Milton*, *Neo-slave Narratives: Studies in the Social Logic of a Literary Form*, *Remembering Generations: Race and Family in Contemporary African American Fiction*, *American Lynching*, and *The End of American Lynching.*

down! You have been watching there quite long enough. Come, instantly; or with my magic I'll turn you into a fantastic, dancing bug, such as those that straddle there upon the waters of the spring, or else into a fat pollywog that wiggles in the black ooze among the dead leaves and rotting bits of wood."

With a quick movement, she tucked her violin under her chin and played a few measures of the worst sort of ragtime, in perfect imitation of a popular performer. The effect, following the music she had just been making, was grotesque and horrible.

"Mercy, mercy!" cried the man at the gate. "I beg! I beg! Do not, I pray, good nymph, torture me with thy dreadful power. I swear that I will obey thy every wish and whim."

Pointing with her bow—as with a wand—to the boulder, she sternly commanded, "Come, then, and sit here upon this rock; and give to me an account of all that thou hast done since I left thee in the rose garden or I will split thy ears and stretch thy soul upon a torture rack of hideous noise."

She lifted her violin again, threateningly. The novelist came down the path, on a run, to seat himself upon the gray boulder.

The artist shouted with laughter. But the novelist and the girl paid no heed to his unseemly merriment.

"Speak,"—she commanded, waving her wand,—"what hast thou done?"

"Did I not obey thy will and, under such terms as I could procure, open for thee the treasure room of thy desire?" growled the man on the rock.

"And still," she retorted, "when I made myself subject to those terms, and obediently looked not upon the hidden mystery—still the room of my desires became a trap betraying me into rude hands from which I narrowly escaped. And you—you fled the scene of your wrong-doing, without so much as by-your-leave, and for these long weeks have wandered, irresponsible, among my hills. Did you not say that my home was under these glowing peaks, and in the purple shadows of these canyons? Did you think that I would not find you here, and charm you again within reach of my power?"

"And what is thy will, good spirit?"—he asked, humbly—"tell me thy will and it shall be done—if thou wilt but make music only upon the instrument that is in thy hand."

With a laugh, she ended the play, saying, "My will is that you and Mr. King come, to-morrow evening, for supper with Miss Willard and me. Brian Oakley and Mrs. Oakley will be there. I want you too."

The men looked at each other in doubt.

"Really, Miss Andrés," said the artist, "we—"

The girl interrupted with one of her flash-like changes. "I have invited you. You must come. I shall expect you." And before either of the men could speak again, she sprang lightly across the little stream, and disappeared through the willow wall.

"Well, I'll be—" The novelist checked himself, solemnly—staring blankly at the spot where she had disappeared.

The artist laughed.

"What do you think of it?" demanded Conrad Lagrange, turning to his friend.

Aaron King, packing up his things, answered, "I think we'd better go."

Which opinion was concurred in by Brian Oakley who dropped in on them that evening.

Chapter XX

Myra's Prayer and the Ranger's Warning

That same afternoon, while Sibyl Andrés was making music for Aaron King in the spring glade, Brian Oakley, on his way down the canyon, stopped at the old place where Myra Willard and the girl were living. Riding into the yard that was fenced only by the wild growth, he was greeted cordially by the woman with the disfigured face, who was seated on the porch.

"Howdy, Myra," he called in return, as he swung from the saddle; and leaving the chestnut to roam at will, he went to the porch, his spurs clinking softly over the short, thick grass.

"Where's Sibyl?" he asked, seating himself on the top step.

"I'm sure I don't know, Mr. Oakley," the woman answered, smiling. "You really didn't expect me to, did you?"

The Ranger laughed. "Did she take gun, basket, rod or violin? If I know whether she's gone shooting berrying, fishing or fiddling, it may give me a clue—or did she take all four?"

The woman watched him closely. "She took only her violin. She went sometime after lunch—down the canyon, I think. Do you wish particularly to see her, Mr. Oakley?"

It was evident to the woman that the officer was relieved. "Oh, no; she wouldn't be going far with her violin. If she went down the canyon, it's all right anyway. But I stopped in to tell the girl that she must be careful, for a while. There's an escaped convict ranging somewhere in my district. I received the word this morning, and have been up around Lone Cabin and Burnt Pine and the head of Clear Creek to see if I could start anything. I didn't find any signs, but the information is reliable. Tell Sibyl that I say she must not go out without her gun—that if I catch her wandering around unarmed, I'll pack her off back to civilization, pronto."

"I'll tell her," said Myra Willard, "and I'll help her to remember. It would be better, I suppose, if she stayed at home; but that seems so impossible."

"She'll be all right if she has her gun," asserted the Ranger, confidently. "I'd back the girl against anything I ever met up with—when she has her artillery. By the way, Myra, have your neighbors below called yet?"

"No—at least, not while I have been at home. I have been berrying, two or three times. They might have come while I was out."

"Has Sibyl met them yet?" came the next question.

"She has not mentioned it, if she has."

"H-m-m," mused Brian Oakley.

The woman's love for the girl prompted her to quick suspicion of the Ranger's manner.

"What is it, Mr. Oakley?" she asked. "Has the child been indiscreet? Has she done anything wrong? Has she been with those men?"

"She has called upon one of them several times," returned Brian, smiling. "Mr. King is painting that little glade by the old spring at the foot of the bank, you know, and I guess she stumbled onto him. The place is one of her favorite spots. But bless your heart, Myra, there's no harm in it. It would be natural for her to get interested in any one making a picture of a place she loves as she does that old spring glade. She has spent days at a time there—ever since she was big enough to go that far from home."

"It's strange that she has not mentioned it to me," said the woman—troubled in spite of the Ranger's reassuring words.

The man directed his attention suddenly to his horse; "Max! You let Sibyl's roses alone." The animal turned his head questioningly toward his master. "Back!" said the Ranger, "back!" At his word, the chestnut promptly backed across the yard until the officer called, "That will do," when he halted, and, with an impatient toss of his head, again looked toward the porch, inquiringly. "You are all right now," said the man. Whereupon the horse began contentedly cropping the grass.

"I met Mr. King, accidentally, once, at the depot in Fairlands," continued the woman with the disfigured face. "He impressed me, then, as being a genuinely good man—a true gentleman. But, judging from his books, Conrad Lagrange is not a man I would wish Sibyl to meet. I have wondered at the artist's friendship with him."

"I tell you, Myra, Lagrange is all right," said Brian Oakley, stoutly. "He's odd and eccentric and rough spoken sometimes; but he's not at all what you would think him from the stuff he writes. He's a true man at heart, and you needn't worry about Sibyl getting anything but good from an acquaintance with him. As for King—well—Conrad Lagrange vouches for him. If you knew Lagrange, you'd understand what that means. He and the young fellow's mother grew up together. He swears the lad is right; and, from what I've seen of him, I believe it. It doesn't follow, though, that you don't need to keep your eyes open. The girl is as innocent as a child—though she is a woman—and—well—accidents have happened, you know." As he spoke he glanced unconsciously at the scars that disfigured the naturally beautiful face of the woman.

Myra Willard blushed as she answered sadly, "Yes, I know that accidents have happened. I will talk with Sibyl; and will you not speak to her too? She loves you so, and is always guided by your wishes. A little word or two from you would be an added safeguard."

"Sure I'll talk to her," said the Ranger, heartily—rising and whistling to the chestnut. "But look here, Myra,"—he said, pausing with his foot in the stirrup,—"the girl must have her head, you know. We don't want to put her in the notion that every man in the world is a villain laying for a chance to do her harm. There are clean fellows—a few—and it will do Sibyl good to meet that kind." He swung himself lightly into the saddle.

The woman smiled; "Sibyl could not think that all men are evil, after knowing her father and you, Mr. Oakley."

The Ranger laughed as he turned Max toward the opening in the cedar thicket. "Will was what God and Nelly made him, Myra; and I—if I'm fairly decent it's because Mary took me in hand in time. Men are mostly what you women make 'em, anyway, I reckon."

"Don't forget that you and Mrs. Oakley are coming for supper to-morrow," she called after him.

"No danger of our forgetting that," he answered. "Adios!" And the chestnut loped easily out of the yard.

Myra Willard kept her place on the porch until the sound of the horse's galloping feet died away down the canyon. But, as she listened to the vanishing sound of the Ranger's going, her eyes were looking far away—as though his words had aroused in her heart memories of days long past. When the last echo had lost itself in the thin mountain air, she went into the house.

Standing before the small mirror that served—in the rude, almost camp-like furnishings of the house—for both herself and Sibyl, she studied the face reflected there—turning her head slowly, as if comparing the beautiful unmarked side with the other that was so hideously disfigured. For some time she stood there, unflinchingly giving herself to the torture of this contemplation of her ruined loveliness; drinking to its bitter dregs the sorrowful cup of her secret memories; until, as though she could bear no more, she drew back—her eyes wide with pain and horror, her marred features twisted grotesquely in an agony of mental suffering. With a pitiful moan she sank upon her knees in prayer.

In the earnestness of her spirit—out of the deep devotion of her love—as she prayed God for wisdom to guide the girl entrusted to her care, she spoke aloud. "Let me not rob her, dear Christ, of love; but help me to help her love aright. Help me, that in my fear for her I do not turn her heart against her mate when he shall come. Help me, that I do not so fill her pure mind with doubt and distrust of all men that she will look for evil, only. Help me, that I do not teach her to associate love wholly with that which is base and untrue. Grant, O God, that her beautiful life may not be marred by a love that is unworthy."

As the woman with the disfigured face rose from her knees, she heard the voice of Sibyl, who was coming up the old road toward the cedars—singing as she came.

When Sibyl entered the house, a moment later, Myra Willard, still agitated, was bathing her face. The girl, seeing, checked the song upon her lips; and going to the woman who in everything but the ties of blood was mother to her, sought to discover the reason for her troubled manner, and tried to soothe her with loving words.

The woman held the girl close in her arms and looked into the lovely, winsome face that was so unmarred by vicious thoughts of the world's teaching.

"Dear child, do you not sometimes hate the sight of my ugliness?" she said. "It seems to me, you must."

With her arms about her companion's neck, Sibyl pressed her pure, young lips to those disfiguring scars, in an impulsive kiss. "Foolish Myra," she cried, "you know I love you too well to see anything but your own beautiful self behind the scars. To me, your face is all like this"—and she softly kissed, in turn, the woman's unmarred cheek. "Whatever made the marks, I know that they are not dishonorable. So I never think of them at all, but see only the beautiful side—which is really you, you know."

"No,"—answered Myra Willard, gently,—"my scars are not dishonorable. But the world does not see with your pure eyes, dear child. The world sees only the ugly, disfigured side of my face. It never looks at the other side. And listen, dear heart, so the world often sees dishonor where there is no dishonor It sees evil in many things where there is only good."

"Yes," returned the girl, "but you have never taught me to see with the eyes of the world. So, to me, what the world sees, does not matter."

"Pray that it may never matter, child," answered the woman with the disfigured face, earnestly.

Then, as they went out to the porch, she asked, "Did you meet Mr. Oakley as you were coming home?"

Sibyl laughed and colored with a confusion that was new to her, as she answered, "Yes, I did—and he scolded me."

"About your going unarmed?"

"No,—but he told me about that too. I don't see why, whenever a poor criminal escapes, he always comes into our mountains. I don't like to 'pack a gun'—unless I'm hunting. But Brian Oakley didn't scold me for that, though—he knows I always do as he says. He scolded because I hadn't told you about my going to see Mr. King, in the spring glade." She laughed, conscious of the color that was in her cheeks. "I told him it didn't matter whether I told you or not, because he always knows every single move I make, anyway."

"Why didn't you tell me, dear?" asked the woman. "You never kept anything from me, before—I'm sure."

"Why dearest," the girl answered frankly, "I don't know, myself, why I didn't tell you"—which, Myra Willard knew, was the exact truth.

Then Sibyl told her foster-mother everything about her acquaintance with the artist and Conrad Lagrange—from the time she first watched the painter, from the arbor in the rose garden, where she met the novelist; until that afternoon, when she had invited them to supper, the next day. Only of her dancing before the artist, the girl did not tell.

Later in the evening, Sibyl—saying that she would sing Myra to sleep—took her violin to the porch, outside the window; and in the dusk made soft music until the woman's troubled heart was calmed. When the moon came up from behind the Galenas, across the canyon, the girl tiptoed into the house, to bend over the sleeping woman, in tender solicitude. With that mother tenderness belonging to all true women, she stooped and softly kissed the disfigured face upon the pillow. At the touch, Myra Willard stirred uneasily; and the girl—careful to make no sound—withdrew.

On the porch, she again took up her violin as if to play; but, instead, sat motionless—her face turned down the canyon—her eyes looking far away. Then, quickly, she put aside the instrument, and—as though with sudden yielding to some inner impulse—slipped out into the grassy yard. And there, in the moon's white light,—with only the mountains, the trees, and the flowers to see,—she danced, again, as she had danced before the artist in the glade—with her face turned down the canyon, and her arms outstretched, longingly, toward the camp in the sycamores back of the old orchard.

Suddenly, from the room where Myra Willard slept, came that shuddering, terror-stricken cry.

The girl, fleet-footed as a deer, ran into the house. Kneeling, she put her strong young arms about the cowering, trembling form on the bed. "There, there, dear, it's all right."

The woman of the disfigured face caught Sibyl's hand, impulsively. "I—I—was dreaming again," she whispered, "and—and this time—O Sibyl—this time, I dreamed that it was you."

Chapter XXI

The Last Climb

That first visit of Aaron King and Conrad Lagrange to the old home of Sibyl Andrés was the beginning of a delightful comradeship.

Often, in the evening, the two men, with Czar, went to spend an hour in friendly intercourse with their neighbors up the canyon. Always, they were welcomed by Myra Willard with a quiet dignity; while Sibyl was frankly delighted to have them come. Always, they were invited with genuine hospitality to "come again." Frequently, Brian Oakley and perhaps Mrs. Oakley would be there when they arrived; or the Ranger would come riding into the yard before they left. At times, the canyon's mountain wall echoed the laughter of the little company as Sibyl and the novelist played their fantastical game of words; or again, the older people would listen to the blending voices of the artist and the girl as, in the quiet hush of the evening, they sang together to Myra Willard's accompaniment on the violin; or, perhaps, Sibyl, with her face upturned to the mountain tops, would make for her chosen friends the music of the hills.

Not infrequently, too, the girl would call at the camp in the sycamore grove—sometimes riding with the Ranger, sometimes alone; or they would hear her merry hail from the gate the other side of the orchard as she passed by. And sometimes, in the morning, she would appear—equipped with rod or gun or basket—to frankly challenge Aaron King to some long ramble in the hills.

So the days for the young man at the beginning of his life work, and for the young woman at the beginning of her womanhood, passed. Up and down the canyon, along the boulder-strewn bed of the roaring Clear Creek, from the Ranger Station to the falls; in the quiet glades under the alders hung with virgin's-bower and wild grape; beneath the live-oaks on the mountains' flanks or shoulders; in dimly lighted, cedar-sheltered gulches, among tall brakes and lilies; or high up on the canyon walls under the dark and fragrant pines—over all the paths and trails familiar to her girlhood she led him—showing him every nook and glade and glen—teaching him to know, as he had asked, the mountains that she herself so loved.

The time came, at last, when the two men must return to Fairlands. With Mr. and Mrs. Oakley they were spending the evening at Sibyl's home when Conrad Lagrange announced that they would leave the mountains, two days later.

"Then,"—said the girl, impulsively,—"Mr. King and I are going for one last good-by climb to-morrow. Aren't we?" she concluded—turning to the artist.

Aaron King laughed as he answered, "We certainly seem to be headed that way. Where are we going?"

"We will start early and come back late"—she returned—"which really is all that any one ought to know about a climb that is just for the climb. And listen—no rod, no gun, no sketch-book. I'll fix a lunch."

"Watch out for my convict," warned the Ranger. "He must be getting mighty hungry, by now."

Early in the morning, they set out. Crossing the canyon, they climbed the Oak Knoll trail—down which the artist and Conrad Lagrange had been led by the uncanny wisdom of Croesus, a few weeks before—to the pipe-line. Where the path from below leads into the pipe-line trail, under the live-oaks, on a shelf cut in the comparatively easy slope of the mountain's shoulder, they paused for a look over the narrow valley that lay a thousand feet below. Across the wide, gray, boulder-strewn wash of the mountain torrent's way, with the gleaming thread of tumbling Clear Creek in its center, they could see the white dots that marked the camp back of the old orchard; and, farther up the stream, could distinguish the little opening with the cedar thicket and the giant sycamores that marked the spot where Sibyl was born.

Aaron King, looking at the girl, recalled that day when he and Conrad Lagrange, in a spirit of venturesome fun, had left the choice of trails to the burro. "Good, old Croesus!" he said smiling.

She knew the story of how they had been guided to their camping place, and laughed in return, as she answered, "He's a dear old burro, is Croesus, and worthy of a better name."

"Plutus would be better," suggested the artist.

"Because a Greek God is better than a Lydian King?" she asked curiously.

"Wasn't Plutus the giver of wealth?" he returned.

"Yes."

"Well, and wasn't he forced by Zeus to distribute his gifts without regard to the characters of the recipients?"

She laughed merrily. "Plutus or Croesus—I'm glad he chose the Oak Knoll trail."

"And so am I," answered the man, earnestly.

Leisurely, they followed the trail that is hung—narrow thread-like path—high upon the mountain wall, invisible from the floor of the canyon below. At a point where the trail turns to round the inward curve of one of the small side canyons—where the pines grow dark and tall—some thoughtful hand had laid a small pipe from the large conduit tunnel, under the trail, to a barrel fixed on the mountainside below the little path. Here they stopped again and, while they loitered, filled a small canteen with the cold, clear water from the mountain's heart. Farther on, where the pipe-line again rounds the inward curve of the wall between two mountain spurs, they turned aside to follow the Government trail that leads to the fire-break on the summit of the Galenas and then down into the valley on the other side. At the gap where the Galena trail crosses the fire-break, they again turned aside to make their leisure way along the broad, brush-cleared break that lies in many a fold and curve and kink like a great ribbon on the thin top of the ridge. With every step, now, they were climbing. Midday found them standing by a huge rock at the edge of a clump of pines on one of the higher points of the western end of the range. Here they would have their lunch.

As they sat in the lee of the great rock, with the wind that sweeps the mountain tops singing in the pines above their heads, they looked directly down upon the wide Galena Valley and far across to the spurs and slopes of the San Jacintos beyond. Sibyl's keen eyes—mountain-trained from childhood—marked a railway train crawling down the grade from San Gorgonio Pass toward the distant ocean. She tried in vain to point it out to her companion. But the city eyes of the man could not find the tiny speck in the vast landscape that lay within the range of their vision. The artist looked at his watch. The train was the Golden State Limited that had brought him from the far away East, a few months before.

Aaron King remembered how, from the platform of the observation car, he had looked up at the mountains from which he now looked down. He remembered too, the woman into whose eyes he had, for the first time, looked that day. Turning his face to the west, he could distinguish under the haze of the distance the dark squares of the orange groves of Fairlands. Before three days had passed he would be in his studio home again. And the woman of the observation car platform—From distant Fairlands, the man turned his eyes to the winsome face of his girl comrade on the mountain top.

"Please"—she said, meeting his serious gaze with a smile of frank fellowship—"please, what have I done?"

Smiling, he answered gravely, "I don't exactly know—but you have done something."

"You look so serious. I'm sure it must be pretty bad. Can't you think what it is?"

He laughed. "I was thinking about down there"—he pointed into the haze of the distant valley to the west.

"Don't," she returned, "let's think about up here"—she waved her hand toward the high crest of the San Bernardinos, and the mountain peaks about them.

"Will you let me paint your portrait—when we get back to the orange groves?" he asked.

"I'm sure I don't know," she returned. "Why do you want to paint me? I'm nobody, you know—but just me."

"That's the reason I want to paint you," he answered.

"What's the reason?"

"Because you are you."

"But a portrait of me would not help you on your road to fame," she retorted.

He flinched. "Perhaps," he said, "that's partly why I want to do it."

"Because it won't help you?"

"Because it won't help me on the road to fame. You will pose for me, won't you?"

"I'm sure I cannot say"—she answered—"perhaps—please don't let's talk about it."

"Why not?" he asked curiously.

"Because"—she answered seriously—"we have been such good friends up here in the mountains; such—such comrades. Up here in the hills, with the canyon gates shut against the world that I don't know, you are like—like Brian Oakley—and like my father used to be—and down there"—she hesitated.

"Yes," he said, "and down there I will be what?"

"I don't know," she answered wistfully, "but sometimes I can see you going on and on and on toward fame and the rewards it will bring you and you seem to get farther and farther and farther away from—from the mountains and our friendship; until you are so far away that I can't see you any more at all. I don't like to lose my mountain friends, you know."

He smiled. "But no matter how famous I might become—no matter what fame might bring me—I could not forget you and your mountains."

"I would not want you to remember me," she answered "if you were famous. That is—I mean"—she added hesitatingly—"if you were famous just because you wanted to be. But I know you could never forget the mountains. And that would be the trouble; don't you see? If you could forget, it would not matter. Ask Mr. Lagrange, he knows."

For some time Aaron King sat, without speaking, looking about at the world that was so far from that other world—the world he had always known. The girl, too,—seeming to understand the thoughts that he himself, perhaps, could not have expressed,—was silent.

Then he said slowly, "I don't think that I care for fame as I did before you taught me to know the mountains. It doesn't, somehow, now, seem to matter so much. It's the work that really matters—after all—isn't it?"

And Sibyl Andrés, smiling, answered, "Yes, it's the work that really matters. I'm sure that must be so."

In the afternoon, they went on, still following the fire-break, down to where it is intersected by the pipe-line a mile from the reservoir on the hill above the power-house; then back to Oak Knoll, again on the pipe-line trail all the way—a beautiful and never-to-be-forgotten walk.

The sun was just touching the tops of the western mountains when they started down Oak Knoll. The canyon below, already, lay in the shadow. When they reached the foot of the trail, it was twilight. Across the road, by a small streamlet—a tributary to Clear Creek—a party of huntsmen were making ready to spend the night. The voices of the men came clearly through the gathering gloom. Under the trees, they could see the camp-fire's ruddy gleam. They did not notice the man who was standing, half hidden, in the bushes beside the road, near the spot where the trail opens into it. Silently, the man watched them as they turned up the road which they would follow a little way before crossing the canyon to Sibyl's home. Fifty yards farther on, they met Brian Oakley.

"Howdy, you two," called the Ranger, cheerily—without stopping his horse. "Rather late to-night, ain't you?"

"We'll be there by dark," called the artist And the Ranger passed on.

At sound of the mountaineer's voice, the man in the bushes drew quickly back. The officer's trained eyes caught the movement in the brush, and he leaned forward in the saddle.

A moment later, the man reappeared in the road, farther down, around the bend. As the Ranger approached, he was hailed by a boisterous, "Hello, Brian! better stop and have a bite."

"How do you do, Mr. Rutlidge?" came the officer's greeting, as he reined in his horse. "When did you land in the hills?"'

"This afternoon," answered the other. "We're just making camp. Come and meet the fellows. You know some of them."

"Thanks, not to-night,"—returned Brian Oakley,—"deer hunt, I suppose."

"Yes—thought we would be in good time for the opening of the season. By the way, do you happen to know where Lagrange and that artist friend of his are camped?"

"In that bunch of sycamores back of the old orchard down there," answered the Ranger, watching the man's face keenly. "I just passed Mr. King, up the road a piece."

"That so? I didn't see him go by," returned the other. "I think I'll run over and say 'hello' to Lagrange in the morning. We are only going as far as Burnt Pine to-morrow, anyway."

"Keep your eyes open for an escaped convict," said the officer, casually. "There's one ranging somewhere in here—came in about a month ago. He's likely to clean out your camp. So long."

"Perhaps we'll take him in for you," laughed the other. "Good night." He turned toward the camp-fire under the trees, as the officer rode away.

"Now what in hell did that fellow want to lie to me like that for," said Brian Oakley to himself. "He must have seen King and Sibyl as they came down the trail. Max, old boy, when a man lies deliberately, without any apparent reason, you want to watch him."

Chapter XXII

Shadows of Coming Events

Aaron King and Conrad Lagrange were idling in their camp, after breakfast the next morning, when Czar turned his head, quickly, in a listening attitude. With a low growl that signified disapproval, he moved forward a step or two and stood stiffly erect, gazing toward the lower end of the orchard.

"Some one coming, Czar?" asked the artist.

The dog answered with another growl, while the hair on his neck bristled in anger.

"Some one we don't like, heh!" commented the novelist. "Or"—he added as if musing upon the animal's instinct—"some one we ought not to like."

A bark from Czar greeted James Rutlidge who at that moment appeared at the foot of the slope leading up to their camp.

The two men—remembering the occasion of their visitor's last call at their home in Fairlands, when he had seen Sibyl in the studio—received the man with courtesy, but with little warmth. Czar continued to manifest his sentiments until rebuked by his master. The coolness of the reception, however, in no way disconcerted James Rutlidge; who, on his part, rather overdid his assumption of pleasure at meeting them again.

Explaining that he had come with a party of friends on a hunting trip, he told them how he had met Brian Oakley, and so had learned of their camp hidden behind the old orchard. The rest of his party, he said, had gone on up the canyon. They would stop at Burnt Pine on Laurel Creek, where he could easily join them before night. He could not think, he declared, of passing so near without greeting his friends.

"You two certainly are expert when it comes to finding snug, out-of-the-way quarters," he commented, searching the camp and the immediate surroundings with a careful and, ostensibly, an appreciative eye. "A thousand people might pass this old, deserted place without ever dreaming that you were so ideally hidden back here."

As he finished speaking, his roving eye came to rest upon a pair of gloves that Sibyl—the last time she had called—had carelessly left lying upon a stump close by a giant sycamore where, in camp fashion, the rods and creels and guns were kept. The artist had intended to return the gloves the day before, together with a book of trout-flies which the girl had also forgotten; but, in his eagerness for the day's outing, he had gone off without them.

The observing Conrad Lagrange did not fail to note that James Rutlidge had seen the telltale gloves. Fixing his peculiar eyes upon the visitor, he asked abruptly, with polite but purposeful interest, after the health of Mr. and Mrs. Taine and Louise.

The faint shadow of a suggestive smile that crossed the heavy features of James Rutlidge, as he turned his gaze from the gloves to meet the look of the novelist was maddening.

"The old boy is steadily going down," he said without feeling. "The doctors tell me that he can't last through the winter. It'll be a relief to everybody when he goes. Mrs. Taine is well and beautiful, as always—remarkable how she keeps up appearances, considering her husband's serious condition. Louise is quite as usual. They will all be back in Fairlands in another month. They sent regards to you both—in case I should run across you."'

The two men made the usual conventional replies, adding that they were returning to Fairlands the next day.

"So soon?" exclaimed their visitor, with another meaning smile. "I don't see how you can think of leaving your really delightful retreat. I understand you have such charming neighbors too. Perhaps though, they are also returning to the orange groves and roses."

Aaron King's face flushed hotly, and he was about to reply with vigor to the sneering words, when Conrad Lagrange silenced him with a quick look. Ignoring the reference to their neighbors, the novelist replied suavely that they felt they must return to civilization as some matters in connection with the new edition of his last novel demanded his attention, and the artist wished to get back to his studio and to his work.

"Really," urged Rutlidge, mockingly, "you ought not to go down now. The deer season opens in two days. Why not join our party for a hunt? We would be delighted to have you."

They were coolly thanking him for the invitation,—that, from the tone in which it was given, was so evidently not meant,—when Czar, with a joyful bark, dashed away through the grove. A moment, and a clear, girlish voice called from among the trees that bordered the cienaga, "Whoo-ee." It was the signal that Sibyl always gave when she approached their camp.

James Rutlidge broke into a low laugh while Sibyl's friends looked at each other in angry consternation as the girl, following her hail and accompanied by the delighted dog, appeared in full view; her fishing-rod in hand, her creel swung over her shoulder.

The girl's embarrassment, when, too late, she saw and recognized their visitor, was pitiful. As she came slowly forward, too confused to retreat, Rutlidge started to laugh again, but Aaron King, with an emphasis that checked the man's mirth, said in a low tone, "Stop that! Be careful!"

As he spoke, the artist arose and with Conrad Lagrange went forward to greet Sibyl in—as nearly as they could—their customary manner.

Formally, Rutlidge was presented to the girl; and, under the threatening eyes of the painter, greeted her with no hint of rudeness in his voice or manner; saying courteously, with a smile, "I have had the pleasure of Miss Andrés' acquaintance for—let me see—three years now, is it not?" he appealed to her directly.

"It was three years ago that I first saw you, sir," she returned coolly.

"It was my first trip into the mountains, I remember," said Rutlidge, easily. "I met you at Brian Oakley's home."

Without replying, she turned to Aaron King appealingly. "I—I left my gloves and fly-book. I was going fishing and called to get them."

The artist gave her the articles with a word of regret for having so carelessly forgotten to return them to her. With a simple "good-by" to her two friends but without even a glance toward their caller, she went back up the canyon, in the direction from which she had come.

When the girl had disappeared among the trees, James Rutlidge said, with his meaning smile, "Really, I owe you an apology for dropping in so unexpectedly. I—"

Conrad Lagrange interrupted him, curtly. "No apology is due, sir."

"No?" returned Rutlidge, with a rising inflection and a drawling note in his voice that was almost too much for the others. "I really must be going, anyway," he continued. "My party will be some distance ahead. Sure you wouldn't care to join us?"

"Thanks! Sorry! but we cannot this time. Good of you to ask us," came from Aaron King and the novelist.

"Can't say that I blame you," their caller returned. "The fishing used to be fine in this neighborhood. You must have had some delightful sport. Don't blame you in the least for not joining our stag party. Delightful young woman, that Miss Andrés. Charming companion—either in the mountains or in civilization Good-by—see you in Fairlands, later."

When he was out of hearing the two men relieved their feelings in language that perhaps it would be better not to put in print.

"And the worst of it is," remarked the novelist, "it's so damned dangerous to deny something that does not exist or make explanations in answer to charges that are not put into words."

"I could scarcely refrain from kicking the beast down the hill," said Aaron King, savagely.

"Which"—the other returned—"would have complicated matters exceedingly, and would have accomplished nothing at all. For the girl's sake, store your wrath against the day of judgment which, if I read the signs aright, is sure to come."

When Sibyl Andrés went down the canyon to the camp in the sycamores, that morning, the world, to her, was very bright. Her heart sang with joyous freedom amid the scenes that she so loved. Care-free and happy, as when, in the days of her girlhood, she had gone to visit the spring glade, she still was conscious of a deeper joy than in her girlhood she had ever known.

When she returned again up the canyon, all the brightness of her day was gone. Her heart was heavy with foreboding fear. She was oppressed with a dread of some impending evil which she could not understand. At every sound in the mountain wild-wood, she started. Time and again, as if expecting pursuit, she looked over her shoulder—poised like a creature of the woods ready for instant panic-stricken flight. So, without pausing to cast for trout, or even to go down to the stream, she returned home; where Myra Willard, seeing her come so early and empty handed, wondered. But to the woman's question, the girl only answered that she had changed her mind—that, after recovering her gloves and fly-book at the camp of their friends, she had decided to come home. The woman with the disfigured face, knowing that Aaron King was leaving the hills the next day, thought that she understood the girl's mood, and wisely made no comment.

The artist and Conrad Lagrange went to spend their last evening in the hills with their friends. Brian Oakley, too, dropped in. But neither of the three men mentioned the name of James Rutlidge in the presence of the women; while Sibyl was, apparently, again her own bright and happy self—carrying on a fanciful play of words with the novelist, singing with the artist, and making music for them all with her violin. But before the evening was over, Conrad Lagrange found an opportunity to tell the Ranger of the incident of the morning, and of the construction that James Rutlidge had evidently put upon Sibyl's call at the camp. Brian Oakley,—thinking of the night before, and how the man must have seen the artist and the girl coming down the Oak Knoll trail in the twilight,—swore softly under his breath.

Chapter XXIII

Outside the Canyon Gates Again

Aaron King and Conrad Lagrange determined to go back from the mountains, the way they had come. Said the novelist, "It is as unseemly to rush pell-mell from an audience with the gods as it is to enter their presence irreverently."

To which the artist answered, laughing, "Even criminals under sentence have, at least, the privilege of going to their prisons reluctantly."

So they went down from the mountains, reverently and reluctantly.

Yee Kee, with the more elaborate equipment of the camp, was sent on ahead by wagon. The two men, with Croesus packed for a one night halt, and Czar, would follow. When all was ready, and they could neither of them invent any more excuses for lingering, Conrad Lagrange gave the word to the burro and they set out—down the little slope of grassy land; across the tiny stream from the cienaga; around the lower end of the old orchard, by the ancient weed-grown road—even Czar went slowly, with low-hung head, as if regretful at leaving the mountains that he, too, in his dog way, loved.

At the gate, Aaron King asked the novelist to go on, saying that he would soon overtake him. It was possible, he said, that he might have left something in the spring glade. He thought he had better make sure. Conrad Lagrange, assenting, went through the gate and down the road, with the four-footed members of the party; and Czar must have thought that there was something very funny about old Croesus that morning, from the way his master laughed; when they were safely around the first turn.

There was, of course, no material thing in the spring glade that the artist wanted. He knew that—quite as well as his laughing friend. Under the mistletoe oak, at the top of the bank, he paused, hesitating—as one will often pause when about to enter a sacred building. Softly, he pushed open the old gate, as he might have pushed open the door of a church. Slowly, reverently, he went down the path; baring his head as he went. He did not search for anything that he might have left. He simply stood for a few minutes under the gray-trunked alders that were so marked by the loving hands of long ago men and maidens—beside the mint bordered spring with the scattered stones of that old foundation—where, through the screen of boughs and vines and virgin's-bower the sunlight fell as through the traceries of a cathedral window, and the low, deep tones of the mountain waters came like the music of a great organ.

It is likely that Aaron King, himself, could not, at that time, have told why, as he was leaving the hills, he had paused to visit once more the spot where Sibyl Andrés had brought to him her three gifts from the mountains—where, in her pure innocence, she had danced before him the dance of the mating butterflies—and where, with the music of her violin, she had saved their friendship from the perils that threatened it—lifting their intimate comradeship into the pure atmosphere of the higher levels, even as she had shown him the trails that lead from the lower canyon to the summits and peaks of the encircling mountain walls. But when he rejoined his friend there was something in his face that prevented the novelist from making any comment in a laughing vein.

As the two men passed outward through the canyon gates and, looking backward as they went, saw those mighty doors close silently behind them, the artist was moved by emotions that were strange and new to the man who, two months before, had watched those gates open to receive him. This, too, is true; as that man, then, knew, but did not know, the mountains; so this man, now, knew, yet still did not know, himself.

Where the road crosses, for the last time, the tumbling stream from the heart of the hills, they halted; and for one night slept again at the foot of the mountains. The next day they arrived at their little home in the orange grove. To Aaron King, it seemed that they had been away for years.

When the traces of their days upon the road had been removed, and they were garbed again in the conventional costume of the world; when their outfit had been put away, and a home found for patient Croesus; the artist went to his studio. The afternoon passed and Yee Kee called dinner; but Aaron King did not come. Then Conrad Lagrange went to find him. Softly, the older man pushed open the studio door to see the painter sitting before the portrait of Mrs. Taine, with the package of his mother's letters in his hand.

Without a sound, the novelist withdrew, leaving the door ajar. Going to the corner of the house, he whistled low, and in answer, Czar come bounding to him from the porch. "Go find Aaron, Czar," said the man, pointing toward the studio. "Go find Aaron."

Obediently, with waving tail, the dog trotted off, and pushing open the door entered the room; followed a few moments later by his master.

Conrad Lagrange smiled as he saw that the easel was without a canvas. The portrait of Mrs. Taine was turned to the wall.

Chapter XXIV

James Rutlidge Makes a Mistake

When Aaron King and Conrad Lagrange had said, "good-by," to their friends, at Sibyl Andrés' home, that evening; and had returned to spend their last night at the camp in the sycamores; the girl's mood was again the mood of one oppressed by a haunting, foreboding fear.

Sibyl could not have expressed, or even to herself defined, her fear. She only knew that in the presence of James Rutlidge she was frightened. She had tried many times to overcome her strange antipathy; for Rutlidge, until that day in the studio, had never been other than kind and courteous in his persistent efforts to win her friendship. Perhaps it was the impression left by the memory of Myra Willard's manner at the time of their first meeting with him, three years before, in Brian Oakley's home; perhaps it was because the woman with the disfigured face had so often warned her against permitting her slight acquaintance with Rutlidge to develop; perhaps it was something else—some instinct, possible, only, to one of her pure, unspoiled nature—whatever it was, the mountain girl who was so naturally unafraid, feared this man who, in his own world, was an acknowledged authority upon matters of the highest spiritual and moral significance.

That night, she slept but little. With the morning, every nerve demanded action, action. She felt as though if she could not spend herself in physical exertion she would go mad. Taking her lunch, and telling her companion that she was going for a good, full day with the trout; she was starting off, when the woman called her back.

"You have forgotten Mr. Oakley's warning, dear. You are not to go unarmed, you know."

"Oh, bother that old convict, Brian Oakley is so worried about," cried the girl. "I don't like to carry a gun when I am fishing. It's only an extra load." But, never-the-less, as she spoke, she went back to the porch; where Myra Willard handed her a belt of cartridges, with a serviceable Colt revolver in the holster. There was no hint of awkwardness when the girl buckled the belt about her waist and settled the holster in its place at her hip.

"You will be careful, won't you, dear," said the woman, earnestly.

Lifting her face for another good-by kiss, the girl answered, "Of course, dear mother heart." Then, with a laugh—"I'll agree to shoot the first man I meet, and identify him afterwards—if it will make you easier in your mind. You won't worry, will you?"

Myra Willard smiled. "Not a bit, child. I know how Brian Oakley loves you, and he says that he has no fear for you if you are armed. He takes great chances himself, that man, but he would send us back to Fairlands, in a minute, if he thought you were in any danger in your rambles."

Beside the roaring Clear Creek, Sibyl seated self upon a great boulder—her rod and flies neglected—apparently unmindful of the purpose that had brought her to the stream. Her eyes were not upon the swirling pool at her feet, but were lifted to a spot, a thousand feet up on Oak Knoll, where she knew the pipe-line trail lay, and where Croesus had made the momentous decision that had resulted in her comradeship with Aaron King. Following the canyon wall with her eyes—as though in her mind she walked the thread-like path—from Oak Knoll to the fire-break a mile from the reservoir; her gaze then traced the crest of the Galenas, resting finally upon that clump of pines high up on the point that was so clearly marked against the sky. Once, she laid aside her rod, and slipped the creel from her shoulder. But even as she set out, she hesitated and turned back; resolutely taking up her fishing-tackle again, as though, angry with herself for her state of mind, she was determined to indulge no longer her mood of indecision.

But the fishing did not go well. To properly cast a trout-fly, one's thoughts must be upon the art. A preoccupied mind and wandering attention tends to a tangled line, a snarled leader, and all sorts of aggravating complications. Sibyl—usually so skillful at this most delicate of sports—was as inaccurate and awkward, this day, as the merest tyro. The many pools and falls and swirling eddies of Clear Creek held for her, now, memories more attractive, by far, than the wary trout they sheltered. The familiar spots she had known since childhood were haunted by a something that made them seem new and strange.

At last,—thoroughly angry with her inability to control her mood, and half ashamed of the thoughts that forced themselves so insistently upon her; with her nerves and muscles craving the action that would bring the relief of physical weariness,—she determined to leave the more familiar ground, for the higher and less frequented waters of Fern Creek. Climbing out of the canyon, by the steep, almost stair-like trail on the San Bernardino side, she walked hard and fast to reach Lone Cabin by noon. But, before she had finished her lunch, she decided not to fish there, after all; but to go on, over the still harder trail to Burnt Pine on Laurel Creek, and, returning to the lower canyon by the Laurel trail, to work down Clear Creek on the way to her home, in the late afternoon and twilight.

The trail up the almost precipitous wall of the gorge at Lone Cabin, and over the mountain spur to Laurel Creek, is one that calls for a clear head and a sure foot. It is not a path for the city bred to essay, save with the ready arm of a guide. But the hill-trained muscles and nerves of Sibyl Andrés gloried in the task. The cool-headed, mountain girl enjoyed the climb from which her city sisters would have drawn back in trembling fear.

Once, at a point perhaps two-thirds of the height to the top, she halted. Her ear had caught a slight noise above her head, as a few pebbles rolled down the almost perpendicular face of the wall and bounded from the trail where she stood, into the depths below. For a few minutes, the girl, on the little, shelf-like path that was scarcely wider than the span of her two hands, was as motionless and as silent as the cliff itself; while, with her face turned upward, she searched with keen eyes the rim of the gorge; her free, right hand resting upon the butt of the revolver at her hip. Then she went on—not timidly, but neither carelessly; not in the least frightened, but still,—knowing that the spot was far from the more frequented paths,—with experienced care.

As her head and shoulders came above the rim, she paused again, to search with careful eyes the vicinity of the trail that from this point leads for a little way down the knife-like ridge of the spur, and then, by easier stages, around the shoulder and the flank of the mountain, to Burnt Pine Camp. When no living object met her eye, and she could hear no sound save the lonely wind in the pines and the faint murmur of the stream in the gorge below, she took the few steps that yet remained of the climb, and seated herself for a moment's well-earned rest. Some small animal, she told herself,—a squirrel or a wood-rat, perhaps,—frightened at her approach, and scurrying hastily to cover, had dislodged the pebbles with the slight noise that she had heard.

From where she sat with her back against the trunk of a great pine, she could see—far below, and beyond the immediate spurs and shoulders of the range, on the farther side of the gorge out of which she had just come—the lower end of Clear Creek canyon, and, miles away, under the blue haze of the distance, the dark squares of the orange groves of Fairlands.

Somewhere between those canyon gates and the little city in the orange groves, the girl knew that Aaron King and his friend were making their way back to the world of men. With her eyes fixed upon the distant scene, as if striving for a wholly impossible strength of vision to mark the tiny, moving spots that she knew were there, the girl upon the high rim of the wild and lonely mountain gorge was lost to her surroundings, in an effort, as vain, to see her comrade of the weeks just past, in the years that were to come. Would the friendship born in the hills endure in the world beyond the canyon gates? Could it endure away from those scenes that had given it birth? Was it possible for a fellowship, established in the free atmosphere of the mountains, to live in the lower altitude of Fairlands? Sibyl Andrés,—as she sat there, alone in the hills she loved,—in her heart of hearts, answered her own questions, "No." But still she searched the years to come—even as her eyes so futilely searched the distant landscape beyond the mighty gates that seemed, now, to shut her in from that world to which Aaron King was returning.

The girl was aroused from her abstraction by a sound behind her and a little to the left of the tree against which she was leaning. In a flash, she was on her feet.

James Rutlidge stood a few steps away. He had been approaching her as she sat under the tree; but when she sprang to her feet and faced him, he halted. Lifting his hat, he greeted her with easy assurance; a confident, triumphant smile upon his heavy features.

White-faced and trembling, the mountain girl—who a few moments before, had been so unafraid—stood shrinking before this cultured representative of the arts. Returning his salutation, she was starting hurriedly away down the trail, when he said, "Wait. Why be in such a hurry?"

As if against her will, she paused. "It is growing late," she faltered; "I must go."

He laughed. "I will go with you presently. Don't be afraid." Coming forward, with an air of making himself very much at home, he placed his rifle against the tree where she had been sitting. Then, as if to calm her fears, he continued, "I am camped at Burnt Pine, with a party of friends. I was up here looking for deer sign when I noticed you below, at the cabin there. I was just starting down to you, when I saw that you were going to come up; so I waited. Beautiful spot—this—don't you think?—so out of the way, too. Just the place for a quiet little visit."

As the man spoke, he was eyeing her in a way that only served to confuse and frighten her the more. Murmuring some inaudible reply, she again started to go. But again he said, peremptorily, "Wait." And again, as if against her will, she paused. "If you have no scruples about wandering over the mountains alone with that artist fellow, I do not see why you should hesitate to favor me."

The man's words were, undoubtedly, prompted by what he firmly believed to be the nature of the relation between the girl and Aaron King—a belief for which he had, to his mind, sufficient evidence. But Sibyl had no understanding of his meaning. In the innocence of her pure mind, the purport of his words was utterly lost. Her very fear of the man was not a reasoning fear, but the instinctive shrinking of a nature that had never felt the unclean touch of the world in which James Rutlidge habitually moved. It was this very unreasoning element in her emotions that made her always so embarrassed in the man's presence. It was because she did not understand her fear of him, that the girl, usually so capable of taking her own part, was, in his presence, so helpless.

James Rutlidge, by the intellectual, moral, and physical atmosphere in which he lived, was made wholly incapable of understanding the nature of Sibyl Andrés. Secure in the convictions of his own debased mind, as to her relation to the artist; and misconstruing her very manner in his presence; he was not long in putting his proposal into words that she could not fail to understand.

When she did grasp his meaning, her fears and her trembling nervousness gave place to courageous indignation and righteous anger that found expression in scathing words of denunciation.

The man, still, could not understand the truth of the situation. To him, there was nothing more in her refusal than her preference for the artist. That this young woman—to him, an unschooled girl of the hills—whom he had so long marked as his own, should give herself to another, and so scornfully turn from him, was an affront that he could not brook. The very vigor of her wrath, as she stood before him,—her eyes bright, her cheeks flushed, and her beautiful body quivering with the vehemence of her passionate outburst,—only served to fan the flame of his desire; while her stinging words provoked his bestial mind to an animal-like rage. With a muttered oath and a threat, he started toward her.

But the woman who faced him now, with full understanding, was very different from the timid, frightened girl who had not at first understood. With a business-like movement that was the result of Brian Oakley's careful training, her hand dropped to her hip and was raised again.

James Rutlidge stopped, as though against an iron bar. In the blue eyes that looked at him, now, over the dark barrel of the revolver, he read no uncertainty of purpose. The small hand that had drawn the weapon with such ready swiftness, was as steady as though at target practice. Instinctively, the man half turned, throwing up his arm as if to shield his face from a menacing blow. "For God's sake," he gasped, "put that down."

In truth, James Rutlidge was nearer death, at that instant, than he had ever been before.

Drawing back a few fearful paces, his hands still uplifted, he said again, "Put it down, I tell you. Don't you see I'm not going to touch you? You are crazy. You might kill me."

Her words came cold and collected, expressing, together with her calm manner, perfect self-possession "If you can give any good reason why I should not kill you, I will let you go."

The man was carefully drawing backward toward the tree against which he had placed his rifle.

She watched him, with a disconcerting smile. "You may as well stop now," she said, in those even, composed tones. "I shall fire, the moment you are within reach of your gun."

He halted with a gesture of despair; his face livid with fear at her apparent indecision as to his fate.

Presently, she spoke again. "Don't worry. I'm not going to kill you—unless you force me to—which I assure you will not be at all difficult for you to do. Move down the trail until I tell you to stop." She indicated the direction, along the ridge of the mountain spur.

He obeyed.

"That will do," she said, when he was some twenty paces away.

He stopped, turning to face her again.

Picking up his Winchester, she skillfully and rapidly threw all of the shells out of the magazine. Then, covering him again with her own weapon, she went a few steps closer and threw the empty rifle at his feet. "Now," she said, "put that gun over your left shoulder, and go on ahead of me down the trail. If you try to dodge or run, or if you change the position of your rifle, I'll kill you."

"What are you going to do?" he asked.

"I'm going to take you down to your camp at Burnt Pine."

James Rutlidge, pale with rage and shame, stood still. "You may as well kill me," he said. "I will never go into camp, this way."

"Don't be uneasy," she returned. "I am no more anxious for the world to know of this, than you are. Do as I say. When we come within sight of your camp, or if we meet any one, I will put up my gun and we will go on together. That's why I am permitting you to carry your rifle."

So they went down the mountainside—the man with his empty rifle over his shoulder; the girl following, a few paces in the rear, with ready weapon.

When they had come within sight of the camp, James Rutlidge said, "There's some one there."

"I see," returned Sibyl, slipping her gun in its holster and stepping forward beside her companion. And there was a note of glad relief in her voice, for it was Brian Oakley who was bending over the camp-fire "Come," she continued to her companion, "and act as though nothing had happened."

The Ranger, on his way down from somewhere in the vicinity of San Gorgonio, had stopped at the hunters' camp for a belated dinner. Finding no one at home, he had started a fire, and had helped himself to coffee and bacon. He was just concluding his appropriated meal, when Sibyl and James Rutlidge arrived.

In a few words, the girl explained to her friend, that she was on her way over the trail from Lone Cabin, and had accidentally met Mr. Rutlidge who had accompanied her as far as the camp. James Rutlidge had little to say beyond assuring the Ranger of his welcome; and very soon, the officer and the girl set out on their way down the Laurel trail to Clear Creek canyon. As they went, Sibyl's old friend asked not a few questions about her meeting with James Rutlidge; but the girl, walking ahead in the narrow trail, evaded him, and was glad that he could not see her face.

Sibyl had spoken the literal truth when she said to Rutlidge, that she did not want any one to know of the incident. She felt ashamed and humiliated at the thought of telling even her father's old comrade and friend. She knew Brian Oakley too well to have any doubts as to what would happen if he knew how the man had approached her, and she shrank from the inevitable outcome. She wished only to forget the whole affair, and, as quickly as possible, turned the conversation into other and safer channels.

The Ranger could not stop at the house with her, but must go on down the canyon, to the Station. So the girl returned to Myra Willard, alone; and, to the woman's surprise, for the second time, with an empty creel.

Sibyl explained her failure to bring home a catch of trout, with the simple statement that she had not fished; and then—to her companion's amazement—burst into tears; begging to return at once to their little home in Fairlands.

Myra Willard thought that she understood, better than the girl herself, why, for the first time in her life, Sibyl wished to leave the mountains. Perhaps the woman with the disfigured face was right.

Chapter XXV

On the Pipe-Line Trail

James Rutlidge spent the day following his experience with Sibyl Andrés, in camp. His companions very quickly felt his sullen, ugly mood, and left him to his own thoughts.

The manner in which Sibyl received his advances had in no way changed the man's mind as to the nature of her relation to Aaron King. To one of James Rutlidge's type,—schooled in the intellectual moral and esthetic tenets of his class,—it was impossible to think of the companionship of the artist and the girl in any other light. If he had even considered the possibility of a clean, pure comradeship existing between them—under all the circumstances of their friendship as he had seen them in the studio, on the trail at dusk, and in the artist's camp—he would have answered himself that Aaron King was not such a fool as to fail to take advantage of his opportunities. The humiliation of his pride, and his rage at being so ignominiously checked by the girl whom he had so long endeavored to win, served only to increase his desire for her. Sibyl's resolute spirit, and vigorous beauty, when aroused by him, together with her unexpected opposition to his advances, were as fuel to the flame of his passion.

His day of sullen brooding over the matter did not improve his temper; and the next morning his friends were relieved to see him setting out alone, with rifle and field-glass and lunch. Ostensibly starting in the direction of the upper Laurel Creek country he doubled back, as soon as he was out of sight of camp, and took the trail leading down to Clear Creek canyon.

It could not be said that the man had any definite purpose in mind. He was simply yielding in a purposeless way to his mood, which, for the time being, could find no other expression. The remote chance that some opportunity looking toward his desire might present itself, led him to seek the scenes where such an opportunity would be most likely to occur.

Crossing the canyon above the Company Headwork he came into the pipe-line trail at a point a little back from the main wagon road and, an hour later, reached the place on Oak Knoll where the Government trail leads down into the canyon below, and where Aaron King and Conrad Lagrange had committed themselves to the judgment of Croesus. Here he left the trail, and climbed to a point on a spur of the mountain, from which he could see the path for some distance on either side and below, and from which his view of the narrow valley was unobstructed. Comfortably seated, with his back against a rock, he adjusted his field-glass and trained it upon the little spot of open green—marked by the giant sycamores, the dark line of cedars, and the half hidden house—where he knew that Sibyl Andrés and Myra Willard were living.

No sooner had he focused the powerful glass upon the scene that so interested him, than he uttered a low exclamation. The two women, surrounded by their luggage and camp equipment, were sitting on the porch with Brian Oakley; waiting, evidently, for the wagon that was crossing the creek toward the house. It was clear to the man on the mountainside, that Sibyl Andrés and the woman with the disfigured face were returning to Fairlands.

For some time, James Rutlidge sat watching, with absorbing interest, the unconscious people in the canyon below. Once, he turned for a brief glance at the grove of sycamores behind the old orchard, farther down the creek. The camp of Conrad Lagrange and Aaron King was no longer there. Quickly he fixed his gaze again upon Sibyl and her friends. Presently,—as one will when looking long through a field-glass or telescope,—he lowered his hands, to rest his eyes by looking, unaided, at the immediate objects in the landscape before him. At that moment, the figure of a man appeared on the near-by trail below. It was a pitiful figure—ill-kempt ragged, half-starved, haggard-faced.

Creeping feebly along the lonely little path—without seeing the man on the mountainside above—crouching as he walked with a hunted, fearful air—the poor creature moved toward the point of the spur around which the trail led beneath the spot where Rutlidge sat.

As the man on the trail drew nearer, the watcher on the rocks above involuntarily glanced toward the distant Forest Ranger; then back to the—as he rightly guessed—escaped convict.

There are, no doubt, many moments in the life of a man like James Rutlidge when, however bad or dominated by evil influences he may be, he feels strongly the impulse of pity and the kindly desire to help. Undoubtedly, James Rutlidge inherited from his father those tendencies that made him easily ruled by his baser passions. His character was as truly the legitimate product of the age, of the social environment, and of the thought that accepts such characters. What he might have been if better born, or if schooled in an atmosphere of moral and intellectual integrity, is an idle speculation. He was what his inheritance and his life had made him. He was not without impulses for good. The pitiful, hunted creature, creeping so wearily along the trail, awoke in this man of the accepted culture of his day a feeling of compassion, and aroused in him a desire to offer assistance. For the legal aspect of the case, James Rutlidge had all the indifference of his kind, who imbibe contempt for law with their mother's milk. For the moment he hesitated. Then, as the figure below passed from his sight, under the point of the spur, he slipped quietly down the mountainside, and, a few minutes later, met the convict face to face.

At the leveled rifle and the sharp command, "Hands up," the poor fellow halted with a gesture of tragic despair. An instant they stood; then the hunted one turned impulsively toward the canyon that, here, lies almost a sheer thousand feet below.

James Rutlidge spoke sharply. "Don't do that. I'm not an officer. I want to help you."

The convict turned his hunted, fearful, starving face in doubtful bewilderment toward the speaker.

The man with the gun continued, "I got the drop on you to prevent accidents—until I could explain—that's all." He lowered the rifle.

The other went a staggering step forward. "You mean that?" he said in a harsh, incredulous whisper. "You—you're not playing with me?"

"Why should I want to play with you?" returned the other, kindly. "Come, let's get off the trail. I have something to eat, up there." He led the way back to the place where he had left his lunch.

Dropping down upon the ground, the starving man seized the offered food with an animal-like cry; feeding noisily, with the manner of a famished beast. The other watched with mingled pity and disgust.

Presently, in stammering, halting phrases, but in words that showed no lack of education, the wretched creature attempted to apologize for his unseemly eagerness, and endeavored to thank his benefactor. "I suppose, sir, there is no use trying to deny my identity," he said, when James Rutlidge had again assured him of his kindly interest.

"Not at all," agreed the other, "and, so far as I am concerned, there is no reason why you should."

"Just what do you mean by that, sir?" questioned the convict.

"I mean that I am not an officer and have no reason in the world for turning you over to them. I saw you coming along the trail down there and, of course, could not help noticing your condition and guessing who you were. To me, you are simply a poor devil who has gotten into a tight hole, and I want to help you out a bit, that's all."

The convict turned his eyes despairingly toward the canyon below, as he answered, "I thank you, sir, but it would have been better if you had not. Your help has only put the end off for a few hours. They've got me shut in. I can keep away from them, up here in the mountains, but I can't get out. I won't go back to that hell they call prison though—I won't." There was no mistaking his desperate purpose.

James Rutlidge thought of that quick movement toward the edge of the trail and the rocky depth below. "You don't seem such a bad sort, at heart," he said invitingly.

"I'm not," returned the other, "I've been a fool—miserably weak fool—but I've had my lesson—only—I have had it too late."

While the man was speaking, James Rutlidge was thinking quickly. As he had been moved, at first, by a spirit of compassion to give temporary assistance to the poor hunted creature, he was now prompted to offer more lasting help—providing, of course, that he could do so without too great a risk to his own convenience. The convict's hopeless condition, his despairing purpose, and his evident wish to live free from the past, all combined to arouse in the other a desire to aid him. But while that truly benevolent inclination was, in his consciousness, unmarred with sinister motive of any sort; still, deeper than the impulse for good in James Rutlidge's nature lay those dominant instincts and passions that were his by inheritance and training. The brutal desire, the mood and purpose that had brought him to that spot where with the aid of his glass he could watch Sibyl Andrés, were not denied by his impulse to kindly service. Under all his thinking, as he considered how he could help the convict to a better life, there was the shadowy suggestion of a possible situation where a man like the one before him—wholly in his power as this man would be—might be of use to him in furthering his own purpose—the purpose that had brought about their meeting.

Studying the object of his pity, he said slowly, "I suppose the most of us are as deserving of punishment as the majority of those who actually get it. One way or another, we are all trying to escape the penalty for our wrong-doing. What if I should help you out—make it possible for you to live like other men who are safe from the law? What would you do if I were to help you to your freedom?"

The hunted man became incoherent in his pleading for a chance to prove the sincerity of his wish to live an orderly, respectable, and honest life.

"You have a safe hiding place here in the mountains?" asked Rutlidge.

"Yes; a little hut, hidden in a deep gorge, over on the Cold Water. I could live there a year if I had supplies."

James Rutlidge considered. "I've got it!" he said at last. "Listen! There must be some peak, at the Cold Water end of this range, from which you can see Fairlands as well as the Galena Valley."

"Yes," the other answered eagerly.

"And," continued Rutlidge, "there is a good 'auto' road up the Galena Valley. One could get, I should think, to a point within—say nine hours of your camp. Do you know anything about the heliograph?"

"Yes," said the man, his face brightening. "That is, I understand the general principle—that it's a method of signaling by mirror flashes."

"Good! This is my plan. I will meet you to-morrow on the Laurel Creek trail, where it turns off from the creek toward San Gorgonio. You know the spot?"

"Yes."

"We will go around the head of Clear Creek, on the divide between this canyon and the Cold Water, to some peak in the Galenas from which we can see Fairlands; and where, with the field-glass, we can pick out some point at the upper end of Galena Valley, that we can both find later."

"I understand."

"When I get back to Fairlands, I will make a night trip in the 'auto' to that point, with supplies. You will meet me there. The day before I make the trip, I'll signal you by mirror flashes that I am coming; and you will answer from the peak. We'll agree on the time of day and the signals to-morrow. When you have kept close, long enough for your beard and hair to grow out well, everybody will have given you up for dead or gone. Then I will take you down and give you a job in an orange grove. There's a little house there where you can live. You won't need to show yourself down-town and, in time, you will be forgotten. I'll bring you enough food to-morrow to last you until I can return to town and can get back on the first night trip."

The man who left James Rutlidge a few minutes later, after trying brokenly to express his gratitude, was a creature very different from the poor, frightened hunted, starving, despairing, wretch that Rutlidge had halted an hour before. What that man was to become, would depend almost wholly upon his benefactor.

When the man was gone, James Rutlidge again took up his field-glass. The old home of Sibyl Andrés was deserted. While he had been talking with the convict, the girl and Myra Willard had started on their way back to Fairlands.

With a peculiar smile upon his heavy features, the man slipped the glass into its case, and, with a long, slow look over the scene, set out on his way to rejoin his friends.

Chapter XXVI

I Want You Just as You Are

The evening of that day after their return from the mountains, when Conrad Lagrange had found Aaron King so absorbed in his mother's letters, the artist continued in his silent, preoccupied, mood. The next morning, it was the same. Refusing every attempt of his friend to engage him in conversation, he answered only with absent-minded mono-syllables; until the novelist, declaring that the painter was fit company for neither beast nor man, left him alone; and went off somewhere with Czar.

The artist spent the greater part of the forenoon in his studio, doing nothing of importance. That is, to a casual observer he would have seemed to be doing nothing of importance. He did, however, place his picture of the spring glade beside the portrait of Mrs. Taine, and then, for an hour or more, sat considering the two paintings. Then he turned the "Quaker Maid" again to the wall and fixed a fresh canvas in place on the easel. That was all.

Immediately after their midday lunch, he returned to the studio—hurriedly, as if to work. He arranged his palette, paints, and brushes ready to his hand, indeed—but he, then, did nothing with them. Listlessly, without interest, he turned through his portfolios of sketches. Often, he looked away through the big, north window to the distant mountain tops. Often, he seemed to be listening. He was sitting before the easel, staring at the blank canvas, when, clear and sweet, from the depths of the orange grove, came the pure tones of Sibyl Andrés' violin.

So soft and low was the music, at first, that the artist almost doubted that it was real, thinking—as he had thought that day when Sibyl came singing to the glade—that it was his fancy tricking him. When he and Conrad Lagrange left the mountains three days before, the girl and her companion had not expected to return to Fairlands for at least two weeks. But there was no mistaking that music of the hills. As the tones grew louder and more insistent, with a ringing note of gladness, he knew that the mountain girl was announcing her arrival and, in the language she loved best, was greeting her friends.

But so strangely selfish is the heart of man, that Aaron King gave the novelist no share in their neighbor's musical greeting. He received the message as if it were to himself alone. As he listened, his eyes brightened; he stood erect, his face turned upward toward the mountain peaks in the distance; his lips curved in a slow smile. He fancied that he could see the girl's winsome face lighted with merriment as she played, knowing his surprise. Once, he started impulsively toward the door, but paused, hesitating, and turned back. When the music ceased, he went to the open window that looked out into the rose garden, and watched expectantly.

Presently, he heard her low-voiced song as she came through the orange grove beyond the Ragged Robin hedge. Then he glimpsed her white dress at the little gate in the corner. Then she stood in full view.

The artist had, so far, seen Sibyl only in her mountain costume of soft brown,—made for rough contact with rocks and underbrush,—with felt hat to match, and high, laced boots, fit for climbing. She was dressed, now, as Conrad Lagrange had seen her that first time in the garden, when he was hiding from Louise Taine. The man at the window drew a little back, with a low exclamation of pleased surprise and wonder. Was that lovely creature there among the roses his girl comrade of the hills? The Sibyl Andrés he had known—in the short skirt and high boots of her mountain garb—was a winsome, fanciful, sometimes serious, sometimes wayward, maiden. This Sibyl Andrés, gowned in clinging white, was a slender, gracefully tall, and beautifully developed woman.

Slowly, she came toward the studio end of the garden; pausing here and there to bend over the flowers as though in loving, tender greeting; singing, the while, her low-voiced melody; unafraid of the sunshine that enveloped her in a golden flood, undisturbed by the careless fingers of the wind that caressed her hair. A girl of the clean out-of-doors, she belonged among the roses, even as she had been at home among the pines and oaks of the mountains. The artist, fascinated by the lovely scene, stood as though fearing to move, lest the vision vanish.

Then, looking up, she saw him, and stretched out her hands in a gesture of greeting, with a laugh of pleasure.

"Don't move, don't move!" he called impulsively. "Hold the pose—please hold it! I want you just as you are!"

The girl, amused at his tragic earnestness, and at the manner of his welcome, understood that the zeal of the artist had brushed aside the polite formalities of the man; and, as unaffectedly natural as she did everything, gave herself to his mood.

Dragging his easel with the blank canvas upon it across the studio, he cried out, again, "Don't move, please don't move!" and began working. He was as one beside himself, so wholly absorbed was he in translating into the terms of color and line, the loveliness purity and truth that was expressed by the personality of the girl as she stood among the flowers. "If I can get it! If I can only get it!" he exclaimed again and again, with a kind of savage earnestness, as he worked.

All his years of careful training, all his studiously acquired skill, all his mastery of the mechanics of his craft, came to him, now, without conscious effort—obedient to his purpose. Here was no thoughtful straining to remember the laws of composition, and perspective, and harmony. Here was no skillful evading of the truth he saw. So freely, so surely, he worked, he scarcely knew he painted. Forgetting self, as he was unconscious of his technic, he worked as the birds sing, as the bees toil, as the deer runs. Under his hand, his picture grew and blossomed as the roses, themselves, among which the beautiful girl stood.

Day after day, at that same hour, Sibyl Andrés came singing through the orange grove, to stand in the golden sunlight among the roses, with hands outstretched in greeting. Every day, Aaron King waited her coming—sitting before his easel, palette and brush in hand. Each day, he worked as he had worked that first day—with no thought for anything save for his picture.

In the mornings, he walked with Conrad Lagrange or, sometimes, worked with Sibyl in the garden. Often, in the evening, the two men would visit the little house next door. Occasionally, the girl and the woman with the disfigured face would come to sit for a while on the front porch with their friends. Thus the neighborly friendship that began in the hills was continued in the orange groves. The comradeship between the two young people grew stronger, hour by hour, as the painter worked at his easel to express with canvas and color and brush the spirit of the girl whose character and life was so unmarred by the world.

A11 through those days, when he was so absorbed in his work that he often failed to reply when she spoke to him, the girl manifested a helpful understanding of his mood that caused the painter to marvel. She seemed to know, instinctively, when he was baffled or perplexed by the annoying devils of "can't-get-at-it," that so delight to torment artist folk; just as she knew and rejoiced when the imps were routed and the soul of the man exulted with the sureness and freedom of his hand. He asked her, once, when they had finished for the day, how it was that she knew so well how the work was progressing, when she could not see the picture.

She laughed merrily. "But I can see you; and I"—she hesitated with that trick, that he was learning to know so well, of searching for a word—"I just feel what you are feeling. I suppose it's because my music is that way. Sometimes, it simply won't come right, at all, and I feel as though I never could do it. Then, again, it seems to do itself; and I listen and wonder—just as if I had nothing to do with it."

So that day came when the artist, drawing slowly back from his easel, stood so long gazing at his picture without touching it that the girl called to him, "What's the matter? Won't it come right?"

Slowly he laid aside his palette and brushes. Standing at the open window, he looked at her—smiling but silent—as she held the pose.

For an instant, she did not understand. "Am I not right?" she asked anxiously. Then, before he could answer—"Oh, have you finished? Is it all done?"

Still smiling, he answered almost sadly, "I have done all that I can do. Come."

A moment later, she stood in the studio door.

Seeing her hesitate, he said again, "Come."

"I—I am afraid to look," she faltered.

He laughed. "Really I don't think it's quite so bad as that."

"Oh, but I don't mean that I'm afraid it's bad—it isn't."

The painter watched her,—a queer expression on his face,—as he returned curiously, "And how, pray tell, do you know it isn't bad—when you have never seen it? It's quite the thing, I'll admit, for critics to praise or condemn without much knowledge of the work; but I didn't expect you to be so modern."

"You are making fun of me," she laughed. "But I don't care. I know your work is good, because I know how and why you did it. You painted it just as you painted the spring glade, didn't you?"

"Yes," he said soberly, "I did. But why are you afraid?"

"Why, that's the reason. I—I'm afraid to see myself as you see me."

The man's voice was gentle with feeling as he answered seriously, "Miss Andrés, you, of all the people I have ever known, have the least cause to fear to look at your portrait for that reason. Come."

Slowly, she went forward to stand by his side before the picture.

For some time, she looked at the beautiful work into which Aaron King had put the best of himself and of his genius. At last, turning full upon him, her eyes blue and shining, she said in a low tone, "O Mr. King, it is too—too—beautiful! It is so beautiful it—it—hurts. She seems to, to"—she searched for the word—"to belong to the roses, doesn't she? It makes you feel just as the rose garden makes you feel."

He laughed with pleasure, "What a child of nature you are! You have forgotten that it is a portrait of yourself, haven't you?"

She laughed with him. "I had forgotten. It's so lovely!" Then she added wistfully, "Am I—am I really like that?—just a little?"

"No," he answered. "But that is just a little, a very little, like you."

She looked at him half doubtfully—sincerely unmindful of the compliment, in her consideration of its truth. Shaking her head, with a serious smile, she returned slowly, "I wish that I could be sure you are not mistaken."

"You will permit me to exhibit the picture, will you?" he asked.

"Why, yes! of course! You made it for people to see, didn't you? I don't believe any one could look at it seriously without having good thoughts, could they?"

"I'm sure they could not," he answered. "But, you see, it's a portrait of you; and I thought you might not care for the—ah—" he finished with a smile—"shall I say fame?"

"Oh! I did not think that you would tell any one that I had anything to do with it. Is it necessary that my name should be mentioned?"

"Not exactly necessary"—he admitted—"but few women, these days, would miss the opportunity."

She shook her head, with a positive air. "No, no; you must exhibit it as a picture; not as a portrait of me. The portrait part is of no importance. It is what you have made your picture say, that will do good."

"And what have I made it say?" he asked, curiously pleased.

"Why it says that—that a woman should be beautiful as the roses are beautiful—without thinking too much about it, you know—just as a man should be strong without thinking too much about his strength, I mean."

"Yes," he agreed, "it says that. But I want you to know that, whatever title it is exhibited under, it will always be, to me, a portrait—the truest I have ever painted."

She flushed with genuine pleasure as she said brightly, "I like you for that. And now let's try it on Conrad Lagrange and Myra Willard. You get him, and I'll run and bring her. Mind you don't let Mr. Lagrange in until I get back! I want to watch him when he first sees it."

When the artist found Conrad Lagrange and told him that the picture was finished, the novelist, without comment, turned his attention to Czar.

The painter, with an amused smile, asked, "Won't you come for a look at it, old man?"

The other returned gruffly, "Thanks; but I don't think I care to risk it."

The artist laughed. "But Miss Andrés wants you to come. She sent me to fetch you."

Conrad Lagrange turned his peculiar, baffling eyes upon the young man. "Does she like it?"

"She seems to."

"If she seems to, she does," retorted the other, rising. "And that's different."

When the novelist, with his three friends, stood before the easel, he was silent for so long that the girl said anxiously, "I—I thought you would like it, Mr. Lagrange."

They saw the strange man's eyes fill with tears as he answered, in the gentle tones that always marked his words to her, "Like it? My dear child, how could I help liking it? It is you—you!" To the artist, he added, "It is great work, my boy, great! I—I wish your mother could have seen it. It is like her—as I knew her. You have done well." He turned, with gentle courtesy, to Myra Willard; "And you? What is your verdict, Miss Willard?"

With her arm around the beautiful original of the portrait, the woman with the disfigured face answered, "I think, sir, that I, better than any one in all the world, know how good, how true, it is."

Conrad Lagrange spoke again to the artist, inquiringly; "You will exhibit it?"

"Miss Andrés says that I may—but not as a portrait."

The novelist could not conceal his pleasure at the answer. Presently, he said, "If it is not to be shown as a portrait, may I suggest a title?"

"I was hoping you would!" exclaimed the painter.

"And so was I," cried Sibyl, with delight. "What is it, Mr. Lagrange?"

"Let it be exhibited as 'The Spirit of Nature—A Portrait'," answered Conrad Lagrange.

As the novelist finished speaking, Yee Kee appeared in the doorway. "They come—big automobile. Whole lot people. Misse Taine, Miste' Lutlidge, sick man, whole lot—I come tell you."

The artist spoke quickly,—"Stop them in the house, Kee; I'll be right in,"—and the Chinaman vanished.

At Yee Kee's announcement, Myra Willard's face went white, and she gave a low cry.

"Never mind, dear," said the girl, soothingly. "We can slip away through the garden—come."

When Sibyl and the woman with the disfigured face were gone, Conrad Lagrange and Aaron King looked at each other, questioningly.

Then the novelist said harshly,—pointing to the picture on the easel,—"You're not going to let that flock of buzzards feed on this, are you? I'll murder some one, sure as hell, if you do."

"I don't think I could stand it, myself," said the artist, laughing grimly, as he drew the velvet curtain to hide the portrait.

Chapter XXVII

The Answer

When Aaron King and Conrad Lagrange entered the house to meet their callers from Fairlands Heights, the artist felt, oddly, that he was meeting a company of strangers.

The carefully hidden, yet—to him—subtly revealed, warmth of Mrs. Taine's greeting embarrassed him with a momentary sense of shame. The frothing gush of Louise's inane ejaculations, and the coughing, choking, cursing of Mr. Taine,—whose feeble grip upon the flesh that had so betrayed him was, by now, so far loosed that he could scarcely walk alone,—set the painter struggling for words that would mean nothing—the only words that, under the circumstances, could serve. Aaron King was somewhat out of practise in the use of meaningless words, and the art of talking without saying anything is an art that requires constant exercise if one would not commit serious technical blunders. James Rutlidge's greeting was insolently familiar; as a man of certain mind greets—in public—a boon companion of his private and unmentionable adventures. Toward the great critic, the painter exercised a cool self-restraint that was at least commendable.

While Aaron King, with James Rutlidge and Mr. Taine, with carefully assumed interest, was listening to Louise's effort to make a jumble of "ohs" and "ahs" and artistic sighs sound like a description of a sunset in the mountains, Mrs. Taine said quietly to Conrad Lagrange, "You certainly have taken excellent care of your protege, this summer. He looks splendidly fit."

The novelist, watching the woman whose eyes, as she spoke, were upon the artist, answered, "You are pleased to flatter me, Mrs. Taine."

She turned to him, with a knowing smile. "Perhaps I am giving you more credit than is due. I understand Mr. King has not been in your care altogether. Shame on you, Mr. Lagrange! for a man of your age and experience to permit your charge to roam all over the country, alone and unprotected, with a picturesque mountain girl!—and that, after your warning to poor me!"

Conrad Lagrange smiled grimly. "I confess I thought of you in that connection several times."

She eyed him doubtfully. "Oh, well," she said easily, "I suppose artists must amuse themselves, occasionally—the same as the rest of us."

"I don't think that, 'amuse' is exactly the word, Mrs. Taine," the other returned coldly.

"No? Surely you don't meant to tell me that it is anything serious?"

"I don't mean to tell you anything about it," he retorted rather sharply.

She laughed. "You don't need to. Jim has already told me quite enough. Mr. King, himself, will tell me more."

"Not unless he's a bigger fool than I think," growled the novelist.

Again, she laughed into his face, mockingly. "You men are all more or less foolish when there's a woman in the case, aren't you?"

To which, the other answered tartly, "If we were not, there would be no woman in the case."

As Conrad Lagrange spoke, Louise, exhausted by her efforts to achieve that sunset in the mountains with her limited supply of adjectives, floundered hopelessly into the expressive silence of clasped hands and heaving breast and ecstatically upturned eyes. The artist, seizing the opportunity with the cunning of desperation, turned to Mrs. Taine, with some inane remark about the summers in California.

Whatever it was that he said, Mrs. Taine agreed with him, heartily, adding, "And you, I suppose, have been making good use of your time? Or have you been simply storing up material and energy for this winter?"

This brought Louise out of the depths of that sunset, with a flop. She was so sure that Mr. King had some inexpressibly wonderful work to show them. Couldn't they go at once to the equally inexpressibly beautiful studio, to see the inexpressibly lovely pictures that she was so inexpressibly sure he had been painting in the inexpressibly grand and beautiful and wonderfully lovely mountains?

The painter assured them that he had no work for them to see; and Louise floundered again into the depths of inexpressible disappointment and despair.

Nevertheless, a few minutes later, Aaron King found himself in his studio, alone with Mrs. Taine. He could not have told exactly how she managed it, or why. Perhaps, in sheer pity, she had rescued him from the floods of Louise's appreciation. Perhaps—she had some other reasons. There had been something said about her right to see her own picture, and then—there they were—with the others safely barred from intruding upon the premises sacred to art.

When there was no longer need to fear the eyes of the world, Mrs. Taine was at no pains to hide the warmth of her feeling. With little reserve, she confessed herself in every look and tone and movement.

"Are you really glad to see me, I wonder," she said invitingly. "All this summer, while I have been forced to endure the company of all sorts of stupid people, I have been thinking of you and your work. And, you see, I have come to you, the first possible moment after my return home."

The man—being a man—could not remain wholly insensible to the alluring physical beauty of the splendid creature who stood so temptingly before him; but, to the honor of his kind, he could and did remain master of himself.

The woman, true to her life training,—as James Rutlidge had been true to his schooling when he approached Sibyl Andrés in the mountains,—construed the artist's manner, not as a splendid self-control but as a careful policy. To her, and to her kind, the great issues of life are governed, not at all by principle, but by policy. It is not at all what one is, or what one may accomplish that matters; it is wholly what one may skillfully appear to be, and what one may skillfully provoke the world to say, that is of vital importance. Turning from the painter to the easel, as if to find in his portrait of her the fuller expression of that which she believed he dared not yet put into words, she was about to draw aside the curtain; when Aaron King checked her quickly, with a smile that robbed his words of any rudeness.

"Please don't touch that, Mrs. Taine. I am not yet ready to show it."

As she turned from the easel to face him, he took her portrait from where it rested, face to the wall; and placed it upon another easel, saying, "Here is your picture."

With the painting before her, she talked eagerly of her plans for the artist's future; how the picture was to be exhibited, and how, because it was her portrait, it would be praised and talked about by her friends who were leaders in the art circles. Frankly, she spoke of "pull" and "influence" and "scheme"; of "working" this and that "paper" for "write-ups"; of "handling" this or that "critic" and "writer"; of "reaching the committees"; of introducing the painter into the proper inside cliques, and clans; and of clever "advertising stunts" that would make him the most popular portrait painter of his day; insuring thus his—as she called it—fame.

The man who had painted the picture of the spring glade, and who had so faithfully portrayed the truth and beauty of Sibyl Andrés as she stood among the roses, listened to this woman's plans for making his portrait of herself famous, with a feeling of embarrassment and shame.

"Do you really think that the work merits such prominence as you say will be given it?" he asked doubtfully.

She laughed knowingly, "Just wait until Jim Rutlidge's 'write-up' appears, and all the others follow his lead, and you'll see! The picture is clever enough—you know it as well as I. It is beautiful. It has everything that we women want in a portrait. I really don't know much about what you painters call art; but I know that when Jim and our friends get through with it, your picture will have every mark of a great masterpiece, and that you will be on the topmost wave of success."

"And then what?" he asked.

Again, she interpreted his words in the light of her own thoughts, and with little attempt to veil the fire that burned in her eyes, answered, "And then—I hope that you will not forget me."

For a moment he returned her look; then a feeling of disgust and shame for her swept over him, and he again turned away, to stand gazing moodily out of the window that looked into the rose garden.

"You seem to be disturbed and worried," she said, in a tone that implied a complete understanding of his mood, and a tacit acceptance of the things that he would say if it were not for the world.

He laughed shortly—"I fear you will think me ungrateful for your kindness. Believe me, I am not."

"I know you are not," she returned. "But don't think that you had better confess, just the same?"

He answered wonderingly, "Confess?"

"Yes." She shook her finger at him, in playful severity. "Oh, I know what you have been up to all summer—running wild with your mountain girl! Really, you ought to be more discreet."

Aaron King's face burned as he stammered something about not knowing what she meant.

She laughed gaily. "There, there, never mind—I forgive you—now that you are safely back in civilization again. I know you artists, and how you must have your periods of ah—relaxation—with rather more liberties than the common herd. Just so you are careful that the world doesn't know too much."

At this frank revelation of her mind, the man stood amazed. For the construction she put upon his relation with the girl whose pure and gentle comradeship had led him to greater heights in his art than he had ever before attained, he could have driven this woman from the studio he felt that she profaned. But what could he say? He remembered Conrad Lagrange's counsel when James Rutlidge had seen the girl at their camp. What could he say that would not injure Sibyl Andrés? To cover his embarrassment, he forced a laugh and answered lightly, "Really, I am not good at confessions."

"Nor I at playing the part of confessor," she laughed with him. "But, just the same, you might tell me what you think of yourself. Aren't you just a little ashamed?"

The artist had moved to a position in front of her portrait; and, as he looked upon the painted lie, his answer came. "Rather let me tell you what I think of you, Mrs. Taine. And let me tell you in the language I know best. Let me put my answer to your charges here," he touched her portrait.

Almost, his reply was worthy of Conrad Lagrange, himself.

"I don't quite understand," she said, a trifle put out by the turn his answer had taken.

"I mean," he explained eagerly, "that I want to repaint your portrait. You remember, I wrote, when I returned Mr. Taine's generous check, that I was not altogether satisfied with it. Give me another chance."

"You mean for me to come here again, to pose for you?—as I did before?"

"Yes," he answered, "just as you did before. I want to make a portrait worthy of you, as this is not. Let me tell you, on the canvas, what I cannot—" he hesitated then said deliberately—"what I dare not put into words."

The woman received his words as a veiled declaration of a passion he dared not, yet, openly express. She thought his request a clever ruse to renew their meetings in the privacy of his studio, and was, accordingly delighted.

"Oh, that will be wonderful!—heavenly!" she cried, springing to her feet. "Can we begin at once? May I come to-morrow?"

"Yes," he answered, "come to-morrow."

"And may I wear the Quaker gown?"

"Yes, indeed! I want you just as you were before—the same dress, the same pose. It is to be the same picture, you understand, only a better one—one more worthy of us, both. And now," he continued hurriedly "don't you think that we should return to the house?"

"I suppose so," she answered regretfully—lingering.

The artist was already opening the door.

As they passed out, she placed her hand on his arm, and looked up into his face admiringly. "What a clever, clever man you are, to think of it! And what a story it will make for the papers—when my picture is shown—how you were not satisfied with the portrait and refused to let it go—and how, after keeping it in your studio for months, you repainted it, to satisfy your artistic conscience!"

Aaron King smiled.

The announcement in the house that the artist was to repaint Mrs. Taine's picture, provoked characteristic comment. Louise effervesced a frothy stream of bubbling exclamations. James Rutlidge gave a hearty, "By Jove, old man, you have nerve! If you can really improve on that canvas, you are a wonder." And Mr. Taine, under the watchful eye of his beautiful wife, responded with a husky whisper, "Quite right—my boy—quite right! Certainly—by all means—if you feel that way about it—" his consent and approval ending in a paroxysm of coughing that left him weak and breathless, and nearly eliminated him from the question, altogether.

When the Fairlands Heights party had departed, Conrad Lagrange looked the artist up and down.

"Well,"—he growled harshly, in his most brutal tones,—"what is it? Is the dog returning to his vomit?—or is the prodigal turning his back on his hogs and his husks?"

Aaron King smiled as he answered, "I think, rather, it's the case of the blind beggar who sat by the roadside, helpless, until a certain Great Physician passed that way."

And Conrad Lagrange understood.

Chapter XXVIII

You're Ruined, My Boy

It was no light task to which Aaron King had set his hand. He did not doubt what it would cost him. Nor did Conrad Lagrange, as they talked together that evening, fail to point out clearly what it would mean to the artist, at the very beginning of his career, to fly thus rudely in the face of the providence that had chosen to serve him. The world's history of art and letters affords too many examples of men who, because they refused to pay court to the ruling cliques and circles of their little day, had seen the doors of recognition slammed in their faces; and who, even as they wrought their great works, had been forced to hear, as they toiled, the discordant yelpings of the self-appointed watchdogs of the halls of fame. Nor did the artist question the final outcome,—if only his work should be found worthy to endure,—for the world's history establishes, also, the truth—that he who labors for a higher wage than an approving paragraph in the daily paper, may, in spite of the condemnation of the pretending rulers, live in the life of his race, long after the names to which he refused to bow are lost in the dust of their self-raised thrones.

The painter was driven to his course by that self-respect, without which, no man can sanely endure his own company; together with that reverence—I say it deliberately—that reverence for his art, without which, no worthy work is possible. He had come to understand that one may not prostitute his genius to the immoral purposes of a diseased age, without reaping a prostitute's reward. The hideous ruin that Mr. Taine had, in himself, wrought by the criminal dissipation of his manhood's strength, and by the debasing of his physical appetites and passions, was to Aaron King, now, a token of the intellectual, spiritual, and moral ruin that alone can result from a debased and depraved dissipation of an artist's creative power. He saw clearly, now, that the influence his work must wield upon the lives of those who came within its reach, must be identical with the influence of Sibyl Andrés, who had so unconsciously opened his eyes to the true mission and glory of the arts, and thus had made his decision possible. In that hour when Mrs. Taine had revealed herself to him so clearly, following as it did so closely his days of work and the final completion of his portrait of the girl among the roses, he saw and felt the woman, not as one who could help him to the poor rewards of a temporary popularity, but as the spirit of an age that threatens the very life of art by seeking to destroy the vital truth and purpose of its existence. He felt that in painting the portrait of Mrs. Taine—as he had painted it—he had betrayed a trust; as truly as had his father who, for purely personal aggrandizement, had stolen the material wealth intrusted to him by his fellows. The young man understood, now, that, instead of fulfilling the purpose of his mother's sacrifice, and realizing for her her dying wish, as he had promised; the course he had entered upon would have thwarted the one and denied the other.

The young man had answered the novelist truly, that it was a case of the blind beggar by the wayside. He might have carried the figure farther; for that same blind beggar, when his eyes had been opened, was persecuted by the very ones who had fed him in his infirmity. It is easier, sometimes, to receive blindly, than to give with eyes that see too clearly.

When Mrs. Taine went to the artist, in the studio, the next day, she found him in the act of re-tying the package of his mother's letters. For nearly an hour, he had been reading them. For nearly an hour before that, he had been seated, motionless, before the picture that Conrad Lagrange had said was a portrait of the Spirit of Nature.

When Mrs. Taine had slipped off her wrap, and stood before him gowned in the dress that so revealed the fleshly charms it pretended to hide, she indicated the letters in the artist's hands, with an insinuating laugh; while there was a glint of more than passing curiosity in her eyes. "Dear me," she said, "I hope I am not intruding upon the claims of some absent affinity."

Aaron King gravely held out his hand with the package of letters, saying quietly, "They are from my mother."

And the woman had sufficient grace to blush, for once, with unfeigned shame.

When he had received her apologies, and, putting aside the letters, had succeeded in making her forget the incident, he said, "And now, if you are ready, shall we begin?"

For some time the painter stood before the picture on his easel, without touching palette or brush, studying the face of the woman who posed for him. By a slight movement of her eyes, without turning her head, she could look him fairly in the face. Presently as he continued to gaze at her so intently, she laughed; and, with a little shrug of her shoulders and a pretense as of being cold, said, "When you look at me that way, I feel as though you had surprised me at my bath."

The artist turned his attention instantly to his color-box. While setting his palette, with his eyes upon his task, he said deliberately, "'Venus Surprised at the Bath.' Do you know that you would make a lovely Venus?"

With a low laugh, she returned, daringly. "Would you care to paint me as the Goddess of Love?"

He, still, did not look at her; but answered, while, with deliberate care, he selected a few brushes from the Chinese jar near the easel, "Venus is always a very popular subject, you know."

She did not speak for a moment or two; and the painter felt her watching him. As he turned to his canvas—still careful not to look in her direction—she said, suggestively, "I suppose you could change the face so that no one would know it was I who posed."

The man remembered her carefully acquired reputation for modesty, but held to his purpose, saying, as if considering the question seriously, "Oh, as for that part; it could be managed with perfect safety." Then, suddenly, he turned his eyes upon her face, with a gaze so sharp and piercing that the blood slowly colored neck and cheek.

But the painter did not wait for the blush. He had seen what he wanted and was at work—with the almost savage intensity that had marked his manner while he had worked upon the portrait of Sibyl Andrés.

And so, day after day, as he painted, again, the portrait of the woman who Conrad Lagrange fancifully called "The Age," the artist permitted her to betray her real self—the self that was so commonly hidden from the world, under the mask of a pretended culture, and the cloak of a fraudulent refinement. He led her to talk of the world in which she lived—of the scandals and intrigues among those of her class who hold such enviable positions in life. He drew from her the philosophies and beliefs and religions of her kind. He encouraged her to talk of art—to give her understanding of the world of artists as she knew it, and to express her real opinions and tastes in pictures and books. He persuaded her to throw boldly aside the glittering, tinsel garb in which she walked before the world, and so to stand before him in all the hideous vulgarity, the intellectual poverty and the moral depravity of her naked self.

At times, when, under his intense gaze, she drew the cloak of her pretenses hurriedly about her, he sat before his picture without touching the canvas, waiting; or, perhaps, he paced the floor; until, with skillful words, her fears were banished and she was again herself. Then, with quick eye and sure, ready hand, he wrought into the portrait upon the easel—so far as the power was given him—all that he saw in the face of the woman who—posing for him, secure in the belief that he was painting a lie—revealed her true nature, warped and distorted as it was by an age that, demanding realism in art, knows not what it demands. Always, when the sitting was finished, he drew the curtain to hide the picture; forbidding her to look at it until he said that it was finished.

Much of the time, when he was not in the studio at work, the painter spent with Mrs. Taine and her friends, in the big touring car, and at the house on Fairlands Heights. But the artist did not, now, enter into the life of Fairlands' Pride for gain or for pleasure—he went for study—as a physician goes into the dissecting room. He justified himself by the old and familiar argument that it was for his art's sake.

Sibyl Andrés, he seldom saw, except occasionally, in the early morning, in the rose garden. The girl knew what he was doing—that is, she knew that he was painting a portrait of Mrs. Taine—and so, with Myra Willard, avoided the place. But Conrad Lagrange now, made the neighboring house in the orange grove his place of refuge from Louise Taine, who always accompanied Mrs. Taine,—lest the world should talk,—but who never went as far as the studio.

But often, as he worked, the artist heard the music of the mountain girl's violin; and he knew that she, in her own beautiful way, was trying to help him—as she would have said—to put the mountains into his work. Many times, he was conscious of the feeling that some one was watching him. Once, pausing at the garden end of the studio as he paced to and fro, he caught a glimpse of her as she slipped through the gate in the Ragged Robin hedge. And once, in the morning, after one of those afternoons when he had gone away with Mrs. Taine at the conclusion of the sitting, he found a note pinned to the velvet curtain that hid the canvas on his working easel. It was a quaint little missive; written in one of the girl's fanciful moods, with a reference to "Blue Beard," and the assurance that she had been strong and had not looked at the forbidden picture.

As the work progressed, Mrs. Taine remarked, often, how the artist was changed. When painting that first picture, he had been so sure of himself. Working with careless ease, he had been suave and pleasant in his manner, with ready smile or laugh. Why, she questioned, was he, now, so grave and serious? Why did he pause so often, to sit staring at his canvas, or to pace the floor? Why did he seem to be so uncertain—to be questioning, searching, hesitating? The woman thought that she knew. Rejoicing in her fancied victory—all but won—she looked forward to the triumphant moment when this splendid man should be swept from his feet by the force of the passion she thought she saw him struggling to conceal. Meanwhile she tempted him by all the wiles she knew—inviting him with eyes and lips and graceful pose and meaning gesture.

And Aaron King, with clear, untroubled eye seeing all; with cool brain understanding all; with steady, skillful hand, ruled supremely by his purpose, painted that which he saw and understood into his portrait of her.

So they came to the last sitting. On the following evening, Mrs. Taine was giving a dinner at the house on Fairlands Heights, at which the artist was to meet some people who would be—as she said—useful to him. Eastern people they were; from the accredited center of art and literature; members of the inner circle of the elect. They happened to be spending the season on the Coast, and she had taken advantage of the opportunity to advance the painter's interests. It was very fortunate that her portrait was to be finished in time for them to see it.

The artist was sorry, he said, but, while it would not be necessary for her to come to the studio again, the picture was not yet finished, and he could not permit its being exhibited until he was ready to sign the canvas.

"But I may see it?" she asked, as he laid aside his palette and brushes, and announced that he was through.

With a quick hand, he drew the curtain. "Not yet; please—not until I am ready."

"Oh!" she cried with a charming air of submitting to one whose wish is law, "How mean of you! I know it is splendid! Are you satisfied? Is it better than the other? Is it like me?"

"I am sure that it is much better than the other," he replied. "It is as like you as I can make it."

"And is it as beautiful as the other?"

"It is beautiful—as you are beautiful," he answered.

"I shall tell them all about it, to-morrow night—even if I haven't seen it. And so will Jim Rutlidge."

Aaron King and Conrad Lagrange spent that evening at the little house next door. The next morning, the artist shut himself up in his studio. At lunch time, he would not come out. Late in the afternoon, the novelist went, again, to knock at the door.

The artist called in a voice that rang with triumph, "Come in, old man, come in and help me celebrate."

Entering, Conrad Lagrange found him; sitting, pale and worn, before his picture—his palette and brushes still in his hand.

And such a picture!

A moment, the novelist who knew—as few men know—the world that was revealed with such fidelity in that face upon the canvas, looked; then, with weird and wonderful oaths of delight, he caught the tired artist and whirled him around the studio, in a triumphant dance.

"You've done it! man—you've done it! It's all there; every rotten, stinking shred of it! Wow! but it's good—so damned good that it's almost inhuman. I knew you had it in you. I knew it was in you, all the time—if only you could come alive. God, man! if that could only be exhibited alongside the other! Look here!"

He dragged the easel that held Sibyl Andrés' portrait to a place beside the one upon which the canvas just finished rested, and drew back the curtain. The effect was startling.

"'The Spirit of Nature' and 'The Spirit of the Age'," said Conrad Lagrange, in a low tone.

"But you're ruined, my boy," he added gleefully. "You're ruined. These canvases will never be exhibited Her own, she'll smash when she sees it; and you'll be artistically damned by the very gods she has invoked to bless you with fame and wealth. Lord, but I envy you! You have your chance now—a real chance to be worthy your mother's sacrifice.

"Come on, let's get ready for the feast."

Chapter XXIX

The Hand Writing on the Wall

It was November. Nearly a year had passed since that day when the young man on the Golden State Limited—with the inheritance he had received from his mother's dying lips, and with his solemn promise to her still fresh in his mind—looked into the eyes of the woman on the platform of the observation car. That same day, too, he first saw the woman with the disfigured face, and, for the first time, met the famous Conrad Lagrange.

Aaron King was thinking of these things as he set out, that evening, with his friend, for the home of Mrs. Taine. He remarked to the novelist that the time seemed, to him, many years.

"To me, Aaron," answered the strange man, "it has been the happiest and—if you would not misunderstand me—the most satisfying year of my life. And this"—he added, his deep voice betraying his emotion—"this has been the happiest day of the year. It is your independence day. I shall always celebrate it as such—I—I have no independence day of my own to celebrate, you know."

Aaron King did not misunderstand.

As the two men approached the big house on Fairlands Heights, they saw that modern palace, from concrete foundation to red-tiled roof, ablaze with many lights. Situated upon the very topmost of the socially graded levels of Fairlands, it outshone them all; and, quite likely, the glittering display was mistaken by many dwellers in the valley below for a new constellation of the heavenly bodies. Quite likely, too, some lonely dweller, high up among the distant mountain peaks, looked down upon the sparkling bauble that lay for the moment, as it were, on the wide lap of the night, and smiled in quiet amusement that the earth children should attach such value to so fragile a toy.

As they passed the massive, stone pillars of the entrance to the grounds, Conrad Lagrange said, "Really, Aaron, don't you feel a little ashamed of yourself?—coming here to-night, after the outrageous return you have made for the generous hospitality of these people? You know that if Mrs. Taine had seen what you have done to her portrait, you could force the pearly gates easier than you could break in here."

The artist laughed. "To tell the truth, I don't feel exactly at home. But what the deuce can I do? After my intimacy with them, all these months, I can't assume that they are going to make my picture a reason for refusing to recognize me, can I? As I see it, they, not I, must take the initiative. I can't say: 'Well, I've told the truth about you, so throw me out'."

The novelist grinned. "Thus it is when 'Art' becomes entangled with the family of 'Materialism.' It's hard to break away from the flesh-pots—even when you know you are on the road to the Promised Land. But don't worry—'The Age' will take the initiative fast enough when she sees your portrait of her. Wow! In the meantime, let's play their game to-night, and take what spoils the gods may send. There will be material here for pictures and stories a plenty." As they went up the wide steps and under the portal into the glare of the lights, and caught the sound of the voices within, he added under his breath, "Lord, man, but 'tis a pretty show!—if only things were called by their right names. That old Babylonian, Belshazzar, had nothing on us moderns after all, did he? Watch out for the writing upon the wall."

When Aaron King and his companion entered the spacious rooms where the pride of Fairlands Heights and the eastern lions were assembled, a buzz of comment went round the glittering company. Aside from the fact that Mrs. Taine, with practised skill, had prepared the way for her protege, by subtly stimulating the curiosity of her guests—the appearance of the two men, alone, would have attracted their attention The artist, with his strong, splendidly proportioned, athletic body, and his handsome, clean-cut intellectual face—calmly sure of himself—with the air of one who knows that his veins are rich with the wealth of many generations of true culture and refinement; and the novelist—easily the most famous of his day—tall, emaciated, grotesquely stooped—with his homely face seamed and lined, world-worn and old, and his sharp eyes peering from under his craggy brows with that analyzing, cynical, half-pathetic half-humorous expression—certainly presented a contrast too striking to escape notice.

For an instant, as comrades side by side upon a battle-field might do, they glanced over the scene. To the painter's eye, the assembled guests appeared as a glittering, shimmering, scintillating, cloud-like mass that, never still, stirred within itself, in slow, graceful restless motions—forming always, without purpose new combinations and groupings that were broken up, even as they were shaped, to be reformed; with the black spots and splashes of the men's conventional dress ever changing amid the brighter colors and textures of the women's gowns; the warm flesh tints of bare white arms and shoulders, gleaming here and there; and the flash and sparkle of jewels, threading the sheen of silks and the filmy softness of laces. Into the artist's mind—fresh from the tragic earnestness of his day's work, and still under the enduring spell of his weeks in the mountains—flashed a sentence from a good old book; "For what is your life? It is even a vapor, that appeareth for a little time, and then vanisheth away."

Then they were greeting, with conventional nothings their beautiful hostess; who, with a charming air of triumphant—but not too triumphant—proprietorship received them and passed them on, with a low spoken word to Aaron King; "I will take charge of you later."

Conrad Lagrange, before they drifted apart, found opportunity to growl in his companion's ear; "A near-great musician—an actress of divorce court fame—an art critic, boon companion of our friend Rutlidge—two free-lance yellow journalists—a poet—with leading culture-club women of various brands, and a mob of mere fashion and wealth. The pickings should be good. Look at 'Materialism', over there."

In a wheeled chair, attended by a servant in livery, a little apart from the center of the scene,—as though the pageant of life was about to move on without him,—but still, with desperate grip, holding his place in the picture, sat the genius of it all—the millionaire. The creature's wasted, skeleton-like limbs, were clothed grotesquely in conventional evening dress. His haggard, bestial face—repulsive with every mark of his wicked, licentious years—grinned with an insane determination to take the place that was his by right of his money bags; while his glazed and sunken eyes shone with fitful gleams, as he rallied the last of his vital forces, with a devilish defiance of the end that was so inevitably near.

As Aaron King, in the splendid strength of his inheritance, went to pay his respects to the master of the house, that poor product of our age was seized by a paroxysm of coughing, that shook him—gasping and choking—almost into unconsciousness. The ready attendant held out a glass of whisky, and he clutched the goblet with skinny hands that, in their trembling eagerness, rattled the crystal against his teeth. In the momentary respite afforded by the powerful stimulant, he lifted his yellow, claw-like hand to wipe the clammy beads of sweat that gathered upon his wrinkled, ape-like brow; and the painter saw, on one bony, talon-like finger, the gleaming flash of a magnificent diamond.

Mr. Taine greeted the artist with his husky whisper "Hello, old chap—glad to see you!" Peering into the laughing, chattering, glittering, throng he added, "Some beauties here to-night, heh? Gad! my boy, but I've seen the day I'd be out there among them! Ha, ha! Mrs. Taine, Louise, and Jim tried to shelve me—but I fooled 'em. Damn me, but I'm game for a good time yet! A little off my feed, and under the weather; but game, you understand, game as hell!" Then to the attendant—"Where's that whisky?" And, again, his yellow, claw-like hand—with that beautiful diamond, a gleaming point of pure, white light—lifted the glass to his grinning lips.

When Mrs. Taine appeared to claim the artist, her husband—huddled in his chair, an unclean heap of all but decaying flesh—watched them go, with hidden, impotent rage.

A few moments later, as Mrs. Taine and her charge were leaving one group of celebrities in search of another they encountered Conrad Lagrange. "What's this I see?" gibed the novelist, mockingly. "Is it 'Art being led by Beauty to the Judges and Executioners'? or, is it 'Beauty presenting an Artist to the Gods of Modern Art'?"

"You had better be helping a good cause instead of making fun, Mr. Lagrange," the woman retorted. "You weren't always so famous yourself that you could afford to be indifferent, you know."

Aaron King laughed as his friend replied, "Never fear, madam, never fear—I shall be on hand to assist at the obsequies."

In the shifting of the groups and figures, when dinner was announced, the young man found himself, again, within reach of Conrad Lagrange; and the novelist whispered, with a grin, "Now for the flesh-pots in earnest. You will be really out of place in the next act, Aaron. Only we artists who have sold our souls have a right to the price of our shame. You should dine upon a crust, you know. A genius without his crust, huh! A devil without his tail, or an ass without his long ears!"

Most conspicuous in the brilliant throng assembled in that banquet hall, was the horrid figure of Mr. Taine who sat in his wheeled chair at the head of the table; his liveried attendant by his side. Frequently—as though compelled—eyes were turned toward that master of the feast, who was, himself, so far past feasting; and toward his beautiful young wife—the only woman in the room, whose shoulders and arms were not bare.

At first, the talk moved somewhat heavily. Neighbor chattered nothings to neighbor in low tones. It was as though the foreboding presence of some grim, unbidden guest overshadowed the spirits of the company But gradually the scene became more animated The glitter of silver and crystal on the board; the sparkle of jewels and the wealth of shimmering colors that costumed the diners; with the strains of music that came from somewhere behind a floral screen that filled the air with fragrance; concealed, as it were, the hideous image of immorality which was the presiding genius of the feast. As the glare of a too bright light blinds the eyes to the ditch across one's path, so the brilliancy of their surroundings blinded the eyes of his guests to the meaning of that horrid figure in the seat of highest honor. But rich foods and rare wines soon loose the tongues that chatter the thoughts of those who do not think. As the glasses were filled and refilled again, the scene took color from the sparkling goblets. Voices were raised to a higher pitch. Shrill or boisterous laughter rang out, as jest and story went the rounds. It was Mrs. Taine, now, rather than her husband, who dominated the scene. With cheeks flushed and eyes bright she set the pace, nor permitted any laggards.

Conrad Lagrange watched, cool and cynical—his worn face twisted into a mocking smile; his keen, baffling eyes, from under their scowling brows, seeing all, understanding all. Aaron King, weary with the work of the past days, endured—wishing it was over.

The evening was well under way when Mrs. Taine held up her hand. In the silence, she said, "Listen! I have a real treat for you, to-night, friends. Listen!" As she spoke the last word, her eyes met the eyes of the artist, in mocking, challenging humor. He was wondering what she meant, when,—from behind that screen of flowers,—soft and low, poignantly sweet and thrilling in its purity of tone, came the music of the violin that he had learned to know so well.

Instantly, the painter understood. Mrs. Taine had employed Sibyl Andrés to play for her guests that evening; thinking to tease the artist by presenting his mountain comrade in the guise of a hired servant. Why the girl had not told him, he did not know. Perhaps she had thought to enjoy his surprise. The effect of the girl's presence—or rather of her music, for she, herself, could not be seen—upon the artist was quite other than Mrs. Taine intended.

Under the spell of the spirit that spoke in the violin, Aaron King was carried far from his glittering surroundings. Again, he stood where the bright waters of Clear Creek tumbled among the granite boulders, and where he had first moved to answer the call of that music of the hills. Again, he followed the old wagon road to the cedar thicket; and, in the little, grassy opening with its wild roses, its encircling wilderness growth, and its old log house under the sheltering sycamores, saw a beautiful girl dancing with the unconscious grace of a woodland sprite, her arms upheld in greeting to the mountains. Once again, he was painting in the sacred quiet of the spring glade where she had come to him with her three gifts; where, in maidenly innocence, she had danced the dance of the butterflies; and, later, with her music, had lifted their friendship to heights of purity as far above the comprehension of the company that listened to her now, as the mountain peaks among the stars that night were high above the house on Fairlands Heights.

The music ceased. It was followed by the loud clapping of hands—with exclamations in high-pitched voices. "Who is it?" "Where did you find him?" "What's his name?"—for they judged, from Mrs. Taine's introductory words, that she expected them to show their appreciation.

Mrs. Taine laughed, and, with her eyes mockingly upon the artist's face answered lightly, "Oh, she is a discovery of mine. She teaches music, and plays in one of the Fairlands churches."

"You are a wonder," said one of the illustrious critics, admiringly. And lifting his glass, he cried, "Here's to our beautiful and talented hostess—the patron saint of all the arts—the friend of all true artists."

In the quiet that followed the enthusiastic endorsement of the distinguished gentleman's words, another voice said, "If it's a girl, can't we see her?" "Yes, yes," came from several. "Please, Mrs. Taine, bring her out." "Have her play again." "Will she?"

Mrs. Taine laughed. "Certainly, she will. That's what she's here for—to amuse you." And, again, as she spoke, her eyes met the eyes of Aaron King.

At her signal, a servant left the room. A moment later, the mountain girl, dressed in simple white, with no jewel or ornament other than a rose in her soft, brown hair, stood before that company. Unconscious of the eyes that fed upon her loveliness; there was the faintest shadow of a smile upon her face as she met, in one swift glance, the artist's look; then, raising her violin, she made music for the revelers, at the will of Mrs. Taine. As she stood there in the modest naturalness of her winsome beauty—innocent and pure as the flowers that formed the screen behind her; hired to amuse the worthy friends and guests of that hideously repulsive devotee of lust and licentiousness who, from his wheeled chair, was glaring at her with eyes that burned insanely—she seemed, as indeed she was, a spirit from another world.

James Rutlidge, his heavy features flushed with drink, was gazing at the girl with a look that betrayed his sensual passion. The face of Conrad Lagrange was dark and grim with scowling appreciation of the situation. Mrs. Taine was looking at the artist. And Aaron King, watching his girl comrade of the hills as she seemed to listen for the music which she in turn drew from the instrument, felt,—by the very force of the contrast between her and her surroundings he had never felt before, the power and charm of her personality—felt—and knew that Sibyl Andrés had come into his life to stay.

In the flood of emotions that swept over him, and in the mental and spiritual exultation caused by her music and by her presence amid such scenes; it was given the painter to understand that she had, in truth, brought to him the strength, the purity, and the beauty of the hills; that she had, in truth, shown him the paths that lead to the mountain heights; that it was her unconscious influence and teaching that had made it impossible for him to prostitute his genius to win favor in the eyes of the world. He knew, now, that in those days when he had painted her portrait, as she stood with outstretched hands in the golden light among the roses, he had mixed his colors with the best love that a man may offer a woman. And he knew that the repainting of that false portrait of Mrs. Taine, with all that it would cost him, was his first offering to that love.

The girl musician finished playing and slipped away. When they would have recalled her, Mrs. Taine—too well schooled to betray a hint of the emotions aroused by what she had just seen as she watched Aaron King—shook her head.

At that instant, Mr. Taine rose to his feet, supporting himself by holding with shaking hands to the table. A hush, sudden as the hush of death, fell upon the company. The millionaire's attendant put out his hand to steady his master, and another servant stepped quickly forward. But the man who clung so tenaciously to his last bit of life, with a drunken strength in his dying limbs, shook them off, saying in a hoarse whisper, "Never mind! Never mind—you fools—can't you see I'm game!"

In the quiet of the room, that a moment before rang with excited voices and shrill laughter, the man's husky, straining, whispered boast sounded like the mocking of some invisible, fiendish presence at the feast.

Lifting a glass of whisky with that yellow, claw-like hand upon which the great diamond gleamed—a spot of flawless purity; with his repulsive features twisted into a grewsome ugliness by his straining effort to force his diseased vocal chords to make his words heard; the wretched creature said: "Here's to our girl musician. The prettiest—lassie that I—have seen for many a day—and I think I know a pretty girl—when I see one too. Who comes bright and fresh—from her mountains, to amuse us—and to add, to the beauty—and grace and wit and genius—that so distinguishes this company—the flavor and the freedom of her wild-wood home. Her music—is good, you'll all agree—" he paused to cough and to look inquiringly around, while every one nodded approval and smiled encouragingly. "Her music is good—but I—maintain that she, herself, is better. To me—her beauty is more pleasing to the eye—than—her fiddling can possibly—be to the ear!" Again he was forced to pause, while his guests, with hand and voice, applauded the clever words. Lifting the glass of whisky toward his lips that, by his effort to speak, were drawn back in a repulsive grin, he leered at the celebrities sitting nearest. "I suppose to-morrow—if we desire the company of these distinguished artists—we will have to follow—them to the mountains. I don't blame you, gentlemen—if I was not—ah—temporarily incapacitated—I would certainly—go for a little trip to the inspiring hills—myself. Even if I don't know—as much about music and art as some of you." Again his words were interrupted by that racking cough, the sound of which was lost in the applause that greeted his witticism. Lifting the glass once more, he continued, "So here's to our girl musician—who is her own—lovely self so much more attractive than any music—she can ever make." He drained the glass, and sank back into his chair, exhausted by his effort.

Aaron King was on the point of springing to his feet, when Conrad Lagrange caught his eye with a warning look. Instantly, he remembered what the result would be if he should yield to his impulse. Wild with indignation, rage, and burning shame, he knew that to betray himself would be to invite a thousand sneering questions and insinuations to besmirch the name of the girl he loved.

In the continued applause and laughter that followed the drinking of the millionaire's toast, the artist caught the admiring words, "Bully old sport." "Isn't he game?" "He has certainly traveled some pace in his day." "The girl is a beauty." "Let's have her in again." This last expression was so insistently echoed that Mrs. Taine—who, through it all, had been covertly watching Aaron King's face, and whose eyes were blazing now with something more than the effect of the wine she had been drinking—was forced to yield. A servant left the room, and, a moment later, reappeared, followed by Sibyl.

The girl was greeted, now, by hearty applause which she, accepting as an expression of the company's appreciation of her music, received with smiling pleasure. The artist, his heart and soul aflame with his awakening love, fought for self-control. Conrad Lagrange, catching his eye, again, silently bade him wait.

Sibyl lifted her violin and the noisy company was stilled. Slowly, under the spell of the music that, to him, was a message from the mountain heights, Aaron King grew calm. His tense muscles relaxed. His twitching nerves became steady. He felt himself as it were, lifted out of and above the scene that a moment before had so stirred him to indignant anger. His brain worked with that clearness and precision which he had known while repainting Mrs. Taine's portrait. Wrath gave way to pity; indignation to contempt. In confidence, he smiled to think how little the girl he loved needed his poor defense against the animalism that dominated the company she was hired to amuse. With every eye in the room fixed upon her as she played, she was as far removed from those who had applauded the suggestive words of the dying sensualist as her music was beyond their true comprehension.

Then it was that the genius of the artist awoke. As the flash of a search-light in the darkness of night brings out with startling clearness the details of the scene upon which it is turned, the painter saw before him his picture. With trained eye and carefully acquired skill, he studied the scene; impressing upon his memory every detail—the rich appointments of the room; the glittering lights; the gleaming silver and crystal; the sparkling jewels and shimmering laces; the bare shoulders; the wine-flushed faces and feverish eyes; and, in the seat of honor, the disease-wasted form and repulsive, sin-marked countenance of Mr. Taine who—almost unconscious with his exertion—was still feeding the last flickering flame of his lustful life with the vision of the girl whose beauty his toast had profaned: and in the midst of that company—expressing as it did the spirit of an age that is ruled by material wealth and dominated by the passions of the flesh—the center of every eye, yet, still, in her purity and innocence, removed and apart from them all; standing in her simple dress of white against the background of flowers—the mountain girl with her violin—offering to them the highest, holiest, gift of the gods—her music. Upon the girl's lovely, winsome face, was a look, now, of troubled doubt. Her wide, blue eyes, as she played, were pleading, questioning, half fearful—as though she sensed, instinctively the presence of the spirit she could not understand; and felt, in spite of the pretense of the applause that had greeted her, the rejection of her offering.

Not only did the artist, in that moment of conception see his picture and feel the forces that were expressed by every character in the composition, but the title, even, came to him as clearly as if Conrad Lagrange had uttered it aloud, "The Feast of Materialism."

Sibyl Andrés finished her music, and quickly withdrew as if to escape the noisy applause. Amid the sound of the clapping hands and boisterous voices, Mr. Taine, summoning the last of his wasted strength, again struggled to his feet. With those claw-like hands he held to the table for support; while—shaking in every limb, his features twisted into a horrid, leering grin—he looked from face to face of the hushed and silent company; with glazed eyes in which the light that flickered so feebly was still the light of an impotent lust.

Twice, the man essayed to speak, but could not. The room grew still as death. Then, suddenly—as they looked—he lifted that yellow, skinny hand, to his wrinkled, ape-like brow, and—partially loosing, thus, his supporting grip upon the table—fell back, in a ghastly heap of diseased flesh and fine raiment; in the midst of which blazed the great diamond—as though the cold, pure beauty of the inanimate stone triumphed in a life more vital than that of its wearer.

His servants carried the unconscious master of the house from the room. Mrs. Taine, excusing herself, followed.

In the confusion that ensued, the musicians, hidden behind the floral screen, struck up a lively air. Some of the guests made quiet preparations for leaving. A group of those men—famous in the world of art and letters—under the influence of the wine they had taken so freely, laughed loudly at some coarse jest. Others, thinking, perhaps,—if they could be said to think at all,—that their host's attack was not serious, renewed conversations and bravely attempted to restore a semblance of animation to the interrupted revelries.

Aaron King worked his way to the side of Conrad Lagrange, "For God's sake, old man, let's get out of here."

"I'll find Rutlidge or Louise or some one," returned the other, and disappeared.

As the artist waited, through the open door of an adjoining room, he caught sight of Sibyl Andrés; who, with her violin-case in her hand, was about to leave. Obeying his impulse, he went to her.

"What in the world are you doing here?" he said almost roughly—extending his hand to take the instrument she carried.

She seemed a little bewildered by his manner, but smiled as she retained her violin. "I am here to earn my bread and butter, sir. What are you doing here?"

"I beg your pardon," he said. "I did not mean to be rude."

She laughed, then, with a troubled air—"But is it not right for me to be here? It is all right for me to play for these people, isn't it? Myra didn't want me to come, but we needed the money, and Mrs. Taine was so generous. I didn't tell you and Mr. Lagrange because I wanted the fun of surprising you." As he stood looking at her so gravely, she put out her hand impulsively to his arm. "What is it, oh, what is it? How have I done wrong?"

"You have done no wrong, my dear girl," he answered "It is only that—"

He was interrupted by the cold, clear voice of Mrs. Taine, who had entered the room, unnoticed by them. "I see you are going, Miss Andrés. Good-night. I will mail you a check to-morrow. Your music was very satisfactory. An automobile is waiting to take you home. Good night."

Before Aaron King could speak, the girl was gone.

"Mr. Lagrange and I were just about to go," said the artist, as the woman faced him. "I hope Mr. Taine has not suffered severely from the excitement of the evening?"

The woman's cheeks were flushed, and her eyes were bright with feverish excitement. Going close to him, she said in a low, hurried tone, "No, no, you must not go. Mr. Taine is all right in his room. Every one else is having a good time. You must not go. Come, I have had no opportunity, at all, to have you to myself for a single moment. Come, I—"

As she had interrupted Aaron King's reply to Sibyl Andrés, the cool, sarcastic tones of Conrad Lagrange's deep voice interrupted her. "Mrs. Taine, they are hunting for you all over the house. Your husband is calling for you. I'm sure that Mr. King will excuse you, under the circumstances."

Chapter XXX

In the Same Hour

In a splendid chamber, surrounded by every comfort and luxury that dollars could buy, and attended by liveried servants, Mr. Taine was dying.

The physician who met Mrs. Taine at the door, answered her look of inquiry with; "Your husband is very near the end, madam." Beside the bed, sat Louise, wringing her hands and moaning. James Rutlidge stood near. Without speaking, Mrs. Taine went forward.

The doctor, bending over his patient, with his fingers upon the skeleton-like wrist, said, "Mr. Taine, Mr. Taine, your wife is here."

In response, the eyes, deep sunken under the wrinkled brow, opened; the loosely hanging, sensual lips quivered.

The physician spoke again; "Your wife is here, Mr. Taine."

A sudden gleam of light flared up in the glazed eyes. The doctor could have sworn that the lips were twisted into a shadow of a ghastly, mocking smile. As if summoning, by a supreme effort of his will, from some unguessed depths of his being, the last remnant of his remaining strength, the man looked about the room and, in a hoarse whisper, said, "Send the others away—everybody—but her."

"O papa, papa!" exclaimed poor Louise, protestingly.

"Never mind, daughter," came the whispered answer from the bed. "Try to be game, girl—game as your father. Take her away, Jim."

As the physician passed Mrs. Taine, who had thus far stood like a statue, seemingly incapable of thought or feeling or movement, he said in a low tone, "I will be just outside the door, madam; easily within call."

When only the woman was left in the room with her husband, the dying man spoke again; "Come here. Stand where I can see you."

Mechanically, she obeyed; moving to a position near the foot of the bed.

After a moment's silence, during which he seemed to be rallying the very last of his vital forces for the effort, he said, "Well—the game is played—out. You think—you're the winner. You're—wrong—damn you—you're wrong. I wasn't—so drunk to-night that—I couldn't see." His face twisted in a hideous, malicious grin. "You—love—that artist fellow. Your—interest in his art is—all rot. It's him you want—and you—you have been thinking—you'd get him—with my money—the same as I got you. But you won't.

You've—lost him already. I'm glad—you love him—damn glad—because—I know that after—what he's seen of me—even if he didn't love—that mountain—girl, he wouldn't wipe—his feet on you. You've tortured me—you've mocked—and sneered and laughed—at me—in my suffering—you fiend—and I've—tried my damnedest—to pay you back. What I couldn't do—the man you love—will—do for me. You'll suffer—now in earnest. You thought you'd be a—sure winner—as soon—as I was out of—the game. But you've lost—you've lost—you've lost! I saw your love for him—in your—face to-night—as I have seen—it every time—you two were together. I saw his love—for the girl—too—and I—saw—that you—saw it. I—I—wouldn't—wouldn't die—until I'd told you—that I knew." He paused to gather his strength for the last evil effort of his evil life.

The woman—who had stood, frozen with horror, her eyes fixed upon the face of the dying man, as though under a dreadful spell—cowered before him, livid with fear. Cringing, helpless—as though before some infernal monster—she hid her face; while her husband, struggling for breath to make her hear, called her every foul name he could master—derided her with fiendish glee—mocked her, taunted her, cursed her—with words too vile to print. With an oath and a profane wish for her future upon his lips, the end came. The sensual mouth opened—the diseased wasted limbs shuddered—the insane light in the lust-worn eyes went out.

With a scream, Mrs. Taine sank unconscious upon the floor beside the bed.

From the lower part of the house came the faint sounds of the few remaining revelers.

When Aaron King and Conrad Lagrange left the house on Fairlands Heights that night, they walked quickly, as though eager to escape from the brilliantly lighted vicinity. Neither spoke until they were some distance away. Then the novelist, checking his quick stride, pointed toward the shadowy bulk of the mountains that heaved their mighty crests and peaks in solemn grandeur high into the midnight sky.

"Well, boy," he said, "the mountains are still there. It's good to see them again, isn't it?"

Reaching home, the older man bade his friend good night. But the artist, declaring that he was not yet ready to turn in, went, with pipe and Czar for company, to sit for a while on the porch.

Looking away over the dark mass of the orange groves to the distant peaks, he lived over again, in his thoughts, those weeks of comradeship with Sibyl Andrés in the hills. Every incident of their friendship he recalled—every hour they had spent together amid the scenes she loved—reviewing every conversation—questioning searching, wondering, hoping, fearing.

Later, he went out into the rose garden—her garden—where the air was fragrant with the perfume of the flowers she tended with such loving care. In the soft, still darkness of the night, the place seemed haunted by her presence. Quietly, he moved here and there among the roses—to the little gate in the Ragged Robin hedge, through which she came and went; to the vine-covered arbor where she had watched him at his work; and to the spot where she had stood, day after day, with hands outstretched in greeting, while he worked to make the colors and lines upon his canvas tell the secret of her loveliness. He remembered how he had felt her presence in those days when he had laughingly insisted to Conrad Lagrange that the place was haunted. He remembered how, even when she was unknown to him, her music had always moved him—how her message from the hills had seemed to call to the best that was in him.

So it was, that, as he recalled these things,—as he lived again the days of his companionship with her and realized how she had come into his life, how she had appealed always to the best of him, and satisfied always his best needs,—he came to know the answer to his questions—to his doubts and fears and hopes. There, in the rose garden, with its dark walls of hedge and vine and grove, in the still night under the stars, with his face to the distant mountains, he knew that the mountain girl would not deny him—that, when she was ready, she would come to him.

In the hour when Mr. Taine, with the last strength of his evil life, profanely cursed the woman that his gold had bought to serve his licentious will—and cursing—died; Aaron King—inspired by the character and purity of the woman he loved, and by whom he knew he was loved, and dreaming of their comradeship that was to be—dedicated himself anew to the ministry of his art and so entered into that more abundant life which belongs by divine right to all who will claim it.

But it was not given Aaron King to know that before Sibyl Andrés could come to him he must be tested by a trial that would tax his manhood's best strength to the uttermost. In that night of his awakened love, as he dreamed of the days of its realization, the man did not know that the days of his testing were so near at hand.

Chapter XXXI

As the World Sees

It was three days after the incidents just related when an automobile from Fairlands Heights stopped at the home of Aaron King and the novelist.

Mrs. Taine, dressed in black and heavily veiled, went, alone, to the house, where Yee Kee appeared in answer to her ring.

There was no one at home, the Chinaman said. He did not know where the artist was. He had gone off somewhere with Mr. Lagrange and the dog. Perhaps they would return in a few minutes; perhaps not until dinner time.

Mrs. Taine was exceedingly anxious to see Mr. King. She was going away, and must see him, if possible, before she left. She would come in, and, if Yee Kee would get her pen and paper, would write a little note, explaining—in case she should miss him. The Chinaman silently placed the writing material before her, and disappeared.

Before sitting down to her letter, the woman paced the floor restlessly, in nervous agitation. Her face, when she had thrown back the veil, appeared old and worn, with dark circles under the eyes, and a drawn look to the weary, downward droop of the lips. As she moved about the room, nervously fingering the books and trifles upon the table or the mantle, she seemed beside herself with anxiety. She went to the window to stand looking out as if hoping for the return of the artist. She went to the open door of his bedroom, her hands clenched, her limbs trembling, her face betraying the agony of her mind.

With Louise, she was leaving that evening, at four o'clock, for the East—with the body of her husband. She could not go without seeing again the man whom, as Mr. Taine had rightly said, she loved—loved with the only love of which—because of her environment and life—she was capable. She still believed in her power over him whose passion she had besieged with all the lure of her physical beauty, but that which she had seen in his face as he had watched the girl musician the night of the dinner, filled her with fear. Presently, in her desperation, when the artist did not return, she seated herself at the table to put upon paper, as best she could, the things she had come to say.

Her letter finished, she looked at her watch. Calling the Chinaman, she asked for a key to the studio, explaining that she wished to see her picture. She still hoped for the artist's return and that her letter would not be necessary. She hoped, too, that in her portrait, which she had not yet seen, she might find some evidence of the painter's passion for her. She had not forgotten his saying that he would put upon the canvas what he thought of her, nor could she fail to recall his manner and her interpretation of it as he had worked upon the picture.

In the studio, she stood before the easel, scarce daring to draw the curtain. But, calling up in her mind the emotions and thoughts of the hours she had spent in that room alone with the artist, she was made bold by her reestablished belief in his passion and by her convictions that were founded upon her own desires. Under the stimulating influence of her thoughts, a flush of color stole into her cheeks, her eyes grew bright with the light of triumphant anticipation. With an eager hand she boldly drew aside the curtain.

The picture upon the easel was the artist's portrait of Sibyl Andrés.

With an exclamation that was not unlike fear, Mrs. Taine drew back from the canvas. Looking at the beautiful painting,—in which the artist had pictured, with unconscious love and an almost religious fidelity, the spirit of the girl who was so like the flowers among which she stood,—the woman was moved by many conflicting emotions. Surprise, disappointment admiration, envy, jealousy, sadness, regret, and anger swept over her. Blinded by bitter tears, with a choking sob, in an agony of remorse and shame, she turned away her face from the gaze of those pure eyes. Then, as the flame of her passion withered her shame, hot rage dried her tears, and she sprang forward with an animal-like fierceness, to destroy the picture. But, even as she put forth her hand, she hesitated and drew back, afraid. As she stood thus in doubt—halting between her impulse and her fear—a sound at the door behind her drew her attention. She turned to face the beautiful original of the portrait Instantly the woman of the world had herself perfectly in hand.

Sibyl Andrés drew back with an embarrassed, "I beg your pardon. I thought—" and would have fled.

But Mrs. Taine, with perfect cordiality, said quickly, "O how do you do, Miss Andrés; come in."

She seemed so sincere in the welcome that was implied in her voice and manner; while her face, together with her somber garb of mourning, was so expressive of sadness and grief that the girl's gentle heart was touched. Going forward, with that natural, dignity that belongs to those whose minds and hearts are unsullied by habitual pretense of feeling and sham emotions, Sibyl spoke a few well chosen words of sympathy.

Mrs. Taine received the girl's expression of condolence with a manner that was perfect in its semblance of carefully controlled sorrow and grief, yet managed, skillfully, to suggest the wide social distance that separated the widow of Mr. Taine from the unknown, mountain girl. Then, as if courageously determined not to dwell upon her bereavement, she said, "I was just looking, again, at Mr. King's picture—for which you posed. It is beautiful, isn't it? He told me that you were an exceptionally clever model—quite the best he has ever had."

The girl—disarmed by her own genuine feeling of sympathy for the speaker—was troubled at something that seemed to lie beneath the kindly words of the experienced woman. "To me, it is beautiful," she returned doubtfully. "But, of course, I don't know. Mr. Lagrange thinks, though, that it is really a splendid portrait."

Mrs. Taine smiled with a confident air, as one might smile at a child. "Mr. Lagrange, my dear, is a famous novelist—but he really knows very little of pictures."

"Perhaps you are right," returned Sibyl, simply. "But the picture is not to be shown as a portrait of me, at all."

Again, that knowing smile. "So I understand, of course. Under the circumstances, you would scarcely expect it, would you?"

Sibyl, not in the least understanding what the woman meant, answered doubtfully, "No. I—I did not wish it shown as my portrait."

Mrs. Taine, studying the girl's face, became very earnest in her kindly interest; as if, moved out of the goodness of her heart, she stooped from her high place to advise and counsel one of her own sex, who was so wholly ignorant of the world. "I fear, my dear, that you know very little of artists and their methods."

To which the girl replied, "I never knew an artist before I met Mr. King, this summer, in the mountains."

Still watching her face closely, Mrs. Taine said, with gentle solicitude, "May I tell you something for your own good, Miss Andrés?"

"Certainly, if you please, Mrs. Taine."

"An artist," said the older woman, carefully, with an air of positive knowledge, "must find the subjects for his pictures in life. As he goes about, he is constantly on the look-out for new faces or figures that are of interest to him—or, that may be used by him to make pictures of interest. The subjects—or, I should say, the people who pose for him—are nothing at all to the artist—aside from his picture, you see—no more than his paints and brushes and canvas. Often, they are professional models, whom he hires as one hires any sort of service, you know. Sometimes—" she paused as if hesitating, then continued gently—"sometimes they are people like yourself, who happen to appeal to his artistic fancy, and whom he can persuade to pose for him."

The girl's face was white. She stared at the woman with pleading, frightened dismay. She made a pitiful attempt to speak, but could not.

The older woman, watching her, continued, "Forgive me, dear child. I do not wish to hurt you. But Mr. King is so careless. I told him he should be careful that you did not misunderstand his interest in you. But he laughed at me. He said that it was your innocence that he wanted to paint, and cautioned me not to warn you until his picture was finished." She turned to look at the picture on the easel with the air of a critic. "He really has caught it very well. Aaron—Mr. King is so good at that sort of thing. He never permits his models to know exactly what he is after, you see, but leads them, cleverly, to exhibit, unconsciously, the particular thing that he wishes to get into his picture."

When the tortured girl had been given time to grasp the full import of her words, the woman said again,—turning toward Sibyl, as she spoke, with a smiling air that was intended to show the intimacy between herself and the artist,—"Have you seen his portrait of me?"

"No," faltered Sibyl. "Mr. King told me not to look at it. It has always been covered when I have been in the studio."

Again, Mrs. Taine smiled, as though there was some reason, known only to herself and the painter, why he did not wish the girl to see the portrait. "And do you come to the studio often—alone as you came to-day?" she asked, still kindly, as though from her experience she was seeking to counsel the girl. "I mean—have you been coming since the picture for which you posed was finished?"

The girl's white cheeks grew red with embarrassment and shame as she answered, falteringly, "Yes."

"You poor child! Really, I must scold Aaron for this. After my warning him, too, that people were talking about his intimacy with you in the mountains It is quite too bad of him! He will ruin himself, if he is not more careful." She seemed sincerely troubled over the situation.

"I—I do not understand, Mrs. Taine," faltered Sibyl. "Do you mean that my—that Mr. King's friendship for me has harmed him? That I—that it is wrong for me to come here?"

"Surely, Miss Andrés, you must understand what I mean."

"No, I—I do not know. Tell me, please."

Mrs. Taine hesitated as though reluctant. Then, as if forced by her sense of duty, she spoke. "The truth is, my dear, that your being with Mr. King in the mountains—going to his camp as familiarly as you did, and spending so much time alone with him in the hills—and then your coming here so often, has led people to say unpleasant things."

"But what do people say?" persisted Sibyl.

The answer came with cruel deliberateness; "That you are not only Mr. King's model, but that you are his mistress as well."

Sibyl Andrés shrank back from the woman as though she had received a blow in the face. Her cheeks and brow and neck were crimson. With a little cry, she buried her face in her hands.

The kind voice of the older woman continued, "You see, dear, whether it is true or not, the effect is exactly the same. If in the eyes of the world your relations to Mr. King are—are wrong, it is as bad as though it were actually true. I felt that I must tell you, child, not alone for your own good but for the sake of Mr. King and his work—for the sake of his position in the world. Frankly, if you continue to compromise him and his good name by coming like this to his studio, it will ruin him. The world may not care particularly whether Mr. King keeps a mistress or not, but people will not countenance his open association with her, even under the pretext that she is a model."

As she finished, Mrs. Taine looked at her watch. "Dear me, I really must be going. I have already spent more time than I intended. Good-by, Miss Andrés. I know you will forgive me if I have hurt you."

The girl looked at her with the pain and terror filled eyes of some gentle wild creature that can not understand the cruelty of the trap that holds it fast. "Yes—yes, I—I suppose you know best. You must know more than I. I—thank you, Mrs. Taine. I—"

When Mrs. Taine was gone, Sibyl Andrés sat for a little while before her portrait; wondering, dumbly, at the happiness of that face upon the canvas. There were no tears. She could not cry. Her eyes burned hot and dry. Her lips were parched. Rising, she drew the curtain carefully to hide the picture, and started toward the door. She paused. Going to the easel that held the other picture, she laid her hand upon the curtain. Again, she paused. Aaron King had said that she must not look at that picture—Conrad Lagrange had said that she must not—why? She did not know why.

Perhaps—if the mountain girl had drawn aside the curtain and had looked upon the face of Mrs. Taine as Aaron King had painted it—perhaps the rest of my story would not have happened.

But, true to the wish of her friends, even in her misery, Sibyl Andrés held her hand. At the door of the studio, she turned again, to look long and lingeringly about the room. Then she went out, closing and locking the door, and leaving the key on a hidden nail, as her custom was.

Going slowly, lingeringly, through the rose garden to the little gate in the hedge, she disappeared in the orange grove.

Aaron King and Conrad Lagrange, returning from a long walk, overtook Myra Willard, who was returning from town, just as the woman of the disfigured face arrived at the gate of the little house in the orange grove. For a moment, the three stood chatting—as neighbors will,—then the two men went on to their own home. Czar, racing ahead, announced their coming to Yee Kee and the Chinaman met them as they entered the living-room. Telling them of Mrs. Taine's visit, he gave Aaron King the letter that she had left for him.

As the artist, conscious of the scrutinizing gaze of his friend, read the closely written pages, his cheeks flushed with embarrassment and shame. When he had finished, he faced the novelist's eyes steadily and, without speaking, deliberately and methodically tore Mrs. Taine's letter into tiny fragments. Dropping the scraps of paper into the waste basket, he dusted his hands together with a significant gesture and looked at his watch. "Her train left at four o'clock. It is now four-thirty."

"For which," returned Conrad Lagrange, solemnly, "let us give thanks."

As the novelist spoke, Czar, on the porch outside, gave a low "woof" that signalized the approach of a friend.

Looking through the open door, they saw Myra Willard coming hurriedly up the walk. They could see that the woman was greatly agitated, and went quicklv forward to meet her.

Women of Myra Willard's strength of character—particularly those who have passed through the furnace of some terrible experience as she so evidently had—are not given to loud, uncontrolled expression of emotion. That she was alarmed and troubled was evident. Her face was white, her eyes were frightened and she trembled so that Aaron King helped her to a seat; but she told them clearly, with no unnecessary, hysterical exclamations, what had happened. Upon entering the house, after parting from the two men at the gate, a few minutes before, she had found a letter from Sibyl. The girl was gone.

As she spoke, she handed the letter to Conrad Lagrange who read it and gave it to the artist. It was a pitiful little note—rather vague—saying only that she must go away at once; assuring Myra that she had not meant to do wrong; asking her to tell Mr. King and the novelist good-by; and begging the artist's forgiveness that she had not understood.

Aaron King looked from the letter in his hand to the faces of his two friends, in consternation. "Do you understand this, Miss Willard?" he asked, when he could speak.

The woman shook her head. "Only that something has happened to make the child think that her friendship with you has injured you; and that she has gone away for your sake. She—she thought so much of you, Mr. King."

"And I—I love her, Miss Willard. I should have told you soon. I tell you now to reassure you. I love her."

Aaron King made his declaration to his two friends with a simple dignity, but with a feeling that thrilled them with the force of his earnestness and the purity and strength of his passion.

Conrad Lagrange—world-worn, scarred by his years of contact with the unclean, the vicious, and debasing passions of mankind—grasped the young man's hand, while his eyes shone with an emotion his habitual reserve could not conceal. "I'm glad for you, Aaron"—he said, adding reverently—"as your mother would be glad."

"I have known that you would tell me this, sometime Mr. King," said Myra Willard. "I knew it, I think, before you, yourself, realized; and I, too, am glad—glad for my girl, because I know what such a love will mean to her. But why—why has she gone like this? Where has she gone? Oh, my girl, my girl!" For a moment, the distracted woman was on the point of breaking down; but with an effort of her will, she controlled herself.

"It's clear enough what has sent her away," growled Conrad Lagrange, with a warning glance to the artist. "Some one has filled her mind with the notion that her friendship with Aaron has been causing talk. I think there's no doubt as to where she's gone."

"You mean the mountains?" asked Myra Willard, quickly.

"Yes. I'd stake my life that she has gone straight to Brian Oakley. Think! Where else would she go?"

"She has sometimes borrowed a saddle-horse from your neighbor up the road, hasn't she, Miss Willard?" asked Aaron King.

"Yes. I'll run over there at once."

Conrad Lagrange spoke quickly; "Don't let them think anything unusual has happened. We'll go over to your house and wait for you there."

Fifteen minutes later, Myra Willard returned. Sibyl had borrowed the horse; asking them if she might keep it until the next day. She did not say where she was going. She had left about four o'clock.

"That will put her at Brian's by nine," said the novelist.

"And I will arrive there about the same time," added Aaron King, eagerly. "It's now five-thirty. She has an hour's start; but I'll ride an hour harder."

"With an automobile you could overtake her," said Myra Willard.

"I know," returned the artist, "but if I take a horse, we can ride back together."

He started through the grove, toward the other house, on a run.

Chapter XXXII

The Mysterious Disappearance

By the time Aaron King had found a saddle-horse and was ready to start on his ride, it was six o'clock.

Granting that Conrad Lagrange was right in his supposition that the girl had left with the intention of going to Brian Oakley's, the artist could scarcely, now, hope to arrive at the Ranger Station until some time after Sibyl had reached the home of her friends—unless she should stop somewhere on the way, which he did not think likely. Once, as he realized how the minutes were slipping away, he was on the point of reconsidering his reply to Myra Willard's suggestion that he take an automobile. Then, telling himself that he would surely find Sibyl at the Station and thinking of the return trip with her, he determined to carry out his first plan.

But when he was finally on the road, he did not ride with less haste because he no longer expected to overtake Sibyl. In spite of his reassuring himself, again and again, that the girl he loved was safe, his mind was too disturbed by the situation to permit of his riding leisurely. Beyond the outskirts of the city, with his horse warmed to its work, the artist pushed his mount harder and harder until the animal reached the limit of a pace that its rider felt it could endure for the distance they had to go. Over the way that he and Conrad Lagrange had walked with Czar and Croesus so leisurely, he went, now, with such hot haste that the people in the homes in the orange groves, sitting down to their evening meal, paused to listen to the sharp, ringing beat of the galloping hoofs. Two or three travelers, as he passed, watched him out of sight, with wondering gaze. Those he met, turned their heads to look after him.

Aaron King's thoughts, as he rode, kept pace with his horse's flying feet. The points along the way, where he and the famous novelist had stopped to rest, and to enjoy the beauty of the scene, recalled vividly to his mind all that those weeks in the mountains had brought to him. Backward from that day when he had for the first time set his face toward the hills, his mind traveled—almost from day to day—until he stood, again, in that impoverished home of his boyhood to which he had been summoned from his studies abroad. As he urged his laboring horse forward, in the eagerness and anxiety of his love for Sibyl Andrés, he lived again that hour when his dying mother told her faltering story of his father's dishonor; when he knew, for the first time, her life of devotion to him, and learned of her sacrifice—even unto poverty—that he might, unhampered, be fitted for his life work; and when, receiving his inheritance, he had made his solemn promise that the purpose and passion of his mother's years of sacrifice should, in him and in his work, be fulfilled. One by one, he retraced the steps that had led to his understanding that only a true and noble art could ever make good that promise. Not by winning the poor notice of the little passing day, alone; not by gaining the applause of the thoughtless crowd; not by winning the rewards bestowed by the self-appointed judges and patrons of the arts; but by a true, honest, and fearless giving of himself in his work, regardless alike of praise or blame—by saying the thing that was given him to say, because it was given him to say—would he keep that which his mother had committed to him. As mile after mile of the distance that lay between him and the girl he loved was put behind him in his race to her side, it was given him to understand—as never before—how, first the friendship of the world-wearied man who had, himself, profaned his art; and then, the comradeship of that one whose life was so unspotted by the world; had helped him to a true and vital conception of his ministry of color and line and brush and canvas.

It was twilight when the artist reached the spot where the road crosses the tumbling stream—the spot where he and Conrad Lagrange had slept at the foot of the mountains. Where the road curves toward the creek, the man, without checking his pace, turned his head to look back upon the valley that, far below, was fast being lost in the gathering dusk. In its weird and gloomy mystery,—with its hidden life revealed only by the sparkling, twinkling lights of the towns and cities,—it was suggestive, now, to his artist mind, of the life that had so nearly caught him in its glittering sensual snare. A moment later, he lifted his eyes to the mountain peaks ahead that, still in the light of the western sun, glowed as though brushed with living fire. Against the sky, he could distinguish that peak in the Galena range, with the clump of pines, where he had sat with Sibyl Andrés that day when she had tried to make him see the train that had brought him to Fairlands.

He wondered now, as he rode, why he had not realized his love for the girl, before they left the hills. It seemed to him, now, that his love was born that evening when he had first heard her violin, as he was fishing; when he had watched her from the cedar thicket, as she made her music of the mountains and as she danced in the grassy yard. Why, he asked himself, had he not been conscious of his love in those days when she came to him in the spring glade, and in the days that followed? Why had he not known, when he painted her portrait in the rose garden? Why had the awakening not come until that night when he saw her in the company of revelers at the big house on Fairlands Heights—the night that Mr. Taine died?

It was dark before he reached the canyon gates. In the blackness of the gorge, with only the light of a narrow strip of stars overhead, he was forced to ride more slowly. But his confidence that he would find her at the Ranger Station had increased as he approached the scenes of her girlhood home. To go to her friends, seemed so inevitably the thing that she would do. A few miles farther, now, and he would see her. He would tell her why he had come. He would claim the love that he knew was his. And so, with a better heart, he permitted his tired horse to slacken the pace. He even smiled to think of her surprise when she should see him.

It was a little past nine o'clock when the artist saw, through the trees, the lights in the windows at the Station, and dismounted to open the gate. Hiding up to the house, he gave the old familiar hail, "Whoo-e-e." The door opened, and with the flood of light that streamed out came the tall form of Brian Oakley.

"Hello! Seems to me I ought to know that voice."

The artist laughed nervously. "It's me, all right, Brian—what there is left of me."

"Aaron King, by all that's holy!" cried the Ranger, coming quickly down the steps and toward the shadowy horseman. "What's the matter? Anything wrong with Sibyl or Myra Willard? What brings you up here, this time of night?"

Aaron King heard the questions with sinking heart. But so certain had he come to feel that the girl would be at the Station, that he said mechanically, as he dropped wearily from his horse to grasp his friend's hand, "I followed Sibyl. How long has she been here?"

Brian Oakley spoke quickly; "Sibyl is not here, Aaron."

The artist caught the Ranger's arm. "Do you mean, Brian, that she has not been here to-day?"

"She has not been here," returned the officer, coolly.

"Good God!" exclaimed the other, stunned and bewildered by the positive words. Blindly, he turned toward his horse.

Brian Oakley, stepping forward, put his hand on the artist's shoulder. "Come, old man, pull yourself together and let a little light in on this matter," he said calmly. "Tell me what has happened. Why did you expect to find Sibyl here?"

When Aaron King had finished his story, the other said, still without excitement, "Come into the house. You're about all in. I heard Doctor Gordan's 'auto' going up the canyon to Morton's about an hour ago. Their baby's sick. If Sibyl was on the road, he would have passed her. I'll throw the saddle on Max, and we'll run over there and see what he knows. But first, you've got to have a bite to eat."

The young man protested but the Ranger said firmly, "You can eat while I saddle; come. I wish Mary was home," he added, as he set out some cold meat and bread. "She is in Los Angeles with her sister. I'll call you when I'm ready." He spoke the last word from the door as he went out.

The artist tried to eat; but with little success. He was again mounted and ready to go when the Ranger rode up from the barn on the chestnut.

When they reached the point where the road to Morton's ranch leaves the main canyon road, Brian Oakley said, "It's barely possible that she went on up to Carleton's. But I think we better go to Morton's and see the Doctor first. We don't want to miss him. Did you meet any one as you came up? I mean after you got within two or three miles of the mouth of the canyon?"

"No," replied the other. "Why?"

"A man on a horse passed the Station about seven o'clock, going down. Where did the Doctor pass you?"

"He didn't pass me."

"What?" said the Ranger, sharply.

"No one passed me after I left Fairlands."

"Hu-m-m. If Doc left town before you, he must have had a puncture or something, or he would have passed the Station before he did."

It was ten o'clock when the two men arrived at the Morton ranch.

"We don't want to start any excitement," said the officer, as they drew rein at the corral gate. "You stay here and I'll drop in—casual like."

It seemed to Aaron King, waiting in the darkness, that his companion was gone for hours. In reality, it was only a few minutes until the Ranger returned. He was walking quickly, and, springing into the saddle he started the chestnut off at a sharp lope.

"The baby is better," he said. "Doctor was here this afternoon—started home about two o'clock. That 'auto' must have gone on up the canyon. Morton knew nothing of the man on horseback who went down. We'll cut across to Carleton's."

Presently, the Ranger swung the chestnut aside from the wagon road, to follow a narrow trail through the chaparral. To the artist, the little path in the darkness was invisible, but he gave his horse the rein and followed the shadowy form ahead. Three-quarters of an hour later, they came out into the main road, again; near the Carleton ranch corral, a mile and a half below the old camp in the sycamores behind the orchard of the deserted place.

It was now eleven o'clock and the ranch-house was dark. Without dismounting, Brian Oakley called, "Hello, Henry!" There was no answer. Moving his horse close to the window of the room where he knew the rancher slept, the Ranger tapped on the sash. "Henry, turn out; I want to see you; it's Oakley."

A moment later the sash was raised and Carleton asked, "What is it, Brian? What's up?"

"Is Sibyl stopping with you folks, to-night?"

"Sibyl! Haven't seen her since they went down from their summer camp. What's the matter?"

Briefly, the Ranger explained the situation. The rancher interrupted only to greet the artist with a "howdy, Mr. King," as the officer's words made known the identity of his companion.

When Brian Oakley had concluded, the rancher said, "I heard that 'auto' going up, and then heard it going back down, again, about an hour ago. You missed it by turning off to Morton's. If you'd come on straight up here you'd a met it."

"Did you see the man on horseback, going down, just before dusk?" asked the officer.

"Yes, but not near enough to know him. You don't suppose Sibyl would go up to her old home do you, Brian?"

"She might, under the circumstances. Aaron and I will ride up there, on the chance."

"You'll stop in on your way back?" called the rancher, as the two horsemen moved away.

"Sure," answered the Ranger.

An hour later, they were back. They had found the old home under the giant sycamores, on the edge of the little clearing, dark and untenanted.

Lights were shining, now, from the windows of the Carleton ranch-house. Down at the corral, the twinkling gleam of a lantern bobbed here and there. As the Ranger and his companion drew near, the lantern came rapidly up the hill. At the porch, they were met by Henry Carleton, his two sons, and a ranch hand. As the four stood in the light of the window, and of the lantern on the porch, listening to Brian Oakley's report, each held the bridle-reins of a saddle-horse.

"I figured that the chance of her being up there was so mighty slim that we'd better be ready to ride when you got back," said the mountain ranchman. "What's your program, Brian?" Thus simply he put himself and his household in command of the Ranger.

The officer turned to the eldest son, "Jack, you've got the fastest horse in the outfit. I want you to go down to the Power-House and find out if any one there saw Sibyl anywhere on the road. You see," he explained to the group, "we don't know for sure, yet, that she came into the mountains. While I haven't a doubt but she did, we've got to know."

Jack Carleton was in the saddle as the Ranger finished The officer turned to him again. "Find out what you can about that automobile and the man on horseback. We'll be at the Station when you get back." There was a sharp clatter of iron-shod hoofs, and the rider disappeared in the darkness of the night.

The other members of the little party rode more leisurely down the canyon road to the Ranger Station. When they arrived at the house, Brian Oakley said, "Make yourselves easy, boys. I'm going to write a little note." He went into the house where, as they sat on the porch, they saw him through the window, his desk.

The Ranger had finished his letter and with the sealed official envelope in his hand, appeared in the doorway when his messenger to the Power-House returned. Without dismounting, the rider reined his horse up to the porch. "Good time, Jack," said the officer, quietly.

The young man answered, "One of the company men saw Sibyl. He was coming up with a load of supplies and she passed him a mile below the Power-House just before dark. When he was opening the gate, the automobile went by. It was too dark to see how many were in the machine. They heard the 'auto' go down the canyon, again, later. No one noticed the man on horseback. Three Company men will be up here at daybreak."

"Good boy," said Brian Oakley, again. And then, for a little, no sound save the soft clinking of bit or bridle-chain in the darkness broke the hush that fell over the little group. With faces turned toward their leader, they waited his word. The Ranger stood still, the long official envelope in his hand. When he spoke, there was a ring in his voice that left in the minds of his companions no doubt as to his view of the seriousness of the situation. "Milt," he said sharply.

The youngest of the Carleton sons stepped forward. "Yes, sir."

"You will ride to Fairlands. It's half past one, now. You should be back between eight and nine in the morning. Give this letter to the Sheriff and bring me his answer. Stop at Miss Willard's and tell her what you know. You'll get something to eat there, while you're talking. If I'm not at your house when you get back, feed your horse and wait."

"Yes, sir," came the answer, and an instant later the boy rider vanished into the night.

While the sound of the messenger's going still came to them, the Ranger spoke again. "Henry, you'll ride to Morton's. Tell him to be at your place, with his crowd, by daylight. Then go home and be ready with breakfast for the riders when they come in. We'll have to make your place the center. It'll be hard on your wife and the girls, but Mrs. Morton will likely go over to lend them a hand. I wish to God Mary was here."

"Never mind about my folks, Brian," returned the rancher as he mounted. "You know they'll be on the job."

"You bet I know, Henry," came the answer as the mountaineer rode away. Then—"Bill, you'll take every one between here and the head of the canyon. If there's a man shows up at Carleton's later than an hour after sunup, we'll run him out of the country. Tom, you take the trail over into the Santa Ana, circle around to the mouth of the canyon, and back up Clear Creek. Turn out everybody. Jack, you'll take the Galena Valley neighborhood. Send in your men but don't come back yourself until you've found that man who went down the canyon on horseback."

When the last rider was gone in the darkness, the Ranger said to the artist, "Come, Aaron, you must get some rest. There's not a thing more that can be done, until daylight."

Aaron King protested. But, strong as he was, the unusual exertion of his hours in the saddle, together with his racking anxiety, had told upon muscles and nerves. His face, pale and drawn, gave the lie to his words that he was not tired.

"You must rest, man," said Brian Oakley, shortly. "There may be days of this ahead of us. You've got to snatch every minute, when it's possible, to conserve your strength. You've already had more than the rest of us. Jerk off your boots and lie down until I call you, even if you can't sleep. Do as I say—I'm boss here."

As the artist obeyed, the Ranger continued, "I wrote the Sheriff all I knew—and some things that I suspect. It's that automobile that sticks in my mind—that and some other things. The machine must have left Fairlands before you did, unless it came over through the Galena Valley, from some town on the railroad, up San Gorgonio Pass way—which isn't likely. If it did come from Fairlands, it must have waited somewhere along the road, to enter the canyon after dark. Do you think that any one else besides Myra Willard and Lagrange and you know that Sibyl started up here?"

"I don't think so. The neighbor where she borrowed the horse didn't know where she was going."

"Who saw her last?"

"I think Mrs. Taine did."

The artist had already told the Ranger about the possible meeting of Mrs. Taine and Sibyl in his studio.

"Hu-m-m," said the other.

"Mrs. Taine left for the East at four o'clock, you know," said the artist.

"Jim Rutlidge didn't go, you said." The Ranger spoke casually. Then, as if dismissing the matter, he continued, "You get some rest now, Aaron. I'll take care of your horse and saddle a fresh one for you. As soon as it's light, we'll ride. I'm going to find out where that automobile went—and what for."

Chapter XXXIII

Beginning the Search

Aaron King lay with closed eyes, but not asleep. He was thinking, thinking, thinking In a weary circle, his tired brain went round and round, finding no place to stop. The man on horseback, the automobile, some accident that might have befallen the girl in her distraught state of mind—he could find no place in the weary treadmill of conjecture to rest. While it was still too dark to see, Brian Oakley called him. And the call was a relief.

As the artist pulled on his boots, the Ranger said, "It'll be light enough to see, by the time we get above Carleton's. We know the automobile went that far anyway."

At the Carleton ranch, as they passed, they saw, by the lights, that the mountaineer's family were already making ready for the gathering of the riders. A little beyond, they met two men from the Company Head-Work, on their way to the meeting place. Soon, in the gray, early morning light, the tracks of the automobile were clearly seen. Eagerly, they followed to the foot of the Oak Knoll trail, where the machine had stopped and, turning around, had started back down the canyon. With experienced care, Brian Oakley searched every inch of the ground in the vicinity.

Shaking his head, at last, as though forced to give up hope of finding any positive signs pointing to the solution of the puzzle, the officer remounted, slowly. "I can't make it out," he said. "The road is so dry and cut up with tracks, and the trail is so gravelly, that there are no clear signs at all. Come, we better get back to Carleton's, and start the boys out. When Milt returns from Fairlands he may know something."

With the rising of the sun, the mountain folk, summoned in the night by the Ranger's messengers, assembled at the ranch; every man armed and mounted with the best his possessions afforded. Tied to the trees in the yard, and along the fence in front, or standing with bridle-reins over their heads, the horses waited. Lying on the porch, or squatting on their heels, in unconscious picturesque attitudes, the mountain riders who had arrived first and had finished their breakfast were ready for the Ranger's word. In the ranch kitchen, the table was filled with the later ones; and these, as fast as they finished their meal, made way for the new arrivals. There was no loud talk; no boisterous laughter; no uneasy restlessness. Calm-eyed, soft-voiced, deliberate in movement, these hardy mountaineers had answered Brian Oakley's call; and they placed themselves, now, under his command, with no idle comment, no wasteful excitement but with a purpose and spirit that would, if need be, hold them in their saddles until their horses dropped under them, and would, then, send them on, afoot, as long as their iron nerves and muscles could be made to respond to their wills.

There was scarce a man in that company, who did not know and love Sibyl Andrés, and who had not known and loved her parents. Many of them had ridden with the Ranger at the time of Will Andrés' death. When the officer and his companion appeared, they gathered round their leader with simple words of greeting, and stood silently ready for his word.

Briefly, Brian Oakley divided them into parties, and assigned the territory to be covered by each. Three shots in quick succession, at intervals of two minutes, would signal that the search was finished. Two men, he held to go with him up Oak Knoll trail, after his messenger to the Sheriff had returned. At sunset, they were all to reassemble at the ranch for further orders. When the officer finished speaking, the little group of men turned to the horses, and, without the loss of a moment, were out of sight in the mountain wilderness.

A half hour before he was due, young Carleton appeared with the Sheriff's answer to the Ranger's letter. "Well done, boy," said Brian Oakley, heartily. "Take care of your horse, now, and then get some rest yourself, and be ready for whatever comes next."

He turned to those he had held to go with him; "All right, boys, let's ride. Sheriff will take care of the Fairlands end. Come, Aaron."

All the way up the Oak Knoll trail the Ranger rode in the lead, bending low from his saddle, his gaze fixed on the little path. Twice he dismounted and walked ahead, leaving the chestnut to follow or to wait, at his word. When they came out on the pipe-line trail, he halted the party, and, on foot, went carefully over the ground either way from the point where they stood.

"Boys," he said at last, "I have a hunch that there was a horse on this trail last night. It's been so blamed dry, and for so long, though, that I can't be sure. I held you two men because I know you are good trailers. Follow the pipe-line up the canyon, and see what you can find. It isn't necessary to say stay with it if you strike anything that even looks like it might be a lead. Aaron and I will take the other way, and up the Galena trail to the fire-break."

While Brian Oakley had been searching for signs in the little path, and the artist, with the others, was waiting, Aaron King's mind went back to that day when he and Conrad Lagrange had sat there under the oaks and, in a spirit of irresponsible fun, had committed themselves to the leadership of Croesus. To the young man, now, that day, with its care-free leisure, seemed long ago. Remembering the novelist's fanciful oration to the burro, he thought grimly how unconscious they had been, in their merriment, of the great issues that did actually rest upon the seemingly trivial incident. He recalled, too, with startling vividness, the times that he had climbed to that spot with Sibyl, or, reaching it from either way on the pipe-line, had gone with her down the zigzag path to the road in the canyon below. Had she, last night, alone, or with some unwelcome companions, paused a moment under those oaks? Had she remembered the hours that she had spent there with him?

As he followed the Ranger over the ground that he had walked with her, that day of their last climb together, it seemed to him that every step of the way was haunted by her sweet personality. The objects along the trail—a point of rock, a pine, the barrel where they had filled their canteen, a broken section of the concrete pipe left by the workmen, the very rocks and cliffs, the flowers—dry and withered now—that grew along the little path—a thousand things that met his eyes—recalled her to his mind until he felt her presence so vividly that he almost expected to find her waiting, with smiling, winsome face, just around the next turn. The officer, who, moving ahead, scanned with careful eyes every foot of the way, seemed to the artist, now, to be playing some fantastic game. He could not, for the moment, believe that the girl he loved was—God! where was she? Why did Brian Oakley move so slowly, on foot, while his horse, leisurely cropping the grass, followed? He should be in the saddle! They should be riding, riding riding—as he had ridden last night. Last night! Was it only last night?

Where the Government trail crosses the fire-break on the crest of the Galenas, Brian Oakley paused. "I don't think there's been anything over this way," he said. "We'll follow the fire-break to that point up there, for a look around."

At noon, they stood by the big rock, under the clump of pines, where Aaron King and Sibyl Andrés had eaten their lunch.

"We'll be here some time," said the Ranger. "Make yourself comfortable. I want to see if there's anything stirring down yonder."

With his back to the rock, he searched the Galena Valley side of the range, through his powerful glass; commenting, now and then, when some object came in the field of his vision, to his companion who sat beside him.

They had risen to go and the officer was returning his glass to its case on his saddle, when Aaron King—pointing toward Fairlands, lying dim and hazy in the distant valley—said, "Look there!"

The other turned his head to see a flash of light that winked through the dull, smoky veil, with startling clearness. He smiled and turned again to his saddle. "You'll often see that," he said. "It's the sun striking some bright object that happens to be at just the right angle to hit you with the reflection. A bit of new tin on a roof, a window, an automobile shield, anything bright enough, will do the trick. Come, we'll go back to the trail and follow the break the other way."

In the dusk of the evening, at the close of the long, hard day, as Brian Oakley and Aaron King were starting down the Oak Knoll trail on their return to the ranch, the Ranger uttered an exclamation. His quick eyes had caught the twinkling gleam of a light at Sibyl's old home, far below, across the canyon. The next instant, the chestnut, followed by his four-footed companion, was going down the steep trail at a pace that sent the gravel flying and forced the artist, unaccustomed to such riding, to cling desperately to the saddle. Up the canyon road, the Ranger sent the chestnut at a run, nor did he draw rein as they crossed the rough boulder-strewn wash. Plunging through the tumbling water of the creek, the horses scrambled up the farther bank, and dashed along the old, weed-grown road, into the little clearing They were met by Czar with a bark of welcome. A moment later, they were greeted by Conrad Lagrange and Myra Willard.

"But why don't you stay down at the ranch, Myra?" asked the Ranger, when he had told them that his day's work was without results.

"Listen, Mr. Oakley," returned the woman with the disfigured face. "I know Sibyl too well not to understand the possibilities of her temperament. Natures, fine and sensitive as hers, though brave and cool and strong under ordinary circumstances, under peculiar mental stress such as I believe caused her to leave us, are easily thrown out of balance. We know nothing. The child may be wandering, alone—dazed and helpless under the shock of a cruel and malicious attempt to wreck her happiness. Only some terrible stress of emotion could have caused her to leave me as she did. If she is alone, out here in the hills, there is a chance that—even in her distracted state of mind—she will find her way to her old home." The woman paused, and then, in the silence, added hesitatingly, "I—I may say that I know from experience the possibilities of which I speak."

The three men bowed their heads. Brian Oakley said softly, "Myra, you've got more heart and more sense than all of us put together." To Conrad Lagrange, he added, "You will stay here with Miss Willard?"

"Yes," answered the novelist, "I would be little good in the hills, at such work as you are doing, Brian. I will do what I can, here."

When the Ranger and the artist were riding down the canyon to the ranch, the officer said, "There's a big chance that Myra is right, Aaron. After all, she knows Sibyl better than any of us, and I can see that she's got a fairly clear idea of what sent the child off like this. As it stands now, the girl may be just wandering around. If she is, the boys will pick her up before many hours. She may have met with some accident. If that's it, we'll know before long. She may have been—I tell you, Aaron, it's that automobile acting the way it did that I can't get around."

The searchers were all at the ranch when the two men arrived. No one had a word of encouragement to report. A messenger from the Sheriff brought no light on the mystery of the automobile. The two men who had followed the pipe-line trail had found nothing. A few times, they thought they had signs that a horse had been over the trail the night before, but there was no certainty; and after the pipe-line reached the floor of the canyon there was absolutely nothing. Jack Carleton was back from the Galena Valley neighborhood, and, with him, was the horseman who had gone down the canyon the evening before. The man was known to all. He had been hunting, and was on his way home when Henry Carleton and the Ranger had seen him. He had come, now, to help in the search.

Picking a half dozen men from the party, Brian Oakley sent them to spend the night riding the higher trails and fire-breaks, watching for camp-fire lights. The others, he ordered to rest, in readiness to take up the search at daylight, should the night riders come in without results.

Aaron King, exhausted, physically and mentally, sank into a stupor that could scarcely be called sleep.

At daybreak, the riders who had been all night on the higher trails and fire-breaks, searching the darkness for the possible gleam of a camp-fire's light, came in.

All that day—Wednesday—the mountain horsemen rode, widening the area of their search under the direction of the Ranger. From sundown until long after dark, they came straggling wearily back; their horses nearly exhausted, the riders beginning to fear that Sibyl would never be found alive. There was no further word from the Sheriff at Fairlands.

Then suddenly, out of the blackness of the night, a rider from the other side of the Galenas arrived with the word that the girl's horse had been found. The animal was grazing in the neighborhood of Pine Glen. The saddle and the horse's sides were stained with dirt, as if the animal had fallen. The bridle-reins had been broken. The horse might have rolled on the saddle; he might have stepped on the bridle-reins; he might have fallen and left his rider lying senseless. In any case, they reasoned, the animal would scarcely have found his way over the Galena range after he had been left to wander at will.

Brian Oakley decided to send the main company of riders over into the Pine Glen country, to continue the search there. He knew that the men who found the horse would follow the animal's track back as far as possible. He knew, also, that if the animal had been wandering several hours, as was likely, it would be impossible to back-track far. Late as it was, Aaron King rode up the canyon to tell Myra Willard and Conrad Lagrange the result of the day's work.

The artist's voice trembled as he told the general opinion of the mountaineers; but Myra Willard said, "Mr. King, they are wrong. My baby will come back. There's harm come to her no doubt; but she is not dead or—I would know it."

In spite of the fact that Aaron King's reason told him the woman of the disfigured face had no ground for her belief, he was somehow helped, by her words, to hope.

Chapter XXXIV

The Tracks on Granite Peak

The searching party was already on the way over to Pine Glen, when Brian Oakley stopped at Sibyl's old home for Aaron King. The Ranger, himself, had waited to receive the morning message from the Sheriff.

When the two men, following the Government trail that leads to the neighborhood where the girl's horse had been found, reached the fire-break on the summit of the Galenas, the officer said, "Aaron, you'll be of little use over there in that Pine Glen country, where you have never been." He had pulled up his horse and was looking at his companion, steadily.

"Is there nothing that I can do, Brian?" returned the young man, hopelessly. "God, man! I must do something! I must, I tell you!"

"Steady, old boy, steady," returned the mountaineer's calm voice. "The first thing you must do, you know, is to keep a firm grip on yourself. If you lose your nerve I'll have you on my hands too."

Under his companion's eye, the artist controlled himself. "You're right, Brian," he said calmly. "What do you want me to do? You know best, of course."

The officer, still watching him, said slowly, "I want you to spend the day on that point, up there,"—he pointed to the clump of pines,—"with this glass." He turned to take an extra field-glass from his saddle. Handing the glass to the other, he continued "You can see all over the country, on the Galena Valley side of this range, from there." Again he paused, as though reluctant to give the final word of his instructions.

The young man looked at him, questioningly. "Yes?"

The Ranger answered in a low tone, "You are to watch for buzzards, Aaron."

Aaron King went white. "Brian! You think—"

The answer came sharply, "I am not thinking. I don't dare think. I am only recognizing every possibility and letting nothing, nothing, get away from me. I don't want you to think. I want you to do the thing that will be of greatest service. It's because I am afraid you will think, that I hesitate to assign you to the position."

The sharp words acted like a dash of cold water in the young man's face. Unconsciously, he straightened in his saddle. "Thank you, Brian. I understand. You can depend upon me."

"Good boy!" came the hearty and instant approval. "If you see anything, go to it; leaving a note here, under a stone on top of this rock; I'll find it to-night, when I come back. If nothing shows up, stay until dark, and then go down to Carleton's. I'll be in late. The rest of the party will stay over at Pine Glen."

Alone on the peak where he had sat with Sibyl the day of their last climb, Aaron King watched for the buzzards' telltale, circling flight—and tried not to think.

It was one o'clock when the artist—resting his eyes for a moment, after a long, searching look through the glass—caught, again, that flash of light in the blue haze that lay over Fairlands in the distant valley. Brian Oakley had said,—when they had seen it that first day of the search,—that it was a common sight; but the artist, his mind preoccupied, watched the point of light with momentary, idle interest.

Suddenly, he awoke to the fact that there seemed to be a timed regularity in the flashes. Into his mind came the memory of something he had read of the heliograph, and of methods of signalling with mirrors Closely, now, he watched—three flashes in quick succession—pause—two flashes—pause—one flash—pause—one flash—pause—two flashes—pause—three flashes—pause. For several minutes the artist waited, his eyes fixed on the distant spot under the haze. Then the flashes began again, repeating the same order: —- — - - — —-.

At the last flash, the man sprang to his feet, and searched the mountain peaks and spurs behind him. On lonely Granite Peak, at the far end of the Galena Range, a flash of light caught his eye—then another and another. With an exclamation, he lifted his glass. He could distinguish nothing but the peak from which had come the flashes. He turned toward the valley to see a long flash and then—only the haze and the dark spot that he knew to be the orange groves about Fairlands.

Aaron King sank, weak and trembling, against the rock. What should he do? What could he do? The signals might mean much. They might mean nothing. Brian Oakley's words that morning, came to him; "I am recognizing every possibility, and letting nothing nothing, get away from me." Instantly, he was galvanized into life. Idle thinking, wondering, conjecturing could accomplish nothing.

Riding as fast as possible down to the boulder beside the trail, where he was to leave his message, he wrote a note and placed it under the rock. Then he set out, to ride the fire-break along the top of the range, toward the distant Granite Peak. An hour's riding took him to the end of the fire-break, and he saw that from there on he must go afoot.

Tying the bridle-reins over the saddle-horn, and fastening a note to the saddle, in case any one should find the horse, he turned the animal's head back the way he had come, and, with a sharp blow, started it forward. He knew that the horse—one of Carleton's—would probably make its way home. Turning, he set his face toward the lonely peak; carrying his canteen and what was left of his lunch.

There was no trail for his feet now. At times, he forced his way through and over bushes of buckthorn and manzanita that seemed, with their sharp thorns and tangled branches, to be stubbornly fighting him back. At times, he made his way along some steep slope, from pine to pine, where the ground was slippery with the brown needles, and where to lose his footing meant a fall of a thousand feet. Again, he scaled some rocky cliff, clinging with his fingers to jutting points of rock, finding niches and projections for his feet; or, with the help of vine and root and bush, found a way down some seemingly impossible precipice. Now and then, from some higher point, he sighted Granite Peak. Often, he saw, far below, on one hand the great canyon, and on the other the wide Galena Valley. Always he pushed forward. His face was scratched and stained; his clothing was torn by the bushes; his hands were bloody from the sharp rocks; his body reeked with sweat; his breath came in struggling gasps; but he would not stop. He felt himself driven, as it were, by some inner power that made him insensible to hardship or death. Far behind him, the sun dropped below the sky-line of the distant San Gabriels, but he did not notice. Only when the dusk of the coming night was upon him, did he realize that the day was gone.

On a narrow shelf, in the lee of a great cliff, he hastily gathered material for a fire, and, with his back to the rock, ate a little of the food he carried. Far up on that wind-swept, mountain ridge, the night was bitter cold. Again and again he aroused himself from the weary stupor that numbed his senses, and replenished the fire, or forced himself to pace to and fro upon the ledge. Overhead, he saw the stars glittering with a strange brilliancy. In the canyon, far below, there were a few twinkling lights to mark the Carleton ranch, and the old home of Sibyl, where Conrad Lagrange and Myra Willard waited. Miles away, the lights of the towns among the orange groves, twinkled like feeble stars in another feeble world. The cold wind moaned and wailed in the dark pines and swirled about the cliff in sudden gusts. A cougar screamed somewhere on the mountainside below. An answering scream came from the ledge above his head. The artist threw more fuel upon his fire, and grimly walked his beat.

In the cold, gray dawn of that Friday morning, he ate a few mouthfuls of his scanty store of food and, as soon as it was light,—even while the canyon below was still in the gloom,—started on his way.

It was eleven o'clock when, almost exhausted, he reached what he knew must be the peak that he had seen through his glass the day before. There was little or no vegetation upon that high, wind-swept point. The side toward the distant peak from which the artist had seen the signals, was an abrupt cliff—hundreds of feet of sheer, granite rock. From the rim of this precipice, the peak sloped gradually down and back to the edge of the pines that grew about its base. The ground in the open space was bare and hard.

Carefully, Aaron King searched—as he had seen the Ranger do—for signs. Beginning at a spot near the edge of the cliff, he worked gradually, back and forth, in ever widening arcs, toward the pines below. He was almost ready to give up in despair, cursing himself for being such a fool as to think that he could pick up a trail, when, clearly marked in a bit of softer soil, he saw the print of a hob-nailed boot.

Instantly the man's weariness was gone. The long, hard way he had come was forgotten. Insensible, now, to hunger and fatigue, he moved eagerly in the direction the boot-track pointed. He was rewarded by another track. Then, as he moved nearer the softer ground, toward the trees, another and another and then—

The man—worn by his physical exertion, and by his days of mental anguish—for a moment, lost control of himself. Clearly marked, beside the broad track of the heavier, man's boot, was the unmistakable print of a smaller, lighter foot.

For a moment he stood with clenched fists and heaving breast; then, with grim eagerness, with every sense supernaturally alert, with nerves tense, quick eyes and ready muscles, he went forward on the trail.

It was after dark, that night, when Brian Oakley, on his way back to Clear Creek, stopped at the rock where the artist had left his note.

Reaching the floor of the canyon, he crossed to tell Myra Willard and the novelist the result of the day's search. The men riding in the vicinity of Pine Glen had found nothing. It had been—as the Ranger expected—impossible to follow back for any distance on the track of the roaming horse, for the animal had been grazing about the Pine Glen neighborhood for at least a day. Over the note left by Aaron King, the mountaineer shook his head doubtfully. Aaron had done right to go. But for one of his inexperience, the way along the crest of the Galenas was practically impossible. If the young man had known, he could have made the trip much easier by returning to Clear Creek and following up to the head of that canyon, then climbing to the crest of the divide, and so around to Granite Peak. The Ranger, himself, would start, at daybreak, for the peak, by that route; and would come back along the crest of the range, to find the artist.

At Carleton's, they told the officer that Aaron's horse had come in. Jack Carleton and his father arrived from the country above Lone Cabin and Burnt Pine, a few minutes after Brian Oakley reached the ranch. It was agreed that Henry should join the searchers at Pine Glen, at daybreak—lest any one should have seen the artist's camp-fire, that night, and so lose precious time going to it—and that Jack should accompany the Ranger to Granite Peak.

Henry Carleton had gone on his way to Pine Glen, and Brian Oakley and Jack were in the saddle, ready to start up the canyon, the next morning, when a messenger from the Sheriff arrived. An automobile had been seen returning from the mountains, about two o'clock that night. There was only one man in the car.

"Jack," said the Ranger, "Aaron has got hold of the right end of this, with his mirror flashes. You've got to go up the canyon alone. Get to Granite Peak as quick as God will let you, and pick up the trail of whoever signalled from there; keeping one eye open for Aaron. I'm going to trail that automobile as far as it went, and follow whatever met or left it. We'll likely meet somewhere, over in the Cold Water country."

A minute later the two men who had planned to ride together were going in opposite directions.

Following the Fairlands road until he came to where the Galena Valley road branches off from the Clear Creek way, three miles below the Power-House at the mouth of the canyon, Brian Oakley found the tracks of an automobile—made without doubt, during the night just past. The machine had gone up the Galena Valley road, and had returned.

A little before noon, the officer stood where the automobile had stopped and turned around for the return trip. The place was well up toward the head of the valley, near the mouth of a canyon that leads upward toward Granite Peak. An hour's careful work, and the Ranger uncovered a small store of supplies; hidden a quarter of a mile up the canyon. There were tracks leading away up the side of the mountain. Turning his horse loose to find its way home; Brian Oakley, without stopping for lunch, set out on the trail.

High up on Granite Peak, Aaron King was bending over the print of a slender shoe, beside the track of a heavy hob-nailed boot. Somewhere in Clear Creek canyon, Jack Carleton was riding to gain the point where the artist stood. At the foot of the mountain, on the other side of the range, Brian Oakley was setting out to follow the faint trail that started at the supplies brought by the automobile, in the night, from Fairlands.

Chapter XXXV

A Hard Way

When Sibyl Andrés left the studio, after meeting Mrs. Taine, her mind was dominated by one thought—that she must get away from the world that saw only evil in her friendship with Aaron King—a friendship that, to the mountain girl, was as pure as her relations to Myra Willard or Brian Oakley.

Under the watchful, experienced care of the woman with the disfigured face, only the worthy had been permitted to enter into the life of this child of the hills. Sibyl's character—mind and heart and body and soul—had been formed by the strength and purity of her mountain environment; by her association with her parents, with Myra Willard, and with her parents' life-long friends; and by her mental comradeship with the greatest spirits that music and literature have given to the world. As her physical strength and beauty was the gift of her free mountain life, the beauty and strength of her pure spirit was the gift of those kindred spirits that are as mountains in the mental and spiritual life of the race.

Love had come to Sibyl Andrés, not as it comes to those girls who, in the hot-house of passion we call civilization, are forced into premature and sickly bloom by an atmosphere of sensuality. Love had come to her so gently, so naturally, so like the opening of a wild flower, that she had not yet understood that it was love. Even as her womanhood had come to fulfill her girlhood, so Aaron King had come into her life to fulfill her womanhood. She had chosen her mate with an unconscious obedience to the laws of life that was divinely reckless of the world.

Myra Willard, wise in her experience, and in her more than mother love for Sibyl, saw and recognized that which the girl herself did not yet understand. Satisfied as to the character of Aaron King, as it had been tested in those days of unhampered companionship; and seeing, as well, his growing love for the girl, the woman had been content not to meddle with that which she conceived to be the work of God. And why not the work of God? Should the development, the blossoming, and the fruiting of human lives, that the race may flower and fruit, be held less a work of divinity than the plants that mature and blossom and reproduce themselves in their children?

The character of Mrs. Taine represented those forces in life that are, in every way, antagonistic to the forces that make the character of a Sibyl Andrés possible. In a spirit of wanton, selfish cruelty, that was born of her worldly environment and training, "The Age" had twisted and distorted the very virtues of "Nature" into something as hideously ugly and vile as her own thoughts. The woman—product of gross materialism and sensuality—had caught in her licentious hands God's human flower and had crushed its beauty with deliberate purpose. Wounded, frightened, dismayed, not understanding, unable to deny, the girl turned in reluctant flight from the place that was, to her, because of her love, holy ground.

It was impossible for Sibyl not to believe Mrs. Taine—the woman had spoken so kindly; had seemed so reluctant to speak at all; had appeared so to appreciate her innocence. A thousand trivial and unimportant incidents, that, in the light of the worldly woman's words, could be twisted to evidence the truth of the things she said, came crowding in upon the girl's mind. Instead of helping Aaron King with his work, instead of truly enjoying life with him, as she had thought, her friendship was to him a menace, a danger. She had believed—and the belief had brought her a strange happiness—that he had cared for her companionship. He had cared only to use her for his pictures—as he used his brushes. He had played with her—as she had seen him toy idly with a brush, while thinking over his work. He would throw her aside, when she had served his purpose, as she had seen him throw a worn-out brush aside.

The woman who was still a child could not blame the artist—she was too loyal to what she had thought was their friendship; she was too unselfish in her yet unrecognized love for her chosen mate. No, she could not blame him—only—only—she wished—oh how she wished—that she had understood. It would not have hurt so, perhaps, if she had understood.

In all the cruel tangle of her emotions, in all her confused and bewildering thoughts, in all her suffering one thing was clear; she must get away from the world that could see only evil—she must go at once. Conrad Lagrange and Aaron King might come at any moment. She could not face them; now that she knew. She wished Myra was home. But she would leave a little note and Myra—dear Myra with her disfigured face—would understand.

Quickly, the girl wrote her letter. Hurriedly, she dressed in her mountain costume. Still acting under her blind impulse to escape, she made no explanations to the neighbors, when she went for the horse. In her desire to avoid coming face to face with any one, she even chose the more unfrequented streets through the orange groves. In her humiliation and shame, she wished for the kindly darkness of the night. Not until she had left the city far behind, and, in the soft dusk, drew near the mouth of the canyon, did she regain some measure of her self-control.

As she was overtaking the Power Company's team and wagon of supplies, she turned in her saddle, for the first time, to look back. A mile away, on the road, she could see a cloud of dust and a dark, moving spot which she knew to be an automobile. One of the Company machines, she thought; and drew a breath of relief that Fairlands was so far away.

It was quite dark as she entered the canyon; but, as she drew near, she could see against the sky, those great gates, opening silently, majestically to receive her. From within the canyon, she watched, as she rode, to see them slowly close again. The sight of the encircling peaks and ridges, rising in solemn grandeur out of the darkness into the light of the stars, comforted her. The night wind, drawing down the canyon, was sweet and bracing with the odor of the hills. The roar of the tumbling Clear Creek, filling the night with its deep-toned music, soothed and calmed her troubled mind. Presently, she would be with her friends, and, somehow, all would be well.

The girl had ridden half the distance, perhaps, from the canyon gates to the Ranger Station when, above the roar of the mountain stream, her quick ear caught the sound of an automobile, behind her. Looking back, she saw the gleam of the lights, like two great eyes in the darkness. A Company machine, going up to the Head-Work, she thought. Or, perhaps the Doctor, to see some one of the mountain folk.

As the automobile drew nearer, she reined her horse out of the road, and halted in the thick chaparral to let it pass. The blazing lights, as her horse turned to face the approaching machine, blinded her. The animal restive under the ordeal, demanded all her attention. She scarcely noticed that the automobile had slowed down, when within a few feet of her, until a man, suddenly, stood at her horse's head; his hand on the bridle-rein as though to assist her. At the same instant, the machine moved past them, and stopped; its engine still running.

Still with the thought of the Company men in her mind, the girl saw only their usual courtesy. "Thank you," she said, "I can handle him very nicely."

But the man—whom she had not had time to see, blinded as she had been by the light, and who was now only dimly visible in the darkness—stepped close to the horse's shoulder, as if to make himself more easily heard above the noise of the machine, his hand still holding the bridle-rein.

"It is Miss Andrés, is it not?" He spoke as though he was known to her; and the girl—still thinking that it was one of the Company men, and feeling that he expected her to recognize him—leaned forward to see his face, as she answered.

Instantly, the stranger—standing close and taking advantage of the girl's position as she stooped toward him from the saddle—caught her in his powerful arms and lifted her to the ground. At the same moment, the man's companion who, under cover of the darkness and the noise of the machine, had drawn close to the other side of the horse, caught the bridle-rein.

Before the girl, taken so off her guard could cry out, a softly-rolled, silk handkerchief was thrust between her lips and skillfully tied in place. She struggled desperately; but, against the powerful arms of her captor, her splendid, young strength was useless. As he bound her hands, the man spoke reassuringly; "Don't fight, Miss. I'm not going to hurt you. I've got to do this; but I'll be as easy as I can. It will do you no good to wear yourself out."

Frightened as she was, the girl felt that the stranger was as gentle as the circumstances permitted him to be. He had not, in fact, hurt her at all; and, in his voice, she caught a tone of genuine regret. He seemed to be acting wholly against his will; as if driven by some power that rendered him, in fact, as helpless as his victim.

The other man, still standing by the horse's head, spoke sharply; "All right there?"

"All right, sir," gruffly answered the man who held Sibyl, and lifting the helpless girl gently in his arms he seated her carefully in the machine. An automobile-coat was thrown around her, the high collar turned up to hide the handkerchief about her lips, and her hat was replaced by an "auto-cap," pulled low. Then her captor went back to the horse; the other man took the seat beside her; and the car moved forward.

The girl's fright now gave way to perfect coolness. Realizing the uselessness of any effort to escape, she wisely saved her strength; watchful to take quick advantage of any opportunity that might present itself. Silently, she worked at her bonds, and endeavored to release the bandage that prevented her from crying out. But the hands that had bound her had been too skillful. Turning her head, she tried to see her companion's face. But, in the darkness, with upturned collar and cap pulled low over "auto-glasses," the identity of the man driving the car was effectually hidden.

Only when they were passing the Ranger Station and Sibyl saw the lights through the trees, did she, for a moment, renew her struggle. With all her strength she strained to release her hands. One cry from her strong, young voice would bring Brian Oakley so quickly after the automobile that her safety would be assured. On that mountain road, the chestnut would soon run them down. She even tried to throw herself from the car; but, bound as she was, the hand of her companion easily prevented, and she sank back in the seat, exhausted by her useless exertion.

At the foot of the Oak Knoll trail the automobile stopped. The man who had been following on Sibyl's horse came up quickly. Swiftly, the two men worked; placing sacks of supplies and blankets—as the girl guessed—on the animal. Presently, the one who had bound her, lifted her gently from the automobile "Don't hurt yourself, Miss," he said in her ear, as he carried her toward the horse. "It will do you no good." And the girl did not again resist, as he lifted her to the saddle.

The driver of the car said something to his companion in a low tone, and Sibyl heard her captor answer, "The girl will be as safe with me as if she were in her own home."

Again, the other spoke, and the girl heard only the reply; "Don't worry; I understand that. I'll go through with it. You've left me no chance to do anything else."

Then, stepping to the horse's head and taking the bridle-rein, the man who seemed to be under orders, led the way up the canyon. Behind them, the girl heard the automobile starting on its return. The sound died away in the distance. The silence of the night was disturbed only by the sound of the man's hob-nailed boots and the horse's iron-shod feet on the road.

Once, her captor halted a moment, and, coming to the horse's shoulder, asked if she was comfortable. The girl bowed her head. "I'm sorry for that gag," he said. "As soon as it's safe, I'll remove it; but I dare not take chances." He turned abruptly away and they went on.

Dimly, Sibyl saw, in her companion's manner, a ray of hope. That no immediate danger threatened, she was assured. That the man was acting against his will, was as evident. Wisely, she resolved to bend her efforts toward enlisting his sympathies,—to make it hard for him to carry out the purpose of whoever controlled him,—instead of antagonizing him by continued resistance and repeated attempts to escape, and so making it easier for him to do his master's bidding.

Leaving the canyon by the Laurel Creek trail, they reached Burnt Pine, where the man removed the handkerchief that sealed the girl's lips.

"Oh, thank you," she said quietly. "That is so much better."

"I'm sorry that I had to do it," he returned, as he unbound her arms. "There, you may get down now, and rest, while I fix a bit of lunch for you."

The girl sprang to the ground. "It is a relief to be free," she said. "But, really, I'm not a bit tired. Can't I help you with the pack?"

"No," returned the other, gruffly, as though he understood her purpose and put himself on his guard. "We'll only be here a few minutes, and it's a long road ahead. You must rest."

Obediently, she sat down on the ground, her back against a tree.

As they lunched, in the dim light of the stars, she said, "May I ask where you are taking me?"

"It's a long road, Miss Andrés. We'll be there to-morrow night," he answered reluctantly.

Again, she ventured timidly; "And is, is—some one waiting for—for us, at the end of our journey?"

The man's voice was kinder as he answered, "no, Miss Andrés; there'll he just you and me, for some time. And," he added, "you don't need to fear me."

"I am not at all afraid of you," she returned gently. "But I am—" she hesitated—"I am sorry for you—that you have to do this."

The man arose abruptly. "We must he going."

For some distance beyond Burnt Pine, they kept to the Laurel Creek trail, toward San Gorgonio; then they turned aside to follow some unmarked way, known only to the man. When the first soft tints of the day shone in the sky behind the peaks and ridges, while Sibyl's friends were assembling at the Carleton Ranch in Clear Creek Canyon, and Brian Oakley was directing the day's search, the girl was following her guide in the wild depths of the mountain wilderness, miles from any trail. The country was strange to her, but she knew that they were making their way, far above the canyon rim, on the side of the San Bernardino range, toward the distant Cold Water country that opened into the great desert beyond.

As the light grew stronger, Sibyl saw her companion a man of medium height, with powerful shoulders and arms; dressed in khaki, with mountain boots. Under his arm, as he led the way with a powerful stride that told of almost tireless strength, the girl saw the familiar stock of a Winchester rifle. Presently he halted, and as he turned, she saw his face. It was not a bad face. A heavy beard hid mouth and cheek and throat, but the nose was not coarse or brutal, and the brow was broad and intelligent. In the brown eyes there was, the girl thought, a look of wistful sadness, as though there were memories that could not be escaped.

"We will have breakfast here, if you please, Miss Andrés," he said gravely.

"I'm so hungry," she answered, dismounting. "May I make the coffee?"

He shook his head. "I'm sorry; but there must be no telltale smoke. The Ranger and his riders are out by now, as like as not."

"You seem very familiar with the country," she said, moving easily toward the rifle which he had leaned against a tree, while he busied himself with the pack of supplies.

"I am," he answered. "I have been forced to learn it thoroughly. By the way, Miss Andrés,"—he added, without turning his head, as he knelt on the ground to take food from the pack,—"that Winchester will do you no good. It is not loaded. I have the shells in my belt." He arose, facing her, and throwing open his coat, touched the butt of a Colt forty-five that hung in a shoulder holster under his left armpit. "This will serve in case quick action is needed, and it is always safely out of your reach, you see."

The girl laughed. "I admit that I was tempted," she said. "I might have known that you put the rifle within my reach to try me."

"I thought it would save you needless disappointment to make things clear at once," he answered. "Breakfast is ready."

The incident threw a strong light upon the character with which Sibyl had to deal. She realized, more than ever, that her only hope lay in so winning this man's sympathies and friendship that he would turn against whoever had forced him into his present position. The struggle was to be one of those silent battles of the spirit, where the forces that war are not seen but only felt, and where those who fight must often fight with smiling faces. The girl's part was to enlist her captor to fight for her, against himself. She saw, as clearly, the need of approaching her object with caution. Eager to know who it was that ruled this man, and by what peculiar power a character so strong could be so subjected, she dared not ask. Hour after hour, as they journeyed deeper and deeper into the mountain wilds, she watched and waited for some sign that her companion's mood would make it safe for her to approach him. Meanwhile, she exercised all her womanly tact to lead him to forget his distasteful position, and so to make his uncongenial task as pleasant as possible.

The girl did not realize how far her decision, in itself, aroused the admiring sympathy of her captor. Her coolness, self-possession, and bravery in meeting the situation with calm, watchful readiness, rather than with hysterical moaning and frantic pleading, did more than she realized toward accomplishing her purpose.

During that long forenoon, she sought to engage her guide in conversation, quite as though they were making a pleasure trip that was mutually agreeable. The man—as though he also desired his thoughts removed as far as might be from his real mission—responded readily, and succeeded in making himself a really interesting companion. Only once, did the girl venture to approach dangerous ground.

"Really," she said, "I wish I knew your name. It seems so stupid not to know how to address you. Is that asking too much?"

The man did not answer for some time, and the girl saw his face clouded with somber thought.

"I beg your pardon," she said gently. "I—I ought not to have asked."

"My name is Henry Marston, Miss Andrés," he said deliberately. "But it is not the name by which I am known these days," he added bitterly. "It is an honorable name, and I would like to hear it again—" he paused—"from you."

Sibyl returned gently, "Thank you, Mr. Marston—believe me, I do appreciate your confidence, and—" she in turn hesitated—"and I will keep the trust."

By noon, they had reached Granite Peak in the Galenas, having come by an unmarked way, through the wild country around the head of Clear Creek Canyon.

They had finished lunch, when Marston, looking at his watch, took a small mirror from his pocket and stood gazing expectantly toward the distant valley where Fairlands lay under the blue haze. Presently, a flash of light appeared; then another and another. It was the signal that Aaron King had seen and to which he had called Brian Oakley's attention, that first day of their search.

With his mirror, the man on Granite Peak answered and the girl, watching and understanding that he was communicating with some one, saw his face grow dark with anger. She did not speak.

They had traveled a half mile, perhaps, from the peak, when the man again stopped, saying, "You must dismount here, please."

Removing the things from the saddle, he led the horse a little way down the Galena Valley side of the ridge, and tied the reins to a tree. Then, slapping the animal about the head with his open hand, he forced the horse to break the reins, and started him off toward the distant valley. Again, the girl understood and made no comment.

Lifting the pack to his own strong shoulders, her companion—his eyes avoiding hers in shame—said gruffly, "Come."

Their way, now, led down from the higher levels of peak and ridge, into the canyons and gorges of the Cold Water country. There was no trail, but the man went forward as one entirely at home. At the head of a deep gorge, where their way seemed barred by the face of an impossible cliff that towered above their heads a thousand feet and dropped, another thousand, sheer to the tops of the pines below, he halted and faced the girl, enquiringly. "You have a good head, Miss Andrés?"

Sibyl smiled. "I was born in the mountains, Mr. Marston," she answered. "You need not fear for me."

Drawing near to the very brink of the precipice, he led her, by a narrow ledge, across the face of the cliff; and then, by an easier path, down the opposite wall of the gorge.

It was late in the afternoon when they arrived at a little log cabin that was so hidden in the wild tangle of mountain growth at the bottom of the narrow canyon as to be invisible from a distance of a hundred yards.

The girl knew that they had reached the end of their journey. Nearly exhausted by the hours of physical exertion, and worn with the mental and nervous strain, she sank down upon the blankets that her companion spread for her upon the ground.

"As soon as it is dark, I will cook a hot supper for you," he said, regarding her kindly. "Poor child, this has been a hard, hard, day for you. For me—"

Fighting to keep back the tears, she tried to thank him. For a moment he stood looking down at her. Then she saw his face grow black with rage, and, clenching his great fists, he turned away.

While waiting for the darkness that would hide the smoke of the fire, the man gathered cedar boughs from trees near-by, and made a comfortable bed in the cabin, for the girl. As soon as it was dark, he built a fire in the rude fire-place, and, in a few minutes, announced supper. The meal was really excellent; and Sibyl, in spite of her situation, ate heartily; which won an admiring comment from her captor.

The meal finished, he said awkwardly, "I want to thank you, Miss Andrés, for making this day as easy for me as you have. We will be alone here, until Friday, at least; perhaps longer. There is a bar to the cabin door. You may rest here as safely as though you were in your own room. Good night."

Before she could answer, he was gone.

A few minutes later, Sibyl stood in the open door. "Mr. Marston," she called.

"Yes, Miss Andrés," came, instantly, out of the darkness.

"Please come into the cabin."

There was no answer.

"It will be cold out there. Please come inside."

"Thank you, Miss Andrés; but I will do very nicely. Bar the door and go to sleep."

"But, Mr. Marston, I will sleep better if I know that you are comfortable."

The man came to her and she saw him in the dim light of the fire, standing hat in hand. He spoke wonderingly. "Do you mean, Miss Andrés, that you would not be afraid to sleep, if I occupied the cabin with you?"

"No," she answered, "I am not afraid. Come in."

But he did not move to cross the threshold. "And why are you not afraid?" he asked curiously.

"Because," she answered, "I know that you are a gentleman."

The man laughed harshly—such a laugh as Sibyl had never before heard. "A gentleman! This is the first time I have heard that word in connection with myself for many a year, Miss Andrés. You have little reason for using it—after what I have done to you—and am doing."

"Oh, but you see, I know that you are forced to do what you are doing. You are a gentleman, Mr. Marston.—Won't you please come in and sleep by the fire? You will be so uncomfortable out there. And you have had such a hard day."

"God bless you, for your good heart, Miss Andrés," the man said brokenly. "But I will not intrude upon your privacy to-night. Don't you see," he added savagely, "don't you see that I—I can't? Bar your door, please, and let me play the part assigned to me. Your kindness to me, your confidence in me, is wasted."

He turned abruptly away and disappeared in the darkness.

Chapter XXXVI

What Should He Do

The next morning, it was evident to Sibyl Andrés that the man who said his name was Henry Marston had not slept.

All that day, she watched the battle—saw him fighting with himself. He kept apart from her, and spoke but little. When night came, as soon as supper was over, he again left the cabin, to spend the long, dark hours in a struggle that the girl could only dimly sense. She could not understand; but she felt him fighting, fighting; and she knew that he fought for her. What was it? What terrible unseen force mastered this man,—compelled him to do its bidding,—even while he hated and loathed himself for submitting?

Watchful, ready, hoping, despairing, the helpless girl could only pray that her companion might be given strength.

The following morning, at breakfast, he told her that he must go to Granite Peak to signal. His orders were to lock her in the cabin, and to go alone; but he would not. She might go with him, if she chose.

Even this crumb of encouragement—that he would so far disobey his master—filled the girl's heart with hope. "I would love to go with you, Mr. Marston," she said, "but if it is going to make trouble for you, I would rather stay."

"You mean that you would rather be locked up in the cabin all day, than to make trouble for me?" he asked.

"It wouldn't be so terrible," she answered, "and I would like to do something—something to—to show you that I appreciate your, kindness to me. There's nothing else I can do, is there?"

The man looked at her wonderingly. It was impossible to doubt her sincerity. And Sibyl, as she saw his face, knew that she had never before witnessed such mental and spiritual anguish. The eyes that looked into hers so questioningly, so pleadingly, were the eyes of a soul in torment. Her own eyes filled with tears that she could not hide, and she turned away.

At last he said slowly, "No, Miss Andrés, you shall not stay in the cabin to-day. Come; we must go on, or I shall be late."

At Granite Peak, Sibyl watched the signal flashes from distant Fairlands—the flashes that Aaron King was watching, from the peak where they had sat together that day of their last climb. As the man answered the signals with his mirror, and the girl beside him watched, the artist was training his glass upon the spot where they stood; but, partially concealed as they were, the distance was too great.

When Sibyl's captor turned, after receiving the message conveyed by the flashes of light, his face was terrible to see; and the girl, without asking, knew that the crisis was drawing near. Deadly fear gripped her heart; but she was strangely calm. On the way back to the cabin, the man scarcely spoke, but walked with bent head; and the girl felt him fighting, fighting. She longed to cry out, to plead with him, to demand that he tell her why he must do this thing; but she dared not. She knew, instinctively that he must fight alone. So she watched and waited and prayed. As they were crossing the face of the canyon wall, on the narrow ledge, the man stopped and, as though forgetting the girl's presence, stood looking moodily down into the depths below. Then they went on. That night, he did not leave the cabin as soon as they had finished their evening meal, but sat on one of the rude seats with which the little hut was furnished, gazing into the fire.

The girl's heart beat quicker, as he said, "Miss Andrés, I would like to ask your opinion in a matter that I cannot decide satisfactorily to myself."

She took the seat on the other side of the rude fireplace.

"What is it, Mr. Marston?"

"I will put it in the form of a story," he answered. Then, after a wait of some minutes, as though he found it hard to begin, he said, "It is an old story, Miss Andrés; a very common one, but with a difference. A young man, with every chance in the world to go right, went wrong. He was well-born. He was fairly well educated. His father was a man of influence and considerable means. He had many friends, good and bad. I do not think the man was intentionally bad, but I do not excuse him. He was a fool—that's all—a fool. And, as fools must, he paid the price of his foolishness.

"A sentence of thirty years in the penitentiary is a big price for a young man to pay for being a fool, Miss Andrés. He was twenty-five when he went in—strong and vigorous, with a good mind; the prospects years of prison life—but that's not the story. I could not hope to make you understand what a thirty years sentence to the penitentiary means to a man of twenty-five. But, at least, you will not wonder that the man watched for an opportunity to escape. He prayed for an opportunity. For ten years,—ten years,—Miss Andrés, the man watched and prayed for a chance to escape. Then he got away.

"He was never a criminal at heart, you must understand. He had no wish, now, to live a life of crime. He wished only to live a sane, orderly, useful, life of freedom. They hunted him to the mountains. They could not take him, but they made it impossible for him to escape—he was starving—dying. He would not give himself up to the twenty years of hell that waited him. He did not want to die—but he would die rather than go back.

"Then, one day, when he was very near the end, a man found him. The poor hunted devil of a convict aroused his pity. He offered help. He gave the wretched, starving creature food. He arranged to furnish him with supplies, until it would be safe for him to leave his hiding place. He brought him food and clothing and books. Later, when the convict's prison pallor was gone, when his hair and beard were grown, and the prison manner and walk were, in some measure, forgotten; when the officers, thinking that he had perished in the mountains, had given up looking for him; his benefactor gave him work—beautiful work in the orange groves—where he was safe and happy and useful and could feel himself a man.

"Do you wonder, Miss Andrés, that the man was grateful? Do you wonder that he worshipped his benefactor—that he looked upon his friend as upon his savior?"

"No," said the girl, "I do not wonder. It was a beautiful thing to do—to help the poor fellow who wanted to do right. I do not wonder that the man who had escaped, loved his friend."

"But listen," said the other, "when the convict was beginning to feel safe; when he saw that he was out of danger; when he was living an honorable, happy life, instead of spending his days in the hell they call prison; when he was looking forward to years of happiness instead of to years of torment; then his benefactor came to him suddenly, one day, and said, 'Unless you do what I tell you, now—unless you help me to something that I want, I will send you back to prison. Do as I say, and your life shall go on as it is—as you have planned. Refuse, and I will turn you over to the officers, and you will go back to your hell for the remainder of your life.'

"Do you wonder, Miss Andrés, that the convict obeyed his master?"

The girl's face was white with despair, but she did not lose her self-control. She answered the man, thoughtfully—as though they were discussing some situation in which neither had a vital interest. "I think, Mr. Marston," she said, "that it would depend upon what it was that the man wanted the convict to do. It seems to me that I can imagine the convict being happier in prison, knowing that he had not done what the man wanted, than he would he, free, remembering what he had done to gain his freedom. What was it the man wanted?"

Breathlessly, Sibyl waited the answer.

The man on the other side of the fire did not speak.

At last, in a voice hoarse with emotion, Henry Marston said, "Freedom and a life of honorable usefulness purchased at a price, or hell, with only the memory of a good deed—which should the man choose, Miss Andrés?"

"I think," she replied, "that you should tell me, plainly, what it was that the man wanted the convict to do."

"I will go on with the story," said the other.

"The convict's benefactor—or, perhaps I should say, master—loved a woman who refused to listen to him. The girl, for some reason, left home, very suddenly and unexpectedly to any one. She left a hurried note, saying, only, that she was going away. By accident, the man found the note and saw his opportunity. He guessed that the girl would go to friends in the mountains. He saw that if he could intercept her, and keep her hidden, no one would know what had become of her. He believed that she would marry him rather than face the world after spending so many days with him alone, because her manner of leaving home would lend color to the story that she had gone with him. Their marriage would save her good name. He wanted the man whom he could send back to prison to help him.

"The convict had known his benefactor's kindness of heart, you must remember, Miss Andrés. He knew that this man was able to give his wife everything that seems desirable in life—that thousands of women would have been glad to marry him. The man assured the convict that he desired only to make the girl his wife before all the world. He agreed that she should remain under the convict's protection until she was his wife, and that the convict should, himself, witness the ceremony." The man paused.

When the girl did not speak, he said again, "Do you wonder, Miss Andrés, that the convict obeyed his master?"

"No," said the girl, softly, "I do not wonder. But, Mr. Marston," she continued, hesitatingly, "what do you think the convict in your story would have done if the man had not—if he had not wanted to marry the girl?"

"I know what he would have done in that case," the other answered with conviction. "He would have gone back to his twenty years of hell. He would have gone back to fifty years of hell, if need be, rather than buy his freedom at such a price."

The girl leaned forward, eagerly; "And suppose—suppose—that after the convict had done his master's bidding—suppose that after he had taken the girl away from her friends—suppose, then, the man would not marry her?"

For a moment there was no sound in the little room, save the crackling of the fire in the fire-place, and the sound of a stick that had burned in two, falling in the ashes.

"What would the convict do if the man would not marry the girl?" persisted Sibyl.

Her companion spoke with the solemnity of a judge passing sentence; "If the man violated his word—if he lied to the convict—if his purpose toward the girl was anything less than an honorable marriage—if he refused to keep his promise after the convict had done his part—he would die, Miss Andrés. The convict would kill his benefactor—as surely as there is a just God who, alone, can say what is right and what is wrong."

The girl uttered a low cry.

The man did not seem to notice. "But the man will do as he promised, Miss Andrés. He wishes to make the girl his wife. He can give her all that women, these days, seem to desire in marriage. In the eyes of the world, she would be envied by thousands. And the convict would gain freedom and the right to live an honorable life—the right to earn his bread by doing an honest man's work. Freedom and a life of honorable service, at the price; or hell, with only the memory of a good deed—which should he choose, Miss Andrés? The convict is past deciding for himself."

The troubled answer came out of the honesty of the girl's heart; "Mr. Marston, I do not know."

A moment, the man on the other side of the fireplace waited. Then, rising, he quietly left the cabin. The girl did not know that he was gone, until she heard the door close.

In that log hut, hidden in the deep gorge, in the wild Cold Water country, Sibyl Andrés sat before the dying fire, waiting for the dawn. On a high, wind-swept ledge in the Galena mountains, Aaron King grimly walked his weary beat. In Clear Creek Canyon, Myra Willard and Conrad Lagrange waited, and Brian Oakley planned for the morrow. Over in the Galena Valley, an automobile from Fairlands stopped at the mouth of a canyon leading toward Granite Peak. Somewhere, in the darkness of the night, a man strove to know right from wrong.

Chapter XXXVII

The Man Was Insane

Neither Sibyl Andrés nor her companion, the next morning, reopened their conversation of the night before. Each was preoccupied and silent, with troubled thoughts that might not be spoken.

Often, as the forenoon passed, Sibyl saw the man listening, as though for a step on the mountainside above. She knew, without being told, that the convict was expecting his master. It was, perhaps, ten o'clock, when they heard a sound that told them some one was approaching.

The man caught up his rifle and slipped a round of cartridges into the magazine; saying to the girl, "Go into the cabin and bar the door; quick, do as I say! Don't come out until I call you."

She obeyed; and the convict, himself, rifle in hand, disappeared in the heavy underbrush.

A few minutes later, James Rutlidge parted the bushes and stepped into the little open space in front of the cabin. The convict reappeared, his rifle under his arm.

The new-comer greeted the man whom Sibyl knew as Henry Marston, with, "Hello, George, everything all right? Where is she?"

"Miss Andrés is in the cabin. When I heard you coming, I asked her to go inside, and took cover in the brush, myself, until I knew for sure that it was you."

Rutlidge laughed. "You are all right, George. But you needn't worry. Everything is as peaceful as a graveyard. They've found the horse, and they think now that the girl killed herself, or met with an accident while wandering around the hills in a state of mental aberration."

"You left the supplies at the same old place, I suppose?" said the convict.

"Yes, I brought what I could," Rutlidge indicated a pack which he had slipped from his shoulder as he was talking. "You better hike over there and bring in the rest to-night. If you leave at once, you will make it back by noon, to-morrow."

The girl in the cabin, listening, heard every word and trembled with fear. The convict spoke again.

"What are your plans, Mr. Rutlidge?"

"Never mind my plans, now. They can wait until you get back. You must start at once. You say Miss Andrés is in the cabin?" He turned toward the door.

But the other said, shortly, "Wait a minute, sir. I have a word to say, before I go."

"Well, out with it."

"You are not going to forget your promise to me?"

"Certainly not, George. You are safe."

"I mean regarding Miss Andrés."

"Oh, of course not! Why, what's the matter?"

"Nothing, only she is in my care until she is your wife."

James Rutlidge laughed. "I will take good care of her until you get back. You need have no fear. You're not doubting my word, are you?"

"If I doubted your word, I would take Miss Andrés with me," answered the convict, simply.

James Rutlidge looked at him, curiously; "Oh, you would?"

"Yes, sir, I would; and I think I should tell you, too, that if you should forget your promise—"

"Well, what would you do if I should forget?"

The answer came deliberately; "If you do not keep your promise I will kill you, Mr. Rutlidge."

James Rutlidge did not reply.

Stepping to the cabin door, the convict knocked.

Sibyl's voice answered, "Yes?"

"You may come out now, please, Miss Andrés."

As the girl opened the door, she spoke to him in a low tone. "Thank you, Mr. Marston. I heard."

"I meant you to hear," he returned in a whisper. "Do not be afraid." In a louder tone he continued. "I must go for supplies, Miss Andrés. I will be back to-morrow noon."

He stepped around the corner of the cabin, and was gone.

Sibyl Andrés faced James Rutlidge, without speaking. She was not afraid, now, as she had always been in his presence, until that day when he had so plainly declared himself to her and she met his advances with a gun. The convict's warning to the man who could send him back to prison for practically the remaining years of his life, had served its purpose in giving her courage. She did not believe that, for the present, Rutlidge would dare to do otherwise than heed the warning.

[Illustration: Still she did not speak.]

James Rutlidge regarded her with a smile of triumphant satisfaction. "Really," he said, at last, "you do not seem at all glad to see me."

She made no reply.

"I am frightfully hungry"—he continued, with a short laugh, moving toward her as she stood in the door of the cabin—"I've been walking since midnight I was in such a hurry to get here that I didn't even stop for breakfast."

She stepped out, and moved away from the door.

With another laugh, he entered the cabin.

Presently, when he had helped himself to food, he went back to the girl who had seated herself on a log, at the farther side of the little clearing. "You seem fairly comfortable here," he said.

She did not speak.

"You and my man get along nicely, I take it. He has been kind to you?"

Still she did not speak.

He spoke sharply, "Look here, my girl, you can't keep this up, you know. Say what you have to say, and let's get it over."

All the time, she had been regarding him intently—her wide, blue eyes filled with wondering pain. "How could you?" she said at last. "Oh, how could you do such a thing?"

His face flushed. "I did it because you have driven me mad, I guess. From the first time I saw you, I have wanted you. I have tried again and again, in the last three years, to approach you; but you would have nothing to do with me. The more you spurned me, the more I wanted you. Then this man, King, came. You were friendly enough, with him. It made me wild. From that day when I met you in the mountains above Lone Cabin, I have been ready for anything. I determined if I could not win you by fair means, I would take you in any way I could. When my opportunity came, I took advantage of it. I've got you. The story is already started that you were the painter's mistress, and that you have committed suicide. You shall stay here, a while, until the belief that you are dead has become a certainty; then you will go East with me."

"But you cannot do a thing so horrible!" she exclaimed "I would tell my story to the first people we met."

He laughed grimly, as he retorted with brutal meaning, "You do not seem to understand. You will be glad enough to keep the story a secret—when the time comes to go."

Bewildered by fear and shame, the girl could only stammer, "How could you—oh how could you! Why, why—"

"Why!" he echoed. Then, as he went a step toward her, he exclaimed, with reckless profanity, "Ask the God who made me what I am, why I want you! Ask the God who made you so beautiful, why!"

He moved another step toward her, his face flushed with the insane passion that mastered him, his eyes burning with the reckless light of one past counting the cost; and the girl, seeing, sprang to her feet, in terror. Wheeling suddenly, she ran into the cabin, thinking to shut and bar the door. She reached the door, and swung it shut, but the bar was gone. While he was in the cabin he had placed it out of her reach. Putting his shoulder to the door, the man easily forced it open against her lighter weight. As he crossed the threshold, she sprang to the farthest corner of the little room, and cowered, trembling—too shaken with horror to cry out. A moment he paused; then started toward her.

At that instant, the convict burst through the underbrush into the little opening.

Hearing the sound, Rutlidge wheeled and sprang to the open door.

The convict was breathing heavily from the exertion of a hard run.

"What are you doing here?" demanded Rutlidge, sharply. "What's the matter?"

"Some one is following my trail down from Granite Peak."

"Well, what are you carrying that rifle for?" said Rutlidge, harshly, with an oath.

"There may be others near enough to hear a shot," answered the convict. "Besides, Mr. Rutlidge, this is your part of the game—not mine. I did not agree to commit murder for you."

"Where did you see him?"

"A half mile beyond the head of the gulch, where we turn off to go to the supply point."

Rutlidge, rifle in hand, stepped from the house. "You stay here and take care of the girl—and see that she doesn't scream." With the last word he set out at a run.

The convict sprang into the cabin, where Sibyl still crouched in the corner. The man's voice was imploring as he said, "Miss Andrés, Miss Andrés, what is the matter? Did he touch you? Tell me, did he harm you?"

Sobbing, the girl held out her hands, and he lifted her to her feet. "You—you came—just in time, Mr. Marston."

An instant he stood there, then muttering something under his breath, he turned, caught up his rifle, and started toward the door.

But, as he reached the threshold, she cried out, "Mr. Marston, don't, don't leave me again."

The convict stopped, hesitated, then he said solemnly "Miss Andrés, can you pray? I know you can. You are a good girl. If God can hear a prayer he will surely hear you. Come with me. Come—and pray girl—pray for me."

The most charitable construction that can be put upon the action of James Rutlidge, just related, is to accept the explanation of his conduct that he, himself made to Sibyl. The man was insane—as Mr. Taine was insane—as Mrs. Taine was insane.

What else can be said of a class of people who, in an age wedded to materialism, demand of their artists not that they shall set before them ideals of truth and purity and beauty, but that they shall feed their diseased minds with thoughts of lust and stimulate their abnormal passions with lascivious imaginings? Can a class—whatever its pretense to culture may be—can a class, that, in story and picture and music and play, counts greatest in art those who most effectively arouse the basest passions of which the human being is capable, be rightly judged sane?

James Rutlidge was bred, born, and reared in an atmosphere that does not tolerate purity of thought. It was literally impossible for him to think sanely of the holiest, most sacred, most fundamental facts of life. Education, culture, art, literature,—all that is commonly supposed to lift man above the level of the beasts,—are used by men and women of his kind to so pervert their own natures that they are able to descend to bestial depths that the dumb animals themselves are not capable of reaching. In what he called his love for Sibyl Andrés, James Rutlidge was insane—but no more so than thousands of others. The methods of securing the objects of their desires vary—the motive that prompts is the same—the end sought is identical.

As he hurriedly climbed the mountainside, out of the deep gorge that hid the cabin, the man's mind was in a whirl of emotions—rage at being interrupted at the moment of his triumph; dread lest the approaching one should be accompanied by others, and the girl be taken from him; fear that the convict would prove troublesome, even should the more immediate danger be averted; anger at himself for being so blindly precipitous; and a maddening indecision as to how he should check the man who was following the tracks that led from Granite Peak to the evident object of his search. The words of the convict rang in his ears. "This is your job. I did not agree to commit murder for you."

Murder had no place in the insanity of James Rutlidge To destroy innocence, to kill virtue, to murder a soul—these are commonplaces in the insane philosophy of his kind. But to kill—to take a life deliberately—the thought was abhorrent to him. He was not educated to the thought of taking life—he was trained to consider its perversion. The heroes in his fiction did not kill men—they betrayed women. The heroines in his stories did not desire the death of their betrayers—they loved them, and deserted their husbands for them.

But to stand idly aside and permit Sibyl Andrés to be taken from him—to face the exposure that would inevitably follow—was impossible. If the man who had struck the trail was alone, there might still be a chance—if he could be stopped. But how could he check him? What could he do? A rifle-shot might bring a dozen searchers.

While these thoughts were seething in his hot brain, he was climbing rapidly toward the cliff at the head of the gorge, across which, he knew, the man who was following the tracks that led to the cabin below, must come.

Gaining the end of the ledge that leads across the face of that mighty wall of rock, less than a hundred feet to the other side, he stopped. There was no one in sight. Looking down, he saw, a thousand feet below the tops of the trees in the bottom of the gorge. Lifting his head, he looked carefully about, searching the mountainsides that slope steeply back from the rim of the narrow canyon. He looked up at the frowning cliff that towered a thousand feet above his head. He listened. He was thinking, thinking. The best of him and the worst of him struggled for supremacy.

A sound on the mountainside, above the gorge, and beyond the other end of the ledge, caught his ear. With a quick step he moved behind a projecting corner of the cliff. Rifle in hand, he waited.

Chapter XXXVIII

An Inevitable Conflict

When Aaron King set out to follow the tracks he had found at Granite Peak, after his long, hard trip along the rugged crest of the Galenas, his weariness was forgotten. Eagerly, as if fresh and strong, but with careful eyes and every sense keenly alert, he went forward on the trail that he knew must lead him to Sibyl Andrés.

He did not attempt to solve the problem of how the girl came there, nor did he pause to wonder about her companion. He did not even ask himself if Sibyl were living or dead. He thought of nothing; knew nothing; was conscious of nothing; but the trail that led away into the depths of the mountain wilderness. Insensible to his own physical condition; without food; unacquainted with the wild country into which he was going; reckless of danger to himself but with all possible care and caution for the sake of the girl he loved, he went on.

Coming to the brink of the gorge in which the cabin was hidden, the trail, following the rim, soon led him to the ledge that lay across the face of the cliff at the head of the narrow canyon. A moment, he paused, to search the vicinity with careful eyes, then started to cross. As he set foot upon the ledge, a voice at the other end called sharply, "Stop."

At the word, Aaron King halted.

A moment passed. James Rutlidge stepped from behind the rocks at the other end of the ledge. He was covering the artist with a rifle.

In a flash, the man on the trail understood. The automobile, the mirror signals from Fairlands—it was all explained by the presence and by the menacing attitude of the man who barred his way. The artist's hand moved toward the weapon that hung at his hip.

"Don't do that," said the man with the rifle. "I can't murder you in cold blood; but if you attempt to draw your gun, I'll fire."

The other stood still.

James Rutlidge spoke again, his voice hoarse with emotion; "Listen to me, King. It's useless for me to deny what brought me here. The trail you are following leads to Sibyl Andrés. You had her all summer. I've got her now. If you hadn't stumbled onto the trail up there, I would have taken her out of the country, and you would never have seen her again. I might have killed you before you saw me, but I couldn't. I'm not that kind. Under the circumstances there is no possible compromise. I'll give you a fighting chance for your life and the girl. I'll take a fighting chance for my life and the girl. Throw your gun out of reach and I'll leave mine here. We'll meet on the ledge there."

James Rutlidge was no coward. Mr. Taine, also,—it will be remembered,—on the night of his death, boasted that he was game.

Without an instant's hesitation, Aaron King unbuckled the belt that held his weapon and, turning, tossed it behind him, with the gun still in its holster. At the other end of the ledge, James Rutlidge set his rifle behind the rock.

Deliberately, the two men removed their coats and threw aside their hats. For a moment they stood eyeing each other. Into Aaron King's mind flashed the memory of that scene at the Fairlands depot, when, moved by the distress of the woman with the disfigured face, he had first spoken to the man who faced him now. With startling vividness, the incidents of their acquaintance came to him in flash-like succession—the day that Rutlidge had met Sibyl in the studio; the time of his visit to the camp in the sycamore grove; the night of the Taine banquet—a hundred things that had strengthened the feeling of antagonism which had marked their first meeting. And, through it all, he seemed to hear Conrad Lagrange saying that in his story of life this character's name was "Sensual." The artist, in that instant, knew that this meeting was inevitable.

It was only for a moment that the two men—who in their lives and characters represented forces so antagonistic—stood regarding each other, each knowing that the duel would be—must be—to the death. Deliberately, they started toward the center of the ledge. Over their heads towered the great cliff. A thousand feet below were the tops of the trees in the bottom of the gorge. About them, on every hand, the silent, mighty hills watched—the wild and lonely wilderness waited.

As they drew closer together, they moved, as wrestlers, warily—crouching, silent, alert. Stripped to their shirts and trousers, they were both splendid physical types. James Rutlidge was the heavier, but Aaron King made up for his lack in weight by a more clean-cut, muscular firmness.

They grappled. As two primitive men in a savage age might have met, bare handed, they came together. Locked in each other's arms, their limbs entwined, with set faces, tugging muscles, straining sinews, and taut nerves they struggled. One moment they crushed against the rocky wall of the cliff—the next, and they swayed toward the edge of the ledge and hung over the dizzy precipice. With pounding hearts, laboring breath, and clenched teeth they wrestled.

James Rutlidge's foot slipped on the rocky floor; but, with a desperate effort, he regained his momentary loss. Aaron King—worn by his days of anxiety, by his sleepless nights and by the long hours of toil over the mountains, without sufficient food or rest—felt his strength going. Slowly, the weight and endurance of the heavier man told against him. James Rutlidge felt it, and his eyes were beginning to blaze with savage triumph.

They were breathing, now, with hoarse, sobbing gasps, that told of the nearness of the finish. Slowly, Aaron King weakened. Rutlidge, spurred to increase his effort, and exerting every ounce of his strength, was bearing the other downward and back.

At that instant, the convict and Sibyl Andrés reached the cliff. With a cry of horror, the girl stood as though turned to stone.

Motionless, without a word, the convict watched the struggling men.

With a sob, the girl stretched forth her hands. In a low voice she called, "Aaron! Aaron! Aaron!"

The two men on the ledge heard nothing—saw nothing.

Sibyl spoke again, almost in a whisper, but her companion heard. "Mr. Marston, Mr. Marston, it is Aaron King. I—I love him—I—love him."

Without taking his eyes from the struggling men, the convict answered, "Pray, girl; pray, pray for me." As he spoke, he steadily raised his rifle to his shoulder.

Aaron King went down upon one knee. Rutlidge his legs braced, his body inclined toward the edge of the precipice, was gathering his strength for the last triumphant effort.

The convict, looking along his steady rifle barrel, was saying again, "Pray, pray for me, girl." As the words left his lips, his finger pressed the trigger, and the quiet of the hills was broken by the sharp crack of the rifle.

James Rutlidge's hold upon the artist slipped. For a fraction of a second, his form half straightened and he stood nearly erect; then, as a weed cut by the sharp scythe of a mower falls, he fell; his body whirling downward toward the trees and rocks below. The sound of the crashing branches mingled with the reverberating report of the shot. On the ledge, Aaron King lay still.

The convict dropped his rifle and ran forward. Lifting the unconscious man in his arms, he carried him a little way down the mountain, toward the cabin; where he laid him gently on the ground. To Sibyl, who hung over the artist in an agony of loving fear, he said hurriedly, "He'll be all right, presently, Miss Andrés. I'll fetch his coat and hat."

Running back to the ledge, he caught up the dead man's rifle, coat, and hat, and threw them over the precipice, as he swiftly crossed for the artist's things. Recovering his own rifle, he ran back to the girl.

"Listen, Miss Andrés," said the convict, speaking quickly. "Mr. King will be all right in a few minutes. That rifle-shot will likely bring his friends; if not, you are safe, now, anyway. I dare not take chances. Good-by."

From where she sat with the unconscious man's head in her lap, she looked at him, wonderingly. "Good-by?" she repeated questioningly.

Henry Marston smiled grimly. "Certainly, good-by What else is there for me?"

A moment later, she saw him running swiftly down the mountainside, like some hunted creature of the wilderness.

Chapter XXXIX

The Better Way

Alone on the mountainside with the man who had awakened the pure passion of her woman heart, Sibyl Andrés bent over the unconscious object of her love. She saw his face, unshaven, grimy with the dirt of the trail and the sweat of the fight, drawn and thin with the mental torture that had driven him beyond the limit of his physical strength; she saw how his clothing was stained and torn by contact with sharp rocks and thorns and bushes; she saw his hands—the hands that she had watched at their work upon her portrait as she stood among the roses—cut and bruised, caked with blood and dirt—and, seeing these things, she understood.

In that brief moment when she had watched Aaron King in the struggle upon the ledge,—and, knowing that he was fighting for her, had realized her love for him,—all that Mrs. Taine had said to her in the studio was swept away. The cruel falsehoods, the heartless misrepresentations, the vile accusations that had caused her to seek the refuge of the mountains and the protection of her childhood friends were, in the blaze of her awakened passion, burned to ashes; her cry to the convict—"I love him, I love him"—was more than an expression of her love; it was a triumphant assertion of her belief in his love for her—it was her answer to the evil seeing world that could not comprehend their fellowship.

As the life within the man forced him slowly toward consciousness, the girl, natural as always in the full expression of herself, bent over him with tender solicitude. With endearing words, she kissed his brow, his hair, his hands. She called his name in tones of affection. "Aaron, Aaron, Aaron." But when she saw that he was about to awake, she deftly slipped off her jacket and, placing it under his head, drew a little back.

He opened his eyes and looked wonderingly up at the dark pines that clothed the mountainsides. His lips moved and she heard her name; "Sibyl, Sibyl."

She leaned forward, eagerly, her cheeks glowing with color. "Yes, Mr. King."

"Am I dreaming, again?" he said slowly, gazing at her as though struggling to command his senses.

"No, Mr. King," she answered cheerily, "you are not dreaming."

Carefully, as one striving to follow a thread of thought in a bewildering tangle of events, he went over the hours just past. "I was up on that peak where you and I ate lunch the day you tried to make me see the Golden State Limited coming down from the pass. Brian Oakley sent me there to watch for buzzards." For a moment he turned away his face, then continued, "I saw flashes of light in Fairlands and on Granite Peak. I left a note for Brian and came over the range. I spent one night on the way. I found tracks on the peak. There were two, a man and a woman. I followed them to a ledge of rock at the head of a canyon," he paused. Thus far the thread of his thought was clear. "Did some one stop me? Was there—was there a fight? Or is that part of my dream?"

"No," she said softly, "that is not part of your dream."

"And it was James Rutlidge who stopped me, as I was going to you?"

"Yes."

"Then where—" with quick energy he sat up and grasped her arm—"My God! Sibyl—Miss Andrés, did I, did I—" He could not finish the sentence, but sank back, overcome with emotion.

The girl spoke quickly, with a clear, insistent voice that rallied his mind and forced him to command himself.

"Think, Mr. King, think! Do you remember nothing more? You were struggling—your strength was going—can't you remember? You must, you must!"

Lifting his face he looked at her. "Was there a rifle-shot?" he asked slowly. "It seems to me that something in my brain snapped, and everything went black. Was there a rifle-shot?"

"Yes," she answered.

"And I did not—I did not—?"

"No. You did not kill James Rutlidge. He would have killed you, but for the shot that you heard."

"And Rutlidge is—?"

"He is dead," she answered simply.

"But who—?"

Briefly, she told him the story, from the time that she had met Mrs. Taine in the studio until the convict had left her, a few minutes before. "And now," she finished, rising quickly, "we must go down to the cabin. There is food there. You must be nearly starved. I will cook supper for you, and when you have had a night's sleep, we will start home."

"But first," he said, as he rose to his feet and stood before her, "I must tell you something. I should have told you before, but I was waiting until I thought you were ready to hear. I wonder if you know. I wonder if you are ready to hear, now."

She looked him frankly in the eyes as she answered, "Yes, I know what you want to tell me. But don't, don't tell me here." She shuddered, and the man remembering the dead body that lay at the foot of the cliff, understood. "Wait," she said, "until we are home."

"And you will come to me when you are ready? When you want me to tell you?" he said.

"Yes," she answered softly, "I will go to you when I am ready."

At the cabin in the gulch, the girl hastened to prepare a substantial meal. There was no one, now, to fear that the smoke would be seen. Later, with cedar boughs and blankets, she made a bed for him on the floor near the fire-place. When he would have helped her she forbade him; saying that he was her guest and that he must rest to be ready for the homeward trip.

Softly, the day slipped away over the mountain peaks and ridges that shut them in. Softly, the darkness of the night settled down. In the rude little hut, in the lonely gulch, the man and the woman whose lives were flowing together as two converging streams, sat by the fire, where, the night before, the convict had told that girl his story.

Very early, Sibyl insisted that her companion lie down to sleep upon the bed she had made. When he protested, she answered, laughing, "Very well, then, but you will be obliged to sit up alone," and, with a "Good night," she retired to her own bed in another corner of the cabin. Once or twice, he spoke to her, but when she did not answer he lay down upon his woodland couch and in a few minutes was fast asleep.

In the dim light of the embers, the girl slipped from her bed and stole quietly across the room to the fire-place, to lay another stick of wood upon the glowing coals. A moment she stood, in the ruddy light, looking toward the sleeping man. Then, without a sound, she stole to his side, and kneeling, softly touched his forehead with her lips. As silently, she crept back to her couch.

All that afternoon Brian Oakley had been following with trained eyes, the faintly marked trail of the man whose dead body was lying, now, at the foot of the cliff. When the darkness came, the mountaineer ate a cold supper and, under a rude shelter quickly improvised by his skill in woodcraft, slept beside the trail. Near the head of Clear Creek, Jack Carleton, on his way to Granite Peak, rolled in his blanket under the pines. Somewhere in the night, the man who had saved Sibyl Andrés and Aaron King, each for the other, fled like a fearful, hunted thing.

At daybreak, Sibyl was up, preparing their breakfast But so quietly did she move about her homely task that the artist did not awake. When the meal was ready, she called him, and he sprang to his feet, declaring that he felt himself a new man. Breakfast over, they set out at once.

When they came to the cliff at the head of the gulch, the girl halted and, shrinking back, covered her face with trembling hands; afraid, for the first time in her life, to set foot upon a mountain trail. Gently, her companion led her across the ledge, and a little way back from the rim of the gorge on the other side.

Five minutes later they heard a shout and saw Brian Oakley coming toward them. Laughing and crying, Sibyl ran to meet him; and the mountaineer, who had so many times looked death in the face, unafraid and unmoved, wept like a child as he held the girl in his arms.

When Sibyl and Aaron had related briefly the events that led up to their meeting with the Ranger, and he in turn had told them how he had followed the track of the automobile and, finding the hidden supplies, had followed the trail of James Rutlidge from that point, the officer asked the girl several questions. Then, for a little while he was silent, while they, guessing his thoughts, did not interrupt. Finally, he said, "Jack is due at Granite Peak, sometime about noon. He'll have his horse, and with Sibyl riding, we'll make it back down to the head of Clear Creek by dark. You young folks just wait for me here a little. I want to look around below there, a bit."

As he started toward the gulch, Sibyl sprang to her feet and threw herself into his arms. "No, no, Brian Oakley, you shall not—you shall not do it!"

Holding her close, the Ranger looked down into her pleading eyes, smilingly. "And what do you think I am going to do, girlie?"

"You are going down there to pick up the trail of the man who saved Aaron—who saved me. But you shall not do it. I don't care if you are an officer, and he is an escaped convict! I will not let you do anything that might lead to his capture."

"God bless you, child," answered Brian Oakley, "the only escaped convict I know anything about, this last year, according to my belief, died somewhere in the mountains. If you don't believe it, look up my official reports on the matter."

"And you're not going to find which way he went?"

"Listen, Sibyl," said the Ranger gravely. "The disappearance of James Rutlidge, prominent as he was, will be heralded from one end of the world to the other. The newspapers will make the most of it. The search is sure to be carried into these hills, for that automobile trip in the night will not go unquestioned, and Sheriff Walters knows too much of my suspicions. In a few days, the body will be safely past recognition, even should it be discovered through the buzzards. But I can't take chances of anything durable being found to identify the man who fell over the cliff."

When he returned to them, two hours later, he said, quietly, "It's a mighty good thing I went down. It wasn't a nice job, but I feel better. We can forget it, now, with perfect safety. Remember"—he charged them impressively—"even to Myra Willard and Conrad Lagrange, the story must be only that an unknown man took you, Sibyl, from your horse. The man escaped, when Aaron found you. We'll let the Sheriff, or whoever can, solve the mystery of that automobile and Jim Rutlidge's disappearance."

A half mile from Granite Peak, they met Jack Carleton and, by dark, as Brian Oakley had said, were safely down to the head of Clear Creek; having come by routes, known to the Ranger, that were easier and shorter than the roundabout way followed by the convict and the girl.

It was just past midnight when the three friends parted from young Carleton and crossed the canyon to Sibyl's old home.

Chapter XL

Facing the Truth

As Brian Oakley had predicted, the disappearance of James Rutlidge occupied columns in the newspapers, from coast to coast. In every article he was headlined as "A Distinguished Citizen;" "A Famous Critic;" "A Prominent Figure in the World of Art;" "One of the Greatest Living Authorities;" "Leader in the Modern School;" "Of Powerful Influence Upon the Artistic Production of the Age." The story of the unknown mountain girl's abduction and escape was a news item of a single day; but the disappearance of James Rutlidge kept the press busy for weeks. It may be dismissed here with the simple statement that the mystery has never been solved.

Of the unknown man who had taken Sibyl away into the mountains, and who had escaped, the world has never heard. Of the convict who died but did not die in the hills, the world knows nothing. That is, the world knows nothing of the man in this connection. But Aaron and Sibyl, some years later, knew what became of Henry Marston—which does not, at all, belong to this story.

Upon his return with Conrad Lagrange to their home in the orange groves, Aaron King plunged into his work with a purpose very different from the motive that had prompted him when first he took up his brushes in the studio that looked out upon the mountains and the rose garden.

Day after day, as he gave himself to his great picture,—"The Feast of Materialism,"—he knew the joy of the worker who, in his art, surrenders himself to a noble purpose—a joy that is very different from the light, passing pleasure that comes from the mere exercise of technical skill. The artist did not, now, need to drive himself to his task, as the begging musician on the street corner forces himself to play to the passing crowd, for the pennies that are dropped in his tin cup. Rather was he driven by the conviction of a great truth, and by the realization of its woeful need in the world, to such adequate expression as his mastery of the tools of his craft would permit He was not, now, the slave of his technical knowledge; striving to produce a something that should be merely technically good. He was a master, compelling the medium of his art to serve him; as he, in turn, was compelled to serve the truth that had mastered him.

Sometimes, with Conrad Lagrange, he went for an evening hour to the little house next door. Sometimes Sibyl and Myra Willard would drop in at the studio, in the afternoon. The girl never, now, came alone. But every day, as the artist worked, the music of her violin came to him, out of the orange grove, with its message from the hills. And the painter at his easel, reading aright the message, worked and waited; knowing surely that when she was ready she would come.

Letters from Mrs. Taine were frequent. Aaron King, reading them—nearly always under the quizzing eyes of Conrad Lagrange, whose custom it was to bring the daily mail—carefully tore them into little pieces and dropped them into the waste basket, without comment.

Once, the novelist asked with mock gravity, "Have you no thought for the day of judgment, young man? Do you not know that your sins will surely find you out?"

The artist laughed. "It is so written in the law, I believe."

The other continued solemnly, "Your recklessness is only hastening the end. If you don't answer those letters you will be forced, shortly, to meet the consequences face to face."

"I suppose so," returned the painter, indifferently. "But I have my answer ready, you know."

"You mean that portrait?"

"Yes."

The novelist laughed grimly. "I think it will do the trick. But, believe me, there will be consequences!"

The artist was in his studio, at work upon the big picture, when Mrs. Taine called, the day of her return to Fairlands.

It was well on in the afternoon. Conrad Lagrange and Czar had started for a walk, but had gone, as usual, only as far as the neighboring house. Yee Kee, meeting Mrs. Taine at the door, explained, doubtfully, that the artist was at his work. He would go tell Mr. King that Mrs. Taine was here.

"Never mind, Kee. I will tell him myself," she answered; and, before the Chinaman could protest, she was on her way to the studio.

"Damn!" said the Celestial eloquently; and retired to his kitchen to ruminate upon the ways of "Mellican women."

Mrs. Taine pushed open the door of the studio, so quietly, that the painter, standing at his easel and engrossed with his work, did not notice her presence. For several moments the woman stood watching him, paying no heed to the picture, seeing only the man. When he did not look around, she said, "Are you too busy to even look at me?"

With an exclamation, he faced her; then, as quickly, turned again; with hand outstretched to draw the easel curtain. But, as though obeying a second thought that came quickly upon the heels of the first impulse, he did not complete the movement. Instead, he laid his palette and brushes beside his color-box, and greeted her with, "How do you do, Mrs. Taine? When did you return to Fairlands? Is Miss Taine with you?"

"Louise is abroad," she answered. "I—I preferred California. I arrived this afternoon." She went a step toward him. "You—you don't seem very glad to see me."

The painter colored, but she continued impulsively, without waiting for his reply. "If you only knew all that I have been doing for you!—the wires I have pulled; the influences I have interested; the critics and newspaper men that I have talked to! Of course I couldn't do anything in a large public way, so soon after Mr. Taine's death, you know; but I have been busy, just the same, and everything is fixed. When our picture is exhibited next season, you will find yourself not only a famous painter, but a social success as well." She paused. When he still did not speak, she went on, with an air of troubled sadness; "I do miss Jim's help though. Isn't it frightful the way he disappeared? Where do you suppose he is? I can't—I won't—believe that anything has happened to him. It's all just one of his schemes to get himself talked about. You'll see that he will appear again, safe and sound, when the papers stop filling their columns about him. I know Jim Rutlidge, too well."

Aaron King thought of those bones, picked bare by the carrion birds, at the foot of the cliff. "It seems to be one of the mysteries of the day," he said. "Commonplace enough, no doubt, if one only had the key to it."

Mrs. Taine had evidently not been in Fairlands long enough to hear the story of Sibyl's disappearance—for which the artist mentally gave thanks.

"I am glad for one thing," continued the woman, her mind intent upon the main purpose of her call. "Jim had already written a splendid criticism of your picture—before he went away—and I have it. All this newspaper talk about him will only help to attract attention to what he has said about you. They are saying such nice things of him and his devotion to art, you know—it is all bound to help you." She waited for his approval, and for some expression of his gratitude.

"I fear, Mrs. Taine," he said slowly, "that you are making a mistake."

She laughed nervously, and answered with forced gaiety. "Not me. I'm too old a hand at the game not to know just how far I dare or dare not go."

"I do not mean that"—he returned—"I mean that I can not do my part. I fear you are mistaken in me."

Again, she laughed. "What nonsense! I like for you to be modest, of course—that will be one of your greatest charms. But if you are worried about the quality of your work—forget it, my dear boy. Once I have made you the rage, no one will stop to think whether your pictures are good or bad. The art is not in what you do, but in how you get it before the world. Ask Conrad Lagrange if I am not right."

"As to that," returned the artist, "Mr. Lagrange agrees with you, perfectly."

"But what is this that you are doing now? Will it be ready for the exhibition too?" She looked past him, at the big canvas; and he, watching her curiously stepped aside.

Parts of the picture were little more than sketched in, but still, line and color spoke with accusing truth the spirit of the company that had gathered at the banquet in the home on Fairlands Heights, the night of Mr. Taine's death. The figures were not portraits, it is true, but they expressed with striking fidelity, the lives and characters of those who had, that night, been assembled by Mrs. Taine to meet the artist. The figure in the picture, standing with uplifted glass and drunken pose at the head of the table—with bestial, lust-worn face, disease-shrunken limbs, and dying, licentious eyes fixed upon the beautiful girl musician—might easily have been Mr. Taine himself. The distinguished writers, and critics; the representatives of the social world and of wealth; Conrad Lagrange with cold, cynical, mocking, smile; Mrs. Taine with her pretense of modest dress that only emphasized her immodesty; and, in the midst of the unclean minded crew, the lovely innocence and the unconscious purity of the mountain girl with her violin, offering to them that which they were incapable of receiving—it was all there upon the canvas, as the artist had seen it that night. The picture cried aloud the intellectual degradation and the spiritual depravity of that class who, arrogating to themselves the authority of leaders in culture and art, by their approval and patronage of dangerous falsehood and sham in picture or story, make possible such characters as James Rutlidge.

Aaron King, watching Mrs. Taine as she looked at the picture on the easel, saw a look of doubt and uncertainty come over her face. Once, she turned toward him, as if to speak; but, without a word, looked again at the canvas. She seemed perplexed and puzzled, as though she caught glimpses of something in the picture that she did not rightly understand Then, as she looked, her eyes kindled with contemptuous scorn, and there was a pronounced sneer in her cold tones as she said, "Really, I don't believe I care for you to do this sort of thing." She laughed shortly. "It reminds one a little of that dinner at our house. Don't you think? It's the girl with the violin, I suppose."

"There are no portraits in it, Mrs. Taine," said the artist, quietly.

"No? Well, I think you'd better stick to your portraits. This is a great picture though," she admitted thoughtfully. "It, it grips you so. I can't seem to get away from it. I can see that it will create a sensation. But just the same, I don't like it. It's not nice, like your portrait of me. By the way"—and she turned eagerly from the big canvas as though glad to escape a distasteful subject—"do you remember that I have never seen my picture yet? Where do you keep it?"

The painter indicated another easel, near the one upon which he was at work, "It is there, Mrs. Taine."

"Oh," she said with a pleased smile. "You keep it on the easel, still!" Playfully, she added, "Do you look at it often?—that you have it so handy?"

"Yes," said the artist, "I must admit that I have looked at it frequently." He did not explain why he looked at her portrait while he was working upon the larger picture.

"How nice of you," she answered "Please let me see it now. I remember when you wanted to repaint it, you said you would put on the canvas just what you thought of me; have you? I wonder!"

"I would rather that you judge for yourself, Mrs. Taine," he answered, and drew the curtain that hid the painting.

As the woman looked upon that portrait of herself, into which Aaron King had painted, with all the skill at his command, everything that he had seen in her face as she posed for him, she stood a moment as though stunned. Then, with a gesture of horror and shame, she shrank back, as though the painted thing accused her of being what, indeed, she really was.

Turning to the artist, imploringly, she whispered, "Is it—is it—true? Am I—am I that?"

Aaron King, remembering how she had sent the girl he loved so nearly to a shameful end, and thinking of those bones at the foot of the cliff, answered justly; "At least, madam, there is more truth in that picture than in the things you said to Miss Andrés, here in this room, the day you left Fairlands."

Her face went white with quick rage, but, controling herself, she said, "And where is the picture of your mistress? I should like to see it again, please."

"Gladly, madam," returned the artist. "Because you are a woman, it is the only answer I can make to your charge; which, permit me to say, is as false as that portrait of you is true."

Quickly he pushed another easel to a position beside the one that held Mrs. Taine's portrait, and drew the curtain.

The effect, for a moment, silenced even Mrs. Taine—but only for a moment. A character that is the product of certain years of schooling in the thought and spirit of the class in which Mrs. Taine belonged, is not transformed by a single exhibition of painted truth. From the two portraits, the woman turned to the larger canvas. Then she faced the artist.

"You fool!" she said with bitter rage. "O you fool! Do you think that you will ever be permitted to exhibit such trash as this?" she waved her hand to include the three paintings. "Do you think that I am going to drag you up the ladder of social position to fame and to wealth for such reward as that?" she singled out her own portrait. "Bah! you are impossible—impossible! I have been mad to think that I could make anything out of you. As for your idiotic claim that you have painted the truth—" She seized a large palette knife that lay with the artist's tools upon the table, and springing to her portrait, hacked and mutilated the canvas. The artist stood motionless making no effort to stop her. When the picture was utterly defaced she threw it at his feet. "That, for your truth, Mr. King!" With a quick motion, she turned toward the other portrait.

But the artist, who had guessed her purpose, caught her hand. "That picture was yours, madam—this one is mine." There was a significant ring of triumph in his voice.

Neither Aaron King nor Mrs. Taine had noticed three people who had entered the rose garden, from the orange grove, through the little gate in the corner of the hedge. Conrad Lagrange, Myra Willard and Sibyl were going to the studio; deliberately bent upon interrupting the artist at his work. They sometimes—as Conrad Lagrange put it—made, thus, a life-saving crew of three; dragging the painter to safety when the waves of inspiration were about to overwhelm him. Czar, of course, took an active part in these rescues.

As the three friends approached the trellised arch that opened from the garden into the yard, a few feet from the studio door, the sound of Mrs. Taine's angry voice, came clearly through the open window.

Conrad Lagrange stopped. "Evidently, Mr. King has company," he said, dryly.

"It is Mrs. Taine, is it not?" asked Sibyl, quietly, recognizing the woman's voice.

"Yes," answered the novelist.

The woman with the disfigured face said hurriedly, "Come, Sibyl, we must go back. We will not disturb Mr. King, now, Mr. Lagrange. You two come over this evening." They saw her face white and frightened.

"I believe I'll go back with you, if you don't mind," returned Conrad Lagrange, with his twisted grin; "I don't think I want any of that in there, either." To the dog who was moving toward the studio door, he added; "Here, Czar, you mustn't interrupt the lady. You're not in her class."

They were moving away, when Mrs. Taine's voice came again, clearly and distinctly, through the window.

"Oh, very well. I wish you joy of your possession. I promise you, though, that the world shall never hear of this portrait of your mistress. If you dare try to exhibit it, I shall see that the people to whom you must look for your patronage know how you found the original, an innocent, mountain girl, and brought her to your studio to live with you. Fairlands has already talked enough, but my influence has prevented it from going too far. You may be very sure that from now on I shall not exert myself to deny it."

The artist's friends in the rose garden, again, stopped involuntarily. Sibyl uttered a low exclamation.

Conrad Lagrange looked at Myra Willard. "I think," he said in a low tone, "that the time has come. Can you do it?"

"Yes. I—I—must," returned the woman. She spoke to the girl, who, being a little in advance, had not heard the novelist's words, "Sibyl, dear, will you go on home, please? Mr, Lagrange will stay with me. I—I will join you presently."

At a look from Conrad Lagrange, the girl obeyed.

"Go with Sibyl, Czar," said the novelist; and the girl and the dog went quickly away through the garden.

In the studio, Aaron King gazed at the angry woman in amazement. "Mrs. Taine," he said, with quiet dignity, "I must tell you that I hope to make Miss Andrés my wife."

She laughed harshly. "And what has that to do with it?"

"I thought that if you knew, it might help you to understand the situation," he answered simply.

"I understand the situation, very well," she retorted, "but you do not appear to. The situation is this: I—I was interested in you—as an artist. I, because my position in the world enabled me to help you, commissioned you to paint my portrait. You are unknown, with no name, no place in the world. I could have given you success. I could have introduced you to the people that you must know if you are to succeed. My influence would insure you a favorable reception from those who make the reputations of men like you. I could have made you the rage. I could have made you famous. And now—"

"Now," he said calmly, "you will exert your influence to hinder me in my work. Because I have not pleased you, you will use whatever power you have to ruin me. Is that what you mean, Mrs. Taine?"

"You have made your choice. You must take the consequences," she replied coldly, and turned to leave the studio.

In the doorway, stood the woman with the disfigured face.

Conrad Lagrange stood near.

XLI

Marks of the Beast

When Mrs. Taine would have passed out of the studio, the woman with the disfigured face said, "Wait madam, I must speak to you."

Aaron King recalled that strange scene at the depot, the day of his arrival in Fairlands.

"I have nothing to say to you"—returned Mrs. Taine, coldly—"stand aside please."

But Conrad Lagrange quietly closed the door. "I think, Mrs. Taine," he remarked dryly, "than you will be interested in what Miss Willard has to say."

"Oh, very well," returned the other, making the best of the situation. "Evidently, you heard what I just said to your protege."

The novelist answered, "We did. Accept my compliments madam; you did it very nicely."

"Thanks," she retorted, "I see you still play your role of protector. You might tell your charge whether or not I am mistaken as to the probable result of his—ah—artistic conscientiousness."

"Mr. King knows that you are not. You have, indeed, put the situation rather mildly. It is a sad fact, but, never-the-less, a fact, that the noblest work is often forced to remain unrecognized and unknown to the world by the same methods that are used to exalt the unworthy. You undoubtedly have the power of which you boast, Mrs. Taine, but—"

"But what?" she said triumphantly. "You think I will hesitate to use my influence?"

"I know you will not use it—in this case," came the unexpected answer.

She laughed mockingly, "And why not? What will prevent?"

"The one thing on earth, that you fear, madam"—answered Conrad Lagrange—"the eyes of the world."

Aaron King listened, amazed.

"I don't think I understand," said Mrs. Taine, coldly.

"No? That is what Miss Willard proposes to explain," returned the novelist.

She turned haughtily toward the woman with the disfigured face. "What can this poor creature say to anything I propose?"

Myra Willard answered gently, sadly, "Have you no kindness, no sympathy at all, madam? Is there nothing but cruel selfishness in your heart?"

"You are insolent," retorted the other, sharply. "Say what you have to say and be brief."

Myra Willard drew close to the woman and looked long and searchingly into her face. The other returned her gaze with contemptuous indifference.

"I have been sorry for you," said Myra Willard slowly. "I have not wished to speak. But I know what you said to Sibyl, here in the studio; and I overheard what you said to Mr. King, a few minutes ago. I cannot keep silent."

"Proceed," said Mrs. Taine, shortly. "Say what you have to say, and be done with it."

Myra Willard obeyed. "Mrs. Taine, twenty-six years ago, your guardian, the father of James Rutlidge won the love of a young girl. It does not matter who she was. She was beautiful and innocent That was her misfortune. Beauty and innocence often bring pain and sorrow, madam, in a world where there are too many men like Mr. Rutlidge, and his son. The girl thought the man—she did not know him by his real name—her lover. She thought that he became her husband. A baby was born to the girl who believed herself a wife; and the young mother was happy. For a short time, she was very happy.

"Then, the awakening came. The girl mother was holding her baby to her breast, and singing, as happy mothers do, when a strange woman appeared in the open door of the room. She was a beautiful woman, richly dressed; but her face was distorted with passion. The young mother did not understand. She did not know, then, that the woman was Mrs. Rutlidge—the true wife of the father of her child. She knew that, afterward. The woman, in the doorway lifted her hand as though to throw something, and the mother, instinctively, bowed her head to shield her baby. Then something that burned like fire struck her face and neck. She screamed in agony, and fainted.

"The rest of the story does not matter, I think. The injured mother was taken to the hospital. When she recovered, she learned that Mrs. Rutlidge was dead—a suicide. Later, Mr. Rutlidge took the baby to raise as his ward; telling the world that the child was the daughter of a relative who had died at its birth. You must understand that when the disfigured mother of the baby came to know the truth, she believed that it would be better for the little one if the facts of its birth were never known. The wealthy Mr. Rutlidge could give his ward every advantage of culture and social position. The child would grow to womanhood with no stain upon her name. Because she felt she owed her baby this, the only thing that she could give her, the mother consented and disappeared.

"Madam," finished Myra Willard, slowly, "a little of the acid that burned that mother's face fell upon the shoulder of her illegitimate baby."

"God!" exclaimed the artist.

Throughout Myra Willard's story, Mrs. Taine stood like a woman of stone. At the end, she gazed at the woman's disfigured face, as though fascinated with horror, while her hands moved to finger the buttons of her dress. Unconscious of what she was doing, as though under some strange spell, without removing her gaze from Myra Willard's marred features she opened the waist of her dress and bared to them her right shoulder. It was marked by a broad scar like the scars that disfigured the face of her mother.

Myra Willard started forward, impelled by the mother instinct. "My baby, my poor, poor girl!"

The words broke the spell. Drawing back with an air of cold, unconquerable pride, the woman looked at Conrad Lagrange. "And now," she said, as she swiftly rearranged her dress, "perhaps you will be good enough to tell me why you have done this."

Myra Willard turned away to sink into a chair, white and trembling. Aaron King stepped quickly to her side, and, placing his hand gently on her shoulder waited for the novelist to speak.

"Miss Willard told you this story because I asked her to," said Conrad Lagrange. "I asked her to tell you because it gives me the power to protect the two people who are dearer to me than all the world."

"Still in your role of protector, I see," sneered Mrs. Taine.

"Exactly, madam. It happens that I was a reporter on a certain newspaper when the incidents just related occurred. I wrote the story for the press. In fact, it was the story that gave me my start in yellow journalism, from which I graduated the novelist of your acquaintance. I know the newspaper game thoroughly, Mrs. Taine. I know the truth of this story that you have just heard. Permit me to say, that I know how to write in the approved newspaper style, and to add that my name insures a wide hearing. Proceed to carry out your threats, and I promise you that I will give this attractive bit of news, in all its colorful details, to every newspaper in the land. Can't you see the headlines? 'Startling Revelation,' 'The Secret of the Beautiful Mrs. Taine's Shoulders,' 'Why a Leader in the Social World makes Modesty her Fad,' 'The Parentage of a Social Leader.' Do you understand, madam? Use your influence to interfere with or to hinder Mr. King in his work; or fail to use your influence to contradict the lies you have already started about the character of Miss Andrés; and I will use the influence of my pen and the prestige of my name to put you before the eyes of the world for what you are."

For a moment the woman looked at him, defiantly. Then, as she grasped the full significance of what he had said, she slowly bowed her head.

Conrad Lagrange opened the door.

As she went out, the woman with the disfigured face started forward, holding out her hands appealingly.

Mrs. Taine did not look back, but went quickly toward the big automobile that was waiting in front of the house.

Chapter XLII

Aaron King's Success

The winter months were past.

Aaron King was sitting before his finished picture. The colors were still fresh upon the canvas that, to-day, hangs in an honored place in one of the great galleries of the world. To the last careful touch, the artist had put into his painted message, the best he had to give. Back of every line and brush-stroke there was the deep conviction of a worthy motive. For an hour, he had been sitting there, before the easel, brush and palette in hand, without touching the canvas. He could do no more.

Laying aside his tools, he went to his desk, and took from the drawer, that package of his mother's letters. He pushed a deep arm-chair in front of his picture, and again seated himself. As he read letter after letter, he lifted his eyes, at almost every sentence from the written pages to his work. It was as though he were submitting his picture to a final test—as, indeed, he was. He had reached the last letter when Conrad Lagrange entered the studio; Czar at his heels.

Every day, while the picture was growing under the artist's hand, his friend had watched it take on beauty and power. He did not need to speak of the finished painting, now.

"Well, lad," he said, "the old letters again?"

The artist, caressing the dog's silky head as it was thrust against his knee, answered, "Yes, I finished the picture two hours ago. I have been having a private exhibition all on my own hook. Listen." From the letter in his hand he read:

"It is right for you to be ambitious, my son. I would not have you otherwise. Without a strong desire to reach some height that in the distance lifts above the level of the present, a man becomes a laggard on the highway of life—a mere loafer by the wayside—slothful, indolent—slipping easily, as the years go, into the most despicable of places—the place of a human parasite that, contributing nothing to the wealth of the race, feeds upon the strength of the multitude of toilers who pass him by. But ambition, my boy, is like to all the other gifts that lead men Godward. It must be a noble ambition, nobly controlled. A mere striving for place and power, without a saving sense of the responsibility conferred by that place and power, is ignoble. Such an ambition, I know—as you will some day come to understand—is not a blessing but a curse. It is the curse from which our age is suffering sorely; and which, if it be not lifted, will continue to vitiate the strength and poison the life of the race.

"Because I would have your ambition, a safe and worthy ambition, Aaron, I ask that the supreme and final test of any work that comes from your hand may be this; that it satisfy you, yourself—that you may be not ashamed to sit down alone with your work, and thus to look it squarely in the face. Not critics, nor authorities, not popular opinion, not even law or religion, must be the court of final appeal when you are, by what you do, brought to bar; but by you, yourself, the judgment must be rendered. And this, too, is true, my son, by that judgment and that judgment alone, you will truly live or you will truly die."

"And that"—said the novelist—so famous in the eyes of the world, so infamous in his own sight—"and that is what she tried to make me believe, when she and I were young together. But I would not. I would not accept it. I thought if I could win fame that she—" he checked himself suddenly.

"But you have led me to accept it, old man," cried the artist heartily. "You have opened my eyes. You have helped me to understand my mother, as I never could have understood her, alone."

Conrad Lagrange smiled. "Perhaps," he admitted whimsically. "No doubt good may sometimes be accomplished by the presentation of a horrible example. But go on with your private exhibition. I'll not keep you longer. Come, Czar."

In spite of the artist's protests, he left the studio.

While the painter was putting away his letters, the novelist and the dog went through the rose garden and the orange grove, straight to the little house next door. They walked as though on a definite mission.

Sibyl and Myra Willard were sitting on the porch.

"Howdy, neighbor," called the girl, as the tall, ungainly form of the famous novelist appeared. "You seem to be the bearer of news. What is the latest word from the seat of war?"

"It is finished," said Conrad Lagrange, returning Myra's gentle greeting, and accepting the chair that Sibyl offered.

"The picture?" said the girl eagerly, a quick color flushing her cheeks. "Is the picture finished?"

"Finished," returned the novelist. "I just left him mooning over it like a mother over a brand-new baby."

They laughed together, and when, a moment later, the girl slipped into the house and did not return, the woman with the disfigured face and the famous novelist looked at each other with smiling eyes. When Czar, with sudden interest, started around the corner of the house, his master said suggestively, "Czar, you better stay here with the old folks."

Passing through the house, and out of the kitchen door, Sibyl ran, lightly, through the orange grove, to the little gate in the corner of the Ragged Robin hedge. A moment she paused, hesitating, then, stealing cautiously into the rose garden, she darted in quick flight to the shelter of the arbor; where she parted the screen of vines to gain a view of the studio.

Between the big, north window and the window that opened into the garden, she saw the artist. She saw, too, the big canvas upon the easel. But Aaron King was not, now, looking at his work just finished. He was sitting before that other picture into which he had unconsciously painted, not only the truth that he saw in the winsome loveliness of the girl who posed for him with outstretshed hands among the roses, but his love for her as well.

With a low laugh, Sibyl drew back. Swiftly, as she had reached the arbor, she crossed the garden, and a moment later, paused at the studio door. Again she hesitated—then, gently,—so gently that the artist, lost in his dreams, did not hear,—she opened the door. For a little, she stood watching him. Softly, she took a few steps toward him. The artist, as though sensing her presence, started and looked around.

She was standing as she stood in the picture; her hands outstretched, a smile of welcome on her lips, the light of gladness in her eyes.

As he rose from his chair before the easel, she went to him.

Not many days later, there was a quiet wedding, at Sibyl's old home in the hills. Besides the two young people and the clergyman, only Brian Oakley, Mrs. Oakley, Conrad Lagrange and Myra Willard were present. These friends who had prepared the old place for the mating ones, after a simple dinner following the ceremony, returned down the canyon to the Station.

Standing arm in arm, where the old road turns around the cedar thicket, and where the artist had first seen the girl, Sibyl and Aaron watched them go. From the other side of roaring Clear Creek, they turned to wave hats and handkerchiefs; the two in the shadow of the cedars answered; Czar barked joyful congratulations; and the wagon disappeared in the wilderness growth.

Instead of turning back to the house behind them, the two, without speaking, as though obeying a common impulse, set out down the canyon.

A little later they stood in the old spring glade, where the alders bore, still, in the smooth, gray bark of their trunks, the memories of long-ago lovers; where the light fell, slanting softly through the screen of leaf and branch and vine and virgin's-bower, upon the granite boulder and the cress-mottled waters of the spring, as through the window traceries of a vast and quiet cathedral; and where the distant roar of the mountain stream trembled in the air like the deep tones of some great organ.

Sibyl, dressed in her brown, mountain costume, was sitting on the boulder, when the artist said softly, "Look!"

Lifting her eyes, as he pointed, she saw two butterflies—it might almost have been the same two—with zigzag flight, through the opening in the draperies of virgin's-bower. With parted lips and flushed cheeks, the girl watched. Then—as the beautiful creatures, in their aerial waltz, whirled above her head—she rose, and lightly, gracefully,—almost as her winged companions,—accompanied them in their dance.

The winged emblems of innocence and purity flitted away over the willow wall. The girl, with bright eyes and smiling lips—half laughing, half serious—looked toward her mate. He held out his arms and she went to him.

Harold Bell Wright – A Concise Bibliography

That Printer of Udell's (1902–03)
The Shepherd of the Hills (1907)
The Calling of Dan Matthews (1909)
The Uncrowned King (1910)
The Winning of Barbara Worth (1911)
Their Yesterdays (1912)
The Eyes of the World (1914)
When a Man's a Man (1914)
The Re-Creation of Brian (1919)
Helen of the Old House (1921)
The Mine with the Iron Door (1923)
A Son of His Father (1925)
God and the Groceryman (1927)
Long Ago Told: Legends of the Papago Indians (1929)
Exit (1930)
The Devil's Highway (1932)
Ma Cinderella (1932)
To My Sons (1934)
The Man Who Went Away (1942)

Filmography
The Eyes of the World (1917)
The Shepherd of the Hills (1919, also director)
When a Man's a Man (1924 film) (1924)

The Mine with the Iron Door (1924)
The Re-Creation of Brian Kent (1925)
A Son of His Father (1925)
The Winning of Barbara Worth (1926)
The Shepherd of the Hills (1928)
The Eyes of the World (1930)
When a Man's a Man (1935)
The Calling of Dan Matthews (1935)
The Mine with the Iron Door (1936)
Wild Brian Kent (1936)
Secret Valley (1937)
It Happened Out West (1937)
The Californian (1937, uncredited)
Western Gold (1937)
The Shepherd of the Hills (1941)
Massacre River (1949, uncredited)
The Shepherd of the Hills (1964)

Made in the USA
Coppell, TX
01 July 2021